Elementary Science Methods

A Constructivist Approach

Elementary Science Methods
A Constructivist Approach

David Jerner Martin

Kennesaw State College

Delmar Publishers

I⊤P™ An International Thomson Publishing Company

Albany • Bonn • Boston • Cincinnati • Detroit • London • Madrid
Melbourne • Mexico City • New York • Pacific Grove • Paris
San Francisco • Singapore • Tokyo • Toronto • Washington

NOTICE TO THE READER

Publisher does not warrant or guarantee any of the products described herein or perform any independent analysis in connection with any of the product information contained herein. Publisher does not assume, and expressly disclaims, any obligation to obtain and include information other than that provided to it by the manufacturer.

The reader is expressly warned to consider and adopt all safety precautions that might be indicated by the activities herein and to avoid all potential hazards. By following the instructions contained herein, the reader willingly assumes all risks in connection with such instructions.

The publisher makes no representation or warranties of any kind, including but not limited to, the warranties of fitness for particular purpose or merchantability, nor are any such representations implied with respect to the material set forth herein, and the publisher takes no responsibility with respect to such material. The publisher shall not be liable for any special, consequential, or exemplary damages resulting, in whole or part, from the readers' use of, or reliance upon, this material.

Cover Design: Alexander Piejko

Delmar Staff
Publisher: Diane L. McOscar
Associate Editor: Erin J. O'Connor
Project Editor: Timothy Coleman
Production Coordinator: James Zayicek
Art and Design Coordinator: Carol Keohane
Editorial Assistant: Glenna Stanfield

COPYRIGHT © 1997
By Delmar Publishers
a division of International Thomson Publishing Inc.

The ITP logo is a trademark under license.

Printed in the United States of America

For more information, contact:

Delmar Publishers
3 Columbia Circle, Box 15015
Albany, New York 12212-5015

International Thomson Publishing Europe
Berkshire House 168-173
High Holborn
London, WC1V 7AA
England

Thomas Nelson Australia
102 Dodds Street
South Melbourne, 3205
Victoria, Australia

Nelson Canada
1120 Birchmont Road
Scarborough, Ontario
Canada, M1K 5G4

International Thomson Editores
Campos Eliseos 385, Piso 7
Col Polanco
11560 Mexico D F Mexico

International Thomson Publishing GmbH
Konigswinterer Strasse 418
53227 Bonn
Germany

International Thomson Publishing Asia
221 Henderson Road
#05-10 Henderson Building
Singapore 0315

International Thomson Publishing—Japan
Hirakawacho Kyowa Building, 3F
2-2-1 Hirakawacho
Chiyoda-ku, Tokyo 102
Japan

1 2 3 4 5 6 7 8 9 10 XXX 02 01 00 99 98 97 96

Library of Congress Cataloging-in-Publication Data
Martin, David Jerner.
   Elementary science methods : a constructivist approach / David
Jerner Martin.
       p.   cm.
   Includes bibliographical references and index.
   ISBN 0-8273-7174-8
   1. Science—Study and teaching (Elementary)—United States.
2. Constructivism (Education)—United States. I. Title.
LB1585.3.M37   1996
372.3'5044—dc20   95-46332
                                                 CIP

Contents

CHAPTER 6   *Learner Differences*   *217*

CHAPTER 7   *Assessment*   *253*

CHAPTER 10   *Technology in Elementary Science   359*

It is with love and gratitude
that I dedicate this work
to my wife, Mary.

Preface

Children learn science by *doing* science . . . by asking their own questions about things which interest them, exploring answers to their questions through applying the processes of science in open-ended inquiries, and combining new experiences with information they already possess as they form personally-constructed meanings. This is the essence of constructivism: building personal knowledge from one's own experience and thought.

This text prepares students to teach science from a constructivist perspective in preschool through sixth grade. It utilizes a constructivist approach to teach students to teach in a constructivist manner. A wealth of open-ended inquiry activities are suggested for students to do in class to construct their own personal conceptualizations about teaching science in the elementary school. Students pursue these activities and discuss their outcomes in small groups and with the whole class—much as teachers conduct their elementary science classes.

In the end, teachers must be able to apply the methodology they have constructed in their classrooms. Over 150 process-oriented inquiry activities are suggested, each keyed to a range of grade levels, and each open-ended so teachers can encourage children to develop and perform their own investigations. The activities are placed in the text where the concepts they illustrate are discussed so students can see immediately how to apply the concepts in the classroom. Children's literature is referenced extensively throughout the text to encourage the tandem construction of scientific understandings and literacy.

The text is divided into three parts. In Part I, students construct basic understandings of how they will teach science. They consider goals and objectives of quality elementary science education, the processes of science, the role of content in teaching the processes, the constructivist paradigm, methods of encouraging student inquiry, ways of accommodating learner differences, including multicultural dimensions, and methods of assessing authentically. Part II extends the students' explorations of the basic science program to include literature and other interdisciplinary topics, technological applications, concept mapping, concepts and principles of science appropriate for elementary grades, and professional aspects of science teaching. Part III describes a model of science that may represent the ultimate in constructivist science education.

The text is suitable for both undergraduate and graduate work. The inexperienced undergraduate student will construct sound conceptualizations of constructivistic, inquiry-oriented science teaching through the use of this text. The graduate student will consider advanced models of inquiry and interdisciplinary studies, including science-technology-society, the use of technology, issues of content and methodology, ways of contributing to the profession through action research, and the sophisticated model of teaching by listening.

In my 30 years in the field of science education at all levels from kindergarten through college, it has been my experience that the only science children learn is the science they do themselves. Consequently, in this practical text, I have taken the bold and uncompromising position that hands-on, process-oriented, constructivist-focused inquiry must be fostered in science education in the elementary schools. Preservice and inservice teachers who construct their science education conceptualizations and methodologies through the guidance offered in this text will find science teaching to be fun, stimulating, rewarding, and extremely successful.

Acknowledgements

This work would not have been possible without the support and help of many people. I am especially grateful to the following people:

Dr. Linda Webb, who reviewed and critiqued countless drafts and whose encouragement kept me going.

Ms. Bonnie Higgins, a first year teacher committed to interdisciplinary constructivism, who did much of the research for this book and whose interest in children's literature motivated her to provide the vast majority of the literature connections cited.

Mr. William M. Reynolds, an undergraduate art education major at Kennesaw State College with much potential for an illustrious career, for all the line drawings and the computer-generated concept maps found in Chapter Eleven.

Mr. Paul Hultberg, who understands both children and education, for the photography which so skillfully brings the two together.

Dr. Jonelle Pool and Dr. Jean Ketter who contributed the interdisciplinary case study in Chapter Nine, and who urged me to write these ideas down in the first place.

Sedalia Park Elementary School in Cobb County, Georgia, their teachers, their children, and Ms. Judy Thigpen, their principal, for welcoming me as a colleague, providing me with much valuable experience, and allowing us to take the photographs there.

Professor Ernst Von Glasersfeld for his critical review of the material in Chapter Four.

Dr. Loretta McMillon Howell who reviewed, critiqued, and provided much valuable input to the multicultural material.

Dr. Ronghua Ouyang who reviewed, critiqued, and provided much valuable input to the material on educational technology, and who patiently helped prepare many of the computer images.

Dr. Edward C. Lucy, professor, mentor, colleague, and friend, who reviewed, critiqued, and provided much valuable input.

Dr. Pam Rhyne who reviewed and critiqued and provided much valuable input to the life sciences section of Chapter Twelve.

Dr. Gary Lewis who reviewed, critiqued, and provided much valuable input to the physical and earth and space sciences section of Chapter Twelve.

Dr. Anita VanBrackle who provided help on the material dealing with mathematics.

Ms. Jane Comer, Ms. Ashley Mize, and Ms. Betty Hesrick whose reviews of an early draft provided much encouragement.

Associate Editor Erin O'Connor Traylor of Delmar Publishers who kept encouraging and who knew just when to say what.

Art and Design Coordinator Tim Conners of Delmar Publishers who understands what a quality elementary science methods text should look like.

All the many professional colleagues who have supported my work through the years in many diverse ways.

The students in my college classes who have shown me what works and what doesn't. I have used many of their ideas and vignettes in this text.

The many professional colleagues who provided critique through their reviews:

Rosemary Cameron
College of St. Rose
Albany, New York

Margaret King
Ohio University
Athens, Ohio

George M. Christ, Ed.D.
University of Dallas
Ivring, Texas

Shirley Raines, Ph.D.
University of South Florida
Tampa, Florida

Norman Dee, Ph.D.
Lesley College
Cambridge, Massachusetts

Marilyn Shelton
California State University
Fresno, California

Joseph Jesunathadas, Ed.D.
California State University
San Bernardino, California

JoAnn Simmons
Greenville Central School
Greenville, New York

To all these people, and many more, "Thank you."

To The Student

Welcome to this exploration of elementary science education!

Teaching science in the elementary grades need not be difficult. Science is one of the most fascinating pursuits experienced by children. Elementary children love to tinker, to explore, to try things out, to observe things, to talk about what they observe, to find out what makes things work. They love to play with magnets, discovering that some things are attracted to magnets and some things are not—even through water, plastic, and sand; discovering the idea that some ends of straight magnets attract each other and some ends repel. They are enthralled by the metamorphosis of a caterpillar into a beautiful butterfly. They get excited watching things that swing and things that balance. They are thrilled by the changes that occur during the seasons, by the setting of the sun, by the countless stars in the night sky, by the many shapes of the moon, by the different colors of rocks, by the magic of seeds sprouting. They love to act like scientists, exploring this or that phenomenon and trying something new such as blowing bubbles designed to be bigger or to last longer than anyone else's.

However, in spite of children's natural fascination with exploring on their own, for many years the teaching of science has consisted of the skillful impartation of scientific knowledge to students. Textbooks have contained information for children to learn, and it has been the job of the teacher to interpret the textbook and augment it such that every child learns the material presented.

Science education of the 2000s takes a radically different view from this teacher-focused approach. Science education today capitalizes on children's natural curiosity. It encourages children to construct information in ways that are meaningful to them. It comprises experiences children do themselves. The focus is on *doing* rather than *acquiring*. The competent teacher of elementary science encourages children to wonder, to ask questions, to explore possible answers to these questions, and to construct their own conclusions.

The way children learn science is through doing science; the way children do science is through using the processes of science in personally-constructed inquiries. Therefore, this book is about constructing the process-oriented inquiry method of science teaching. The emphasis is on process skills and hands-on experiences in which children ask their own questions about phenomena which interest them, and seek their own answers to their questions through doing activities which they, themselves, devise. As you will see, inquiry is the agent of constructivism.

The text utilizes a constructivist approach; you will learn to teach science in the same manner as children in your classroom will learn how to do science. You will develop your own personally-constructed conceptualizations about teaching elementary science. Many questions and issues are raised for you to grapple with; there are many more questions than answers, for you have to come to your own conclusions.

Each topic begins with one or more case studies or hands-on activities to help you begin to construct your conceptualizations. Topics are treated inductively, which means you will explore a variety of specific situations pertaining to a phenomenon before the concept is introduced or defined. In this way, you will construct your own generalizations and conclusions as you move through a topic, rather than rely on the preconstructed conclusions of the author. Periodically, you will be asked to compare your conclusions with the author's. Hopefully there will be a degree of congruence.

Disagreement and debate are encouraged—this is the only way people can crystallize their own ideas. This is the essence of constructivism.

Many class activities called "Constructing Your Ideas" are suggested throughout the text. They are designed to help you in your constructions of your conceptualizations, and it is strongly suggested that you actually do as many as time allows. It also is suggested that you do the "Constructing Your Ideas" activities in small groups of four to six students and share group results with the class as a whole. As you will see, small group work fosters children's abilities to come to their own valid conclusions, and doing the activities in small groups models the actual elementary class.

Many "In The Schools" activities are included to illustrate the concepts under consideration and show how they are actually used in classrooms. In addition, many suggested children's activities called "Constructing Science In the Classroom" occur throughout the text near the science learning principle they can be used to teach. The "In The Schools" activities and the "Constructing Science In the Classroom" activities are meant to be suggestions only—points of departure; they are not intended to be duplicated. In the constructivist approach, science investigations are designed to meet the unique needs of children in a particular classroom, and often are developed jointly between the teacher and the children. Suggested ranges of grade levels for each activity are shown with icons. Most of the activities contain suggested literary connections to help you utilize an interdisciplinary approach to science.

Many facets of today's science teaching are examined in this text: what to teach, how to teach it, developmental appropriateness, interdisciplinary and multicultural aspects, the use of language arts strands in the science program, the use of technology, and the assessment of children, the program, and your teaching.

The book is divided into three sections. The first section sets the stage for contemporary science teaching and leads you from consideration of the goals and objectives of the elementary science program, the processes of science, and the role of content in teaching the processes, to the constructivist paradigm, the development of the process-oriented inquiry methodology, ways of accommodating learner differences including multicultural dimensions, ways of assessing, and special considerations regarding the elementary science classroom. The second section presents explorations of adjuncts to the basic science program: reading, writing, and interdisciplinary dimensions, the use of educational technology, concept mapping, basic concepts and principles of science appropriate for elementary science programs, and the essence of the elementary science professional. In the third section, a model which synthesizes the material is presented. Resources available to the elementary science teacher are cited in Appendix A; cross-references of activities to basic scientific principles and concepts are given in Appendix B; works of children's literature cited in the text are indexed in Appendix C.

The goals of this book are for you to construct your own personal philosophy of teaching science, lose any fears or lack of confidence that may have accompanied you into this course, and construct a methodology and curriculum base that will enable you to enter the classroom a competent teacher of science for elementary children.

Enjoy your explorations!

PART 1

Constructing the Elementary Science Program

CHAPTER 1

The Science Education Imperative

The goal of this chapter is to stimulate your thinking about elementary science education in general
terms. The constructivist viewpoint suggests that
learning occurs best when you question your own
preconceived ideas, and that the best way for this
to occur is through exposure to experiences you
cannot reconcile readily in your own mind with
the understandings and experiences available to
you. Thus, in the first chapter, we set the stage for
you to begin to question your current understandings about science education.

A fundamental issue is raised: How much
science does a competent elementary science
teacher need to know? Teachers often perceive their
intellectual authority as dependent on their knowledge of "the truth." The issue of content is examined from several viewpoints, and the proposition

is offered that competent teachers of elementary science do not have to know as much science content as they may have thought, but, instead, need such skills as observing, predicting, and hypothesizing.

Attention is given to the nebulosity of "right" and "wrong" answers. Answers teachers may consider wrong may, to some degree, be "right." Thus, it is suggested that it is more important for teachers to listen to children and elicit from them their reasons for their responses than to declare responses either right or wrong.

The processes of science are introduced as the most important outcome of science education in elementary grades because using the processes in inquiry investigations is the means by which new knowledge can be produced. It is suggested that quality elementary science education programs utilize basic scientific concepts and facts as the *vehicles* to teach the processes.

Preconceived notions about science and about science teaching are examined, and you are encouraged to find your own preconceptions in order to begin your study of elementary science teaching with an open mind.

In summary, the goal of the first chapter is to stimulate your questioning about the best way to teach science to elementary children. In keeping with the constructivist inquiry paradigm promoted in this text, you are encouraged to answer your own questions.

How Much Science Does the Elementary Science Teacher Need to Know?

What do you remember from your science experiences in school?

CONSTRUCTING YOUR IDEAS 1.1
Remembering Science

Try this. For about a minute, think back to your elementary school years, say 4th or 5th grade. Try to remember what you learned in science. Write down one or two things that come to mind, and share these with the rest of your class. Which experiences were positive? Which were negative? Do you see a commonality?

Here are some of the things students have said in classes like yours: Going on a field trip to the river bed. Dissecting frogs. Watching caterpillars hatch into butterflies. Collecting rocks.

The chances are that neither you nor other members of your class listed such notions as the composition of an atom of oxygen, the hardness of quartz, the probability of obtaining yellow pea plants from crossing two hybrids, the number of chromosomes in a normal human cell, the nature of friction, the class of lever represented by a pair of scissors, or the freezing point of water in degrees Celsius.

If you were to think back to your more recent high school years, or even to your college years, in all probability you would not include this kind of factual information in a list of things you remember having learned in science. Yet, without doubt, this material was taught!

This little exercise, of course, suggests a very important question. If we can not remember those facts and concepts and pieces of information that were undoubtedly taught to us in our school days, why were they taught? (Maybe we also need to ask *how* they were taught.) It appears that teaching factual material does not promote either lasting learning of science or enjoyment and appreciation of science.

You are undertaking to learn how to teach science to children in the elementary grades. You want your children to remember what they have learned. If they were asked the question 14 or 15 years from now, "What do you remember learning in science?" you would want them to be able to list some of what they learned in *your* classes! You also would want them to remember the joy they experienced in learning science.

Teachers of elementary science typically perceive their job to be directly related to the amount of scientific content to which they can expose children. It is generally understood that science is factual in nature and that there are certain concepts, generalizations, facts, and bits of information that every elementary child must know. It is the purpose of this section to examine how realistic this truly is.

Amount of Science Known Today

One of the difficulties involved with focusing on factual information in science education is the sheer volume of information known. The amount of science known today is enormous. There are over 50,000 distinct research fields in science (Hurd, 1990, pp. 423–424). With over 120,000 technical journals in regular print devoted to reporting currently-known scientific information, it has been calculated that a person would have to read at the rate of four million words per hour to keep up-to-date with all of science (Hurd, 1985, p. 1). In 1982, John Naisbitt reported that "between 6000 and 7000 scientific articles are written each day" (1982, p. 17). He continued:

> Scientific and technical information now increases 13 percent per year, which means it doubles every 5.5 years. But the rate will soon jump to perhaps 40 percent per year because of new, more powerful information systems and an increasing population of scientists. That means that data will double every twenty months. By 1985 the volume of information will be somewhere between four and seven times what it was only a few years earlier. (Naisbitt, 1982, p. 17)

It has been estimated that, by the year 2020, the amount of knowledge in the world will double every 73 days. That means the amount of knowledge available to the world in mid-March will be twice that which was available on New Year's Day!

You can see that there is a gargantuan amount of science known today and that the amount of scientific knowledge is increasing at an unprecedented rate.

Since there is so much science known to mankind, it should not surprise us that children may very well ask questions to which we do not know the answers. Let us say, for example, you decide you might have to teach metamorphosis. So you study the stages of metamorphosis of caterpillars in your science classes, committing them to memory, and you observe the application of these stages in beetles, moths, and butterflies. You are all set to teach metamorphosis. Now, let us say you are presenting a well-prepared lesson on the metamorphosis of caterpillars into butterflies. Unexpectedly, some child asks a question about earwigs, perhaps because his family has just discovered a colony of these pests. Now what? You know a lot about your subject, but you do not know about earwigs. How do you respond?

Here is another scenario. This time, you are dealing with simple machines. As you are having the children "invent" their own machines, a child asks about cranes. Not having studied cranes, you are in a quandary. What do you do?

By now you see the problem: *No matter how much science you study and learn, it will never be enough.*

Obsolescence of Scientific Knowledge

There is another difficulty with focusing on factual information in science: scientific knowledge may become obsolete. What we know today may be replaced in a few years with different information. For example, prior to 1956, biology teachers insisted their students memorize the *fact* that the normal cells in the human body had 48 chromosomes (24 pairs). Woe be unto any student who did not know this indisputable fact! But, in 1956, it was discovered that the human chromosome number is 46 instead of 48 (Therman, 1986, p. 8). What happens to all those students of biology in the 1950s who are roaming the globe with the so-called indisputable knowledge that the human body has 48 chromosomes in each normal cell? What can we do about that factual error?

It has been estimated that half the specialized knowledge learned by engineers will be replaced by more current knowledge in the first 3.2 years of their careers (Braun, 1991, pp. 24–25). So again we must ask if it is important to learn scientific facts, especially given that these facts may become obsolete as new discoveries are made.

Changing Scientific Knowledge

There is yet another difficulty with focusing on factual information in science: scientific knowledge changes. Scientific inquiry often results in the rejection of one previously accepted theory and in the adoption of another.[1] Our understandings of basic phenomena change with additional research, new technology, refined investigations, and deeper probing. A good example of this involves the theory of light. Today's science textbooks teach students that light is made of photons that exhibit characteristics of both particles and waves. However, this characterization of light is barely seventy years old. Before it was developed by Max Planck, Albert Einstein and others in the early 1900s, science texts taught that light was strictly a wave in nature.

In another example, the modern concept of plate tectonics that suggests the earth's continents and oceans lie on plates that move, is scarcely thirty years old and replaces the previously well-established view that continents and ocean basins are permanent.

These are but two examples of the way scientific knowledge is constantly changing.

How Much Science Does the Elementary Teacher Need to Know?

This discussion has shown there are at least three difficulties with elementary science teachers learning "enough" content:

1. There is too much science known today for any one person to be able to know it all, or even a small part of it.
2. Scientific knowledge considered factual today may become obsolete in the future.
3. Scientific conceptualizations tend to change with time.

Since this is the case, what science should the elementary science teacher know? It was agreed in the beginning of this book that there would be more questions than answers. This is the first such case. There is absolutely no answer to the question, "What science should the elementary science teacher know?" Nor is there any universally agreed-upon answer to the question "What is the *minimum* amount of science the elementary science teacher needs to know in order to be a competent science teacher?" It seems a good idea for elementary science teachers to have studied the three basic fields: life science, physical science, and earth-space science. Life science includes the study of cells, plants, animals, life cycles, genetics, evolution, and ecology. Physical science includes topics related to matter, energy, and chemistry. Earth-space science includes topics related to geology, rocks and minerals, the earth, weather, and space. Summaries of basic concepts in these areas are presented in Chapter Twelve. For now, it seems prudent to offer the following proposition: *Elementary science teachers do not have to have extensive knowledge about science in order to be able to teach it well.*

Before you throw this book away on charges of blasphemy, let me hasten to add that there most definitely are certain basic, fundamental, overarching principles of science all teachers, and, for that matter, all citizens of the world should be familiar with. But elementary teachers do not need to master a huge collection of facts, concepts, generalizations, theories, and laws about science. Rather, they need to know how children learn science and how to teach children. As Robert Yager said, "Apparently what a teacher does and how he/she does it in the classroom is far more important than what a teacher knows or the curriculum he/she uses." (1990, p. 146)

There is a solution to this dilemma presented above. Rather than children learning vast amounts of scientific information, they must learn how to *do* science. They must learn how to observe, how to create, how to come up with new ideas, how to synthesize, how to analyze, how to evaluate. They must be able to construct their own conceptualizations. They must be able to ferret out for themselves what is important and what is unimportant *for them*.

It is not necessary for teachers to clutter children's minds with myriads of facts and principles and concepts to be learned under the mistaken impression that these are essential for survival in tomorrow's (or today's) society. Children must learn how to *do* science.

Right and Wrong

In the traditional paradigm of education, teachers present information for children to learn, and children demonstrate they have learned this information with their responses to questions and situations. Some responses are considered "right," and some are considered "wrong."

Let us consider two questions that are fundamental for all of elementary science education. *Are there **right** answers? Are there **wrong** answers?*

THE GUMMY BEARS LESSON

A student teacher had developed a fine interdisciplinary math and science lesson for first grade using gummy bears. The object of the lesson was for children to sort various-colored gummy bears given to them in individual plastic bags by color, lay them head-to-toe on vertical columns previously drawn on chart paper, and draw an elementary histogram of the numbers of each of the gummy bear colors in their bags. After they were finished, they would get to eat their lesson. The student teacher passed out bags of different colored gummy bears, one to each student. Seizing on a "teachable moment," she asked each child to estimate how many gummy bears there were in his bag as she handed it to him. (Prior to this lesson, the class had explored estimation using common classroom objects.) It was obvious that there were 15 to 20 gummy bears in each bag. She went from child to child. "How many gummy bears do you suppose there are in your bag?" she asked. "Twenty," said one child. "Twenty five," said another. "Seventeen." "Twenty." "Thirty." "Twenty five." "Five." "Eighteen." Wait a minute! Didn't Melissa just say "five?" Wisely, the student teacher moved to the rest of the children, not commenting on what Melissa or anyone else had estimated. The class did the lesson while the student teacher facilitated. No one commented on the estimating activity. When they were finished, Melissa raised her hand. "I said there were five gummy bears in the bag," she said. "I thought you meant 'How many colors!'"

This anecdote illustrates a principle that is to be found over and over again in education, not only in science education: *There are no right answers!*

Suppose a teacher asks a child in her second grade class how much five plus two is. She expects the answer to be seven, of course. Suppose the child answered ten. Is that wrong? Let's ask the child. "How did you get ten?" From what the child says, the teacher infers that the child employed multiplication rather than addition. There was an error in operation, and one can easily tell what happened to produce the "wrong" answer. Suppose the child answers "three." Obviously, he must have subtracted. Note that the need to stress the importance of the +, −, ×, and ÷ signs is highlighted by these responses.

How about "52?" We all know the magnificent riddle that says "How much is five plus two?" "It's fifty-two!" So, again the child's answer is understandable. Suppose the child answers "nine." The teacher searches her mind for a way the child could come up with "nine" for an answer, but she can not find a single possible way. So, the typical teacher dismisses the answer as being an invalid one. This dismissal did not occur when the responses of "ten," or "two," or "fifty-two" were heard; this was because the teacher could construct in her own mind the way the child probably was thinking. But, she finds it impossible to construct a method in her mind by which one can obtain the answer of "nine." Does that make the "nine" wrong? This question is left for you.

Recognizing the Unexpected

New knowledge is produced as a result of new thinking—thinking that rejects the limitations of "right" and "wrong." Scientists doing science are not locked in to right and wrong answers. Rather, they continuously search for new and unexpected occurrences which do not fit previously-conceived patterns. To illustrate this point, let us consider stories of some of the more famous inventions and discoveries.

Charles Goodyear had been working for several years on how to preserve and cure raw rubber so it would maintain its elastic characteristics regardless of temperature. His discovery of vulcanization, the process by which the rubber for tires is processed, occurred by following an instinct he said had come to him in a dream: combine sulfur with the rubber. He wrote:

> I was encouraged in my efforts by the reflection that what is hidden and unknown, and cannot be discovered by scientific research, will most

likely be discovered by accident, if at all, and by the man who applies himself most perseveringly to the subject, and is most observing of everything related thereto. (Iles, 1968, p. 166)

Samuel Morse conceived the telegraph after a chance conversation about electricity with a fellow passenger aboard a steamship returning to the United States (Iles, p. 82).

The telephone was developed from an accidental occurrence. Alexander Graham Bell and his associate, Thomas Watson, were experimenting with the possibility that a vibrating membrane might be made to produce changes in electric current similar to the way the human eardrum transmits vibrations to the hammer, anvil, and stirrup in the inner ear. One day in 1875, Watson was working on the transmitting part of the apparatus while Bell was in another room listening at the receiving end. Suddenly Bell heard a twang over the receiver. One of the springs in the transmitter had become stuck, and Watson had caused it to twang while trying to get it free. This had generated a small electric current which was transmitted along the wire to the receiver. This accident ultimately resulted in the development of the telephone (Evans, 1966, pp. 96–97).

The production of penicillin can be traced to a chance observation by Sir Alexander Fleming in 1928 that some air-borne material, later shown to be mold, had contaminated petri dishes of culture medium on which colonies of *staphylococcus* bacteria were growing, killing the bacteria (Macfarlane, 1984, pp. 118–119). Fleming did not understand the medical implications of this discovery, and several years later, Gladys Hobby, together with Martin Henry and Karl Meyer, perfected penicillin, becoming the first to cure a patient with the drug. Hobby subsequently developed Terramycin, a more powerful antibiotic.

In each of these cases, the discovery was made because people were able to recognize the significance of something they had never seen before! This is one of the primary characteristics of scientists. New knowledge is not produced simply by committing old knowledge to memory, though certainly some prior knowledge is necessary as a foundation. New knowledge is produced by being able to observe what others have not observed, ask questions no one has thought to ask, try things no one has thought to try, make inferences no one has thought to make, sort things in different ways, and focus less on *right* answers and more on *sensible* answers. New knowledge is produced as the result of being able to *do* science.

Perception

CONSTRUCTING YOUR IDEAS 1.2
Meanings of a Word

Try this. Pick a word that is a little unusual, but that everyone knows, and ask the rest of the class to write the first word that comes to mind. For example, you might ask the students to write the first thing that comes to mind when you say the word "Jaguar."

Responses might include "tiger," "animal," "car," "silver," "money," "rich," "cat." Each response represents the initial association made with the word. Notice the different ways people in your class perceive the same stimulus.

CONSTRUCTING YOUR IDEAS 1.3
Meanings of Pairs of Words

Try this. Create pairs of words from the following, and tell WHY you paired them.

ants — cats — monkeys — buildings —
plastic — rocks — bananas — tacks

Pair #1: _____ and _____

Why? _____

Pair #2 _____ and _____

Why? _____

Compare the responses of different members of your class. Who paired something with the word, "monkeys?" Perhaps someone paired "bananas" with "monkeys," because monkeys *eat* bananas. Perhaps someone else paired "rocks" with "monkeys," because monkeys like to climb rocks. Did anyone pair "buildings" with "monkeys?" Who paired something with the word "cats?" A student once paired "tacks" with "cats" because they had four letters in common. How about other pairs? Different people perceive these words in different ways.

CONSTRUCTING YOUR IDEAS 1.4
Meanings of a Sentence

Try this. Read the following sentence out loud to a group of people, and ask them to write down the first thing that comes to mind.

There is a man at home with a mask,
and another man coming home.

Some of the responses might include "robbers," "Halloween," "rape," and so on. One student wrote "baseball." All individuals in your group heard precisely the same thing (namely the sentence), and yet perceived the meaning in a variety of different ways.

Optical illusions also show that different people perceive the same stimulus in different ways. (See Figure 1.1.)

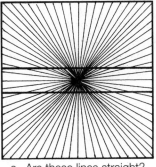

a. Are these lines straight?

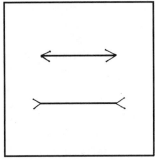

b. Are these lines of different lengths?

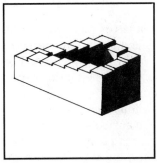

c. Where is the top of the stairs?

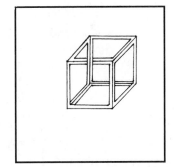

d. Can you build this box?

FIGURE 1.1 Optical illusions

Perception is "the detection and interpretation of sensory stimuli" (Solso, 1988, p. 6). It is the mental image formed when information is received through the senses and is attended to. No two people, when exposed to the same stimulus, perceive it in the same way.[2] This is because we all have different prior experiences of different strengths which influence how we perceive things. Different people in your class associated the word "Jaguar" with different phenomena. Different people formed different pairs of words from the same list. Different people attached different meanings to the "man with a mask."

If this is true with simple things like words, then it is also true with more complex concepts like "volcano eruption." Ask a class of third graders to respond to the word "volcano," and the children will talk about all sorts of things, from explosions, lava, and cones to Mt. St. Helens (if they have a relative who lives in Washington) and Hawaii (if they have visited there, or have relatives there, or have become interested in Hawaii). Is any one of these responses the *right* one? Is any one of these responses *wrong*? How about "Jaguars?" Which response is right? Which is wrong? It would be very difficult, indeed, to say that any of these responses was either *right* or *wrong*. The best we can say is that *to the individual* the response is right. Students are likely to respond in very different ways from what we teachers expect. That does not make the student's response wrong; it simply makes it *theirs*.

This is one of the main reasons why standardized testing is being examined, particularly at the pre-school level; different children associate different meanings with the same words. For example, when asked "When do you go swimming?" some three-year-olds reply "summer," and others, who swim indoors, reply "winter." (Assessment is discussed in detail in Chapter Seven.)

Listening

It is a fundamental premise of this text that teachers of elementary science education must listen to children—listen to their responses—so they can understand what *their* prior experiential base is, how *they* are combining new information with their prior experiences, and how *they* are constructing information.

In this way, we see that there are no "right" answers and there are no "wrong" answers; the answers children offer are representative of the way they are thinking. It is far more important for teachers to listen to children and elicit from them their reasons for their responses than to declare their responses either right or wrong.

The Process of Science

We have tried to make the point that it is better for children to learn how to do science than it is for them to learn the facts, generalizations, concepts, theories, and laws someone else has concluded—that it is better for children to learn to do science than to learn about science. What does it mean to do science? What do children do when they do science?

To answer these questions, we turn our attention to the *processes of science*.

CONSTRUCTING YOUR IDEAS 1.5
What Did You See On Your Way to School Today?

Try this. Take about one minute, and think about what you saw on your way to school today. Then, write down one or two things and share them in your class.

What did you see? Responses in other classes have included "traffic," "signal lights," "rain," "fog," "an accident." However, many people have difficulty recalling what they saw on the way to school. Why is that? Certainly there were countless stimuli! It is because we did not pay attention to what we were seeing. We have not sharpened our powers of *observation*. Observations are made by employing our senses, and observing is the most fundamental of the processes of science.

The *Random House Dictionary* defines the term *process* as "a systematic series of actions directed to some end," (Stein, 1967). In science, the processes are directed to the end of understanding a phenomenon, answering a question, developing a theory, or discovering more information about something. Twelve processes make up the scientific endeavor:

1. Observing
2. Classifying
3. Communicating
4. Measuring
5. Predicting
6. Inferring
7. Identifying and Controlling Variables
8. Formulating and Testing Hypotheses
9. Interpreting Data
10. Defining Operationally
11. Experimenting
12. Constructing Models

Learning to do science means learning to do the processes in inquiry situations. The processes are discussed in detail in Chapter Three.

History of the Process Approach to Science Education

Let us take a short historical excursion to see how the processes of science came to be recognized as the foundation for scientific activity. In October, 1959, the United States felt deeply humiliated by the launching of the Soviet spaceship, Sputnik. American scientists had been working on launching an American space craft for a number of years; yet the Soviets were first. Great was the gnashing of teeth, long were the faces of the scientists, the citizenry, and the government. The question was asked, "How did this happen? How did the United States, with all its technological capabilities, all its talent and all its money, not achieve the goal of being first in space?" As so often happens, education took much of the blame. This was a turning point in science education.

One month prior to the launching of Sputnik, Jerome Bruner, a renowned professor of psychology at Harvard, chaired the now-famous ten-day "Woods Hole" conference in Woods Hole, Massachusetts. The conference was held at the request of the National Academy of Sciences which, for several years, had been examining the state of science education in America. The intent of the conference was "not to institute a crash program, but rather to examine the fundamental processes involved in imparting to young students a sense of the substance and method of science" (Bruner, 1965, p. vii). The conference was unprecedented in that it dealt with education, yet was chaired by a psychologist and was attended by experts in several science disciplines, psychology, mathematics, and cinematography, in addition to education.

The question was asked, "How do scientists *do* science?" Though there had been brief forays into process-oriented science curricula prior to the conference, science education had largely consisted of imparting those facts, concepts, generalizations, theories, and laws of chemistry, biology, physics, geology, astronomy, and other scientific fields which had been deemed important for children to learn. Since this scientific information often was too advanced for elementary children, science education was concentrated in the upper grades. At the Woods Hole conference, the conclusion was reached that students should learn science the way science is done. Chemistry should be learned the way chemists practice their profession; physics should be learned the way physicists do physics; biology should be learned the way biologists explore their world.

These convictions manifested themselves in the continuation of bold new approaches to science education that focused more on process than content. Often called the "alphabet soup curricula" of the 1960s, the new science programs included BSCS biology, CHEM-Study Chemistry, and PSSC Physics among others. As the process approach to science education rippled to the lower grades, a host of new elementary science curriculum projects became available: ESS (Elementary Science Study), SCIS (Science Curriculum Improvement Study), SAPA (Science A Process Approach), and others. They were "hands-on" programs that encouraged students at all levels to predict and experiment first and conclude later. This was in direct contrast to the verification model of laboratory "experiments" where the teacher explained what was supposed to happen based on some theory or principle, and then set the students to work on a carefully outlined laboratory activity designed to demonstrate that the theory or principle was correct.

For example, you may recall adding a drop of iodine to various food materials in biology class. You had already learned that iodine turns blue-black in the presence of starch, and that this was the test for starch. So, in the laboratory activity, you were directed to place one drop of iodine on each of several foods (potato, sugar, cornstarch, and bread) and record the resulting color. Then you were to record your conclusions, which, in this case, were that the potato, cornstarch, and bread contained starch. In essence, you *verified* what someone else had already concluded.

Hands-On Elementary Science Approaches of the 1960s

In the new hands-on elementary science approaches of the 1960s, children were led through a series of activities to make many of these discoveries for themselves. The whole idea was for children to master the processes of science—to learn how to *do* science. These new science programs rapidly replaced the former content-oriented programs. They became the solution to the perceived deterioration of science knowledge and scientific expertise of America's youth.

Of the programs developed in the late 1950s and 1960s, only the BSCS—Biological Sciences Curriculum Study—still maintains a national office and is active in curriculum issues. Why did the new programs fail? Why are we in the same basic state of affairs today that we were in forty years ago?

This is a complex question, and there is no simple answer to it. It appears, however, that there were several contributing factors to the failure of the "Alphabet Soup" science programs. One had to do with teacher commitment. Often, the new programs were handed to teachers who were instructed to replace the old programs with the new ones. Teachers were not trained in the use of the new materials; they did not know the rationales for them; they did not know the program goals or what the new programs were supposed to accomplish. Using the new materials was expensive; teacher preparation time was extensive. Teachers were afraid of losing control of their classes by allowing children freedom to explore, for, at that time, classrooms were highly structured with teachers as focal points. Teachers are the most important factor in a classroom, and if they are not involved in materials adoption decisions, they are likely to shelve new materials and continue using the old familiar textbooks. This is exactly what happened with the hands-on inquiry programs of the 1960s.

Then, too, there was the perceived necessity of pleasing the school administration and the school district; those districts that continued to place high emphasis on content acquisition found teachers reluctant to implement new programs in which the focus on content was diminished. Consequently, and tragically, the new programs were abandoned. But did they fail? Shymansky, Kyle, and Alport synthesized performance data from earlier studies that focused on ESS, SCIS, and SAPA. They compared performance improvements for students in classrooms that used ESS, SCIS, and SAPA with that of students in traditional classrooms. Six performance areas were considered: achievement, attitude, facility in process skills, facility in related skills, creativity, and performance on Piagetian tasks. They concluded,

> When the cumulative results of the research were considered, students in new programs outperformed those in traditional textbook-based classrooms on every criterion measured . . . The average student in the ESS, SCIS, or SAPA classroom performed better than 62% of the students in traditional classrooms across all performance criteria measured—a 12 percentile-point gain. (1982, p. 14–15)

Over time, educators began to dissect the ways scientists do science to find its roots; this resulted in the identification of the processes of science.

It seems logical that because the processes of science are the fundamental building blocks of the scientific enterprise, our children ought to be developing facility in these processes. The scientific facts, generalizations, principles, theories, and laws are springboards for children to use as they explore the processes and develop mastery of them. Processes are mastered using content as the vehicle. For example, the process of observing can be taught using plants, animals, rocks, and moving objects. Children can learn to classify using leaves, pictures of seasons, shells, and minerals. Children communicate the results of their scientific inquiries; they measure items they use in their experiments; they predict what would happen if a plant is deprived of light; and they infer why soil is composed of many different things.

Once again, it is a fundamental premise of this text that it is far more important for children to learn the process skills than to learn facts; it is far more important that they learn to *do* science than to learn *about* science.

Ownership of Knowledge and Thought

Science education, as all education, should lead to independent self-activity. It should empower individuals to think and act. (DeBoer, 1991, p. 249)

In order to be self-empowered, children must develop confidence in their thinking abilities. They must take ownership of their knowledge and their thinking. Children know a lot of science before they enter school, such as properties of toys, characteristics of seasons, the difference between heat and cold, what cooking does to food, and so on. They need to be told that they know a lot of science so they can develop confidence and take ownership of their abilities to learn.

Mystery Box

CONSTRUCTING YOUR IDEAS 1.6
A Mystery Box

Try this. Before you go any further, please STOP and do this activity.

Obtain a small box that has a cover, and place two or three small objects in it. The objects may be any size and any shape, and may be made of any material. *Do not tell anyone what is in the box!* Put the cover on the box, tape it shut, and give this Mystery Box to four or five other students in a group. Ask them to draw or write or describe what is in the box. If you put magnetic items in the box, you may wish to provide them with a magnet to help them in their observations.

A typical box might contain a 1-inch washer taped to the bottom of the box, a loose metal screw, and a small irregularly-shaped stone. (See Figure 1.2) You may wish to include coins or marbles. *Do not put too many items in the box!*

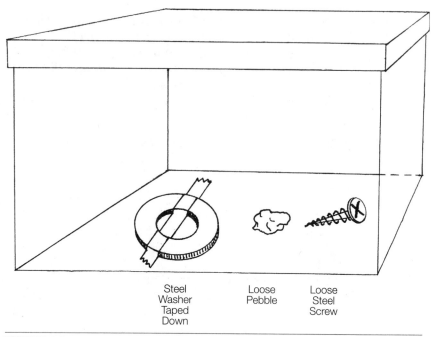

Steel	Loose	Loose
Washer	Pebble	Steel
Taped		Screw
Down		

FIGURE 1.2   A Typical mystery box

What do you have to do to figure out what is in the box? You prob-ably will shake it. You will tilt it, sometimes rapidly, sometimes very slowly, sometimes at different angles. You will listen to what is happen-ing inside as you tilt it. You will try to balance it. You will try the magnet to see if there is anything magnetic in it. Can you feel a magnetic force? You have been using the sense of feel (magnetic pull), sound (listening to what happens when you tilt the box), and sight (checking for balance). What other senses do you use? Try smelling it. Any odors? As you pro-ceed with your investigation, you will get more and more refined in focus. You will discuss your ideas with others in your group, arguing, defending, changing your mind in response to the input of others, and so on.

Please notice that, in this activity, you used several processes: observa-tion, classification (identifying objects as magnetic or non-magnetic), com-munication (with members in your group), maybe some measurement (locations of permanent objects; relative strength of magnetic pull), predi-cation, inference, formulating and testing hypotheses (if you compared the magnetic strength of known objects with the magnetic strength of objects in the box), interpreting data, and, possibly, constructing models.

Now you can make some preliminary generalizations about what is in the box. Let us refine these conclusions. How big is each item? What shape? How thick? What color?

Keep pursuing your investigations. (In an elementary science classroom, the teacher would possibly keep the box or boxes in the science center for several weeks, continually challenging the children to refine their conclusions about what is in the box. Children would work in cooperative groups, challenging each other's perceptions and asking for reasons why they inferred what they did.)

Eventually you will have formulated your very best idea. Are you *right*? How sure are you? What is your confidence percentage? How could you increase your confidence percentage? You could make a model—create an identical box with the same things in yours that you think are in the Mystery Box, and compare the two boxes carefully to see if they exhibit the same characteristics.

There probably are several notions as to what is in the box. Who is right? Who is wrong? Remember, the box is closed. "Rightness" and "wrongness" take on different perspectives—they are no longer the function of correctness of answer, but rather are the function of your best thinking and the way you interrelate your observations and your thinking to form your conclusions. Each student's conclusion is accepted as representative of his best thinking.

This Mystery Box activity also is analogous to children's minds. You, the teacher, can never know with certainty what is in a child's mind. You can ask questions, you can listen, you can ask for clarification, drawings, logic, observations, and personal feelings in an effort to discover what and how the children are thinking. But your conclusion as to what is in a child's mind is no more accurate than your conclusion as to what is in the Mystery Box. You can only *infer*.

Ownership

Should you open the boxes? Suppose they were sealed shut, never to be opened! How would you feel? Frustrated? Cheated? You would never know if you were right or wrong. If you do not open the boxes, you will be required to rely on your own powers of observation, your own reasoning, and your own conclusions that you, yourself, reach from your own and others' thinking. You will be forced to validate your conclusions from your own thinking. You will be forced to *assume ownership* of your observations and thoughts and conclusions.

However, suppose you know you will be allowed to open the box at some point in time. Suddenly *your* thinking is de-valued. Instead of observing and thinking and reasoning, you are trying to "guess." The motivation becomes to compare your answer with the "right" answer, not with your own conclusion. There is a "right" answer, and you compare your answer with IT. If you guessed correctly, great! If not, Oh Well!

Should you open the box? Do you have faith in the ability of the scientific processes you used in this activity to provide a "best" answer? Each class will have to decide for themselves. As you are deciding, please cite your arguments.

Valuing Children's Thinking

CONSTRUCTING YOUR IDEAS 1.7
Whose Knowledge Is Valued?

Here is a question for you to wrestle with. Is it more important that elementary children value the teacher's knowledge, or their own?

Many students answer "their own." This response comes from a belief that one of the primary jobs of the teacher is to help children think for themselves. But, what about the teacher? Isn't the teacher's thinking more valid than the children's? Hasn't the teacher had many years of education learning how to think? Shouldn't the teacher teach the children how to think? Shouldn't the teacher encourage the children to emulate correct thinking? This is a question for you to ponder.

If you truly believe it is important for children to take ownership of their own knowledge, then you will be asking how teachers can foster children's beliefs that their thinking is valuable.

Let us digress briefly. The typical elementary teacher asks between 64 and 348 questions a day in elementary school (Orlich et al., 1985, p. 163). The idea is that questioning, as a teaching-learning strategy, stimulates student thinking, enables teachers to better understand what children are thinking, helps teachers know where to provide clarification.

Consider a typical series of questions a kindergarten teacher might ask in introducing a lesson on animals:

Name one animal.
Name another kind of animal.
Name an animal that flies.
Name an animal that has four legs.
Name an animal that lives at home.
Name an animal that lives in the forest.
Name an animal that lives in water.
Name an animal with fur.

It is easy to see how a teacher can fit 348 such questions in the course of a day.

Let us take a look at these questions. Each question implies there are one or more right answers, and that any other answers are wrong.

"Name an animal that flies."
"Bird?"
"Right!"
"Duck?"
"Right!"
"Dog?"
"Wrong!"
"Name an animal that has four legs."
"Dog?"
"Right!"
"Spider?"
"Wrong!"
"Name an animal that lives at home."
"Cat?"
"Right!"
"Lion?"
"Wrong!"

You get the idea: for each question, there are Right answers and there are Wrong answers. Who knows the Right answers? The teacher, of course. Note in the above questioning scenario, the children answered in a questioning tone of voice, and the teacher told them whether they were right or wrong. Teachers indicate "right" or "wrong" answers in a variety of subtle ways, like "Oh, really?" "That's a good answer." "Thank you for answering." and so on until finally a right answer comes along, and the teacher says "Right" or "That's what I was looking for," or "The other answers were good ones, but that is the one I wanted to hear."

In this type of situation, it is the teacher who owns the knowledge. The teacher encourages the children to compare their answers (maybe right and maybe wrong) with the teacher's (always right), thereby giving the children the unmistakable notion that their job is to supply the answers the teacher wants to hear. The teacher owns the knowledge. The teacher is in charge. It is the teacher's thinking that is valued. The same thing happens in hands-on settings that involve children doing activities whose end results are already known, where it is the job of the child to come up with the result the teacher expects. "I don't think that's quite right; try it again and see what you get." (Translation: "You haven't yet gotten the result I wanted you to get.")

How can that be reversed? Using Bloom's higher levels in questioning promotes discussion, whereas using Bloom's lower levels leads to right and wrong answers (Bloom, 1956). The use of open ended questions with longer wait time and longer think time goes a long way toward fostering children's beliefs that their own thinking is important. But, of course, you can't ask 348 questions a day in that manner.

CONSTRUCTING YOUR IDEAS 1.8
Questioning

Try this. Someone be the "teacher," and the rest of the class be the students. Ask a number of factual questions about plants such as these:

> What are the three main parts of plants?
> Which part holds the plant in the ground?
> Which part makes food for the plant?
> Which part holds the plant up?
> What do plants need in order to live?
> Do plants grow better in the light or in the dark?

Keep this line of questioning going for half a minute or so. You will find you get instant responses, and that a "rhythm" becomes established. Question — answer — question — answer — etc.

> Now, suddenly interject a question like this:
> What would happen to a plant if you exposed it only to red light?

The response to the last question is slower to come. First there are a few "silly" responses; that is because people don't want to interrupt the rhythm, and because they want to fill the awkward silence required for thinking with some sort of sound. However, most students will remain silent as they try to gather their thoughts. After a suitable wait period (say, 15 seconds), the teacher asks for the responses and listens to them without comment. Students will offer their best thinking on the subject, thereby taking ownership of their responses.

When asking questions of children, if you, the teacher, resist the temptation to offer "words of great wisdom" (or, better yet, if you don't know the answer to the question), the children will have to work it out for themselves. They will own the thought processes as well as the conclusion. They will be well on their way to learning that their knowledge is valuable and is valued by the teacher.

Another way to encourage children's ownership of their own thought processes and knowledge is to reduce the number of affirmations offered, such as "right," "good try," "wonderful," etc., for these responses lead the child to believe that responses are given for the teacher's judgement. To foster children's ownership of their thinking, these responses are replaced with simple statements thanking children for their responses. The responses to children's answers that foster the highest degree of ownership are those that probe the children's thinking. "Why did you say that?" "How do you know?" "Give an example of what you just said." "Can you add to Jane's response?" "Do you agree?" Do you disagree?" "What would happen if . . ."

In this course you will construct a way of teaching elementary science that places ownership of thought as well as scientific facts, concepts, generalizations, and theories firmly in the laps (or heads) of your children: the process-oriented inquiry methodology. Under the guidance of the teacher, children ask their own questions, devise their own ways to explore their questions, and develop their own answers to their questions.

It is not within the scope of this book to discuss at length how children learn or how they fail. But, if children are to learn and retain anything, they must own and value what *they* do, not what *we* do. Our job is to lead them to their own sound thinking. We must set the tone in the class that sends the signal to all children that their answers are at least important as anyone else's—including the teacher's.

Attitudes about Science and Attitudes about Science Teaching

All people have preconceived notions shaped by their own prior experiences and learning. Some of these notions are congruent with generally accepted knowledge, and some are not. Some are positive, and some are negative. Many teachers have preconceived ideas about the ability of children to learn, and about the amount of scientific information children possess before coming to school. Preconceived ideas about the natural world strongly influence what people learn; we will discuss this phenomenon and its implications for teaching elementary science in Chapter Four. Furthermore, teachers' preconceptions about the ability of children to learn strongly influence the way they teach.

Teacher Beliefs

Arthur Combs has investigated what makes good "helpers" (which include teachers as well as counselors, clergy, nurses, therapists, etc.) He has concluded that what makes a good helper is *not* knowledge, and is *not* methodology.[3] The effectiveness of a helping professional is a result primarily of the *beliefs* of the individual. Teachers behave in terms of their beliefs. Combs identified five areas of beliefs:

1. *Beliefs about the kind of data we should be tuned to:*
   Good helpers tune into data concerned with *people* questions; poor helpers tune into data concerned with *things* questions.

2. *Beliefs about what people are like:*
   Good helpers believe people are *able*; poor helpers *doubt* that people are able.

3. *Beliefs about self (self-concept):*
   Good helpers see the self in essentially positive ways and are self-actualizing. Poor helpers see the self in essentially negative ways.

4. *Beliefs about purpose (what is truly important):*
   Good helpers see their purpose to be essentially a *freeing* behavior; poor helpers see their purpose to be essentially a *controlling* behavior.

5. *Beliefs about methods:*
   Good helpers utilize *self-revealing* methods; poor helpers utilize *self-concealing* methods.

Teachers' beliefs about science, about science teaching, and about children's ability to succeed in science strongly influence their teaching of science.

CONSTRUCTING YOUR IDEAS 1.9
Attitude Inventories

Try this. Because one's belief system is so strong in influencing teaching behavior, two short inventories are presented in Figure 1.3 and Figure 1.4 that may help you reveal some of your biases, positive as well as negative, toward science and toward your teaching of science. Please take a few minutes to complete them. The directions are simple: using a general approach, write for each item the letter between the pairs of adjectives that best reflects your feelings about science (in the first inventory) or your feeling about science teaching (in the second inventory). An "A" indicates you most agree with the term on the left; an "E" indicates you most agree with the term on the right; a "C" indicates you are uncertain.

Scoring is subjective. Score each inventory separately. Give yourself 5 points for each A, 4 points for each B, 3 points for each C, 2 points for each D, and 1 point for each E. Your score in each inventory could range from 20 (if you marked all "E's") to 100 (if you marked all "A's").

MY ATTITUDES ABOUT SCIENCE

	A	B	C	D	E	
1. GOOD	——	——	——	——	——	BAD
2. PLEASURABLE	——	——	——	——	——	UNPLEASURABLE
3. MEANINGFUL	——	——	——	——	——	UNMEANINGFUL
4. IMPORTANT	——	——	——	——	——	UNIMPORTANT
5. POSITIVE	——	——	——	——	——	NEGATIVE
6. SIMPLE	——	——	——	——	——	COMPLEX
7. BENEFICIAL	——	——	——	——	——	HARMFUL
8. INTERESTING	——	——	——	——	——	BORING
9. EASY	——	——	——	——	——	DIFFICULT
10. OBJECTIVE	——	——	——	——	——	SUBJECTIVE
11. SAFE	——	——	——	——	——	DANGEROUS
12. USEFUL	——	——	——	——	——	USELESS
13. EFFORTLESS	——	——	——	——	——	LABORIOUS
14. ORDERLY	——	——	——	——	——	DISORDERLY
15. COMFORTABLE	——	——	——	——	——	UNCOMFORTABLE
16. VALUABLE	——	——	——	——	——	WORTHLESS
17. STIMULATING	——	——	——	——	——	MONOTONOUS
18. COMFORTING	——	——	——	——	——	THREATENING
19. PRODUCTIVE	——	——	——	——	——	UNPRODUCTIVE
20. ORDERLY	——	——	——	——	——	CLUTTERED

FIGURE 1.3 Inventory about attitudes toward science

MY ATTITUDES ABOUT ME TEACHING SCIENCE

		A	B	C	D	E	
1.	SAFE	——	——	——	——	——	DANGEROUS
2.	HAPPY	——	——	——	——	——	SAD
3.	COMFORTABLE	——	——	——	——	——	UNCOMFORTABLE
4.	SUCCESSFUL	——	——	——	——	——	UNSUCCESSFUL
5.	CLEAN	——	——	——	——	——	DIRTY
6.	ORDERLY	——	——	——	——	——	DISORDERLY
7.	USEFUL	——	——	——	——	——	USELESS
8.	CONTENTED	——	——	——	——	——	DISCONTENTED
9.	PLEASURABLE	——	——	——	——	——	PAINFUL
10.	IMPORTANT	——	——	——	——	——	UNIMPORTANT
11.	REFRESHED	——	——	——	——	——	WEARY
12.	ORGANIZED	——	——	——	——	——	DISORGANIZED
13.	BENEFICIAL	——	——	——	——	——	HARMFUL
14.	OPTIMISTIC	——	——	——	——	——	PESSIMISTIC
15.	EAGER	——	——	——	——	——	INDIFFERENT
16.	STRONG	——	——	——	——	——	WEAK
17.	GOOD	——	——	——	——	——	BAD
18.	SUFFICIENT	——	——	——	——	——	INSUFFICIENT
19.	INFLUENTIAL	——	——	——	——	——	UNINFLUENTIAL
20.	STIMULATING	——	——	——	——	——	MONOTONOUS

FIGURE 1.4 Inventory about attitudes toward teaching science

These inventories may give you a general idea about your current attitudes toward science and the teaching of science. If you scored on the positive side (80–100), you are well on your way to enjoying teaching elementary science. If your score was low, indicating negative attitudes, you may want to look at what you can do to develop a more positive general attitude. You are the only one who knows; no one can tell you what your attitude is.

You also may want to look at individual items. Which ones did you mark D or E? Which ones were you unsure of, thus marking a C? These may indicate areas you might want to pay attention to as you develop your competence in teaching elementary science—fears, likes, dislikes, areas of discomfort, etc. Remember what Arthur Combs said: The most important factor influencing people to be good in the helping professions is their beliefs. These beliefs are manifested in attitudes. The successful elementary science teacher enters the field with a positive attitude and a truly open mind.

Discovering your current beliefs about science and the teaching of science, and being aware that you do have prior beliefs about the natural world, often are all that is necessary to open areas of inquiry that were previously closed.

Metaphors

One last word about prior beliefs involves the use of metaphors. Recent research has dealt with metaphors and teachers' latent beliefs about teaching as indicated by the metaphors they choose to characterize their role as a teacher (Munby, 1986; Pajares, 1992; Tobin, 1990). For example, teachers characterizing themselves as "captain of their ship" may be very strong leaders, reluctant to transfer responsibility for learning to children.

CONSTRUCTING YOUR IDEAS 1.10
Metaphors

Try this. Think for minute or so about a metaphor you would use to characterize your role as a teacher of elementary science. Do you consider yourself the captain of your ship? A bus driver? An explorer? A scout leader? A parent? Record the various metaphors the members of your class come up with, and, from that list (which includes your own metaphor), select the metaphor you believe most closely represents your current thinking about what an elementary science teacher is and does. Write it down.

Refer to this metaphor frequently during this course; see if you want to change it. This may be one of the better indicators of how you are constructing the content of the course.

Research in Science Education

Educational research takes many forms and serves many functions. Its primary purpose is to inform the educator on issues of best practice. Research in science education serves the same purpose as general educational research, and centers essentially on issues of curriculum, the learner, and methodology.

Much research is referred to in this text; the student is advised to study the referenced material, question its validity and its application to the classroom, and become a proactive consumer of the research. Questioning is the key to intelligent consumption of research. Research is a springboard for discussion and a catalyst for questions.

Conclusion

The goal of the first chapter has been to promote your personal inquiry into the "best" way of teaching science to elementary children. You have examined a number of issues, and have drawn tentative conclusions. You have started to ask important questions about content, process, goals, outcomes, and methodology of elementary science teaching. As you progress through this course, make it your goal to formulate answers to these questions, to resolve your concerns, and to develop a system of science education that meets the needs of today's children as we prepare them to live in the 21st Century. No one can do this for you; to try to do so would be doing the same thing we are suggesting you *not* do with children: pump them full of previously-digested information. You have to make up your own mind; you have to construct this business of elementary science education such that it makes sense to you.

The rest of the text will help you in your quest.

CHAPTER 1   Additional Questions for Discussion

1. How much of the huge amount of science known is it necessary for you to know in order to teach science?

2. How much of the huge amount of science known is necessary for elementary children to learn?

3. In his book, *Horace's Compromise*, Theodor Sizer states, "Good teachers and wise students know how to separate performance (you flunked) from person (you're O.K.). Making a child feel stupid is stupid and cruel, but pretending that 2 + 2 = 5 in order to massage the student's ego is cruel, and dishonest in addition." (1985, p. 175) Contrast this proposition with the constructivist viewpoint of no right answers and no wrong answers suggested in this chapter.

Notes

1. For a detailed discussion of changing scientific paradigms, see Kuhn, T. (1970).

2. The concept of uniqueness of perception and its application to education was explored in detail over forty years ago by Earl Kelley and Marie Rasey (1952).

3. From a lecture at Kennesaw State College, July 19, 1993.

References

Bloom, B. S., Englehart, M. D., Furst, E. J., Hill, W. H. & Krathwohl, D. R. (Eds.). (1956). *Taxonomy of Educational Objectives. The Classification of Educational Goals. Handbook I: Cognitive Domain.* New York, NY: McKay.

Braun, L. (1991). School drop-outs, economics, & technology. *Computing Teacher*, March, 1991, pp. 24–25.

Bruner, J. S. (1965). *The Process of Education.* Cambridge, MA: Harvard University Press.

DeBoer, G. E. (1991). *A History of Ideas in Science Education: Implications for Practice.* New York, NY: Teachers College Press.

Evans, I. O. (1966). *Inventors of the World.* London: Frederick Warne & Co. Ltd.

Hurd, P. D. (1990). Guest editorial: Change and challenge in science education. *Journal of Research in Science Teaching 27*(5), 413–414.

———. (1985). *A Changing Society: New Perspectives for Science Education.* Paper adapted from an address delivered at the PACE Seminar on Educational Policy for a Changing California Economy, Sacramento, CA, June 14, 1984. Eric Document Number: ED 271311

Iles, George (1968). *Leading American Inventors.* Freeport, NY: Books for Libraries Press.

Kelley, E. C. & Rasey, M. I. (1952). *Education and the Nature of Man*. New York, NY: Harper & Row.

Kuhn, T. S. (1970). *The Structure of Scientific Revolutions*. Chicago, IL: The University of Chicago Press.

Macfarlane, G. (1984). *Alexander Fleming: The Man and the Myth*. Cambridge, MA: Harvard University Press, p. 118–119.

Munby, H. (1986). Metaphor in the thinking of teachers: An exploratory study. *Journal of Curriculum Studies, 18*, p. 197–209.

Naisbitt, J. (1982). *Megatrends*. New York: Warner Books, Inc., p. 17.

Orlich, D.C., Harder, R. J., Callahan, R.G., Kravas, C. H., Kauchak, D. P., Pendergrass, R. A., & Keogh, A. J. (1985). *Teaching Strategies: A Guide to Better Instruction*. Lexington, MA: D.C. Heath and Company.

Pajares, M. (1992). Teachers' beliefs and educational research: Cleaning up on a messy construct. *Review of Educational Research, 61*, p. 307–332.

Sagan, Carl. In *A Brief History of Time* by Stephen W. Hawking (1988). New York, NY: Bantam Books.

Shymansky, J. A., Kyle, W. C., and Alport, J. M. (1982). How effective were the hands-on science programs of yesterday? *Science and Children*, November–December, 1982, p. 14–15.

Sizer, T. (1985). *Horace's Compromise*. Boston: Houghton Mifflin.

Solso, R. L. (1988). *Cognitive Psychology*, Second Edition. Newton, MA: Allyn and Bacon, Inc., p. 6.

Stein, J. (Ed.) (1967). *The Random House Dictionary of the English Language*. New York: Random House.

Therman, E. (1986). *Human Chromosomes*. New York: Springer-Verlag. p. 8.

Tobin, K. (1990). Research on science laboratory activities: In pursuit of better questions and answers to improve learning. *School Science and Mathematics, 90*, p. 403–418.

Yager, R. E. (1993). The need for reform in science teacher education. *Journal of Science Teacher Education 4*(4), 144–148. p. 146.

CHAPTER 2

Science Education Today

The task of science is to both extend the range of our experience and reduce it to order.

Niels Bohr, in Holton, G. & Roller, H. D. (1958), *Foundations of Modern Physical Science*, Reading, MA: Addison-Wesley, p. 214.

You have been exploring a number of factors related to teaching science to elementary school children. You have considered the propositions that it is better for children to learn to *do* science through mastering the processes than to learn *about* science; that scientific content is the vehicle through which the processes can be taught; that children should learn science in a manner similar to the way scientists actually do science.

Thus far we have not said very much about science itself or about how scientists do science. In this chapter, you will inquire into the nature of science—the scientific enterprise, products, processes, and attitudes—and you will explore goals and objectives appropriate for the quality elementary science program.

The Nature of Science

What we know today as *science* was originally called *philosophy*. The word, *philosophy*, was coined during the time of Aristotle from two words: *philos* (love) and *sophia* (wisdom). Thus, the term, *philosophy*, literally means "love of wisdom." The term, *science*, comes from the Latin word, *scientia*, meaning "to know." The dictionaries ground their primary definitions of *science* in the Latin derivative: "A possession of knowledge" (Webster's, 1973); "A branch of knowledge or study dealing with a body of facts or truths systematically arranged and showing the operation of general laws; skill; proficiency" (Stein, 1967).

In *Science for All Americans* (Rutherford & Ahlgren, 1990, p. 4), the following definition is cited: "Science is a process for producing knowledge." That is what we mean by science in this book: a process for producing knowledge. The implication is that science comprises both process and content.

A major goal of science is to explain and describe phenomena observed in the natural world. These explanations and descriptions are embodied in the concepts, theories, and laws of science, all of which have been tested and have been shown to be reasonably, but tentatively, true. These concepts, theories, and laws are based on systematic observation, solid reasoning, and sound application of the scientific method, and are considered universally applicable.

Characteristics of the Scientific Enterprise

Science has several unique characteristics.

1. *Science rejects authority and authoritarianism.* Many people believe the primary work of scientists is to show that hypotheses are true. Though this occurs in many laboratories, most scientific work tries to *disprove* hypotheses rather than prove them correct. If, over a period of time, no one succeeds in disproving a given hypothesis, it becomes increasingly acceptable.

   A good example of this involves the controversy surrounding the work of Jean Piaget, who studied a very limited sample of subjects, namely children who attended private schools in Switzerland. Many researchers cast dispersions on Piaget's work since the sample was not representative of the population to which he generalized his conclusions; however, as other researchers tried to *disprove* Piaget's theories, they found they were unable to do so. It is this lack of contradiction as much as the affirmation of the theories in subsequent studies that has led to wide acceptance of his theories. (See Chapter Four for a discussion of Piagetian principles applied in the elementary science classroom.)

2. *Science is honest.* Scientists publish their research findings, and these publications encourage others to duplicate experiments and either disprove or fail to disprove the hypotheses. A good example of this occurred in 1989 when two university scientists announced their research on developing a process to produce cold fusion. Fusion is the nuclear reaction that is the source of energy in the sun, and occurs when the nuclei of four hydrogen atoms combine to form the nucleus of a single helium atom. In this process, a great deal of energy is released, for it takes less energy to hold the nucleus of a single atom of helium together than it takes to hold the nuclei of each of the four hydrogen atoms together. The process of fusion would be an ideal source of energy for automobiles, power plants, and factories since it uses hydrogen, an element found in water and thus plentiful on earth, to produce enormous amounts of energy. However, the reaction is too radioactive and too hot for these applications. It would be extremely desirable, therefore, to develop a system for cold fusion. The scientists announced they had discovered a method for producing nuclear fusion at room temperatures and provided details of their experimental procedure. As other researchers tried to develop experiments to duplicate the systems described by the university researchers, they found they were unable to do so. It was with some embarrassment that the university retracted their original findings, for it became apparent the scientists' research had been flawed (Wade, 1993, p. 477).

3. *Science rejects supernatural explanations as primary explanations for observed phenomena.* Examples include witchcraft, astrology, extrasensory perception (ESP), plant emotions, and biorhythms. Often referred to as *pseudoscience*, these beliefs lack the support of systematic observational data, and frequently have been arrived at through faulty reasoning or poor scientific methodology. Significant proportions of Americans hold pseudoscientific beliefs. A nationally representative poll conducted in 1987 showed that 39 percent of those sampled viewed astrology as scientific (Eve & Dunn, 1990, p. 4). Science searches for natural rather than supernatural explanations. For example, brain physiologists are seeking medical explanations for the phenomenon of ESP.

4. *Science is skeptical and rejects the notion that it is possible to attain absolute truth.* Scientists accept that there will always be some degree of uncertainty in the natural world. Even Newton's Laws of Motion, once considered truths, are subject to a degree of skepticism; indeed, Einstein's theories of relativity have shown exceptions to the Newtonian Laws.

5. *Science is parsimonious.* Occam's Razor says "Entities shall not be multiplied beyond necessity," meaning that the simpler explanation is preferred to the more complex. In science, if there are several different explanations for an observation, the simplest one is chosen. Parsimony is evident throughout science: Newton's Laws are very simple (though not simplistic) statements of how things move. For example, Newton's First Law states that an object at rest stays at rest, and an object in motion stays in motion in a straight line, unless acted upon by an external, unbalanced force. Einstein's General Theory of Relativity has been reduced to a single simple (and famous) equation, $e=mc^2$. Darwin's Theory of Evolution is reduced to the simple and very descriptive statement, "survival of the fittest."

   Parsimony also is key to quality science education. *Science For All Americans* urges that "Schools should pick the most important concepts and skills to emphasize so they can concentrate on the quality of understanding rather than on the quantity of information presented" (Rutherford & Ahlgren, 1990, p. 143). The National Science Teachers Association also urges teaching " 'less' but 'better' " (1990, p. 2).

6. *Science seeks consistency.* Science presumes that the things and events in the natural world occur in consistent patterns and that the basic rules everywhere in the universe are the same. For example, scientists believe that everything in the universe is composed of the same elements as those found on earth.

Products of Science

We defined science as a process by which knowledge is produced. Thus, the scientific enterprise is comprised of at least two factors: processes and products. Let us look at the products first.

The products of science are the things, theories, thoughts, and attitudes which occur as a result of doing science: scientific content.

Things as Products of Science

The most conspicuous products of science often are the "things"—jet planes, interplanetary rockets, cellular telephones, remote controls, computers, fax machines, frost-resistant strawberries, laser surgery, and countless other advances that we so often take for granted. "Things" are the outcomes of the interaction between scientific thought and theory and technological applications devised by engineers and inventors—the result of the interface between science and technology, a distinction that is becoming increasingly difficult to make.

Science and technology are closely intertwined, each providing for the other in almost circular patterns. Scientific knowledge is applied technologically by engineers and inventors to produce devices that help people live better. Often these devices help scientists make new discoveries.

A good example of this is Newton's Third Law ("For every force, there is an equal and opposite force.") which was applied by engineers in the development of jet aircraft and rockets. The rockets were able to place satellites in orbit which have enabled meteorologists (those who study weather) to gather more and more weather information; this has spawned the desire for even more weather information, creating the need for faster and more powerful computers, etc., etc., etc.

Advances in communications technology have made rapid exchange of more information possible, and this has enabled scientists to increase their research productivity in the communications arena, which has enabled communications networks to offer more information, which enables even more scientific research, which results in the development of even more efficient communications systems, etc., etc., etc.

In the field of bioengineering, the development of frost-resistant strawberries has spawned the desire for more research in genetic engineering, which has resulted in additional advances in the agriculture field, which generates information that can be used by research geneticists, etc., etc., etc.

Technology can be described as the means by which humans control or modify their environment, and can be traced to paleolithic cultures when humans shaped tools out of stone. In increasingly sophisticated ways, humankind has been utilizing the technological enterprise to change our world to accommodate our needs—better stone tools, the use of metals, the invention of devices for agriculture, transportation, health, communication, and countless other technological advances. (The relationships among science, technology and society, and the implications for curriculum and instructional methodology are discussed in Chapter Nine.)

As we have said, products of science include things, theories, thoughts, and attitudes. Theories and thoughts include facts, concepts, generalizations, theories, and laws.

Scientific Facts

Here are some notions considered to be facts:

1. The earth rotates on its axis once about every 24 hours.
2. Seventy-six percent of all animal species are insects.
3. Green plants contain chlorophyll in the cells of their leaves.
4. Water molecules are made of hydrogen and oxygen atoms.
5. A freely-falling object accelerates toward earth at the rate of 9.8 meters per second every second.
6. The temperature at which pure water freezes is 0° Celsius or 32° Fahrenheit.

As you can tell, a fact is a single piece of information that is simply "known." A fact is concrete and is observable. There is no theory behind a fact; it just "is."

CONSTRUCTING YOUR IDEAS 2.2
Recalling Scientific Facts

Try this. In groups, write as many scientific facts as you can think of in about two minutes. Use the above facts as examples and as a spring-board for your effort.

You probably accumulated quite a number of facts. How long were your lists? How hard did you have to think?

CONSTRUCTING YOUR IDEAS 2.3
Importance of Memorizing Scientific Facts

Consider this question: How important is the memorization of facts to the science education of children?

Can children discover facts for themselves?

IN THE SCHOOLS 2.1
Discovering Facts About Soil

A teacher in a first grade class brought to school a pail of soil from her back yard. She spooned samples of the soil onto paper plates, and asked the children to examine the specimens and list what they found in the soil. The objective was for children to observe the soil and identify what was in it. Children were encouraged to use whatever they needed: fingers, magnifying glasses, sieves, pencils, etc. The teacher moved from group to group, asking what they had found so far, suggesting additional ways of observing. When the children were finished, the teacher made a combined list of what the groups had found in the soil; some of the items identified were leaves, sticks, sand, little stones, bugs, tiny worms, mud. Children had discovered a basic fact about soil: soil is composed of many different things. In conjunction with this lesson, the teacher read the book, *Lots of Rot* by Vicky Cobb (Lippincott, 1981) which discusses how rot is formed in food and soil and how people can grow their own rot. The book also suggests activities children can do to discover information about mold, bacteria, and mildew.

IN THE SCHOOLS 2.2
Discovering Facts About Minerals

In a fourth grade class, a teacher set specimens of quartz at four work stations around the room. In groups, children were to test the hardness of quartz using their fingernail, a penny, and a nail. They were instructed to observe whether each of these items would scratch the quartz, and whether the quartz would scratch the item. From this activity, the children were able to find out for themselves that quartz is harder than any of the other materials supplied. The children were discovering facts about minerals.

The teacher then read *The Magic School Bus Inside the Earth* by Joanna Cole (Scholastic, 1987). In this book, children investigate rocks and minerals—their characteristics, how they formed, where they are found, and what they are used for.

CONSTRUCTING YOUR IDEAS 2.4
Activity For Discovering a Scientific Fact

Now it's your turn: In a group, select one fact from your list of facts, and devise an activity children might be able to do in order to discover this fact for themselves.

Scientific Concepts

Concepts are ideas which combine several facts or observations. For example, the statement "Green plants need light in order to grow" relates the two notions of light and growth of green plants. A concept is an abstraction that explains a regularity in observations. Here are some concepts:

1. Green plants bend toward light.
2. The human body uses food for energy and growth.
3. Some chemicals fizz when they come into contact with other chemicals.
4. It takes more force to slide a book on sandpaper than on smooth paper.
5. Running water cuts gullies in soft rock.
6. The moon causes tides.

CONSTRUCTING YOUR IDEAS 2.5
Recalling Scientific Concepts

Try this. As you did for the notion of "facts," in groups, write as many scientific concepts as you can think of in two minutes. Use the above concepts as examples and as a springboard for your effort.

How long were your lists?

CONSTRUCTING YOUR IDEAS 2.6
Importance of Memorizing Scientific Concepts

Consider this question: How important is the memorization of concepts to the science education of children?

Can children discover concepts for themselves?

IN THE SCHOOLS 2.3
Discovering Concepts About Shadows

In a fifth grade class, a teacher supplied a flashlight, a large sheet of white paper, and several solid wooden shapes for each group. Students were asked to use the flashlight to make shadows from the wooden shapes, and trace the shadows formed as the flashlight was held at various angles. Children observed that as the angle of the flashlight changed, so did the length of the shadow of each shape. They were discovering the concept that shadow length depends on the angle of the source of light. The teacher read the poem, "My Shadow" by Robert Louis Stevenson to show the phenomenon in literature.

Additional literature connections:

There's a Nightmare In My Closet by Mercer Mayer (Dial Press, 1968). A boy faces monsters in the night.

Shadows Here, There, and Everywhere by Ron and Nancy Goor (Crowell, 1981) presents information about shadows, including how they are formed, why they can have different lengths, and how they reveal the shapes of things.

IN THE SCHOOLS 2.4
Discovering Concepts About Pulse and Rate of Respiration

In a third grade class, the teacher taught the children how to count their own pulse by placing two fingers lightly on the wrist or on the side of the neck. She also taught them how to count their respirations. She asked each child to measure and record their pulse and respiration while they were seated at their desks. Then she asked them to undergo light exercise (such as marching in place) for two minutes, and measure and record their pulse and respiration again. Then she asked them to undergo heavy exercise (such as jumping or running in place) for two minutes, and again measure and record their pulse and respiration. The children compared the data, and made graphs of the data for pulse and for rate of respiration. They came to the conclusion that the more one exercises the higher one's pulse rate goes and the faster one breathes. They had discovered this concept for themselves. The teacher then read *The Magic School Bus Inside the Human Body* by Joanna Cole (Scholastic, 1989). Children explore the nature of cells and tour several of the body's systems, including the circulatory, respiratory, and digestive systems.

CONSTRUCTING YOUR IDEAS 2.7
Activity for Discovering a Scientific Concept

Now it's your turn. In a group, select one concept from your lists of concepts, and devise an activity children might be able to do in order to discover this concept for themselves.

Scientific Generalizations

Generalizations are broad notions linking several similar concepts. For example, the notion that plants need food, light and water is a generalization encompassing at least three concepts: plants need food, plants need light, and plants need water. Here are some generalizations:

1. Planets, comets, and interplanetary debris revolve about the sun in elliptical orbits.
2. Green plants are living things.
3. In order to maintain a species, living things must reproduce.
4. All materials on earth are formed from the 92 naturally-occurring elements.
5. Heavy marbles roll farther than light marbles when they are given the same push.
6. Electricity can be used to do work.

In forming generalizations, several instances must be examined for the question that is asked. A sound generalization is characterized by two factors: it has *predictive* power and it has *explanatory* power. A sound generalization predicts accurately what will happen in similar, but different situations, and explains satisfactorily why it happened.

For example, suppose you notice, one day, that the tires on your car are soft. The weather is colder than it has been, and you wonder if the tires became soft because it got cold. You set up an experiment in which you fill balloons with air and put them in the refrigerator, measuring the diameter of the balloons before and after they are chilled. If all the balloons shrink, you begin to form the generalization that air contracts when it is cold. You can try larger balloons, smaller balloons, beach balls, bicycle inner tubes, and so on. If the volume of air in the container shrinks in each case, you can add evidence to the generalization that air contracts when it is cold. How about your car tires? You may have to wait for seasonal changes to conclude your inquiry, but you can measure the pressure in your tire every day, morning and evening, for some time to see if there is a relationship between tire pressure and temperature. You are forming a generalization.

CONSTRUCTING YOUR IDEAS 2.8
Recalling Scientific Generalizations

Try this. As you did for the notions of "facts" and "concepts," in groups, write as many scientific generalizations as you can think of in two minutes. Use the above generalizations as examples and as a springboard for your effort.

How long were your lists?

CONSTRUCTING YOUR IDEAS 2.9
Importance of Memorizing Scientific Generalizations

Consider this question: How important is the memorization of generalizations to the science education of children?

Can children discover generalizations for themselves?

IN THE SCHOOLS 2.5
Discovering Generalizations About Parachutes

In a sixth grade class, a teacher asked the children to experiment with parachutes to see if the area of a parachute would affect the rate at which it falls. She provided directions for making the parachutes, and she provided the same weight (a small toy car) for each. Children made parachutes of different sizes. They measured the side of the square that formed their parachute, and calculated its area using the formula, *area* = s^2 (where *s* equals the length of one side). They then climbed onto their tables and held the parachutes the same distance above the floor. At a given signal, they let them drop. The larger ones reached the floor later than the smaller ones, thus suggesting the possible generalization that the larger the area of the parachute, the slower it falls. They were encouraged to try many variations on the same basic activity: timing the length of fall using stopwatches, starting the parachutes from higher places (such as the top of a ladder), using different materials for the parachute, and so on. In each case, the results were the same: the larger the area of the parachute, the slower it fell. (See Figure 2.1.)

FIGURE 2.1 Children experimenting with parachutes

IN THE SCHOOLS 2.6
Discovering Generalizations About Sound

In a second grade class, the teacher filled empty soda bottles with water to various heights. She tapped each bottle with a wooden stick, and the children noticed that the more water there was in the bottle, the lower the pitch of the sound. The teacher then provided each group with three empty soda bottles and instructed them to experiment with the phenomenon some more, doing what they wanted to in order to see if the pitch of a sound depends on the amount of water in the bottle. Groups tapped the sides of the bottles as they filled them with water, noting the changes in pitch as they proceeded. Other groups borrowed enough bottles to set up a musical scale and were able to play "Mary Had a Little Lamb" on their bottles. When the activity was concluded, the whole class discussed their results. It seemed that everyone noticed the same phenomenon: the more water there was in the bottles, the lower the pitch. These students were now in a position to formulate a generalization: the pitch of sound in soda bottles depends on the depth of the water in them. The music teacher was invited to hear children's explanations of their explorations.

Literature Connection:

Ty's One-Man Band by Mildren Pitts Walter (Scholastic, 1980). Ty utilizes several everyday objects (a washboard, a comb, wooden spoons, and a pail) as musical instruments.

Children can form generalizations from their inquiries; all they need to do is determine the variables that might impact on their inquiry and investigate them.

CONSTRUCTING YOUR IDEAS 2.10
Activity for Discovering a Scientific Generalization

Now it's your turn. In a group, select one generalization from your list of generalizations, and devise an activity children might be able to do in order to discover this generalization for themselves.

Scientific Theories

Theories are generalizations which appear to be true, but which cannot be proved. A famous example of this is the atomic theory. According to the atomic theory, the atom contains a dense nucleus made of protons (with positive electric charges) and neutrons (with no electric charges), and a vast external space filled by rapidly moving electrons with negative charges and almost no mass. (See Figure 2.2.) This theory is based on indirect evidence: no one has actually seen an atom. But, if it is true that atoms are constructed in the way described in the atomic theory, they should behave in certain ways when undergoing chemical or nuclear reactions. Huge numbers of experiments have shown that they do behave as expected. So, even though no one can say they have seen an atom, and even though no one can verify the structure of an atom from direct observation, the atomic theory tells us what an atom ought to look like.

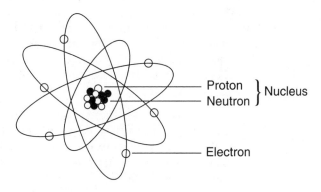

FIGURE 2.2   The atomic model

Here are some examples of theories:

1. The kinetic theory of matter: molecules are in motion, and the rate of motion varies with temperature.
2. The molecular theory: compounds are formed from the interaction of electrons of atoms.
3. Einstein's General Theory of Relativity: The faster an object goes, the greater its mass becomes.
4. Theory of Evolution: Species adapt to their environments, and those that are most fit survive.
5. Theory of Plate Tectonics: The outer shell of the earth consists of several moving plates on which the oceans and the continents lie.
6. Cellular Theory of Life: Living things are made of cells.

You will not be asked to devise ways to have children discover theories. Scientific theories are arrived at after much very complex inquiry, and children are not likely to "discover" these for themselves.

Scientific Laws

Scientific Laws are theories that appear so true that it is believed they can never be disproved. We have mentioned several laws already. Here are some examples of scientific laws:

1. Newton's Third Law of Motion: For every force there is an equal and opposite force.
2. The Law of Universal Gravitation: All objects attract all other objects with a force that depends on their masses and the distance between them.
3. The Law of Conservation of Matter: Matter can neither be created nor destroyed.
4. The Law of Conservation of Energy: Energy can neither be created nor destroyed.
5. The Law of Conservation of Matter and Energy: The sum of the matter and the energy in the universe is constant.
6. The Law of Segregation: During reproduction, the two factors that control each trait separate (segregate), with one factor from each pair passed to the offspring.

Most scientists are reluctant to acknowledge laws as the absolute truths implied by the term "law;" remember that science shuns authority and maintains a skeptical attitude. Laws imply an invariant consistency and an absolute truth that scientists are disinclined to accept. But some of the sweeping theories and generalizations that are proven beyond any reasonable doubt, and that have both predictive and explanatory power, are referred to as laws. There are very few laws in the world of science. In fact, many contemporary texts leave out the term "law" entirely.

Figure 2.3 shows the relationship among scientific facts, concepts, generalizations, theories, and laws.

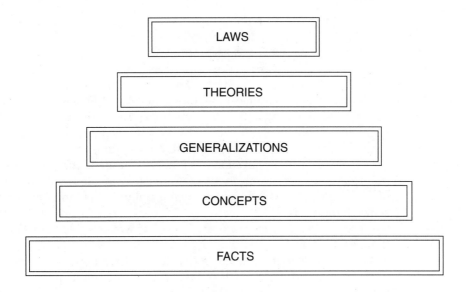

FIGURE 2.3   Relationship among scientific facts, concepts, generalizations, theories, and laws

Attitudes Toward Science

There is another product of science which cannot be described as concretely as facts, concepts, generalizations, theories, and laws. This product is *attitude*. You assessed your attitudes about many characteristics of science and the teaching of science in Chapter One. McCormack & Yager (1989, p. 11–12) suggest that, in addition to knowledge and process outcomes, the science program also should foster positive development in the domain of attitude. People's attitudes about science range from positive when good things happen (such as a life saved by a miracle drug), to negative when something bad happens (such as the fax machine breaking down).[1] The attitudes people possess about science and technology need to be formulated from well-reasoned and carefully thought-out consideration of their own experiences and explorations. Young children having fun in science, having successful experiences, inquiring, asking their own questions, and developing, challenging, and formulating their own sound conclusions, all foster positive attitudes about science in children that, hopefully, will remain with them throughout their lives.

Processes of Science

Much has already been said about the nature of the scientific enterprise: rejection of authority, honesty, rejection of supernatural explanations, skepticism, parsimony, and assumption of consistency. We also have said that children must learn to do science the way scientists do science. This, naturally, suggests the question, "How do scientists do science?"

Many of us committed to memory the "scientific method": problem, hypothesis, experimentation, observations, data collection, and conclusion. Unfortunately, this is not the way scientists do science. A scientist normally starts out with one or more observations or reflections which provoke one or more questions. It is these questions that arise from initial observations and reflections that are experimented with in a variety of ways—not always (maybe not even usually) in the form of a formally-stated hypothesis.

The fact is that there is no single "right" way to do science. However, there are certain features that characterize good scientific inquiry. Variables need to be identified and controlled so the experimenter knows the cause of an effect. Data needs to be collected through a variety of instruments that measure the various factors. Data needs to be interpreted through inferential logic and sound reasoning. Hypotheses are often formulated and tested. Results, methods used to obtain these results, and interpretations of these results need to be communicated to others either to be validated or to be challenged.

Do the above characteristics of the scientific method sound familiar? They should: they are the processes of science introduced in Chapter One.

Scientists do science through careful and appropriate application of the scientific processes to questions that were generated as a result of wondering about something. Science is the process of obtaining knowledge, and scientists do science through the processes of science. The resulting knowledge may be theoretical, subject to verification, validation, and revision; or it may involve discoveries of new facts (like the discovery of new atoms, or the discovery of a new species of insect), or, when technologically developed, it may result in new gizmos.[2]

Interdisciplinary Nature of Science

Though there are thousands of discipline-centered specialties in science, in the broad scheme of the scientific enterprise it is impossible to isolate a single discipline from all the others. To try to do so would be like trying to cook without using anything to measure ingredients, without controlling temperatures, and without paying attention to the selection of proper pans. All disciplines in science depend on other disciplines. For example, it is impossible to study how cells work (traditionally a life science topic) without also investigating the chemical changes that take place, the electron densities at the cell membranes, and the diffusion of substances from high concentrations to low concentrations, all of which traditionally are physical science topics. One cannot study the nature of minerals, an earth science topic, without considering the chemistry and physics of their crystalline structures. Those who study the universe rely heavily on the physics of optics and wave motion to obtain understanding of their data.

Not only does the term "interdisciplinary" refer to integration of the various sciences, it also refers to crossing the traditional subject area borders. One cannot imagine studying science without appropriate facility in language. Most data interpretation from scientific experiments is arrived at mathematically. If science is to be meaningful, it must be learned in social contexts; indeed, technology is largely a socially-motivated discipline. Studies of conservation, health care, weather forecasting, genetic engineering, and sources of energy are all deeply rooted in social contexts.

Science is interdisciplinary in nature, and many theorists advocate teaching science from a Science-Technology-Society (STS) perspective, a scheme which integrates the studies of science, technology, and society in project or thematic approaches. The issue of interdisciplinary and cross-disciplinary approaches to science is addressed more completely in Chapter Nine.

GOALS OF ELEMENTARY SCIENCE EDUCATION

Now that we have looked at the nature of science and the ways scientists do science, let us turn our attention to the goals inherent in a quality elementary science education program.

Carl Sagan (1989) once wrote, "We live in a society exquisitely dependent on science and technology, in which hardly anyone knows anything about science and technology." The ability to understand science and technology in its day-to-day context is called *scientific literacy*; the development of scientific literacy is the basic goal of all science education. Scientific literacy involves developing the information base necessary to arrive at reasoned decisions about scientific and technological issues. Scientifically literate individuals possess "the intellectual skills and knowledge essential . . . to make responsible decisions . . . in situations that require an understanding of science or technology" (Hurd, 1985, p. 88). Scientifically literate people know how and when to ask questions, and how to think critically, and how to make decisions based on reason rather than on emotion or superstition.

A number of national organizations have taken positions on goals of science education that have become widely disseminated. Three of these groups recently have written detailed position statements: the National Science Teachers Association (NSTA), the American Association for the Advancement of Science (AAAS), and the National Commission on Science Education Standards and Assessment (NCSESA). Though the position statements are in a constant state of evolution, it is useful to become familiar with what the national organizations say about science education. The material in this book is grounded, in part, in the philosophies and positions of these national organizations.

All three position statements are similar; all stress teaching less content, teaching more investigation skills, teaching in the inquiry mode, teaching from an interdisciplinary perspective, teaching *all* children, stimulating children's interest in science, and, especially, developing scientifically literate citizens.

National Science Teachers Association

The National Science Teachers Association is extremely active in the reform of science education at all levels. In 1990, the NSTA adopted a position paper on science education in which two major goals of science education are identified: (1) to achieve scientific literacy for all citizens, and (2) to ensure an adequate supply of scientists, engineers, and science teachers. The NSTA says that to achieve these goals, elementary science should emphasize learning science concepts and science processes through the use of activities that involve manipulation of equipment and student thinking about the activity. Curricula should be organized around conceptual themes and should provide opportunities for students to study real-life, personal, and social problems related to science and technology. Students should develop science concepts and processes, see applications of science and technology to everyday life, form positive attitudes toward science, and learn how knowledge of science helps solve personal and societal problems. Programs should integrate science, technology, mathematics, humanities, and the social sciences, and must be responsive to the needs of underrepresented students.

American Association for the Advancement of Science

The American Association for the Advancement of Science, the world's largest federation of scientific and technological societies, engages in a wide variety of activities to advance science and human progress. Responding to grave concerns about the state of science education in America, the AAAS embarked on a project which they named "Project 2061" for the year when Halley's Comet will make its next pass near the earth. The project resulted in the publication of *Science For All Americans* (Rutherford & Algren, 1990) as a first step toward improving scientific literacy. This book suggests that science topics be treated from an interdisciplinary perspective, focusing on systems and interrelationships among the scientific disciplines rather than isolated facts and concepts from isolated fields of study.

Of particular significance is Chapter Thirteen which is devoted entirely to the subject of "Effective Teaching and Learning." In this chapter, teachers are urged to proceed from the concrete to the abstract, start with questions rather than answers, look for prior information, and engage students in collecting evidence and interpreting data in order to answer the questions.

To augment *Science For All Americans*, the AAAS published a companion volume, *Benchmarks for Science Literacy* (1993), which expands the concepts and integration of scientific disciplines. This book presents specific integrated content suggested for children in four grade-level spans: K–2, 3–5, 6–8, and 9–12.

National Commission on Science Education Standards and Assessment

The National Commission on Science Education Standards and Assessment (NCSESA) was formed at the request of the NSTA and other professional societies to take the lead in developing national standards for science education. The resulting *National Science Education Standards* describes what all students should know, understand, and be able to do as a result of their learning experiences, regardless of gender, ethnicity, economic condition, circumstance or ambition. The standards are guided by several principles:

1. Science is for all students.
2. Learning science is an active process.
3. School science reflects the intellectual and cultural traditions that characterize the practice of contemporary science.
4. Improving science is a part of systemic education reform (National Research Council, 1996, p. 19).

The science education standards are not federal mandates, nor do they represent a national curriculum; rather, they offer a coherent vision of what it means to be scientifically literate.

Though the NCSESA emphasizes that the standards are guides to be used to assess quality, there is growing concern over the possibility that the science standards, together with other national standards being developed, may be perceived and treated as a "national curriculum." A national curriculum could work in opposition to the individualization of programs designed to meet children's needs, and could have "deleterious effects on those children, schools, and districts most in need of help" (Fulk, Mantaicopoulos & Hirth, 1994). This is an issue worthy of your attention.[3]

Goals 2000

In 1990, President Bush and the nation's governors met for the first time in America's history to discuss national educational policy. Their discussion was summarized in the now famous six national goals for public education. The goals are as follows:

1. By the year 2000, all children in America will start school ready to learn.
2. By the year 2000, the high school graduate rate will increase to at least 90%.
3. By the year 2000, American students will leave grades 4, 8, and 12 having demonstrated competency over challenging subject matter including English, mathematics, science, history, and geography; and every school in America will ensure that all students use their minds well, so that they may be prepared for responsible citizenship, further learning, and productive employment in our modern society.
4. By the year 2000, U.S. students will be first in the world in mathematics and science achievement.
5. By the year 2000, every adult American will be literate and will possess the knowledge and skills necessary to compete in a global economy and exercise the rights and responsibilities of citizenship.
6. By the year 2000, every school in America will be free of drugs and violence and will offer a disciplined environment conducive to learning.

Goal Four states that U.S. students will be first in the world in mathematics and science achievement. The establishment of this goal has had a major impact on science education in American schools.[4] There has been an increase in emphasis and time spent on science; federal funding for science and mathematics initiatives has been increased; attention to preservice and inservice teacher training has increased; money for equipment and materials has been made more available; and teachers have been encouraged to give attention to all students. Factors such as how science and mathematics are taught, availability of quality instructional materials, and time spent on learning science and mathematics will influence how well this objective will be accomplished. The goal suggests a world-wide comparison, one that often is interpreted in terms of content acquisition.

WHAT DO YOU THINK?

It is time, now, for you to consolidate your thoughts about elementary science education.

CONSTRUCTING YOUR IDEAS 2.11
Preliminary Philosophy of Science Education

Try this. Write your own philosophy of elementary science education. Think through the issues carefully and thoroughly. Consider these kinds of questions:

▌ What is the teacher's role?

▌ What is the student's role?

▌ What are the goals and outcomes of your science program?

▌ What is the role of scientific processes?

▌ What content should be taught?

▌ How will you merge process and content?

▌ What is the role of hands-on activities?

▌ How will you use textual materials and worksheets?

▌ What kinds of materials and equipment will you use?

▌ How involved will the children get in their own learning?

▌ How will children achieve this involvement?

▌ How will children learn to value science?

The statement should be a well thought-out synthesis of your own thinking about your own teaching of science — NOT merely a compilation of answers to the above questions. The questions are offered merely to stimulate your thinking.

This activity is deliberately suggested at the beginning of the course, to give you a chance to reflect on your own thinking and to review your thoughts as you move along. As such, the statement will not be an all-inclusive *opus*, nor will it be definitively refined. Rather, it will be an expression of your ideas about the science teaching/learning experience as you see it at the beginning of your investigations. You will use this statement, together with the metaphor you selected for "science teacher" in Chapter One, to guide you in your construction and reconstruction of your own thinking about appropriate methodology in quality elementary science education.

CHAPTER 2   Additional Questions for Discussion

1. When children work to discover scientific facts, concepts, and gener-
    alizations for themselves, they may come to unexpected conclusions.
    To what extent should teachers ensure that children's conclusions are
    congruent with accepted scientific information?
2. It has been said that teaching is both a science and an art. How does
    the science of teaching parallel the nature of science described in this
    chapter?

Notes

1. There are those who believe science and technology have gone too far—
that we would be much better off if we stopped acquiring new knowledge,
stopped developing new gizmos, and stopped exploration into space and the
oceans. Jacques Ellul (1964) argues that technology is the curse of human life—
that "technique" and standardization have become the way of life and that efficiency is the measure of all aspects of culture. For a detailed discussion of the role
of technology in society, see Pytlik & Johnson (1985).

2. Thomas Kuhn writes "Mopping-up operations are what engage most scientists throughout their careers . . . No part of the aim of normal science is to call
forth new sorts of phenomena; indeed those that will not fit the box are often not
seen at all. Nor do scientists normally aim to invent new theories, and they are
often intolerant of those invented by others. Instead, normal-scentific research is
directed to the articulation of those phenomena and theories that the paradigm
already supplies." (1970, p. 24)

3. The entire Summer 1994 issue of *The Educational Forum* deals with arguments concerning national performance standards. A complete listing of all national standards projects, together with descriptions and status, are found on
p. 421–428 of this issue.

The entire March 1995 issue of *Educational Leadership* (Volume 52, Number 6)
also deals with the problems of national standards.

The standards movement is addressed from several perspectives in the June,
1995 issue of *Phi Delta Kappan* (Volume 76, Number 10).

4. For further discussion on America's Goals 2000, see the Phi Delta Kappa
working paper, "Achieving the Nation's Education Goals."

References

American Association for the Advancement of Science. (1993). *Benchmarks for
    Science Literacy: Project 2061.* New York: Oxford University Press.

Bohr, N. (1958). In *Foundations of Modern Physical Science* by G. Holton and H. D. Roller. Reading, MA: Addison-Wesley.

Cobb, V. (1981). *Lots of Rot.* New York: Lippincott.

Cole, J. (1989). *The Magic School Bus Inside the Human Body.* New York: Scholastic.

———. *The Magic School Bus Inside the Earth.* New York: Scholastic.

Ellul, J. (1964). *The Technological Society.* New York: Vantage Books.

Eve, R. A. and Dunn, D. (1990). Psychic powers, astrology & creationism in the classroom? *The American Biology Teacher 52*(1), 10–21. *Ibid.* p.4.

Fulk, B. M., Mantaicopoulos, P. Y., & Hirth, M. A. (1994). Arguments against national performance standards. *The Educational Forum, 58* (4), p. 365–373.

Goor, R. and Goor, N. (1981). *Shadows Here, There and Everywhere.* New York: Crowell.

Hurd, P. D. (1985). Science education for a new age: The reform movement. *NASSP Bulletin,* September, 1985.

Kuhn, T. S. (1970). *The Structure of Scientific Revolutions.* Chicago, IL: The University of Chicago Press.

Mayer, M. (1968). *There's a Nightmare in My Closet.* New York: Dial Press.

McCormack, A. J. & Yager, R. E. (1989). Towards a taxonomy for science education. *The Georgia Science Teacher 19* (3) p. 11–12.

National Research Council. (1996). *National Science Education Standards.* Washington, DC: National Academy Press.

National Science Teachers Association. (1990). *Science Teachers Speak Out: The NSTA Lead Paper on Science and Technology Education for the 21st Century.* Washington, DC: National Science Teachers Association.

Phi Delta Kappa. *Achieving the Nation's Education Goals.* P.O. Box 789, Bloomington, IN 47402-0789.

Pytlik, E. C., Lauda, D. P., & Johnson, D. L. (1985). *Technology, Change and Society.* Worcester, MA: Davis Publications, Inc.

Rutherford, F. J. & Ahlgren, A. (1990). *Science For All Americans.* New York, NY: Oxford University Press.

Sagan, C. (1989). "Why we need to understand science." *Parade.* September 10, 1989.

Stein, J. (Ed.). (1967). *The Random House Dictionary of the English Language.* New York, NY: Random House.

Wade, N. (1993). The good, bad, and ugly [Review of *Bad Science: The Short Life and Weird Times of Cold Fusion* by Gary Taubes]. *Nature, 364,* 5 August, 1993.

Webster's New Collegiate Dictionary. (1973). Springfield, MA: G. & C. Merriam Company.

Walter, M. P. (1980). *Ty's One-Man Band.* New York: Scholastic.

CHAPTER 3

The Processes of Science

The shrewd guess, the fertile hypothesis, the courageous leap to a tentative conclusion— these are the most valuable coin of the thinker at work.

Jerome Bruner. *The Process of Education* (1960). Cambridge, MA: Harvard University Press. p. 14.

You have been investigating the nature of science, the difference between children learning about science and doing science, the difference between process and product, and the positions taken by the national organizations on science education. We have suggested that it is better for children to learn to do science than to learn the facts, concepts, generalizations, theories, and laws someone else has concluded; that it is far more important for children to master the process skills than to learn facts; and that children should do science the way scientists do science. You have discovered that scientists do science through careful and appropriate application of the scientific processes to questions that were generated as a result of wondering about something. We have suggested that, in a quality elementary science program, children ask their own questions, devise their own ways to explore their questions, and develop their own answers to their questions. They consider themselves scientists.

Science process skills are "a set of broadly transferable abilities, appropriate to many science disciplines and reflective of the behavior of scientists" (Padilla). Elementary children use process skills to find out how scientists think and work and to investigate their own questions in a manner similar to the way scientists conduct their inquiries. Children use the process skills to construct knowledge by asking questions, making observations, taking measurements, collecting data, organizing and interpreting the data, predicting the outcomes of manipulating one variable while keeping the others constant, formulating and testing hypotheses, developing experiments, inferring reasons for what they observe, and communicating their models to others. These activities "lead children to the facts, principles, laws and generalizations which scientists have established" (Renner & Marek, 1990, p. 243). *Doing* science means applying the processes. Process skills form the core of inquiry-based, hands-on science learning. In order to apply the processes, children first have to master them.

In this chapter you will investigate twelve processes that have been identified as basic to scientific investigation:[1]

Observing

Classifying

Communicating

Measuring

Predicting

Inferring

Identifying and controlling variables

Formulating and testing hypotheses

Interpreting data

Defining operationally

Experimenting

Constructing models

Observing

Let us take a short foray into the world of rocks.

CONSTRUCTING YOUR IDEAS 3.1
Observing Rocks

For this activity, please assemble a small collection of 12 to 15 different rocks. You can obtain samples from your school grounds, your back yard, building supply stores, gardening stores, and speciality shops.

Put each rock on a separate paper plate labeled with a number, and spread the plates around the classroom. Also have magnifying glasses available. Now, move around the room from one specimen to another, handling, hefting, looking, and exploring the characteristics of these rocks. Use the magnifying glasses to help you observe.

Spend 10–15 minutes looking at the specimens. Then get together as a class and share what you have observed.

Most people have a difficult time making careful observations of things the first time they see them, so you may wish to use the sheet in Figure 3.1 to help guide you in what to look for. Do not feel compelled to fill in all the boxes; use the sheet only as a guide. Color is self-explanatory. Texture is simply how the rock feels in your hand: rough, slippery, smooth, grainy, etc. "How Heavy" refers to whether it feels heavier or lighter than you expected, or just about right as you "heft" the specimen in the palm of your hand. "How Shiny" is self-explanatory. Other properties will be readily apparent as you look at the specimens.

The purpose of this activity is for you to observe. It is *not* intended that you identify the rocks, or tell the difference between sedimentary and igneous rocks, or learn their names. The sole purpose of this activity is for you to *observe*.

What senses did you use? Certainly you used the sense of sight as you observed the various colors and different subtleties of color. You probably used the sense of touch as you felt how smooth or how rough the specimens are. You probably did *not* use the sense of taste. (SAFETY NOTE: It is important that people be cautioned *not* to taste things unless the instructor specifically says it is okay to do so.) Did you use the sense of smell or hearing? How about other senses? What sense did you use to compare relative weights by "hefting" the specimens? It probably was more of an internal muscular sense than the sense of touch as we commonly know it.

ROCK NUMBER	COLOR	TEXTURE	HOW HEAVY	HOW SHINY	OTHER PROPERTIES
1					
2					
3					
4					
5					
6					

FIGURE 3.1   Data sheet for rock observation activity

As an interesting sideline to this activity, you may have noticed that there might have been one or two students (maybe even you) who were not interested in the rocks. This is important to notice, and it is useful to compare how much these individuals observed with how much those who were interested observed. It seems that we are much better observers when we are interested than when we are not.

IN THE SCHOOLS 3.1
Observation Activities

Activities patterned after this rock-observing activity provide excellent ways for children to begin observing. Use pictures, leaves, cow bells, coins, stamps, buttons, hardware, or just about anything else. Place the specimens on paper plates and put them around the room; children move around and make observations to report back to the class. Do you have a collection? Use it. If you don't have a collection, remember the old dictum, "If you're going to be a teacher, never throw anything away," and use things you have saved.

In observing, we learn to use all our senses. Physiologists tell us we have many more than the five basic senses. We have the senses of sight, sound, taste, smell, and touch. But we also have the sense of balance, the sense of muscle contraction, the sense of muscle memory, the sense of direction, the muscular senses we use when we investigate how heavy something is, and other internal senses. In our skin, we have four different kinds of receptors: receptors for cold, heat, deep pressure, and surface pressure. In all, there are some 30 different kinds of receptor systems in the human body; thus, one can say the human body has over 30 different kinds of senses.

In developing the skill of observation, children learn to use all their senses and attend to stimuli to be recorded in the sensory register, and from there move on for processing. Connections with the memory bank in the long-term memory help people recognize stimuli, making it easier for them to make perceptual sense. Since young children do not have the wealth of experience that older children and adults have, it is important for them to begin obtaining this experiential base. The more observation activities they perform, the more experiences they will add to their long-term memory stores, and the better able they will become to make connections with new things they observe.

CONSTRUCTING YOUR IDEAS 3.2
What Did You See That Made You Wonder About Something?

How good an observer are *you*? What did you see on your way to school today? What did you observe that made you wonder about something? What did you observe that started your mind working on how you could find answers to the questions your observation provoked?

A CASE OF MOON WATCHING

A class of elementary science methods students was asked to describe the moon as they had seen it the night before. Many students had not seen it, and, of those who had, there were different descriptions of what they had seen. Some said the curve of the moon pointed to the right, some said it pointed left, and some said it pointed straight up. In order to clarify the verbal descriptions, several students drew what they had seen on the board. Since there were so many different descriptions, the question was posed, "How could you make accurate observations of the moon?" The class decided they needed to draw the moon exactly as they saw it. The next day, several students shared the moon drawings they had made the previous night. Again there were discrepancies: left vs. right; the angle at which the concave part pointed upward; whether the "dark" part of the moon had been partially visible. The class decided that still more accurate observations were needed, for it was obvious that the moon, itself, was not different from one student to another—it was the observations that were different. It was decided that students could draw an imaginary line connecting the two cusps of the moon and then draw an imaginary perpendicular bisector to show the direction the moon faced. (See Figure 3.2.) Observations were more consistent the following day, but new questions were introduced since it seemed that the moon had changed shape during the three days, getting more and more full. Also, it seemed that the moon had changed position. Indeed, several students reported they could not find the moon, even though it was a clear night.

It became a class project to record observations of the moon every clear night. Concerning the process of observation, the class discovered that they had to record their observations in the form of drawings with detailed descriptions in order to be able to compare what they had seen over the span of several nights. As the class progressed, several generalizations were made from the moon observations: (1) The moon changes shape. (2) The moon changes position in the sky. (3) The way you see the moon depends on where you are. (4) The moon is sometimes visible during the day. In addition, a number of questions were generated by the observations: Why does the moon change shape? Where does it go when it disappears? Why does it move? Why does the moon look different in different places? Though these questions were not answered, several members of the class undertook investigations to try to answer the questions for themselves.[2]

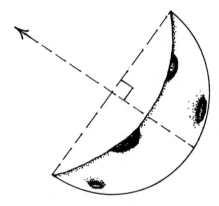

FIGURE 3.2   Moon-watching drawing showing how direction moon faces can be established

The essence of all science is observation. Ultimately, it is observation that determines the procedure and the outcome of any scientific inquiry. It is impossible to inquire scientifically without observing accurately. We must be able to observe not only expected things, but unexpected things as well. Recall that in Chapter One, several inventions were described as having come from unexpected observations.

CONSTRUCTING YOUR IDEAS 3.3
Looking For Things You Haven't Seen Before

To sharpen your ability to observe unexpected things, try this. The next time you travel to school, try to find something along the route you have never seen before, but which has always been there. You will be amazed by how much you have failed to observe during all those trips you have made!

Observation may be qualitative, and it may be quantitative. Your observations were qualitative when you observed the rocks; qualitative observations do not require measurement. In quantitative observation, measurements are required in order to attach specific facts to the observations. For example, measuring the volume and the weight of a certain rock are quantitative observations; from these measurements, you would be able to calculate its density, which is a measure of its weight per volume. The most appropriate type of observation for young children is qualitative; quantitative factors are introduced as the children become ready for the mathematical abstractions involved.

Observation is the first, and, without doubt, the most important scientific process skill for elementary children to master. Elementary teachers must give children the maximum possible opportunity to observe. Observation must be built into every aspect of the daily program. It is our responsibility to help young children develop, sharpen, and master their powers of observation. Observation is the cornerstone of all scientific work.

Several observation activities are suggested in Constructing Science in the Classroom 3.1–3.8. Some are appropriate for young children, and some are more appropriate for older children. The activities suggest ways of providing practice using each of the five basic senses.

CONSTRUCTING SCIENCE IN THE CLASSROOM 3.1
What's In the Sock?

GRADE

6
5
4
3
2
1
K

OBSERVATION ACTIVITY USING
A VARIETY OF SENSES

Objective
The student will use various senses to identify unknown objects placed in a sock.

Secretly put an object that requires more than one sense to identify into a sock. Suggestions are a banana, an apple, a pear, a handful of grapes, a lemon, an onion, a potato, etc. Hold the sock in front of the children, and ask them to guess what they think is in the sock by looking at it, and why they guessed what they did. Then ask what other ways they could use to discover what is in the sock—without looking. Pass the sock around, and allow the children to use their senses to explore the object inside, again emphasizing they cannot look inside the sock. Then ask for their guesses as to what is inside the sock, and ask for the reasons for their guesses. Reveal the surprise object, and discuss how it feels, smells, sounds, looks, and tastes.

Literature connections:
My Five Senses by Aliki (Crowell, 1989). This is a very simple text with clear illustrations of how we use our five senses. "When I bounce a ball, I use three senses. I see, hear, touch."

There Are Rocks In My Socks Said the Ox to the Fox by Patricia Thomas (Lothrop, 1979) describes how the ox felt with rocks in his socks.

CONSTRUCTING SCIENCE IN THE CLASSROOM 3.2
What's In the Bag?

GRADE

6
5
4
3
2
1
K

OBSERVATION ACTIVITY USING THE SENSE OF TOUCH

Objective

The student will use the sense of touch to identify materials in a bag.

Pass out "feely bags" to each child. A "feely bag" is a paper bag in which you secretly have put a familiar object. Children are *not* allowed to look in the bag, but must put their hands in the bag and describe what they feel. They guess what the object is from how it feels. Then they verify their guesses by looking.

Next, give each child a paper bag, and a plastic bag with a variety of small objects (wooden letters, wooden beads, pencils, pieces of cloth, cotton, Q-tips, paper clips, strands of beads, ribbon, wooden shapes, etc.) Each child puts two or three items (some easily identifiable, and some less easily identifiable) into a "feely bag," and exchanges bags with a partner. Observation and identification proceeds as before.

Children can prepare their own bags at home and bring them to school the next day or play the game with family members.

Literature connections:

The poem, "What's In The Sack" in *Where the Sidewalk Ends* by Shel Silverstein (Harper and Row, 1974) is a humorous account of a man carrying a huge sack on his back. It tells of the man's frustrations when people do not really care about him, but only about what's in the sack.

Find Out by Touching by Paul Showers (Thomas Crowell, 1961). Children are encouraged to find something made of wood, metal, cloth, plastic, and rubber, and place the objects in boxes. Using their sense of touch, children determine what is in the box.

CONSTRUCTING SCIENCE IN THE CLASSROOM 3.3
Seeds, Seeds, and More Seeds

GRADE

6
5
4
3
2
1
K

OBSERVATION ACTIVITY USING THE SENSE OF SIGHT

Objective

The student will observe seeds.

Obtain a collection of several different kinds of bean and pea seeds; these are all seeds that come in two parts. (If they haven't been cooked or frozen, you could plant them and they would grow.) Soak them in water for a few hours to loosen up the skin.

Ask children to describe or draw the outsides of the seeds. Then, cut the seeds open. Children should be able to split them with plastic knives; otherwise, you can let them stand in a glass of water until they split open by themselves. Ask children to describe (or draw) what the insides look like. Provide magnifying glasses to aid children in their observations.

To help children sharpen their skills of observation, ask them to compare cooked, packaged, fresh, and frozen vegetables.

Literature connections:
All About Seeds by Melvin Berger (Scholastic, 1992) suggests several activities for collecting, planting, and cooking seeds.

Eat the Fruit, Plant the Seed by Millicent Selsam (Morrow, 1980) is an easy how-to book that shows various stages of development from seed to plant in six different fruits.

FIGURE 3.3 Examining the insides of seeds

CONSTRUCTING SCIENCE IN THE CLASSROOM 3.4
What's In This Dirt?

GRADE

OBSERVATION ACTIVITY USING
THE SENSE OF SIGHT

Objective
The student will observe the composition of dirt.

Bring a bag of soil from your home or from the school yard, and put a spoonful of the soil on a paper plate for each child or group of children. Provide magnifying glasses. Ask the children to look at the soil carefully to identify different kinds of things they can find in the soil.

Urban children might need some background on soil. If soil is not readily available, you can substitute potting soil.

Literature connection:
A Day In the Desert written and illustrated by a first grade class at Robert Taylor Elementary School in Henderson, Nevada (Willowisp, 1994). This story is a wonderful example of children really expressing their observations of what they saw in the desert.

CONSTRUCTING SCIENCE IN THE CLASSROOM 3.5
What's That Sound In the Egg?

GRADE

6
5
4
3
2
1
K

OBSERVATION ACTIVITY USING
THE SENSE OF HEARING

Objective
The student will use the sense of hearing to identify unknown materials.

Put various items in plastic eggs labeled with numbers (marshmallows, rice, beans, pins, cotton, dice, paper clips, a key, marbles, a bottle cap, pennies, toothpicks, macaroni, thread), and close the eggs.
     To be sure children can distinguish between loud and soft sounds and sounds of different qualities, have children close their eyes while you drop familiar objects on the floor or table; children listen to the sounds made, and try to identify the object from its sound. Then pass out the eggs and ask children to shake the eggs and listen carefully. Children try to identify the sounds made in the eggs, and then guess what might be in the egg. Typical inquiry questions might include, "Which eggs have hard sounds?" "Which eggs have soft sounds?" "Which eggs seem empty?" "Which eggs have similar sounds, like metal, glass, plastic, etc.?" "Are some sounds easy to recognize?" "Are some sounds difficult to recognize?" "Are there certain sounds with which we are all familiar?"

Literature connections:
Click, Rumble, Roar: Poems About Machines by Lee Bennett Hopkins (Crowell, 1987) is a book of poetry about the different sounds machines make.

Just Listen by Winifred Morris (Athenium, 1990) is a moving story of a young girl's visit to her grandmother's house. The two ladies would spend time together outside and listen to the "special song" of nature.

CONSTRUCTING SCIENCE IN THE CLASSROOM 3.6
What Did You See Today?

GRADE

6
5
4
3
2
1
K

ONGOING OBSERVATION ACTIVITY

Objective
The students will observe their natural surroundings.

"What did you see on your way to school today?" Ask this question each day. As time goes on, children will start looking for things to report, sharpening their awareness and their observational skills.
     "Did you see the same things on the way home?" Children can discuss with their parents what they see on their way to and from school.

Literature connection:
I'm In Charge of Celebrations by Byrd Taylor (Chas. Scribner's Sons, 1986) is a story of a Native American Girl who makes celebrations of beautiful everyday happenings such as seeing rainbows or coyotes.

Footprints and Shadows by Anne Wescott Dodd (Simon & Schuster, 1992) contains beautiful watercolors and lyrical text that will capture children's attention as the footprints and shadows play their game of hide-and-seek.

Shadows and Reflections by Tana Hoban (Greenwillow, 1990). The collection of pictures in this book offers an opportunity for comparing and contrasting objects with their shadows and reflections.

CONSTRUCTING SCIENCE IN THE CLASSROOM 3.7
What's That Smell?

GRADE

OBSERVATION ACTIVITY USING
THE SENSE OF SMELL

Objective
The student will use the sense of smell to identify materials in film canisters.

Obtain used film canisters from a local photo finishing shop (they are normally free), and number each one. Put a small piece of cotton or paper tissue in each, and place a few drops of substances with different odors in each one (perfume, cinnamon, soap, lemon juice, apple juice, orange juice, chopped onion, instant coffee, herbal tea, etc.) Cover the canister with plastic wrap and poke two or three holes in it. Ask children to describe the odor and try to identify the material in the canister.

Literature connections:
Mucky Moose by Jonathan Allen (Macmillan, 1990) is a humorous story of a foul smelling moose. All the animals in the forest avoid this moose except for the skunks. When a notorious wolf attempts to capture and eat the moose, several hilarious fiascos occur.

Dog Breath by Dav (Blue Sky, 1994) is a story about Hally, the family dog, who is about to be given away because she has bad breath. Fortunately, Hally proves to be indispensable when she foils a robbery attempt.

Breathtaking Noses by Hana Machotka (Morrow Junior Books, 1992) describes specialized animal noses.

CONSTRUCTING SCIENCE IN THE CLASSROOM 3.8
Observing Rocks and Minerals

GRADE

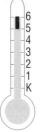

OBSERVATION ACTIVITY USING ALL SENSES

Objective
The student will make observations of rocks and minerals.

This activity expands the initial rock observation activity described in Constructing Your Ideas 3.1, and is suitable as an introduction to a unit on rocks and minerals.
    Assemble a small collections of several different samples of about 15 different rocks and minerals. Here are some suggestions:

Feldspar—2 or 3 different colors
Sandstone—1 or 2 specimens (showing layering of different colors if these specimens are available)
Shale—several colors; some specimens with fossils, and some specimens without
Granite—one or two good-sized specimens of different colors

Conglomerate

Quartz—8 or 10 different kinds of quartz such as clear crystalline quartz, tiger's eye, bloodstone, jasper, geodes, agate, rose quartz, amethyst, etc.

Magnetite and/or lodestone

Gypsum—several varieties, including Iceland Spar if you can get a specimen

Pyrite

Chert

Limestone—several different types

Gneiss

Fluorite

Soapstone

Pumice

Obsidian

You will be able to think of many more. Use what you have available locally, or use your own personal collection.

Put the specimens of each different kind of rock or mineral on paper plates, appropriately labeled with what it is, and spread these around the classroom. Have magnifying glasses available. Also put a magnet by the lodestone, and tie a string around the lodestone so it can dangle. Children move around the room from one specimen to another, handling, hefting, looking, and exploring the characteristics of these rocks and minerals. This activity might give children the opportunity to investigate the principle of magnifying glasses. You may wish to develop a guide sheet similar to that in Figure 3.1 to help children in their observations. For a more structured investigation, you can discuss properties of rocks and minerals such as hard, soft, shiny, glossy, round, flat, bouncy, etc. prior to children investigating on their own.

FIGURE 3-4   Examining specimens of rocks and minerals

After children have spent 20–30 minutes observing and discussing the specimens, get together as a class and share what the children observed. Here are a few typical observations:

Some specimens of the same mineral come in different colors.

Some minerals look alike even though they are different minerals.

Some minerals are very heavy; some are very light.

The magnetite is magnetic and is attracted to the magnet. The lodestone has poles just like a magnet.

Some rocks are made of tiny grains; others are made of crystals that are very large.

Children will notice many more characteristics about the specimens.

Literature connections:

Everybody Needs a Rock by Byrd Taylor (Aladdin, 1974) is a poetic story that prescribes ten rules for finding your own special rock. One of the rules is to sniff a rock. "Some kids can tell by sniffing whether a rock came from the middle of the earth or from an ocean or from a mountain where the wind and sun touched it every day for a million years."

Rocks and Rills—A Look at Geology by Harris Stone and Dale Igmanson (Prentice Hall, 1968). This book poses many questions about rocks, minerals, and other geologic phenomena, and suggests several experiments for students to discover their own answers.

CONSTRUCTING YOUR IDEAS 3.4
An Activity For Observing

Now it's your turn. Write a short activity that can be used to help children sharpen their senses of observation. Specify grade level, and be sure the activity is appropriate to the children in the age/grade group you specify. Cite a process-oriented objective for your lesson; this objective will read something like this: "The student will observe _____." Then get together in small groups, and do the activities each member of the group has prepared.

Classifying

Before you start this section, please assemble a fairly large collection of something: shells, feathers, foreign coins, buttons, stamps, pieces of hardware, etc. Once you have assembled a collection of, say, 50–60 specimens of the same kind of thing for each group in your class, you are ready to do some activities on classification.

CONSTRUCTING YOUR IDEAS 3.5
Classifying a Collection

First, group the items. Group them any way you wish. Compare your arrangement with those of the other groups in the class.

How many different ways were there of sorting the collection? What kinds of arrangements did each group form?

If you had used a collection of foreign coins, you might have formed groups of square coins, round coins, coins with holes in them, coins with pictures of animals, coins with nothing but writing on them, tiny coins, and so on. This is a simple form of classification which young children can do. It requires the ability to abstract common properties of similar objects.

IN THE SCHOOLS 3.2
Grouping Shells

Grouping shells is an excellent way to introduce young children to the process of classification. The teacher asks the children to make piles of shells that look the same. Then she asks children to tell what is the same about the shells in each pile.

FIGURE 3.5 Observing and grouping shells

Young children also have the ability to group objects by *single* characteristics that are readily apparent. For example, a pre-school teacher may put six red squares, six yellow squares, and six green squares in a paper bag, shake them up, and dump them out on the desk in front of the child. Children will be able to sort the squares by color into three piles: red ones, yellow ones, and green ones. Next, the teacher may put six yellow squares, six yellow triangles, and six yellow circles in a paper bag, shake them up, and dump them out on the desk. Children will be able to sort the pile of yellow shapes into three groups: squares, triangles, and circles. (Shapes cut out of velcro provide a tactile stimulus especially useful for young visually impaired children.) Each of these sorting activities requires recognition of a single characteristic: color or shape. However, if the teacher puts three each of red, yellow, and green squares, red, yellow, and green triangles, and red, yellow, and green circles in a bag, and does the same thing, the average pre-schooler will sort them *either* by shape or by color. Those who sort them by shape will not readily understand that those who sorted them by color are also correct; preoperational children do not yet have the ability to recognize that the same object can have more than one attribute.

Piaget describes an activity that illustrates this point. An experimenter shows a preoperational child 20 wooden beads, including 17 brown ones and 3 white ones. The child is asked, "Can you make a longer necklace with the brown beads or the wooden beads?" The preoperational child typically replies "brown beads," unable to recognize that each bead has two attributes: its color and the material it is made of. Preoperational children can deal only with one attribute at a time.

Classifying objects by considering relationships that are subordinate to a larger group as a whole is called *class inclusion*, and is a skill that is learned in the early concrete operational stage of cognitive development. Early concrete operational children recognize that the same object may have more than one attribute (for example, the beads are all wooden and also have different colors, or each of the cut-outs in the paper bag not only has a certain shape, but also a certain color). When children are ready, they are able to start sorting things into two groups that have mutually exclusive attributes using class inclusion skills. Readiness for attempting work requiring more complex thinking often is inferred from children's performance on the Piagetian conservation tasks (see p. 89 and Note 3).

It is important to note that the ability to sort (or classify) does not come spontaneously to children; they must be exposed to the phenomenon. They must be encouraged to do many sorting activities using many different kinds of things to gain experience in the skill of classification. It is a good idea to include classification activities together with observation activities in daily learning centers.

> Now, return to the collection you have been working with, and mix it up. This time, sort the collection into *two* groups, and label each group with a descriptive word or drawing. Again, compare your groups with those of other groups in the class.

What different ways did people have of sorting the collection into two sets? Ask each group to explain *why* they sorted the way they did. Was any of these ways "righter" than any other? Was any wrong?

Take another look at the two sets the groups in your class devised. Each group has two clusters, labeled with a descriptive word or drawing. Are the two clusters *parallel* in construction? In other words, are the two clusters close to being opposites of each other? Suppose, for example, the two clusters identified in the foreign coin collection were (1) copper-colored coins, and (2) silver-colored coins. These two clusters are "opposite" to each other with regard to the color attributes. Suppose, however, the two clusters were (1) copper coins, and (2) coins with faces. These are NOT "opposites." In grouping the coins this way (copper coins and coins with faces), there could be coins that are copper-colored that also have faces on them. The clusters are not *mutually exclusive*. There is no clear line of demarcation between them.

In order for children to devise parallel classification systems, they must be able to abstract the general attributes common to objects in a collection, and also the specific cases of these attributes possessed by each item that make some different from the others. This ability occurs during the mid-concrete operational stage. Children need practice in developing parallel classification systems, and the more activities they can be provided, the better they will learn this skill. These types of classification activities also can be included in the learning centers.

> The next step is for you to form two sub-groups within each mutually-exclusive group you formed above. (If you didn't form mutually-exclusive groups, please re-arrange the objects so you have two mutually-exclusive groups.) Name each of the sub-groups with a word or a drawing. As before, share your arrangements with the class to compare the various ways people had of grouping similar objects.

You will end up with a grouping something like this:

Main Group A	Main Group B
Subgroup 1	Subgroup 1
Subgroup 2	Subgroup 2

Pay special attention to the subgroups. Are Subgroup 1 and Subgroup 2 mutually exclusive within each main group? If not, you will want to rearrange them. Look at each Subgroup 1 under Main Group A and Main Group B. Are they the *same* subgroups? Do the same for each Subgroup 2. For example, if you used the foreign coin collection, you might have a classification system that looks like this:

Copper Colored Coins	Silver Colored Coins
Large	Large
Small	Small

In this arrangement, the subgroups under each of the main groups are the same. You can have large copper coins, small copper coins, large silver coins, or small silver coins. It would be easy (assuming you had defined "large" and "small" fairly precisely) to take a new coin that had not been part of the collection, and place it in one of the four groups. However, consider the following classification:

Copper Colored Coins	Silver Colored Coins
Large	With Faces
Small	Without Faces

What do you think about this system? The subgroups under each main group are mutually exclusive; indeed, it would be possible to take a new coin and place it accurately into one of the four groups: large copper, small copper, silver with faces, or silver without faces. Yet, there is something unsettling about the system. Again, the problem is the lack of parallelism. The subgroupings under the main groups are not parallel to each other. Furthermore, this classification system suggests that the same attributes are not being recognized in *all* the items in the collection.

The primary attribute recognized in the copper coins is size, and the primary attribute recognized in the silver coins is decoration. However, I hasten to add that the absence of parallelism in the subgroups does not make the classification system wrong, or even necessarily weak. Indeed, there are instances when it is more descriptive of a collection to have non-parallel classification systems. For example, a collection of leaves might include broad leaves and pine needles. The attributes found in the broad leaves are different from those found in the pine needles, and so the classification system would necessarily be non-parallel. Such a system might look like this:

Broad Leaves	Pine Needles
Straight Edges	Fat
Crooked Edges	Thin

The important consideration to make when assessing a system of classification is whether it accurately describes the differences among the specimens in the collection. It is critical to *ask* children why they grouped the way they did in order to discover their thinking about the process of classification.

Take your classification activity one step further. For each subgroup, form two or more sub-sub groups. Watch for the use of similar attributes, mutual exclusivity, and parallelism. Check each others' classification systems. As an added challenge, select the "weirdest" item from your own collection, one that you had a hard time deciding where to place, and give this item to a different group, challenging them to place it in their classification system. If their system does the job, they should be able to accomplish this task immediately.

You will end up with a classification system like this:

Main Group A	Main Group B
Subgroup 1	Subgroup 1
a.	a.
b.	b.
Subgroup 2	Subgroup 2
a.	a.
b.	b.

The leaf classification system described above might look like this:

Broad Leaves	Pine Needles
Straight Edges	Fat
Straight veins	Round tips
Radiating veins	Pointed tips
Crooked Edges	Thin
Straight veins	Round tips
Radiating veins	Pointed tips

These multiple groupings are hierarchical systems of classification that require higher levels of cognitive skills than simpler class inclusion systems; children are in the late concrete operational or early formal operational stage of cognitive development when they are able to master these more complex systems of classification.

IN THE SCHOOLS 3.3
The Hardware Store

A fourth grade teacher brought a bag of assorted hardware items to school; items included several kinds of washers, nails, screws, bolts, nuts, and other small items. Groups were provided with about fifty of the items, and were asked to develop a system of organizing them so that a customer would be able to find what he needed readily. They also were asked to label the groups to facilitate the customer's search. The teacher then played the role of the customer and asked each group to locate a specific item.

Literature connection:
Aunt Ippy's Museum of Junk by Rodney Greenblat (Harper Collins, 1991). Two children visit their aunt's museum of junk and discover many reusable materials. This would be an interesting introduction to the process of classification.

IN THE SCHOOLS 3.4
Fingerprinting

A third grade teacher challenged children to be "detectives" by classifying the fingerprints of the class members. Children rubbed the tips of their fingers with a soft lead pencil and rolled their fingertips on the sticky part of transparent adhesive tape. They taped the lifted fingerprints to paper, and compared them with the primary fingerprint characteristics of the loop (fingerprint lines enter and leave on the same side of the finger), the arch (fingerprint lines enter on one side of the finger and leave on the opposite side), and the circle (fingerprint lines enter at one side of the finger and spiral to the center of the finger).

Classification is a skill that is used throughout the scientific enterprise and is a skill that is essential for children to put facts and generalizations together to form concepts.

Several classification activities appropriate for different age groups of children are suggested in Constructing Science in the Classroom 3.9–3.15.

CONSTRUCTING SCIENCE IN THE CLASSROOM 3.9
What's Magnetic? What's Not Magnetic?

GRADE

6
5
4
3
2
1
K

CLASSIFICATION ACTIVITY INVOLVING MAGNETIC OBJECTS

Objective
The student will classify common objects as magnetic or non-magnetic.

Provide each child with a magnet and allow time to explore items in the classroom to see which are attracted to the magnet. Then place a number of objects, both magnetic and non-magnetic, on a tray (nail, paper clip, scissors, rubber band, piece of wood, crayon, leaf, key, screw, metal washer, penny, nickel, dime, quarter, piece of paper, etc.). Ask children to select one item at a time, and tell whether the magnet picks it up. Have a chart available with two columns marked "Magnet Attracts," and "Magnet Did Not Attract" or a suitable pictograph. After testing each item, children place it on the appropriate half of the chart.

Child-constructed bulletin boards showing things that are magnetic and things that are not magnetic can culminate the lesson.

This lesson also can be used as a prediction activity. Children select one object at a time and predict whether it will be attracted to the magnet. Then they try it with the magnet, and place the object on the appropriately labeled card. It is a good idea to have "prediction" and "actual" charts so children can compare their predictions with what actually happened.

Literature connection:
Mickey's Magnet by Franklin Brankley and Eleanor Vaughn (Scholastic, 1956). Mickey discovers some of the properties of magnets when he accidentally spills a box of straight pins and has to pick them up.

FIGURE 3.6 Even batteries are attracted to magnets!

CONSTRUCTING SCIENCE IN THE CLASSROOM 3.10
Classifying Seeds

GRADE

6
5
4
3
2
1
K

CLASSIFICATION ACTIVITY INVOLVING SEEDS

Objective
The student will devise classification systems for seeds.

Use the collection of different kinds of bean and pea seeds you used in the observation activity shown in Constructing Science in the Classroom 3.3 (p. 65). Children have described or drawn the outsides and the insides of the seeds. Now ask them to group them and name the groups. Add other seeds like corn, marigold, pansy, radish, etc., and ask children to group the seeds again. Older children can be asked to form subgroups in their classification system. Have children identify each main group and sub-group with a descriptive name or drawing, and describe their groupings.

As an extension activity, ask children to estimate the number of seeds in each collection.

Literature connections:
Is It Red? Is It Yellow? Is It Blue? and *Is It Rough? Is It Smooth? Is It Shiny?* both by Tana Hoban (Greenwillow, 1978, 1984). The vibrant photographs and wordless text in these books offer many opportunities for introductory classification activities.

Seeds and More Seeds by Millicent Selsam (Harper Row, 1959). An inquisitive young boy discovers through experimentation how to find and plant seeds that grow into beans, fruits, trees, and flowers. The story uses the processes of observation, classification, communication, and measurement.

CONSTRUCTING SCIENCE IN THE CLASSROOM 3.11
Classifying Leaves

GRADE

6
5
4
3
2
1
K

CLASSIFICATION ACTIVITY INVOLVING LEAVES

Objective
The student will classify leaves according to self-identified criteria.

Take children for a walk around the school to collect leaves. Upon return to the classroom, ask children to group them according to one or more characteristics they, themselves, identify. Share the classification systems with the class as a whole.

To enable children to explore other groupings, you may preserve the leaves. Place them between squares of waxed paper (waxed sides toward the leaf), put a cloth over the squares, and iron with a hot iron. Add the preserved specimens to the science center.

Literature connections:
Crinkleroot's Guide to Knowing the Trees by Jim Arnosky (Bradbury, 1992). Take a tour through a forest as Crinkleroot introduces broad-leafed and evergreen trees.

Why Do Leaves Change Color? by Betsy Maestro (Harper Collins, 1994) is a story of how leaves change color when they are exposed to less water and sunlight.

CONSTRUCTING SCIENCE IN THE CLASSROOM 3.12
Classifying Materials In Soil

GRADE

CLASSIFICATION ACTIVITY
INVOLVING SOIL

Objective
The student will devise classification systems for materials found in soil.

Extend the activity in which children made observations on the bag of soil you brought from home or the school yard (Constructing Science in the Classroom 3.4, p. 66), by asking them to group (or classify) the materials they found in the soil. To get started, when children find something recognizable in the soil (such as sand, rocks, bark, leaves, worms, roots, seeds, etc.), they name it and put it on a piece of paper. If children find something they aren't sure of, they place it on a different sheet paper labeled with a question mark. Typical questions the teacher asks as she circulates around the room might include, "Which things are alive?" "Which things used to be alive?" "Which things never were alive?" "Which things are the largest?" "Which things are the smallest?" Having separated and identified the different things in the soil, children can group the things on some basis, and describe their classification system to the rest of the class.

Literature connections:
My Feet by Aliki (Crowell, 1990). In this delightful story, Aliki explains how we use feet and describes the many variations in size and appearance. This would be a great introduction to classification for younger children.

Benny's Animals and How We Put Them In Order by Millicent Selsam (Harper Row, 1966). In this story, a young boy with a passion for neatness and order learns how to classify animals.

CONSTRUCTING SCIENCE IN THE CLASSROOM 3.13
Classifying Soils

GRADE

CLASSIFICATION ACTIVITY
INVOLVING SOIL

Objective
The student will classify soils according to self-identified criteria.

As a continuation of the observational activities with the different kinds of soil you provided where children explored each kind of soil using water, sieves, and magnifying glasses (See In The Schools 2.1, p. 39), ask children to group the soils according to some characteristic they identified. Share the groupings with the class as a whole.
Encourage children to record their findings in their science journals.

Literature connection:
One Small Square Backyard by Donald M. Silver (Freeman, 1993) is a wonderfully illustrated book that encourages the readers to use a notebook to observe, explore, and classify everything in their very own back yard. Utilizing the processes of science is encouraged.

FIGURE 3.7   Making groups of similar things found in soil

CONSTRUCTING SCIENCE IN THE CLASSROOM 3.14
Classifying Smells

GRADE

6
5
4
3
2
1
K

CLASSIFICATION ACTIVITY
INVOLVING SENSE OF SMELL

Objective
The student will classify smells according to self-generated criteria.

Extend the film container odors observation activity (Constructing Science in the Classroom 3.7, p. 68) by asking children to sort canisters by matching the odors in some way. Suggestions include "pleasant and unpleasant odors," "those that are easy to identify and those that are difficult to identify," "fruit-like odors and non-fruit-like odors." Have children come up with their own categories, and ask them to describe their classification systems to the class.

   This activity can be integrated with language arts as children search for descriptive words.

Literature connection:
Frog and Toad Are Friends by Arnold Lobel (Harper and Row, 1970). This is a perfect story to reenact with the class. Frog loses a button and tries to find it with the help of Toad. They find many buttons with different attributes but do not find the actual button until they return home.

CONSTRUCTING SCIENCE IN THE CLASSROOM 3.15
Rock Hardness

GRADE

6
5
4
3
2
1
K

CLASSIFICATION ACTIVITY
INVOLVING HARDNESS OF ROCKS

Objective

The student will classify rocks according to observed properties. (See also In The Schools 2.2, p. 39.)

Provide each group of children with a bag containing specimens of several rocks of different hardnesses (gypsum, coal, quartzite, shale, sandstone, slate, obsidian, limestone, etc.) Also provide each group with a penny, a piece of black construction paper, and a piece of white paper. Children test the hardness of each rock by seeing if it scratches the penny and if the penny scratches the rock. Children also rub each rock on the black and the white paper to see what happens. From the results of the activity, children classify the rocks in descriptive ways, such as "harder than the penny" and "softer than the penny;" "writes on the black paper" and "doesn't write on the black paper," and so on. Children describe their classification system *and the reasons for their system* to the rest of the class.

Note: Strictly speaking, rocks do not have specific hardness since they are made of mixtures of different minerals, each of which has its own hardness. However, for purposes of this activity, this distinction can be disregarded.

Literature connection:
The Big Rock by Bruce Hiscock (Athenium, 1988) traces the origin of a huge granite rock in the Adirondack Mountains that is worn down over the years by outside elements.

CONSTRUCTING YOUR IDEAS 3.6
An Activity For Classifying

Now it's your turn. Write a short activity that can be used to help children develop the skill of classification. Specify grade level, and be sure the activity is appropriate to the children in the age/grade group you specify. Cite a process-oriented objective for your lesson. For lower elementary grades, this objective will read something like this: "The student will group _____." For the upper elementary grades, you may wish, at first, to specify the attributes to be used in the classification system: "The student will classify _____ on the basis of _____." However, with experience children will be able to extract on their own the attributes they will use.

Then get together in small groups, and do the activities each member of the group has prepared.

Communicating

> **CONSTRUCTING YOUR IDEAS 3.7**
> *Directions For Putting On A Jacket*
>
> Try this. Select a partner, and pretend your partner is from a far-away planet and has never seen a jacket and has never seen a human being put one on. Obtain a jacket or a sweater, and give instructions to your partner as to how to put it on. [To the partner: *be sure sure to follow the directions EXACTLY as told to you.*]
>
> How do you start? Do you first tell the partner to be sure the jacket is right-side-out? Then what? "Put your right arm into the right sleeve of the jacket." Great, but you didn't say what end of the sleeve your arm goes into. Try this for a few minutes, and then switch roles with your partner.

This exercise shows what a precise and exquisitely difficult thing it is to communicate accurately. Did you ever have to follow someone's directions to their house? Joke books are filled with such directions as "Turn right about four fence posts before you get to the large maple tree." The skill of accurate and precise communication is essential in all walks of life, including the scientific enterprise.

Communication can be defined as any and all ways people let others know their thoughts. We have already employed the skill of communication in activities involving observation and classification. When children observe something, they let others know what they observed by communicating. Children communicate their explanations for their systems of classification. When children discover something, they let others know what they have discovered by communicating. In fact, probably the *only* way teachers can discover how children are understanding information is to ask them about it, and then listen to what they have to say.

Communication includes verbal as well as non-verbal behavior; people communicate by talking, gesturing, writing, sharing, drawing, telling stories, giving oral presentations, play-acting, pantomiming, singing, puppeteering, and so on. In the classroom, children communicate in small groups, in large groups, in individual conversations with each other, in conferences with the teacher, and so on. Graphs, charts, diagrams, posters, symbols, maps, and mathematical equations are forms of communication of data gathered during an investigation. A graph of daily maximum and minimum temperatures tells legions about temperature trends; a chart of daily food groups eaten by children tells legions about their nutrition habits.

IN THE SCHOOLS 3.5
What's In The Bag?

To sharpen their communications skills, pre-school and kindergarten children can play the game, "What's in the bag?" One child places some object the other children don't know about into a paper bag, and describes one attribute ("It's long." or "It's skinny.") The children try to guess what it is. If they are unsuccessful, the demonstrator provides another clue, and so on until the object has been guessed correctly. The activity can be integrated with language arts so children develop the vocabulary of adjectives needed for adequate descriptions.

Literature connection:
Sense Suspense: A Guessing Game for the Five Senses by Bruce McMillan (Scholastic, 1994). Using close-up pictures, the reader is required to figure out what the whole picture is of and what senses can be used to solve the mystery. The beautiful pictures are from the Caribbean; text is in Spanish and English.

IN THE SCHOOLS 3.6
Funny Figures

In first and second grade, children can provide oral descriptions of unknown objects, such as the funny figures pictured in Figure 3.8. One child holds a funny figure such that the partner cannot see it, and describes it so the other child can make an accurate drawing of it.

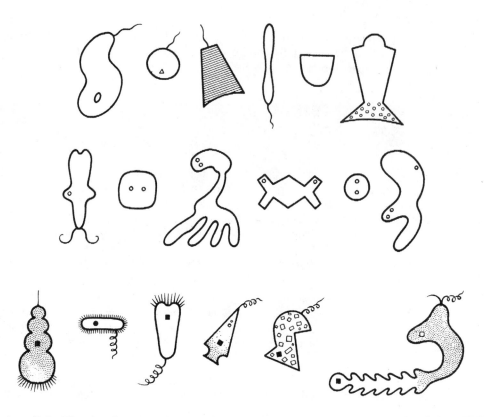

Courtesy: Delta Education, Inc., Hudson, NH 03051, 1-800-258-1302

FIGURE 3.8 Funny figures

A wide variety of such activities designed to foster full and accurate understanding should be included in the science program so children can be given the maximum opportunity to develop accurate communications skills. They can write descriptions of activities for publication in class books. They can write in their science journals regularly, describing and illustrating their science activities. They can share their journals with each other and with the teacher to see if their descriptions are clear and accurate. They can describe their activities and the results of their investigations orally in the form of class presentations. The more opportunity children are given to discuss, describe, and explain, the better their communications skills will become.

Additional communications activities for you to consider using in your classroom are shown in Constructing Science in the Classroom 3.16–3.17.

CONSTRUCTING SCIENCE IN THE CLASSROOM 3.16
Twenty Questions

GRADE

COMMUNICATION GAME

Objective
The student will communicate characteristics of unknown objects and events.

The game, "Twenty Questions," which can be played using all kinds of objects and events, is an excellent way of sharpening children's communications skills. Possible ways of communicating include the following:

> Oral descriptions
> Drawings
> Charts
> Graphs
> Posters
> Written descriptions
> Pantomimes

Literature connection:
The Wise Woman and Her Secret by Eve Merriam (Simon and Schuster, 1991). Many people seek the advice of a wise woman who says, "The secret of wisdom is to be curious; to take the time to look closely; to use all your senses to see and touch and taste and smell and hear; to keep wandering and wondering."

CONSTRUCTING SCIENCE IN THE CLASSROOM 3.17
Sand — Rice — Water

GRADE

COMMUNICATION ACTIVITY ON WATER

The student will communicate characteristics of sand, rice, and water, and will use these characteristics to identify an unknown material.
Provide the following materials for each group of children: 3 containers, sand, water at room temperature, rice, funnels, measuring cups, measuring spoons, paper towels, and a blindfold. Children put sand, rice, and water in each of the three containers, and explore the three materials to discover their characteristics, similarities, and differences. They smell; they observe texture, color, transparency, temperature; they pour; they let the material run through the funnel; they heft, After their initial explorations, they *describe* the sand, the rice, and the water to each other. The group continues the discussion until they agree on accurate descriptions of each. Then, one by one, the members of the group are blindfolded, and put their hands in one of the containers (unknown to the blindfolded student). Based on the accurate descriptions of each material previously agreed upon, the student infers which material his hand is in.

Literature connections:
Sand by Sally Cartwright (Coward, McCann and Geohegan, 1975). Using a question and answer format, Sally Cartwright suggests "stepping barefoot in the sand, warm and dry and crumbly; digging hollows with your hand; a million shiny grains of sand, sliding soft and tumbly."

Communication by Aliki (Greenwillow, 1993). Attractive illustrations and simple language are used to describe the many ways and reasons people and animals communicate. The inside cover includes drawings of sign language and the Braille alphabet.

Measuring

There are five basic entities which elementary children measure in science: length, volume, weight or mass, temperature, and time.

Length

Length is defined as the distance between two points. Examples are the length of a table top, the height of a door, the distance between two cities, the circumference of a beach ball, and so on. Length is the fundamental measurement needed to find area, which is calculated by applying various area formulas such as length times width (for the area of a rectangle) or 1/2 base times height (for the area of a triangle). Length may also be used to find volume by applying various formulas, such as length times width times height (for volume of a rectangular box).

Length may be measured either in metric units or in conventional units. The basic metric unit of length is the meter, which was originally defined as one ten-millionth of the distance from the north pole to the equator measured along a great circle passing through Lyons, France. Today, the meter is defined in more precise terms—the distance light travels in 1/299,792,458th of a second.

The meter is divided into 10 centimeters, and each centimeter is divided into 10 millimeters. One thousand meters makes a kilometer.

PREFIX	MEANING
KILO	1000 times
HECTO	100 times
DECA	10 times
DECI	1/10th
CENTI	1/100th
MILLI	1/1000th

FIGURE 3.9 Table of metric prefixes

The basic unit of length in the conventional system is the foot. Three feet equal a yard. A meter is a little longer than a yard. If you put an inch ruler next to a centimeter ruler, you will find that it takes about 2 1/2 centimeters to make one inch.

Children should be encouraged to measure such things as desk tops, the length and width of the room, the height of the door, their own heights, and anything else in their physical environment. Many instruments are available to assist in measuring: rulers, yardsticks, meter sticks, calipers, etc. When young children find the length of an object they are measuring to be between whole numbers of the units they are using, you can ask them to record the number of *whole* units they measured and disregard the additional fractional part.

MEASURING

FIGURE 3.10 Children measure everything, including walls and their own height.

Systems of measurement generated by children can and should be fostered. In one notable example of some years ago, a class of middle grades children was discussing the meaning of "large." Referring to the system of scientific notation in which the number 10 is raised to different powers (for example, 10^2 is equal to 100 and 10^3 is equal to 1000), the children perceived that an extremely large number would be 10^{100}, which is 10 with 100 zeroes after it. There was no name for this quantity, so they coined the term "googol," a term which is now in use throughout the scientific world.

Children can measure length in terms of number of legos, bears, blocks, paper clips, lengths of string, nose-to-fingertips span, length of feet, and so on. The important thing is that they gain the idea that length can be quantified, and that things can be measured; this is more important than memorizing the rubrics of the metric system, or the number of inches in a foot.

IN THE SCHOOLS 3.7
Graphing Plant Growth

Plant height can be measured in terms of number of squares on a piece of graph paper. Children place strips of graph paper behind the plants they want to measure, and cut the strips off at the top of the plant. The strips are then pasted onto a large chart and the number of squares is counted, showing the relative heights of the plants in graphical form. This procedure also can be used to display plant growth over time.

Literature connection:
The Carrot Seed by Ruth Krauss (Harper & Row, 1945). A little boy plants a carrot seed and cares for it regularly. The seed grows into a huge plant despite everyone telling him it won't come up.

IN THE SCHOOLS 3.8
How Long Is A Kilometer? How Long Is A Mile?

How long is a kilometer? Take a few meter sticks outside to a large but safe region, such as the ball field, the playground, or the sidewalk, and lay the meter sticks end-to-end, one after the other, until 1000 separate meter lengths have been counted off. This is the length of a kilometer. How does it compare with a mile? You can divide 5280 feet in a mile by 3 feet in a yard obtaining 1760 yards, and then do the same thing with yardsticks. In one class, children measured a kilometer and a mile along the street in front of their school, and put markers at the curb so that passers-by could check the accuracy of the odometers of their cars.

Volume

The volume of something is how much space it takes up. Volume can be measured in terms of length (as mentioned above), or in terms of its own units. The basic metric unit for volume is the liter (which is about the same as a quart). One liter contains 1000 milliliters. Since the volume of a milliliter is the same as the volume of a cubic-shaped object that is one centimeter on each side, the term "cubic centimeter," or "c.c." is more commonly used than milliliters. It takes 1000 cc's to equal one liter. The basic unit of liquid volume in the conventional system is the quart, which contains four cups; the cup is equivalent to 8 ounces of liquid. Four quarts make a gallon.

As with length, it is not only possible, but is desirable for children to invent their own units of volume: paper cup, coffee can, and so on are ideal for measuring amount of liquid.

IN THE SCHOOLS 3.9
How Much Soda Is In A Liter?

How many cups will a liter of soda fill? A kindergarten teacher asked a child to pour soda from a one-liter bottle into cups. Other children counted the number of cups that were filled. The question was asked, "If we buy one 1-liter bottle of soda will every child in our class get a cup of soda?"

In dealing with the concept of volume with young children, let us recall the Piagetian experiments relative to conservation. When a ball of clay is rolled into a cigar-shaped cylinder, preoperational children are not able to perceive that the volume of clay stays the same; they perceive there is MORE clay since it occupies greater length. The same is true when water is poured from a tall thin glass into a large tank; since it occupies less depth in the tank than in the glass, young children perceive that there is less water. These experiments show that preoperational children have difficulty in conserving volume. They do not understand that the amount of material in something does not change when it changes shape. These tasks are sometimes used to determine whether children are ready for concrete operational thought. (See Note 3.)

Since preoperational children have difficulty with tasks involving conservation of volume, it is inappropriate to ask them to compare volumes of different materials at the early grades, or to do activities that require they recognize that the volume of a material does not change when its shape changes. In kindergarten, volume activities should consist of counting tasks such as finding the number of cups of sand it takes to fill or empty a pail.

Calculating volume by displacement is a very advanced concept, and there are many children in upper grades who cannot understand the concept. Displacement is a method of determining the volume of an irregularly-shaped object by placing it in a container of a known volume of water and measuring the apparent increase in volume when the object is immersed in the water. This is similar to what you do when you want to measure 1/2 cup of shortening for a cookie recipe. You put, say, 1 1/2 cups of water in a two-cup measuring cup, and completely submerge shortening in the water until the level of water reaches the 2-cup mark. In this way, you have measured 1/2 cup of shortening. This concept is extremely difficult for children to understand, for not only do they have to understand that the volume of water is conserved (none is added, and none is taken away), and the volume of shortening is conserved, but they also have to understand that two things cannot occupy the same place at the same time, and they have to conceive of the subtraction process necessary for calculating the volume. Many fifth grade teachers have reported that even though this concept is presented in the curriculum, their children simply do not understand it. This, of course, is to be expected: many fifth grade children do not yet have the level of conservation reasoning required to understand displacement.

Weight or Mass

There is a difference between weight and mass. Weight is the pull of gravity on something; mass is the amount of material in that something. Weight depends on the strength of gravity. Gravity on the moon is about 1/6 of the gravity on the earth, so things weigh about 1/6 as much on the moon as they do on earth. People can jump higher and hop further on the moon than they can on earth because there is less gravity to hold them down. However, people have the same amount of mass (material) in them whether they are on the earth or on the moon. Weight varies from place to place, but mass does not.

Mass and weight are measured in different ways and have different units. The most common unit of mass is the kilogram, a metric unit. The most common unit of weight is the pound, a conventional system unit. Unfortunately, these units are often used interchangeably in modern society. For example, at home we weigh 125 pounds; when we get to the doctor's office, the nurse tells us we weigh 57 kilograms. The label on a pound package of butter says "NET WEIGHT 1 POUND (454 grams)." Yet, the pound is a unit of *weight* and the kilogram and gram are units of *mass*. The reason people tend to interchange the pound and the kilogram is that, for all practical purposes, the weight of a given mass stays the same everywhere on earth. If a rock has a mass of 5 kilograms, it will weigh 11 pounds on earth (2.2 times its mass in kilograms), no matter where you take it. Of course, there may be slight variations in weight depending on altitude, for the force of gravity decreases the higher you go, but this change in weight is insignificant. As you can imagine, it is difficult for children to understand that mass and weight are two different things. Because of this common, yet technically erroneous, interchangeability of the units for mass and weight, it is suggested that elementary teachers not expend much effort in trying to get children to understand the difference between the two. This concept will certainly come later on.

The basic unit of weight is the pound; there are 16 ounces in a pound, and 2000 pounds in a ton. There are many units in the conventional system to measure large and small amounts of weight: tons, ounces, drams, etc.

The basic unit of mass is the kilogram. The kilogram is defined as the mass of a cylinder made of an alloy of platinum and iridium, kept in Paris, France. A mass of one kilogram weighs 2.2 pounds on earth at sea level. A gram is 1/1000 of a kilogram, and equals the mass of one cubic centimeter of pure water; it is about the mass of a good-sized mosquito. The prefixes shown in Figure 3.9 (p. 86) apply to the gram; the most commonly used sub-units are the milligram (1/1000 of a gram) and the kilogram (1000 grams).

It is not necessary for young children to weigh in terms of grams or ounces or pounds; these concepts are abstract, and are developed in later grades. Instead, they should be encouraged to weigh things in terms of small bears, paper clips, legos, blocks, etc. Simple balances are available that use tiny bears, plastic cubes, or paper clips as units of weight. Children also can compare weights of similar things relative to each other: large rocks vs. small rocks; heavy books vs. light books; large metal washers vs. small metal washers.

IN THE SCHOOLS 3.10
Weighing Cookies

In a second grade class, the teacher gave each child a chocolate chip cookie, and asked the children how they could tell who has the biggest one. Children compared diameters, and then thickness. At the teacher's suggestion, they compared the weights of each others' cookies on the balance scale. Children were then given untouched cookies for a snack.

Temperature

Temperature can be measured either in Celsius degrees (the metric system) or in Fahrenheit degrees (the conventional system). Of course, a certain temperature is the same, whether it is expressed in Fahrenheit or Celsius degrees. Children should become familiar with both the Fahrenheit system and the Celsius system. The points of reference in each system are the freezing point and the boiling point of water (at sea level). The freezing point of water is 0° Celsius or 32° Fahrenheit. The boiling point of water is 100° Celsius or 212° Fahrenheit. The advantage of the Celsius scale is that the difference in temperature between freezing water and boiling water is divided into 100 degrees, whereas, in the Fahrenheit scale, this difference is divided into 180 degrees.

Common temperatures in both Celsius and Fahrenheit are given in Figure 3.11.

COMMON TEMPERATURES IN CELSIUS AND FAHRENHEIT DEGREES

	CELSIUS DEGREES	FAHRENHEIT DEGREES
Boiling Point of Water	100	212
Human Body Normal Temperature	37	98.6
Hot Day Outside	32	90
Comfortable Room Temperature	21	70
Freezing Point of Water	0	32
Cold Day Outside	−18	0

FIGURE 3.11

Temperature is an abstract concept, one with which young children have difficulty. Thus, young children might be encouraged to compare temperatures with their own body temperature: how do things "feel?" Does a cup of water feel hot? Warm? Cool? Cold? Is sand hot in the summer time? How hot? Too hot to walk on? How about the black top on the streets? How about the concrete of the sidewalks? Is a room hot? Cold? Just right? What do you like hot? Soup? Cocoa? Pizza? What do you like cold? Soda? Ice cream?

IN THE SCHOOLS 3.11
Recording Daily Temperatures

Children can be introduced to the conceptual meaning of temperature by recording temperature readings taken from television or radio weather broadcasts on the daily classroom calendars.

As children grow older, they learn to read the thermometer, but, since this requires interpolation (inferring numbers that are not printed on the scales), skill in estimation is required. Thus, temperature readings should be deferred until children can estimate the distance between two known positions. Then, they will be able to count the lines between degrees that are marked on the thermometer, and interpolate the actual reading. Digital thermometers provide accurate temperature readouts, and can be used until children learn how to read regular thermometers.

Time

There are two aspects to measuring time: time of day, and time intervals. One of the tasks children accomplish in the early elementary grades is telling time using clocks. Time is recorded from the wall clocks for many daily routines. Children should be discouraged from using digital clocks until time concepts have been explored using regular clocks. Many science activities involve recording the time of day.

IN THE SCHOOLS 3.12
Recording Time and Temperature

Children record the outdoor temperature at, say, eleven-thirty each day, and construct a histogram to show how the outdoor temperature changes from day to day.

Literature connection:
Temperature and You by Betsy and Guilio Maestro (Lodestar, 1990). This is an introductory story of what temperature is and how it is measured appropriate for lower grades.

A different aspect of time involves measuring intervals of time rather than time of day. The unit used for time intervals is the second; this is a universal unit, and is the same in the conventional system and the metric system. The second was first defined as $1/86,400$ of the mean solar day (the average length of the day over a period of one year). The second now is defined in terms of a type of radiation that is emitted by the element cesium-133.

Intervals of time are measured using stop watches or second hands on a clock.

IN THE SCHOOLS 3.13
How Long Does It Take To Run Across The Playground?

How long does it take a person to run from one end of the playground to the other? One child does the running, and another child either operates a stop watch or counts seconds on a clock.

Literature connection:
Clocks and More Clocks by Pat Hutchins (Macmillan, 1970). Mr. Higgins buys many clocks, but they show different times when he moves from room to room. He consults a clock maker who teaches him about elapsed time.

IN THE SCHOOLS 3.14
Timing How Long It Takes A Ball To Roll Down A Ramp

How much time does it take for a ball to roll down an inclined plane? This requires measurement of time intervals. By second grade, children can either use stopwatches or count seconds on a clock.

As is true for all units of measurement, time is an abstract concept, and children have to build meaning for the concept by doing activities that involve the use of time. Kindergarten is not too early for children to start.

Metric vs. Conventional Units

Many science educators have written about educating our young people in the metric system. The United States is one of very few countries that still use the conventional system. Even Canada and Mexico, our closest neighbors, use the metric system. The U.S. Congress has tried for many years to legislate use of the metric system, but has consistently failed to secure the needed support. (However, in 1988, a law was passed requiring federal agencies to use the metric system whenever practical in order to make the United States more competitive in international trade.) So, in the United States, a person is still five feet three inches tall, and weighs 120 pounds. The temperature is still 72 degrees Fahrenheit.

It is useful to examine the arguments for and against using the metric system. The world of science uses the metric system. Therefore, in keeping with our premise that children should learn science the way scientists do science, children should make all measurements in science using the metric system. The metric system is easier to use than the conventional system, and children enjoy working with it. However, learning theory suggests that children learn best that which is meaningful to them. Children are familiar with the conventional system, and use terms like inches, miles, pounds, ounces, and degrees Fahrenheit. Children do not measure everyday things in meters, weigh things in kilograms, or record temperatures in Celsius degrees. To insist the metric system be used in elementary science education, even though it is not used in the daily lives of the children, is to ask children to think in terms of units that are less meaningful to them than the conventional units. It may also place an aura of mysticism and elitism around the study of science. This is one of the many ambiguities in the field of education with which you must wrestle. So, it is your decision whether the metric system should be used in your science program. You will have support either way. If you use the metric system because of its ease of conversion among subdivisions of the scales and because of its universal use in the scientific enterprise, you have a very strong argument for using the metric system. If you use conventional units in order to foster meaning based on prior experiences and familiarity, you have a very strong argument for using conventional units.

IN THE SCHOOLS 3.15
Comparing Metric and Conventional Units

To help children understand that both the metric and conventional units are in common use, a teacher asked children to list items sold in grocery stores together with the units of measurement used. Children discovered that flour and sugar are sold by the pound and soda is sold by the liter.

Several measurement activities appropriate for various grade levels are suggested in Constructing Science in the Classroom 3.18–3.23.

CONSTRUCTING SCIENCE IN THE CLASSROOM 3.18
How Many Pennies?

GRADE

ACVTIVITY FOR MEASURING LENGTH

Objective

The student will measure length using common objects.

Provide each child with a number of pennies and several objects to be measured, such as a clothes pin, napkin, paper clip, sheet of construction paper, etc. Explain to the children that the unit of measure is "one penny," and ask them to select an object and estimate how many pennies long it is. Then they lay the pennies end-to-end, obtaining an actual length measurement in terms of number of pennies. Estimated and actual penny-lengths are recorded on a chart. Children continue measuring objects in terms of pennies, thereby gaining understanding of the meaning of measurement of length. In addition, their estimates become more and more accurate.

For follow-up, ask children what other items can be used for measurement.

Literature connections:

How Big Is a Foot? by Rolf Mylar (Atheneum, 1962). This is a comical story of the use of non-standard measurement. The king orders a carpenter to build a bed based upon the length of the king's foot; however, the carpenter builds the bed based upon the length of his own foot.

The Hundred Penny Box by Sharon Bell Mathis (Puffin, 1986). An elderly woman explains to her grandson that a penny is placed in a box every year of her life. The passage of time is well explained in this moving story.

CONSTRUCTING SCIENCE IN THE CLASSROOM 3.19
How Much Does A Penny Weigh?

GRADE

ACTIVITY FOR MEASURING WEIGHT

Objective

The student will measure the weight of objects using non-conventional units.

First show children how to use the two-pan balance scale.

Then put a penny in one pan of the balance scale and add paper clips to the other pan until balance is achieved. Children record the number of paper clips. Encourage children to experiment with how much two, three, and four pennies weigh. Also encourage them to explore the weights of many different things using different kinds of "weights" on the balance scale.

Literature connection:

Let's Find Out About What's Light and What's Heavy by Martha and Charles Shapp (Franklin Watts, 1975). With attention-getting pictures and humorous text, children will discover that what may be light for one person may be heavy for another person.

CONSTRUCTING SCIENCE IN THE CLASSROOM 3.20
How Does Ice Affect The Temperature of Water?

GRADE

ACTIVITY FOR MEASURING TEMPERATURE

Objective
The student will measure the temperature of water.

Fill a glass partly full of water, and record its temperature. Add an ice cube to the water, and predict how long it will take to melt. Record the temperature and the time on a chart every minute. Keep recording temperature and time readings until the last three readings stay the same.

Literature connection:
Winter Barn by Peter Parnall (Macmillan, 1986). The winter barn is a safe haven for all of the creatures that seek shelter from the brutal sub-zero winds as they wait for the first signs of spring.

CONSTRUCTING SCIENCE IN THE CLASSROOM 3.21
How Much Does Air Weigh?

GRADE

ACTIVITY FOR MEASURING WEIGHT

Objective
The student will weigh a given amount of air.

Air is a difficult phenomenon for young children to grasp, since we can not see it or smell it. But we can feel it when the wind blows, so we know air is all around us. Does it weigh anything? Since it is a material (we know this since we can feel it when it blows), it must be matter. And, since it is matter, it must have some weight. Take an empty balloon, and put it on the right hand pan of a pan balance. Add weights, paper clips, and tiny pieces of paper to the empty pan until the mechanism is completely balanced. Now, fill the balloon with air by blowing it up. (We understand that what you blow into the balloon isn't strictly air since it contains higher amounts of carbon dioxide and water vapor because it comes from your lungs; however, it still is air.) Put the filled balloon back on the right-hand pan. The scale will be off balance due to the added weight of the air in the balloon. The weight of the air is very small, probably less than a gram. Cut strips of graph paper and add them to the left hand pan of the balance until perfect balance is regained. The weight of the strips of paper is equal to the weight of the air in the balloon.

To find out how much weight this is, weigh a whole sheet of the graph paper, and divide by the number of squares in the sheet. This gives the weight of one square. Multiply this by the number of squares it took to balance the full balloon, and you have calculated the weight of air in the balloon. (This shows integration with mathematics.)

Literature connections:
How Much Is a Million by David Schwartz (Lothrop, Lee & Shepard, 1985). Using humorous illustrations by Steven Kellogg, the author gives understandable representations of the concept of a million, billion, and trillion objects; the method to compute these large scale numbers is explained in the back of the book.

Is It Larger? Is It Smaller? by Tana Hoban (Greenwillow, 1985). This book introduces comparisons of the same object of different sizes and explores the concepts of length, weight, volume, area, time, and money.

CONSTRUCTING SCIENCE IN THE CLASSROOM 3.22
Soda Straw Balance

GRADE

6
5
4
3
2
1
K

ACTIVITY FOR MEASURING WEIGHT

Objective

The student will measure weights of very small objects using the soda straw balance.

With this soda straw balance, children can weigh extremely light objects: a mosquito, a hair, a blade of grass, a square of graph paper, etc. Obtain a plastic or paper soda straw, a bolt or screw that will fit snugly into one end of the straw, a pin, and two wooden blocks. Cut one end of the straw at an angle to form a "pan." Put the bolt in the other end, and screw it part way into the straw. Run the pin through the straw *just barely* forward of the screw, and a little bit above the center of the straw. Balance the straw between the two blocks of wood, and screw the screw in or out very slowly until the straw rests at a suitable incline.

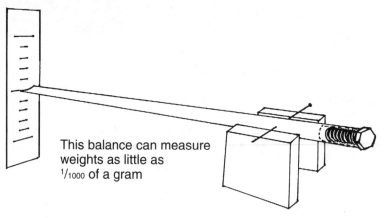

This balance can measure weights as little as $^1/_{1000}$ of a gram

FIGURE 3.12   Soda straw balance

To find the weights of things using this balance, weigh a sheet of graph paper on a gram balance. Count the number of squares in the sheet, and divide the weight by the number of squares to obtain the weight of one square. Cut out one square, and place it in the "pan" of the soda straw balance. Set up a tongue depressor next to the tip of the balance, and record the positions of the tip of the balance without the square of graph paper and with the square of graph paper. Divide these two positions into ten equal divisions, and calculate the weight represented by each division. (Each division is equal to 1/10 of the weight of the square of graph paper.)

Now, use the soda straw balance to measure all sorts of very light things!

Literature connection:

8,000 Stones: A Chinese Folktale retold by Diane Wolkstein (Doubleday, 1972). This story explains the use of non-standard units of measure and how to weigh something very large.

CONSTRUCTING SCIENCE IN THE CLASSROOM 3.23
Which Gets Hotter In The Sun: Soil Or Water?

GRADE

6
5
4
3
2
1
K

ACTIVITY FOR MEASURING TEMPERATURE

Objective
The student will measure temperatures of water and soil, and will infer reasons for any differences.

On a sunny day, set a bucket of cool water and a bucket of planting soil out in the sun. Take temperature readings of both the water and the soil near the surface when you first set them out; remember where you placed the thermometer so you will place it at the same depth each time you take a reading. Take temperature readings every hour throughout the day, and record the time and temperature for both buckets. Was there a difference between the readings taken in the water and those taken in the soil? What do you suppose causes this difference (if any)? Try doing the same thing with buckets of different kinds of soil; with different colors of soil. Try it with a bucket of rocks. What do you notice?

The surface temperature of the soil increases faster than the surface temperature of the water because the soil is darker and absorbs solar radiation more readily. The heat absorbed by the water gets distributed throughout the bucket through convection, resulting in the water retaining the heat longer than the soil. This explains why temperatures are milder near lakes and seashores.

Literature connections:
Environmental America: The Southeastern States by D. J. Herda (Millbrook Press, 1991). This is one of a regional series about how land, air, and water problems can have a national and global impact.

The Weather Classroom by Karen W. Moore (The Weather Channel, 1992). Chapter Three contains details about this activity.

CONSTRUCTING YOUR IDEAS 3.9
An Activity For Measuring

Now it's your turn. Write a short activity that can be used to help children develop skill in one of the measurement skills. Specify grade level, and be sure the activity is appropriate to the children in the age/grade group you specify. Cite a process-oriented objective for your lesson; this objective will read something like this: "The student will measure _____ ." Then get together in small groups, and do the activities each member of the group has prepared.

Predicting

These are questions that involve prediction.

Prediction is an individual's best guess as to what will happen next in a given situation—what would happen if you did something.

It has been said that the most important question elementary science teachers (or any science teacher, for that matter) can ask their students is, "What would happen if _____?" When this question is asked, it seems to require an answer. These "What-would-happen-if-_____" questions stem from observations and curiosity, with the observations leading to questions that someone wants to investigate. And they all involve the process of prediction.

IN THE SCHOOLS 3.16
Predicting Times of Sunrise and Sunset

A class of second grade students recorded sunrise and sunset data every day for 10 school days. Then they made a graph of this data, and, from the graph, predicted the times the sun would rise and set the next school day. They compared their predictions with actual data in the newspaper. The children also predicted the maximum and minimum temperatures and weather for the next day, and compared their predictions with what actually happened.

There are certain things we can predict somewhat accurately. We can predict with reasonable certainty the times of sunrise and sunset. We can predict that in winter the weather will be cold, and that in summertime it will be hot. From complex calculations involving speed and orbit, we can predict that Halley's Comet will return in the year 2061.[4]

However, some predictions are less accurate. For example, meteorologists attempt to provide the public with their best guess as to what will happen to our weather, given the information they have. But many unpredictable variables, such as sudden shifts in atmospheric pressure, wind direction, or atmospheric temperature cause unexpected changes in weather.

Prediction is essential in doing science, and children should be encouraged to predict before they test. For example children should predict whether an item will sink or float before they try it. They should predict whether an item will be attracted or will not be attracted to a magnet before they try it. In this way, children learn to compare what actually happens with what they thought would happen rather than merely accepting what happened without thinking about it. The discrepancies between predicted and actual occurrences are areas worthy of further investigation. For example, if a child predicts that a coin will be attracted to a magnet, and then finds that it is not attracted, the child may want to investigate why this is so.

THE CASE OF THE MYSTERIOUS CRAYONS

Often an activity can have unexpected results, thus opening up whole new avenues of inquiry that no one ever thought of before. In a first grade class, a teacher was engaging his students in a prediction "sink-or-float" activity. Included in the assemblage of items for children to predict and then try were several kinds of crayons. The activity proceeded as expected with the wooden objects, the buttons, the ivory soap, the paper clips, and so on. But a most remarkable thing was observed by the children: some of the crayons sank and some floated. Attempting to understand this newly discovered phenomenon, the teacher asked children to suggest reasons why some crayons would sink and others float. "Maybe it's the paper." So, they removed the paper from all the crayons. Some sank and some floated. "Maybe it's the length." So the children gathered several crayons of the same length with the papers removed. Some sank and some floated. "Maybe it's how fat they are." So the children tried crayons of the same length with their papers removed, but of different thicknesses. Some sank and some floated. After some time of trying several things, someone noticed that the yellow and orange colors floated while the blue and purple colors sank. More experimentation showed that this, indeed, was the case. The darker colors of the same brand of crayon sank and the lighter colors floated. In fact, some of them, the middle colors, floated half way between the top and the bottom of the water.

Why did this happen? I don't know.

Constructing Science in the Classroom 3.24–3.27 describe some activities that focus primarily on the process skill of prediction. Note that all require observation, and that some require classification and measurement as well.

CONSTRUCTING SCIENCE IN THE CLASSROOM 3.24
Sink? Or Float?

GRADE

6
5
4
3
2
1
K

A PREDICTION ACTIVITY

Objective
The student will predict whether given objects sink or float.

Provide a tray with a number of different kinds of objects, some of which sink and some of which float. Suggestions include metal spoon, plastic spoon, metal fork, plastic fork, piece of wood, penny, dime, nickel, quarter, empty shampoo bottle, liquid soap, regular soap, wooden clothes pin, pencil, wooden spoon, paper clip, crayons, etc. Also provide a "Data Sheet" for children to record their results. The data sheet might look like this:

SINK?? OR FLOAT??

OBJECT	PREDICTION		RESULTS	
	SINK	FLOAT	SINK	FLOAT

Children select objects from the tray, predict whether they will sink or float, and record their predictions on the data table. Then they try the item, and record their results. Ask inquiry-oriented questions such as, "What would happen if we changed the shape of an object?" Let children try changing the shapes of the paper clip, the lengths of the crayons, and other things. Try a flat piece of aluminum foil. What would happen if we changed its shape into a boat, a cup, or a tightly-wound-up ball. What actually does happen? "What would happen if we changed the size of things?" Encourage children to try.

Literature connections:
Mr. Gumpy's Outing by John Burningham (Henry Holt, 1970) is a humorous tale of an outdoor adventure on a boat on the river. One by one, children and animals join Mr. Gumpy in the boat. Everything is fine until they upset the balance of weight in the boat.

CONSTRUCTING SCIENCE IN THE CLASSROOM 3.25
Transparent — Translucent — Opaque

GRADE

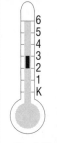

A PREDICTION ACTIVITY

Objective
The student will predict whether given materials are transparent, translucent, or opaque.

When we shine a light on an object, one of three things can happen. (1) All the light can go through the material, and the material is said to be *transparent*. (2) Some of the light can go through the material, and the material is said to be *translucent*. (3) None of the light goes through the material, and the material is said to be *opaque*. (Note: these definitions are not precise, but for purposes of this activity, they are fine.) Provide transparent, translucent, and opaque materials such as a glass jar, a sheet of white paper, overhead transparency film, cardboard, poster board, aluminum foil, waxed paper, tissue paper, facial tissue, a glass of water, a mirror, plastic wrap, an eye glass lens, scotch tape, a magnifying glass, etc. Children predict whether each object is transparent, translucent, or opaque. They then shine flashlight beams at each object to check their predictions. A data table to help children in their exploration might look like the one below; children can either write or draw their predictions.

TRANSPARENT—TRANSLUCENT—OPAQUE

ITEM	TRANSPARENT		TRANSLUCENT		OPAQUE	
	PREDICTED	ACTUAL	PREDICTED	ACTUAL	PREDICTED	ACTUAL

Note: This activity can be integrated with language study as children investigate other words beginning with the prefix "trans."

Literature connections:
Keep the Lights Burning, Abbie by Peter Roop (Carolrhoda, 1985). Abbie keeps the light on in the lighthouse during a storm.

Bouncing and Bending Light by Barbara Taylor (Watts, 1990) presents projects to demonstrate the effects of mirrors and lenses on light rays.

CONSTRUCTING SCIENCE IN THE CLASSROOM 3.26
What Kinds of Materials Absorb Water?

GRADE

A PREDICTION ACTIVITY

Objective
The student will predict whether given materials absorb water.

Provide an assortment of materials such as waxed paper, paper towels, paper bags, napkins, typing paper, plastic wrap, cloth, oil cloth, etc. Children place the material on a piece of cardboard held at an angle. Using an eyedropper or a straw, children place one or two drops of water on the material at the top of the incline. Demonstrate this with one of the materials to show that the water runs down the incline quickly or slowly, depending on how rapidly it is absorbed by the material. Ask children to predict which materials will allow the water to run down the incline rapidly, and which will cause the water to run down the incline slowly. Children record their predictions, and then test them. There are many variations children should be encouraged to explore: What if the material is flat on the table? What if the material is held over the top of an open coffee can? What if we use oil instead of water? Encourage children to try many different substances.

Literature connection:
Desert Giant: The World of the Saguaro Cactus by Barbara Bash (Sierra Club/Little Brown, 1991). This is a wonderful book on the life cycle of the saguaro cactus and the haven it produces for desert life. The book has an abundance of information such as how the cactus skin expands to store rain water for the dry spans.

CONSTRUCTING SCIENCE IN THE CLASSROOM 3.27
How Do Earthworms Behave?

GRADE

A PREDICTION ACTIVITY

Objective
The student will predict the reaction of earthworms under various conditions.

Provide each group with one or two earthworms, and ask them to find out how earthworms behave. Children may do whatever they want to in order to answer the question, with the proviso that they may not cause bodily harm to the worms. Let children predict and test their predictions and write down their conclusions and the reasons for their conclusions. Share with the class.

Literature connection:
Secrets of a Wildlife Watcher by Jim Arnosky (Lothrop, 1983) is a beautifully illustrated guidebook that shares the techniques of finding and observing wildlife behavior.

CONSTRUCTING YOUR IDEAS 3.11
An Activity For Predicting

Now it's your turn. Write a short activity that can be used to help children develop the skill of prediction. Specify grade level, and be sure the activity is appropriate to the children in the age/grade group you specify. Cite a process-oriented objective for your lesson; this objective will read something like this: "The student will predict_____ ." Then get together in small groups, and do the activities each member of the group has prepared.

Inferring

CONSTRUCTING YOUR IDEAS 3.12
Footprints

Consider the illustration in Figure 3.13. Take a piece of paper, and cover the illustration entirely. Then, move the paper slowly from left to right, uncovering more and more of the picture as you move it. What is happening? Write or draw or play-act what you think caused what you observe in the picture. Share your inferences with the rest of the class.

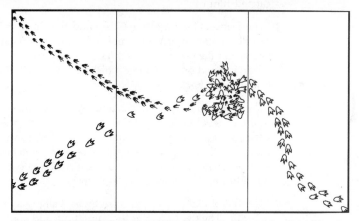

FIGURE 3.13 Footprints

Remember there is no right answer. Some people will say that a small bird and a large bird were coming from opposite directions. The large bird spied the small one, attacked it, and, after a scuffle, ate it, and continued on its trip. Others will infer that the small bird managed to fly away after the scuffle. Still others will suggest that the small bird hopped onto the back of the larger animal and went for a ride. Are these inferences consistent with what is in the picture?

What do you think about the following interpretation:

A small monster was blithely walking down a hill, minding its own business, when all of a sudden it spied a huge monster strolling from the opposite direction. At just that moment, a gigantic snowball rolled down from the top of the hill, and both monsters panicked. The snowball swallowed up the little monster, but the big monster managed to get away. Tired, disoriented, and still panting from its successful attempt to avoid being swallowed up by the huge snowball, the big monster walked away.

The following are actual inferences written by fourth and fifth grade children. As you read each one, check it for validity.

"Two animals were walking. They came together and hit heads because they weren't looking where they were going. They got dizzy and were walking around in circles. Then the dizziness went away. Then they saw each other and started fighting. The bigger one got the smaller one and carried him off."

"The Dance. One night the Gleep and the Glorg were walking through the Pluto Prairie and they met each other and fell in love. Then the Gleep and the Glorg had a romantic weird dance together. After that the Gleep jumped on the Glorge's back and walked off in the night and got a free piggy back ride."

"There was this Apatosaurus and an Archaeopteryx that were walking in the same direction, and the Apatosaurus saw the Archaeopteryx. He tried to get away by taking big steps. The bird saw the dinosaur, ran to him, and they got into a fight. The bird scratched and the dinosaur stomped. The fight finally ended and the Apatosaurus won. However, he didn't eat meat so he walked away."

"The Pot of Gold. A lepercon (sic) was walking to a pot of gold. So was a giraffe. They got there at the same time and started to argue about it. The giraffe ran to the lepercon but the lepercon disappeared with the gold. The giraffe stomped off angrily."

"The Universe formed as a ball and then exploded into big foot-shaped galaxies and spread into little paths. Then all the galaxies got sucked together and the process started again."

Inference is a person's best guess as to *why* something happened. This is contrasted with prediction, which is a person's best guess as to what will happen. In inference, we have to guess what caused something to happen.

Our guess must be based on the evidence we have. Criminal trials often are based on inferential reasoning; the evidence is presented, and the cause of the evidence is inferred from assembling all the evidence.

Inferential reasoning is basic to all scientific understanding. Many times we can observe directly what happens in a scientific activity. For example, we can observe that when we put a drop of vinegar on a piece of limestone, the vinegar fizzes. We can draw the conclusion that vinegar fizzes on limestone directly from the evidence. However, many times we cannot observe what happens directly.

IN THE SCHOOLS 3.17
Burning A Candle In A Goldfish Bowl

A fourth grade teacher fastened a candle to the bottom of a goldfish bowl with wax, and lit it. She then filled the bowl with water, inverted a jar over the candle, and lowered the jar so its rim was below the level of the water. Shortly the flame went out. Children observed the flame being extinguished, but they could not observe *why* this happened. They also observed that water rose up into the jar. They put these two observations together—that the candle went out and the water rose in the jar—and inferred that the reason the candle went out was because it has used up the oxygen in the air. This was an inference.

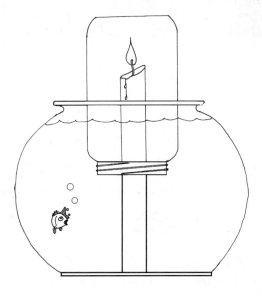

As the candle burns, water rises in the jar.

FIGURE 3.14 Candle in a goldfish bowl

Children's literature is a great source of opportunities for children to reason inferentially.

IN THE SCHOOLS 3.18
Inferring Through Children's Literature

The Mitten: A Ukrainian Folktale adapted by Jan Brett (G. P. Putnam and Sons,1989) is a logical choice to accompany the footprints activity in Constructing Your Ideas 3.12 (p. 105); as each animal comes to crawl inside the lost mitten, it walks across the snow, leaving its footprints. A good activity is for children to infer whether the tracks pictured are those of the animal that has just made its way to the mitten.

Animal Tracks and Traces by Kathleen Kudlinski (Franklin Watts, 1991) also is an excellent accompaniment to the footprints activity. The book encourages children to become good detectives by discovering where to look for animal clues including tracks, nests, skin, feather or fur coverings, and food remnants.

Several activities are shown in Constructing Science in the Classroom 3.28–3.33 that can be used to help children develop the process skill of inference. Note that all require observational skills, and several require other process skills as well.

CONSTRUCTING SCIENCE IN THE CLASSROOM 3.28
The Origin Of Soil

GRADE

6
5
4
3
2
1
K

AN INFERRING ACTIVITY

Objective
The student will infer the origin of a sample of soil.

As you did in the activity on observation (Constructing Science in the Classroom 3.4, p. 66), bring a bag of soil from your home or from the school yard, and put a spoonful of the soil on a paper plate for each child or group of children. Provide magnifying glasses, and tell children they are going to be detectives. Ask the children to look at the soil carefully to try to identify the different kinds of things they can find in the soil. Ask the children to describe what they see in the soil, and ask them to infer where these things came from, citing their reasons for their inferences. Finally, ask them to infer where the soil sample came from, based on what they found in it.

Literature connection:
Who Is the Beast? by Keith Baker (Harcourt Brace, 1990). Several animals identify various parts of a beast. Children infer what the beast is from the progressive clues.

CONSTRUCTING SCIENCE IN THE CLASSROOM 3.29
Cause Of Banding In Sedimentary Rocks

GRADE

AN INFERRING ACTIVITY

Objective
The student will infer the cause of banding in sedimentary rocks.

Provide each group with several specimens of banded sedimentary rocks, and ask them to examine them carefully and describe them. Provide each group with a transparent jar (mayonnaise jar is excellent), enough water to fill the jar about half full, and a plastic bag containing a mixture of fine rocks, sand, and dried mud. Ask them to empty the contents of the plastic bag into the jar, stir or shake it, and let it settle. From the results of this activity, ask them to infer how the bands were formed in the sandstone, share this with the class, and give the reasons for their inferences.

Literature connection:
A River Ran Wild by Lynn Cherry (Harcourt Brace, 1992). This is a true story of the Nashua River Valley in Massachusetts and the impact the industrial revolution had on the river. The book explains how the riverbed changed when the settlers built dams and sawmills.

CONSTRUCTING SCIENCE IN THE CLASSROOM 3.30
The Causes Of Soil Erosion

GRADE

AN INFERRING ACTIVITY

Objective
The student will infer the causes of soil erosion in the environment around the school.

Take the class of children outside, and help them find examples of soil erosion around the school. Ask them for their observations about the soil, the general area, the slope of the ground, etc. Ask them to form inferences as to what caused the soil to erode in the way they observed, and to provide the reasons for their inferences.

In urban settings, it may be more appropriate for children to look for examples of plants growing in unusual places, such as coming up through concrete, and infer reasons for what they observe.

Literature connections:
Follow the Water from Brook to Ocean by Arthur Dorros (Harper Collins, 1991). This story tells of the journey of water and the erosion water causes in the rivers, waterfalls, canyons, dams, and oceans it flows through.

Come a Tide by George Lyon (Orchard, 1990). When the snow melted and the water overflowed by the banks of the creeks and river, the little rural town flooded. Gardens were washed away and homes were full of water, but the townspeople began the slow process of rebuilding their homes.

CONSTRUCTING SCIENCE IN THE CLASSROOM 3.31
What Is That Unknown Substance?

GRADE

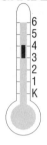

6
5
4
3
2
1
K

AN INFERRING ACTIVITY

Objective
The student will infer the identity of an unknown substance.

Provide each group with a small cup of salt and a small cup of sugar; ask them to describe the similarities and differences between the salt and the sugar. Then give each group a cup of water, some plastic spoons, several small cups, magnifying glasses, and a jar of either salt or sugar, unknown to the children, and ask them to use these tools to infer whether their unknown substance is salt or sugar. Tasting is specifically prohibited except as a last resort. Children then report to the class what their inference was, and why they made their inference.

Literature connection:
Bartholomew and the Oobleck by Dr. Seuss (Random House, 1949). A king is bored with the regularity of rain and snow falling from the sky, so he commands his magicians to change the precipitation. "Oobleck" falls from the sky and causes some amusing situations.

CONSTRUCTING SCIENCE IN THE CLASSROOM 3.32
How Old Is That Tree?

GRADE

6
5
4
3
2
1
K

AN INFERRING ACTIVITY

Objective
The student will infer the age of trees from tree rings.

After a discussion about the nature of tree rings and the seasonal growth of trees which results in tree rings, give children cross-sectional pieces of several branches of the same tree. From the count of the number of rings, ask them to infer which of the branches is oldest, which is youngest, and where on the tree they came from. Depending on the nature of the rings, they may also be able to infer the length and severity of the summer and winter seasons during which the tree grew.

Literature connection:
Outside and Inside Trees by Sandra Markle (Bradbury, 1993) is a beautifully illustrated book that encourages children to discover looking at trees from a new and different perspective.

CONSTRUCTING SCIENCE IN THE CLASSROOM 3.33
Paper Chromatography

GRADE

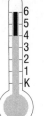

6
5
4
3
2
1
K

AN INFERRING ACTIVITY

Objective
The student will infer the colors that make up black ink.

First, give each group of children a black felt-tip pen. Ask them to make a mark on a sheet of white paper with it and describe what they see. Ask them to infer whether the black ink is one color or is a mixture of several colors.

Next, ask children to test their inferences. Provide each group with a cup about half filled with water and a few thin strips of white paper towel. Children draw a line with the black pen across the strip of paper towel about three inches above the bottom. They hold the strip so that the bottom edge is just below the surface of the water, being careful *not* to let the ink line sink into the water. The water travels up the paper towel, and, as it passes the black line, separates it into its component colors.

Children can try this with different black inks and with inks of different colors.

Literature connection:
The Mystery of the Stranger in the Barn by True Kelley (Dodd, Mead and Co., 1986). Items seem to be disappearing from a barn, but a hat was left behind. Is a mysterious stranger hiding in the barn? This is a good story to demonstrate the difference between evidence and inference.

CONSTRUCTING YOUR IDEAS 3.13
An Activity For Inferring

Now it's your turn. Write a short activity that can be used to help children develop the skill of inferring. Specify grade level, and be sure the activity is appropriate to the children in the age/grade group you specify. Cite a process-oriented objective for your lesson; this objective will read something like this: "The student will infer the reason for _____ ." Then get together in small groups, and do the activities each member of the group has prepared.

Interrelationships Among the Basic Processes

Most of the activities you have done in this chapter have utilized more than one process. For example, you combined the processes of observation and communication to accomplish the rock observing activity. Moon watching required measurement and communication together with observation. In classifying, you also utilized communication. Communication of many different types accompanied inferring in the "footprints" activity.

The processes of observing, classifying, communicating, measuring, predicting, and inferring are the focus of the early elementary science program. They are interdependent and are almost never taught in isolation. The scientific content appropriate to elementary science is used as the vehicles through which mastery of these processes can be attained. After children have acquired facility in the basic processes, they are able to explore scientific concepts the way scientists do.

The Integrated Processes

The processes of scientific inquiry can be classified into *basic* and *integrated* process skills. The six we have discussed thus far are the basic skills and are prerequisite to the integrated skills. Children require development in the basic skills before they are ready to work with the integrated skills. The integrated process skills include the following:

Identifying and controlling variables
Formulating and testing hypotheses
Defining operationally
Experimenting
Interpreting data
Constructing models

There is little doubt that these process skills require deeper levels of thought than the basic skills of observing, classifying, communicating, measuring, predicting, and inferring. However, many children are capable of investigating the integrated skills in early grades. Of course, we must be very careful not to ask children to do something they are not cognitively capable of doing. We cited several examples above: in general, children in lower grades cannot devise complex classification systems, nor can they apply complex principles of conservation. We leave these concepts for later years when the children are ready for them. But, this does not mean that *no* child is ready for these principles at early grades—it means we must be on the lookout for those who are ready and who demonstrate appropriate comprehension before we introduce them. It is the same way with the integrated process skills. Many children in early elementary grades are not capable of the thinking associated with true comprehension of variable identification, variable isolation, hypothesis formulation and testing, operational definition, experiment planning and execution, data interpretation, and model development. However, many elementary children *are* ready to work with these processes. Thus, it is appropriate to encourage children to explore these processes, assess their results, share their conclusions with others, and, in general, validate their perceptions of their application of these skills. As was indicated earlier, readiness can be established through the Piagetian conservation tasks. (See Note 3.)

The Pendulum

CONSTRUCTING YOUR IDEAS 3.14
The Pendulum

Here is an inquiry activity for you to do. It involves investigating factors that might cause a pendulum to swing faster or slower. See Figure 3.15 for a diagram of how to set up the apparatus. The equipment is simple. You will need the following:

     A pencil
     A piece of string about 2–2 1/2 feet long
     8 or 10 metal washers of the same size

Tie one end of the string around the eraser end of the pencil. Tie a washer onto the other end of the string. Hold the pencil on the edge of a desk so the pendulum swings freely, making sure the string does not rub against the desk. If the string is too long, wind a little around the pencil until you get a length that will swing without touching the floor.

Now, let the pendulum swing. Notice that it has a rhythm of its own: back — forth — back — forth. Tap your desk in time with the rhythm to establish it in your mind. Back — forth — back — forth — back — forth. Notice that it takes as long to move back as it does to move forth. Do not do anything with the pendulum yet; just watch it swing.

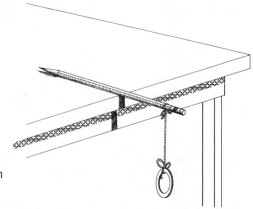

A simple pendulum can enable children to explore all the processes.

FIGURE 3.15 The pendulum

How would you define a "swing?" Some will define it as the total back-and-forth movement (a full cycle); others will define it as either back or forth (a half cycle), since they both take about the same time.

> While you are watching the pendulum swing, discuss this question: What do you suppose will make this pendulum move faster or slower? Brainstorm responses to the question as a class, writing all responses on the board.

Here are some typical responses:

    How hard we push it to get it started
    The weight of the bob
    The color of the string
    The length of the string
    How far we pull it back to get it started
    How much wind there is
    How thick the air is

You are sure to come up with more.

All these ideas as to what might make the pendulum swing faster or slower are called *variables*. In brainstorming the factors that might influence the speed of a pendulum's swing, you have identified variables. It is not necessary to identify *all* variables that could possibly impact on the swing of the pendulum; there are bound to be some you don't think of.

> Next, for each of the factors you have identified as a class, identify the effect you think it would have on the speed of the pendulum. For instance, for the variable "how far back we pull it," you might guess that the further back we pull it, the faster it will swing. For each factor, write what you think will happen. If you don't know what will happen, or if there is disagreement, write that down as well.

Of course, if we *knew* what would happen, there would not be much point in investigating the phenomenon. Your statement of what you think will happen to the pendulum's speed when you change a given variable is called a hypothesis; it takes the form of a statement that says, essentially, "If I do *this* to the pendulum, it will *speed up* or *slow down*." Whether it is written this way or not, it will be thought of this way.

We have one more factor to consider before we can investigate. Our inquiry centers around the question "What will make the pendulum move faster or slower?" That means we are investigating the speed of the swinging pendulum, and we will have to measure its speed. That is difficult to do, since speed is measured in terms of distance per unit of time, such as miles per hour or feet per second. To measure speed, we would have to find the distance the pendulum travels and the time it takes to travel that distance. But, we already have discovered that it has a definite back-and-forth rhythm. Could we measure the *time* without the distance? That would give us a measure that is proportional to speed. The time a pendulum takes to complete one full swing—back *and* forth— is called its *period*. How could we measure the period? Well, we could take a stop watch, and start it as soon as we let the pendulum go, and then stop it as soon as it returns. But there are likely to be inaccuracies with this method. On the other hand, we could count the number of swings in a certain period of time, say one minute. If you try letting it swing for one minute, you will find that a minute is a long time, and the pendulum tends to wander from its original path. How about counting the number of swings in 15 seconds? That way we can finish our swing counting before the pendulum starts to wander.

For purposes of this investigation, let us use the number of swings in 15 seconds as the indication of the speed.[5]

Now you are ready to plan your experiment. Each group can select one of the variables to test, or each group can test them all. Whichever way you choose, it is critical that while you are experimenting with one variable, you keep all the others constant. If, for example, you are investigating the effect of the height of the pull, you must keep the length of the string, the weight of the bob, and all other factors the same throughout your investigation.

Discuss this question: What would happen if you did not keep the variables constant?

How many different values of the variable you are investigating will you need to test? Certainly you will need to experiment with at least three or four different values. In our example, you will want to set the pendulum swinging from at least three or four different heights. How many times will you need to try the same value of the variable? Most scientists do at least three trials for each value of each variable. That is, you would count the number of swings for each different height of drop three different times. There are many factors that can influence your count on any trial—you may miscount; you may count in different ways (starting with "one" when you first let it go, or starting with "one" after a full swing has been completed); you may round up to the next whole number of swings one time and round down a different time; you may ignore a quarter of a swing one time and count a quarter of a swing another time, and so on. So, it is desirable to do each value three times, and then average the three results.

Now, go ahead and do the investigation. Collect the data and write it down in "raw" form. Do any averaging needed after you have the raw data. Your data can be recorded in a data table similar to the one below.

PENDULUM DATA TABLE

VARIABLE: _____

VALUE OF VARIABLE	NUMBER OF SWINGS IN 15 SECONDS	
1. Value: _____	Trial 1	_____
	Trial 2	_____
	Trial 3	_____
	Average	_____
2. Value: _____	Trial 1	_____
	Trial 2	_____
	Trial 3	_____
	Average	_____
3. Value: _____	Trial 1	_____
	Trial 2	_____
	Trial 3	_____
	Average	_____

When all groups are finished, record your average data on the board next to the variable you investigated. You might want to set up a summary data table something like the one below.

CONSOLIDATED DATA FOR PENDULUM SWING INVESTIGATION

Variable: _____
    Value 1 _____   Average Swings _____
    Value 2 _____   Average Swings _____
    Value 3 _____   Average Swings _____
Variable: _____
    Value 1 _____   Average Swings _____
    Value 2 _____   Average Swings _____
    Value 3 _____   Average Swings _____
Variable: _____
    Value 1 _____   Average Swings _____
    Value 2 _____   Average Swings _____
    Value 3 _____   Average Swings _____

Look at the class data. What can you conclude? What effect did changing the height of the drop have on the number of swings in 15 seconds? What effect did the weight of the bob have? How about the length of the string?

Was there any set of data that seemed to be inconclusive? Here is an example:

DATA FOR HEIGHT OF PENDULUM DROP

Variable: __Height of Drop__

Value 1: __3 Centimeters__   Average Swings: _____15_____

Value 2: __4 Centimeters__   Average Swings: _____14_____

Value 3: __5 Centimeters__   Average Swings: _____15_____

In this case, it could be suggested that the number of swings seems to depend on the height of the drop, but there was one item of data that seemed to be anomalous. If Value #3 had been 13, we would have been able to conclude that the higher the drop, the slower it swings. Maybe we need to do a few more trials with a few more values. The data indicates that the effect that seemed to be observed might very well be a function only of the accuracy with which we did the experiment; the data does not tell us conclusively that there was any effect.

You may have decided that each group would explore a different variable. In this case, data from different groups cannot be combined, since each group kept the variables they were not investigating constant, but at different values from those of other groups. For example, one group may have had a constant string length of 8 inches, while another group may have kept their string length constant at 12 inches. The data from all groups could be combined only if each group investigated all the variables, and used the same values for each constant variable. In an actual class setting, it would be preferable for all groups to investigate all the variables. This gives much more data for each variable for the data can be combined; the more data we have, the easier it is to interpret the results.

This investigation into the pendulum leads us to our exploration of the integrated science process skills; you utilized all of them (except formulating models) in the pendulum inquiry. You identified the variables that would affect the swing of the pendulum. You controlled (kept constant) all the variables except the one you were exploring. You formulated hypotheses for each variable ("If I increase the height of the drop, the pendulum will swing faster"). You tested the hypotheses by changing the value of the variable and collecting data from at least three separate trials. You defined operationally when you decided to count number of swings instead of timing the pendulum. You planned the experiment when you decided how you were going to set up the apparatus to investigate the problem, how you were going to investigate all the variables, and how you were going to collect the data. You interpreted data when you looked at the results to see if your variable had any effect.

Identifying and Controlling Variables

IN THE SCHOOLS 3.19
What Do Plants Need In Order To Grow?

In a kindergarten class, the teacher asked the children what plants need in order to grow. After some discussion, it was decided that plants need food, light, and water to grow. "How would we find out?" asked the teacher? A child replied, "We would get two plants. We would put one on the window sill where it could get plenty of light. We would water it every day. We would give it fertilizer every week." The child continued, "We would put the other plant in the closet where it wouldn't get any light. We would not water it. We would not give it any fertilizer." The teacher asked, "What would happen?" The child replied, "The plant in the closet will die." The teacher asked, "Why will it die?" One child replied, "Because it doesn't have any light." Another replied, "Because it doesn't have water." A third replied, "Because it didn't get any fertilizer." The class decided try each of the conditions separately so they could see the effect of each one on the growth of plants.

In our everyday lives, we tend to formulate generalizations without controlling the variables. Consider the person who is coming down with flu-like symptoms. Someone tells her that she ought to take aspirin. Someone else suggests chicken soup. A third friend suggests getting plenty of rest. So the afflicted person goes home, takes two aspirin, eats a bowl of chicken soup for dinner, and goes to bed early. The next day, she feels much better.

CONSTRUCTING YOUR IDEAS 3.15
What Cured The Cold?

Ponder this question: Of the things she did, which cured her?

In many scientific inquiries, we investigate to find out what causes something to happen—to find the effect of one variable on another. In order to pin-point the cause, we must keep all the variables constant except the one we are experimenting with.

Suppose we want to know what causes a toy truck to roll down an inclined board faster or slower. We brainstorm the various conditions that could make a difference (height of the board, surface of the board, and length of the board) to isolate the variables that can have an effect on the speed of the toy truck. When we do the investigation, we investigate the effect of changing only one of the variables; we must keep the others constant. In this way, we can tell which single variable has an effect.

Suppose we have reason to believe more than one variable has an effect. For example, we may suspect that both the surface of the board and the height of the board affect the speed of the toy truck. We investigate the variables one at a time, and we look at the data. If both variables have effects, we may want to carefully devise an experiment that would include manipulating the two variables simultaneously to investigate the double effect.

The idea behind identifying and controlling variables is that we must be sure that what we *think* caused an effect, in fact *did* cause it. We must be able to confirm the cause-and-effect relationship between the two phenomena.

Children do not intuitively know they must identify and control variables in an investigation. It requires the ability to perceive that there is more than one attribute to given objects, and that the attributes are seen not only in their physical characteristics (as we described in the section on classification) but also in their behavior. For example, in the toy truck investigation, children must be able to perceive that the same toy truck may go faster or slower. It also requires the perception of interaction between two occurrences, for example, the understanding that the roughness of the board's surface interacts with the toy truck in such a way as to affect the speed of the truck. When children acquire the ability to perceive multiple physical attributes, multiple behavior attributes, and interactions between and among events, then they can begin to reason that there may be several distinct variables that can influence a particular happening.

Several activities that focus on identifying and controlling variables are provided in Constructing Science in the Classroom 3.34–3.37.

CONSTRUCTING SCIENCE IN THE CLASSROOM 3.34
How Long Can You Keep An Ice Cube Frozen?

GRADE

AN ACTIVITY FOR IDENTIFYING
AND CONTROLLING VARIABLES

Objective

The student will identify and control variables involved in keeping an ice cube frozen.

Hold a contest in which children wrap ice cubes in such a way as to keep them from melting; the one whose ice cube lasts the longest is the winner. What influences the ice cube melting? Heat, of course. How about pressure? What can we do to keep it from melting? What variables need to be controlled so all children have the same advantage? How about opening their apparatus to check whether the ice cube is still frozen? As children develop the rules for the competition, they are actually listing the variables.

Literature connections:

The Frozen Man by David Getz (Holt, 1994)

Iceman by Don Lessem (Crown, 1994). Both these books are about the discovery of a 5,000-year-old body found in glaciers in the Alps.

Einstein Anderson Shocks His Friends by Seymour Simon (Viking, 1980). One chapter deals with Einstein wrapping a snow sculpture in a blanket so it will not melt before the contest.

CONSTRUCTING SCIENCE IN THE CLASSROOM 3.35
How Does Temperature Affect The Movement Of Blue Food Coloring In Water?

GRADE

AN ACTIVITY FOR IDENTIFYING
AND CONTROLLING VARIABLES

Objective

The student will identify and control the variables in an activity relating heat and rate of distribution of food coloring in water.

The idea is for children to devise their own experiments to investigate the effect of water temperature on the movement of blue food coloring in the water. Essentially, they put blue food coloring in glasses of water at different temperatures, and record the time it takes for the water to become completely colored. Before this can be done, children will need to list the variables that can affect the results of the investigation; some variables are density of blue food coloring, how still we hold the glass, temperature of the water, when the food coloring is added, etc.

Literature connection:

Einstein Anderson Tells a Comet's Tale by Seymour Simon (Viking Press, 1981). Using the scientific process of identifying and controlling variables, Einstein is able to make changes to his soap box derby vehicle which allows his team to win the race.

CONSTRUCTING SCIENCE IN THE CLASSROOM 3.36
How Fast Does A Solid Conduct Heat?

GRADE

6
5
4
3
2
1
K

AN ACTIVITY FOR IDENTIFYING
AND CONTROLLING VARIABLES

The student will identify and control variables involved in exploring heat conduction through solids.

The apparatus is simple: a wire or piece of metal suspended between two vertical posts, with small drops of wax fastened to it at various points. One end of the metal wire is held in a candle flame, and children record the time it takes for each drop of wax to fall. Before they get started, children are asked to identify the variables that can influence this investigation; some variables are thickness of wire, length of wire, composition of wire, how hot the flame is, size of wax drop, and other variables they can think of.

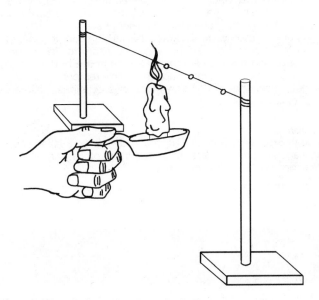

FIGURE 3.16   Apparatus for heat conduction inquiry

CONSTRUCTING SCIENCE IN THE CLASSROOM 3.37
Let's Make A Cloud

GRADE

AN ACTIVITY FOR IDENTIFYING AND CONTROLLING VARIABLES

Objective
The student will identify the variables that influence cloud formation.

Meteorologists tell us that, for clouds to form, we need moisture, a distinct temperature gradient (difference in temperatures between two regions), and small particles for tiny droplets of water to form on. Children can discover these for themselves with a simple activity. Provide each group of children with a transparent plastic cup, some hot water, a plastic bag of ice cubes, some matches, and a small sheet of black paper. Fill the jar to about 1 inch deep with hot water. Light the match and drop it into the jar. It will go out, of course, when it hits the water. IMMEDIATELY cover the top of the cup with the plastic bag of ice. Observe what happens inside the cup. (A cloud will form.) Holding the black paper behind the cup makes it easier to see.

Consider these questions: How do we know the visible vapor in the cup is a cloud, and not just smoke from the match? Is match smoke necessary for the cloud to form? What would happen if we reversed the temperatures (had ice in the bottom of the jar and put a baggy with hot water on the top?) What happens if the temperatures of the top and the bottom of the jar get closer together? From these investigations, children will isolate the variables needed for clouds to form.

Literature connection:
Splish, Splash by Joan Bransfield Graham (Ticknor and Fields, 1994) is a collection of poetry about water in its various states. "Water is a magic potion, it can fill a glass, an ocean, raging river, tiny tear, drops of dew that disappear."

CONSTRUCTING YOUR IDEAS 3.16
An Activity For Identifying and Controlling Variables

Now it's your turn. Write a short activity that can be used to help children develop the skill of identifying and controlling variables. Specify grade level, and be sure the activity is appropriate to the children in the age/grade group you specify. Cite a process-oriented objective for your lesson; this objective will read something like this: "The student will list the variables in _____ and will identify those to be controlled and the one to be investigated in _____ ." Then get together in small groups, and do the activities each member of the group has prepared.

Formulating and Testing Hypotheses

In the pendulum activity, you formulated hypotheses as to what would happen to the period of the pendulum if you varied each of several factors. This was a good example of the science process skill of formulating hypotheses.

CONSTRUCTING YOUR IDEAS 3.17
An Activity For Formulating and Testing Hypotheses

Try this. Set up a wooden board the size of a bookshelf on a stack of books so that it becomes an inclined plane. Hold a toy truck at the top of the plank, and let it roll down. You notice that it takes a certain amount of time to reach the bottom of the plank. Do you suppose it would take the truck a longer, or a shorter period of time to roll down if the plank were lowered? How about if it were raised? Write your tentative answer.

FIGURE 3.17   How long does it take the cart to roll down the ramp?

You will notice that you are considering two separate variables in this activity: (1) the length of time it takes the truck to roll down the plank, and (2) the height of the raised end of the plank. In suggesting a tentative answer to the question, "Will it take the toy truck a longer or a shorter period of time to roll down the plank if it were lowered?" you were formulating a hypothesis. You were saying something like this: "If I raise the plank, the truck will take less time to roll down, and if I lower the plank, it will take a longer time." This is a statement of hypothesis.

A hypothesis is a statement of your best guess as to the *relationship between two variables*. In the case of the toy truck on the plank, it is your best guess as to the relationship between the time it takes the truck to roll down the plank, and the height of the raised end of the plank. Hypothesis formulation is different from prediction. In prediction, we simply ask what would happen if we did something. "I wonder what would happen if I put a drop of vinegar on limestone?" There was only one variable: the vinegar. In hypothesis formation, we ask what would happen to one variable if we change an interacting variable. ("I wonder what would happen to the rate of plant growth if we played music to it.")

Let us return to the plank and the toy truck. How can you obtain a measure of the time it takes? Maybe you can use a stopwatch; start it the instant you let the truck go, and stop it the instant the front wheels touch the floor. If you do this the same way every time, you will probably have a good indication of the time it takes to roll down the plank. You can raise or lower the raised end of the plank, simply by varying the number of books that support it, and you can measure the resulting height of the plank.

> Go ahead and do this activity. Write down your hypothesis. Decide what kind of information you need in order to investigate it, and then test your hypothesis. Record your results, and examine the data after you are finished. What can you conclude?

You probably will need only two items of information for this investigation, since everything else will stay the same. You will need to know the height of the raised end of the plank, and you will need to know how long it takes the truck to roll down. The height of the plank can be measured with a ruler; the time can be measured with a stopwatch. Let us set up a data table to help us record the data. It might look something like this:

DATA TABLE

HEIGHT	TIME	
_____	Trial 1	_____
	Trial 2	_____
	Trial 3	_____
	AVERAGE	_____
_____	Trial 1	_____
	Trial 2	_____
	Trial 3	_____
	AVERAGE	_____
_____	Trial 1	_____
	Trial 2	_____
	Trial 3	_____
	AVERAGE	_____

You will want to place the board at several different heights, and you will want to make at least three trials for each height and average the results.

Setting up the apparatus and getting the data table ready is called hypothesis testing. When we test hypotheses, we assure ourselves we have identified all the variables, have taken steps to control all except the one we are experimenting with, have planned what we are going to do to test the truth of our hypothesis, and have identified the information we need to obtain to allow us to make conclusions about our hypothesis. Often this includes recording data; in many cases we can anticipate what kinds of data we will be recording before we ever get started, but many times we simply have to tinker with the set-up for a while before we can decide how to proceed.

Let us look at another activity which involves formulating and testing hypotheses. We know that the moon has craters on its surface. How do they form? Astronomers tell us that meteoroids rushing through space crash into the moon when they come close enough to be attracted by the moon's gravity, and that the resulting impact forms a crater. Can we investigate this?

CONSTRUCTING YOUR IDEAS 3.18
Moon Craters

Obtain an aluminum pie plate, and fill it with flour. Obtain rocks or marbles of different sizes and weights. One at a time, hold a rock or a marble above the flour in the plate, and drop it. Try dropping the objects from different heights. What do you notice? If you sprinkle a little ground cinnamon on the surface of the flour, you might be able to see what happens better. (See Figure 3.18.) Discuss the effects of your initial investigation with your classmates.

What variables might affect the size of the craters on the moon? Develop a hypothesis, and plan how to test the hypothesis. Then, execute your plan, and report back to the class.

Dropping a ball into a pan of flour

Measuring the depth of the crater

Measuring the diameter of the crater

FIGURE 3.18   Simulating the formation of moon craters

Additional activities designed to aid children in developing the process skill of formulating and testing hypotheses are suggested in Constructing Science in the Classroom 3.38–3.40.

CONSTRUCTING SCIENCE IN THE CLASSROOM 3.38
Which Bubbles Last the Longest?

GRADE

AN ACTIVITY FOR FORMULATING AND TESTING HYPOTHESES

Objective
The student will formulate and test a hypothesis concerning how to keep bubbles the longest.

The teacher may start the activity by blowing some bubbles and asking such questions as, "What is inside a bubble?" "How do you know?" What are bubbles made of?" Provide each group with pipe cleaners or pieces of wire, plastic plates, straws, and "bubble juice" made of 1 cup water, 1 tablespoon sugar, 1 tablespoon white corn syrup, and 2 capfuls of dish-washing detergent. Children are encouraged to "play around" with making bubbles for a few minutes, blowing bubbles on the plates using the straws, and blowing bubbles using the pipe cleaners or wire. Once they get the "hang" of how to blow bubbles, they are asked to formulate a hypothesis as to what method will produce the longest-lasting bubble, and devise a way to test their hypothesis.

Literature connections:
Mr. Archimedes' Bath by Pamela Allen (Harper Collins, 1980). Mr. Archimedes is upset when his bathtub overflows and the water level changes so he decides to use the scientific processes to find answers to his questions.

A Children's Museum Activity Book: Bubbles by Bernie Zubrowski (Little, 1979). This is one in a series of books Zubrowski has written as a staff member at the Children's Museum in Boston to promote the natural curiosity children have of experimenting with objects.

CONSTRUCTING SCIENCE IN THE CLASSROOM 3.39
The Pitch of Sound

GRADE

AN ACTIVITY FOR FORMULATING AND TESTING HYPOTHESES

Objective
The student will formulate and test a hypothesis that describes the relationship between the length of an air column and the pitch of the sound it produces when one blows across its top.

First model the activity with bells to be sure children can recognize different pitches. Then give each group eight identical soda bottles filled with varying amounts of water. Ask children to hypothesize the relationship between the length of the air column and the pitch of the sound resulting from blowing across the bottle tops. To test their hypotheses, children blow across the mouth of each bottle, and observe the pitch of the sound.

Literature connections:
The Magic School Bus in the Haunted Museum: A Book About Sound (Scholastic, 1995). From an episode of the animated TV series, this book describes how children discover the way sound is produced and how it travels.

The Sound of Bells by Eric Sloane (Doubleday, 1966). This is a nostalgic look at the history of bells ringing in our country, from the tinkle of cow bells to the thunderous tones of the town hall bell.

CONSTRUCTING SCIENCE IN THE CLASSROOM 3.40
Strength of Electromagnets

GRADE

6
5
4
3
2
1
K

AN ACTIVITY FOR FORMULATING AND TESTING HYPOTHESES

Objective
The student will formulate and test a hypothesis describing the relationship between number of coils of wire wound around a nail and strength of the resulting electromagnetic field.

Have children wind five or six coils of wire around a nail and connect the free ends of the wire to a nine-volt battery to form an electromagnet (see illustration in Figure 3.19). They use the electromagnet to pick up some paper clips. "How many can you pick up?" Then have children wind more wire around the nail, and see how many paper clips they can pick up. Ask children to formulate a hypothesis showing the relationship between the number of coils of wire and the strength of the electromagnet. Then ask them to test their hypotheses. Children observe that the number of paper clips the electromagnet will pick up depends on the number of times they wind the wire around the nail. From these observations, they may infer that the strength of the electromagnet depends on the number of times the wire is coiled around the nail. From this inference, they can predict that if they increase the number of coils around the wire, they will be able to pick up more paper clips. Children could make a data table that looks something like this in which to record their data:

INITIAL OBSERVATIONS

NUMBER OF COILS	NUMBER OF PAPER CLIPS

PREDICTIONS

NUMBER OF COILS	PREDICTED NUMBER OF PAPER CLIPS	ACTUAL NUMBER OF PAPER CLIPS

Literature connection:
The Secret Life of Dilly McBean by Dorothy Haas (Bradbury Press, 1986). With the help of a professor, Dilly develops secret magnetic powers.

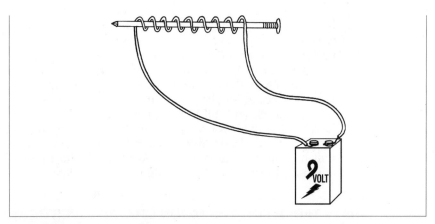

FIGURE 3.19 An electromagnet

CONSTRUCTING YOUR IDEAS 3.19
An Activity for Formulating and Testing Hypotheses

Now it's your turn: Write a short activity that can be used to help children develop the skill of formulating and testing hypotheses. Specify grade level, and be sure the activity is appropriate to the children in the age/grade group you specify. Cite a process-oriented objective for your lesson; this objective will read something like this: "The student will formulate and test a hypothesis concerning the relationship between _____ and _____ ." (Remember that a hypothesis is a student's best guess as to the relationship between two variables.) Then get together in small groups, and do the activities each member of the group has prepared.

Interpreting Data

In the investigation with the rocks dropped on a pan of flour, you collected some data. You probably recorded such items of data as (1) weight of rock, (2) size of rock, (3) height of drop, (4) depth of crater, (5) diameter of crater. You may also have collected some qualitative data, such as noticing that the flour that was displaced from the crater spewed out like rays.

Had you planned to gather all this data? Had you previously set up data tables to record the results?

The first step in interpreting data is to decide what data you want to gather. This comes from the hypothesis you devise. You may do the investigation mentally, visualizing what will happen, and deciding what kinds of information you will need to have in order to tell *why* it happened. Or you may want to "fool around" to see what happens.

For example, in the moon craters investigation, you could state, as a hypothesis, that the higher you hold the rock, the deeper the crater will be. You will need to measure how high the rock is held and how deep the resulting crater is. You could also hypothesize that the higher the rock is held, the wider the crater is. Now you also need to measure the diameter of the crater. You could also hypothesize that the heavier the rock, the deeper and wider the crater is. In this case, you also need to weigh the rocks, and you would investigate the effects of two separate variables: (1) height of drop, and (2) weight of rock. How will you organize your investigation so you can interpret the results?

Let us take the hypothesis that the heavier the rock, the deeper and wider the crater will be. You will need to duplicate the procedure you do with one rock with all the others of different weights. Then, when you have all the data, you will be able to look at the results of each rock to see if height of drop influences depth and diameter of the crater, and you will be able to compare the data from all the rocks to see if size has anything to do with it. You might set up a data table like this:

DATA TABLE FOR THE MOON CRATER INVESTIGATION

	WEIGHT	HEIGHT OF DROP		DEPTH	DIAMETER
#1	_____	_____	Trial 1	_____	_____
			Trial 2	_____	_____
			Trial 3	_____	_____
			AVERAGE	_____	_____
		_____	Trial 1	_____	_____
			Trial 2	_____	_____
			Trial 3	_____	_____
			AVERAGE	_____	_____
		_____	Trial 1	_____	_____
			Trial 2	_____	_____
			Trial 3	_____	_____
			AVERAGE	_____	_____
#2	_____	_____	Trial 1	_____	_____
			Trial 2	_____	_____
			Trial 3	_____	_____
			AVERAGE	_____	_____
		_____	Trial 1	_____	_____
			Trial 2	_____	_____
			Trial 3	_____	_____
			AVERAGE	_____	_____
		_____	Trial 1	_____	_____
			Trial 2	_____	_____
			Trial 3	_____	_____
			AVERAGE	_____	_____
#3	_____	_____	Trial 1	_____	_____
			Trial 2	_____	_____
			Trial 3	_____	_____
			AVERAGE	_____	_____
		_____	Trial 1	_____	_____
			Trial 2	_____	_____
			Trial 3	_____	_____
			AVERAGE	_____	_____
		_____	Trial 1	_____	_____
			Trial 2	_____	_____
			Trial 3	_____	_____
			AVERAGE	_____	_____

Once the data is in a form you can read, you can look at the numbers to see what they tell you. Focusing on only one rock, you would see if the depth of the crater increased, decreased, or remained the same when the height of the drop was increased; you would do the same thing with the diameter of the crater. You would analyze the data from each different rock in the same manner. This enables you to make conclusions about the relationship between height of drop and the depth and diameter of crater. Then you would focus on the different kinds of rocks, and would find the data for the same height of drop for each rock. Comparing the crater depths and diameters made by different rocks dropped from the same height enables you to make conclusions about the effect of the weight of the rock on the crater. Having done this, you can put the two conclusions together to make one generalization, for example: "Craters are deeper and wider when the rock is heavier and is dropped from greater heights."

One of the best ways to organize data for interpretation is to put the data in visual form such as a graph, a chart, or a histogram. Sample data tables from the moon crater investigation together with computer-generated graphs of the data are shown in Figures 3.20 and 3.21. Calculators and computers are very useful aids to constructing graphs. The use of technology is discussed in Chapter Ten.

Young children should be encouraged to create graphs of plant size, numbers of children with certain hair color or eye color, and so forth. Children can line up in rows according to color of sweater (or some other characteristic) to form a "living graph."

Interpreting data is simple once decisions are made to collect the proper data. Suppose you don't know what kind of data to collect? In that case, you simply tinker with the activity to get an idea of what is happening, and then you decide what you need to find out in order to answer the question.

Thus far we have been talking about quantitative data—the kind of data that has numbers or measurements associated with it. Qualitative data can also be collected. The presence or absence of rays from the craters in the pan of flour is a good example of qualitative data. You might decide that you want to see if the size of the rocks or height of drop had any effect on the formation of rays. If the information you gather is either "Yes, rays are formed," or "No, rays are not formed," you are collecting qualitative data.

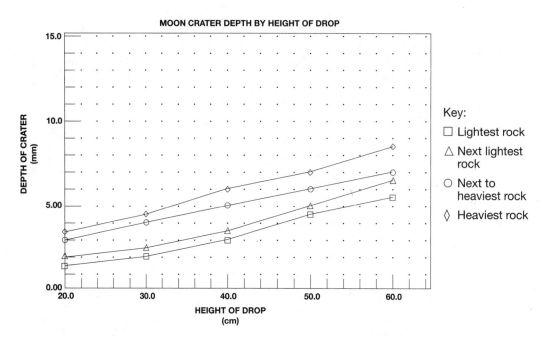

Graphical Analysis application courtesy of Vernier Software, 8565 SW Beaverton-Hillsdale Hwy, Portland, OR 97225-2429

DATA TABLE

Row Number	Series Number	Height of Drop (cm)	Depth of Crater (mm)
1	1	20.0	1.50
2	1	30.0	2.00
3	1	40.0	3.00
4	1	50.0	4.50
5	1	60.0	5.50
6	2	20.0	2.00
7	2	30.0	2.50
8	2	40.0	3.50
9	2	50.0	5.00
10	2	60.0	6.50
11	3	20.0	3.00
12	3	30.0	4.00
13	3	40.0	5.00
14	3	50.0	6.00
15	3	60.0	7.00
16	4	20.0	3.50
17	4	30.0	4.50
18	4	40.0	6.00
19	4	50.0	7.00
20	4	60.0	8.50

FIGURE 3.20   Graph and data table of moon crater depth by height of drop

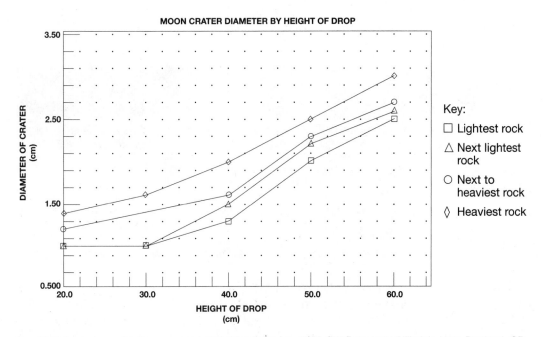

MOON CRATER DIAMETER BY HEIGHT OF DROP

Key:

☐ Lightest rock

△ Next lightest rock

○ Next to heaviest rock

◇ Heaviest rock

Graphical Analysis application courtesy of Vernier Software, 8565 SW Beaverton-Hillsdale Hwy, Portland, OR 97225-2429

DATA TABLE

Row Number	Series Number	Height of Drop (cm)	Diameter of Crater (mm)
1	1	20.0	1.00
2	1	30.0	1.00
3	1	40.0	1.30
4	1	50.0	2.00
5	1	60.0	2.50
6	2	20.0	1.00
7	2	30.0	1.00
8	2	40.0	1.50
9	2	50.0	2.20
10	2	60.0	2.60
11	3	20.0	1.20
12	3	30.0	1.20
13	3	40.0	1.60
14	3	50.0	2.30
15	3	60.0	2.70
16	4	20.0	1.40
17	4	30.0	1.60
18	4	40.0	2.00
19	4	50.0	2.50
20	4	60.0	3.00

FIGURE 3.21   Graph and data table of moon crater diameter by height of drop

In many life science activities, qualitative data is the only kind available.

IN THE SCHOOLS 3.20
Mealworms

A fourth grade teacher asked the children to investigate whether mealworms move toward or away from a stimulus. (Mealworms are available at most pet stores.) Children were asked what stimuli they would want to investigate, and they suggested light, vinegar, and hilly terrain. Children set up the various stimuli on paper plates, and watched the mealworms interact with them. The data they collected was qualitative rather than quantitative. For example, they observed that the mealworms moved away from vinegar, they moved toward the light, and they moved toward the bottom of an incline.

An investigation children can explore to gain facility in interpreting data is shown in Constructing Science in the Classroom 3.41. In this activity, children collect and graph data in order to reach their conclusion.

CONSTRUCTING SCIENCE IN THE CLASSROOM 3.41
How Many Peas Are In a Pod?

GRADE

AN ACTIVITY FOR INTERPETING DATA

Objective
The student will interpret data concerning the number of peas in pea pods.

Provide each group of children several whole pea pods. Ask children to collect data about the length, width, thickness, color, and other external characteristics of the pods. Children then open the pods one by one, and count the number of peas in each. They record their data on the board along with the data collected by other groups. Children then graph the data in such a way as to be able to interpret it. The graph might look like the one in Figure 3.22.
Graphs are interpreted in terms of the relationship between two variables (for example, the longer the pod, the more the peas).

Literature connections:
Discuss the saying, "Alike as two peas in a pod."

Black and White by David Macaulay (Houghton Mifflin, 1990). This book would be an exciting introduction to the process of interpreting data. The book contains four stories, but in reality it may contain only one story. Attention must be given to interpret clues given in the story.

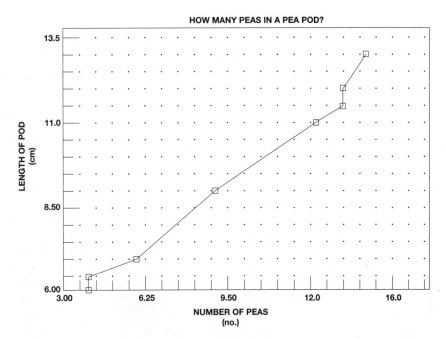

Graphical Analysis application courtesy of Vernier Software, 8565 SW Beaverton-Hillsdale Hwy, Portland, OR 97225-2429

DATA TABLE

Row Number	Series Number	Number of Peas (no.)	Length of Pod (cm)
1	1	4.00	6.00
2	1	4.00	6.50
3	1	6.00	7.00
4	1	9.00	9.00
5	1	13.0	11.0
6	1	14.0	11.5
7	1	14.0	12.0
8	1	15.0	13.0

FIGURE 3.22   Graph and data table of number of peas in a pod

CONSTRUCTING YOUR IDEAS 3.20
An Activity For Interpreting Data

Now it's your turn. Write a short activity that can be used to help children develop the skill of interpreting data. Specify grade level, and be sure the activity is appropriate to the children in the age/grade group you specify. Cite a process-oriented objective for your lesson; this objective will read something like this: "The student will interpret data gathered from an investigation of the effect of _____ on _____ ." Then get together in small groups, and do the activities each member of the group has prepared.

Defining Operationally

In the pendulum activity, we found it necessary to measure the period of the pendulum in terms of the number of swings per 15 seconds because we could not measure the time of one swing conveniently. This is an example of defining a variable operationally. It was impossible, difficult, or inconvenient to measure this quantity directly. So, we had to find an indirect way of measuring it. The measurement we devised had to be equivalent to the measurement we were replacing it with, but it did not have to give the same measurement.

Much scientific work involves exploring variables we can not measure directly. The size of the nucleus of the atom was inferred from the way radioactive rays were deflected from it, causing a fluorescent screen to light up. The rate of expansion of the universe has been measured indirectly by analyzing how much the light emitted by the stars shifts toward the red or blue ends of the spectrum. Polls designed to assess public awareness on recycling are based on indirect questions related to the topic; it would be difficult to obtain accurate data from responses to the question, "Are you aware of recycling?"

In each of these cases, the variable desired was defined in terms of something that could be observed. It was defined operationally.

You will not be asked to devise an activity requiring children to define something operationally; this process is built into many of the investigations.

Experimenting

Experimenting is the scientific process which puts all the processes together. We have suggested several experiments in this chapter. One dealt with factors that influence how fast a pendulum swings. Another dealt with factors that influence how fast a toy truck rolls down a board.

In experimenting, investigators ask questions about something they have observed or have wondered about. The question frequently takes the form of "I wonder why _____?" Often, but not always, this question is cast in the form of a hypothesis. Variables are identified, and those not being investigated but which may contribute to the outcome of the experiment are controlled. If necessary or desirable, the variables to be investigated may be expressed in operational terms. An experimental plan is developed which includes the procedure, the nature of the observations needed, and the data to be collected. The experiment is carried out, and the data is obtained. Modifications often are desirable, and these become part of a modified plan. After the investigation has been carried out and the data and observations have been recorded, the results are analyzed in terms of the original question or hypothesis. Conclusions are made accordingly, and the results of the investigation are communicated to classmates or other individuals for their reactions.

You will recall that science is skeptical. Thus, interaction among children about the conclusions they make and their reasons for making their conclusions represents the essence of the scientific enterprise. Investigators try to convince colleagues that their theories are correct while the colleagues probe with penetrating questions, some of which the investigator may not have thought of. Note that the design and execution of an experiment that is original with a child is located at the synthesis level of Bloom's taxonomy. The child becomes the scientist.

CONSTRUCTING YOUR IDEAS 3.21
Falling Parachutes

Try this experiment. What factors influence the rate of descent of a parachute? An exploratory activity involving parachutes was suggested in In The Schools 2.5, p. 43. Turned into an experiment, the investigation will allow you to put together all the processes. As a group and class activity, design the experiment, obtain the data needed to answer the question, and formulate your conclusion. Share your conclusion and the rationale for your conclusions with the class.

Two additional experiments appropriate for children in elementary grades are suggested in Constructing Science in the Classroom 3.42–3.43.

CONSTRUCTING SCIENCE IN THE CLASSROOM 3.42
An Investigation of Magnetism

GRADE

AN EXPERIMENT

Objective
The student will devise and execute an experiment to show the ability of magnetism to penetrate different materials.

The question is raised, "Do magnets attract through different kinds of materials?" Children design and execute an experiment to answer the question. They decide how to tell if the magnet attracts something (like a paper clip), and they decide what materials to try (paper, cardboard, plastic, overhead projector transparency sheets, sand, water, etc.). They assemble the materials, and they execute the experiment. Data collected is qualitative: for example, the magnet either does or does not attract the paper clip. From the data, children make their conclusions.

Literature connection:
Junior Science: Magnets by Terry Jennings (Gloucester Press, 1990) describes activities children can do to investigate magnetism.

CONSTRUCTING SCIENCE IN THE CLASSROOM 3.43
Electrical Conduction

GRADE

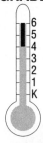

AN EXPERIMENT

Objective

The student will design an experiment to investigate the effects of various materials on the conduction of electricity.

Children are given batteries, wire, bulbs, sockets, and a variety of materials (paper, nails, paper clips, wood, lemon juice, water, salt, and so on). They design an experiment to investigate the relationship between nature of material and the conduction of electricity. Apparatus can be set up as in the diagram in Figure 3.23.

Literature connections:

Dear Mr. Henshaw by Beverly Cleary (Morrow, 1983). Ten year old Leigh is troubled with his parents' divorce and being the new kid in school. In one segment of the story, Leigh earns the respect of his peers when he solves the problem of his lunch box thief by experimenting with batteries and circuits. His battery-powered burglar alarm deters the thief.

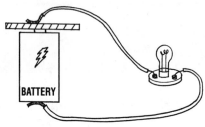

a. Connect wires to both terminals of the battery to be sure the bulb lights.

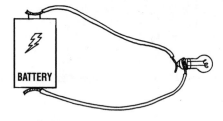

b. Place materials between the wire and one terminal to see what materials conduct electricity.

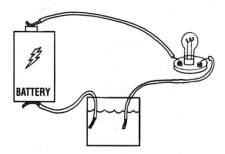

c. Put two wires in different liquids to see what conducts electricity.

FIGURE 3.23

CONSTRUCTING YOUR IDEAS 3.22
An Activity for Experimenting

Now it's your turn. Write a short activity that can be used to help children develop the skill of experimenting. Specify grade level, and be sure the activity is appropriate to the children in the age/grade group you specify. Cite a process-oriented objective for your lesson; this objective will read something like this: "The student will design and execute an experiment to investigate the effect of _____ on _____ ." Then get together in small groups, and do the activities each member of the group has prepared.

Constructing Models

You constructed a model when you investigated crater formation on the moon using a pie plate filled with flour. Models are concrete representations of things or phenomena we cannot readily see. Some good examples of models are the model of the atom (Figure 2.2, p. 45), the model of the cross section of the earth (Figure 12.11, p. 438), and models of sound waves (Figure 12.4, p. 418). In these cases, models have been constructed to enable us to visualize what we cannot see. No one has seen the inside of an atom, no one has seen the inside of the earth, and no one has seen a sound wave. Yet, the atom behaves in certain ways, the earth behaves in certain ways, and sound waves behave in certain ways—ways that permit scientists to devise replicas that represent what they *ought to* look like in order to behave the way they do.

You constructed, or, at least, you thought about constructing, a model of the mystery box in Chapter Two. In this case, your model was a box identical to the mystery box, with things put into it and exchanged and moved around until your model behaved the way the mystery box behaved. Although the model box was not the same thing as the mystery box, the two behaved the same way, and you were reasonably confident that your model box was the same as (or very close to) the mystery box.

Constructing models in the scientific sense is different from building model airplanes or from the models that appear in fashion magazines. Model airplanes and model boats are intended to reduce the size of something we can already see to a size that is manageable to work with. Models in fashion magazines demonstrate what some item of clothing or makeup or hair-do would look like on you *if* you looked like the model. The intent of these kinds of models is not to explain a phenomenon; rather it is to replicate (in the case of model airplanes) or to advertise (in the case of fashion modelling).

One of the earliest ways children get involved in constructing scientific models is to observe some that have already been developed. Two good examples come from the world of the solar system.

How big is the sun? Constructing Science in the Classroom 3.44 shows how to construct a model which compares the size of the earth with the size of the sun. The sun's diameter is 108 times the earth's diameter; it takes 108 earths to cross the sun. This is a model of something we cannot see for ourselves.

CONSTRUCTING SCIENCE IN THE CLASSROOM 3.44
How Big is the Sun?

GRADE

A MODEL-BUILDING ACTIVITY

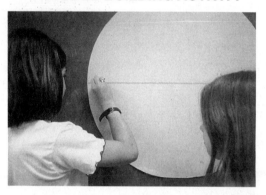

This activity shows a size comparison between the earth and the sun. The earth is approximately 8,000 miles in diameter, and the sun is approximately 865,000 miles in diameter. Thus, the diameter of the sun is about 108 times the diameter of the earth. This means that 108 earths could fit across the surface of the sun if it were flat.

Cut a circular "sun" 2 feet 3 inches in diameter and laminate it. Use 1/4-inch stick-on dots (available from office supply stores) to represent the earth. Have children stick the dots on in a straight line (diameter) across the center of the sun. It will take 108 dots to extend all the way across.

Note: This activity fosters development of the scientific processes of (1) observing, (2) measuring, (3) inferring, and (4) model building.

Directions for constructing a model of the solar system that shows the true relationships among the distances of the planets from the sun are given in Constructing Science in the Classroom 3.45.

CONSTRUCTING SCIENCE IN THE CLASSROOM 3.45
Model of the Solar System

GRADE

6
5
4
3
2
1
K

A MODEL BUILDING ACTIVITY

Objective
The student will construct a model showing the relative distances of the planets from the sun.

Materials: Meter stick, about 12 meters of 4-inch adding machine tape, and a pencil.
      This activity will give an idea of the actual distances of the planets from the sun.
      First, refer to the chart below. The chart gives the actual distances of each planet from the sun in millions of kilometers, and a proportionately scaled distance of each planet from the sun. The chart also provides actual and proportionately scaled diameters of each planet. (Note that the scale for distance is different from the scale for diameter.)

TABLE OF ACTUAL AND RELATIVE DISTANCES OF PLANETS FROM THE SUN AND RELATIVE DIAMETERS OF PLANETS

Planet	Actual Average Distance from Sun (in 10 million km)	Scaled Distance from Outer "Edge" of Sun	Actual Diameter (Km)	Scaled Diameter (Mars = 1.0 mm and Sun = 20 cm)
Mercury	5.8	12 cm	4,900	0.7 mm
Venus	11	22 cm	12,000	1.7 mm
Earth	15	30 cm	12,800	1.8 mm
Mars	23	46 cm	6,800	1.0 mm
Jupiter	78	156 cm	140,000	20.0 mm
Saturn	140	280 cm	120,000	17.0 mm
Uranus	290	580 cm	47,000	6.7 mm
Neptune	450	900 cm	50,000	7.1 mm
Pluto	590	1180 cm	1,500	0.2 mm

1. Cut out a circle 20 cm in diameter to represent the sun, and fasten it to one edge of the tape.
2. Measure from the outer edge of the circle representing the sun to find the positions of each of the planets. Measure the distances given in the column labeled "Scaled Distance" from the outer edge of the sun. Note that the distances given are *from the sun* and *not* from the preceding planet. Subtraction is necessary to find distance from preceding planet.
3. Draw in the planets at their locations using circles of the diameters given in the "Scaled Diameter" columns to show relative sizes of the planets.

Note that the diameters of the planets are given in a different scale than their relative distances from the sun.

Literature connection:
The Magic School Bus Lost In Space by Joanna Cole (Scholastic, 1990). Children travel in the solar system and stop at each of the planets.

One of the difficulties involved in building models is that the spatial relationships that actually exist often are of such gigantic proportions that it becomes necessary to compress the space into something manageable. As a result, distorted models often are designed to fit into the space available, such as a page in a book. The model of the solar system presented on p. 141, though an accurate representation, will not fit on the page of a book, and probably will have to be displayed in the school hall, for it is nearly 12 meters long. This is an inconvenient model, but it is realistic.

IN THE SCHOOLS 3.21
Temperatures of the Planets

An early elementary teacher brought in nine paper bags with costumes representing various climates: (1) dark sunglasses, fan, sun visor; (2) dark sunglasses, fan; (3) dark sunglasses; (4) light sunglasses; (5) jacket; (6) jacket and gloves; (7) jacket, gloves, and cap; (8) jacket, gloves, cap, and scarf; (9) jacket, gloves, cap, scarf, and earmuffs. Costumes were distributed to children, who put them on. Children then lined up and moved around a large paper "sun" in accordance with the costumes they were wearing. Typical discussion questions included, "How does your distance from the "sun" affect how hot or cold you are? "How big does the sun look from different positions?" "If you represented the planets, which would be the coldest? The hottest?" "Which planet would you like to live on? Why?" Then, the teacher passed out name tags for the planets, and the children wore them as they moved around the sun. These children were building a model of the solar system.

Literature connection:
Journey To the Planets (3rd ed.) by Patricia Lauber (Crown, 1990) describes prominent features of planets in our solar system; includes photos and information gathered by the Voyager explorations.

Another model that frequently is presented erroneously is the model of the thickness of the atmosphere. The correct model is shown in Figure 3.24. You will notice that when we use actual measurements of the thickness of the various layers of the atmosphere and construct them proportionately, the thickness of the earth's atmosphere turns out to be very thin—much thinner than people normally assume because of the apparently huge depth of the atmosphere and because of the models we have been exposed to previously in textbooks. Difficult as it is to envision the thickness of the earth's atmosphere the way this model presents it, this model is proportionately correct. We need only look at a photograph of the planet earth taken from outer space to verify this model.

THICKNESS OF THE EARTH'S ATMOSPHERE

The atmosphere is thought of as consisting of several layers. These layers do not have definite separations, but intermingle with one another at their interfaces.

TABLE OF THICKNESSES OF LAYERS OF EARTH'S ATMOSPHERE

EXOSPHERE Beginning of Interplanetary Space	250 – 625 miles (400 – 1000 km)
THERMOSPHERE Contains Very Few Molecules	50 – 250 miles (80–400 km)

MESOSPHERE
    Contains electrically-charged particles (ions) formed by
    collision of cosmic rays with air molecules. Ozone is found in
    lower levels of mesosphere and upper levels of stratosphere.
	30 – 50 miles
	(50–80 km)

STRATOSPHERE	16 – 30 miles (25–50 km)
TROPOSPHERE Contains the weather	0 – 16 miles (0–25 km)

To show the relationship of the thickness of the earth's atmosphere to the diameter of the earth, use the following proportional equation:

$$\frac{\text{Atmospheric Thickness}}{\text{Earth's Diameter}} = \frac{1000 \text{ km}}{12{,}800 \text{ km}}$$

If we convert this to meters, the relationship is 1,000 meters:12,800 meters.

Dividing by 100, the relationship becomes 10 meters:128 meters or 10 cm:128 cm

This gives us the proportion that the earth's atmosphere is 10 cm above the earth's surface if the earth is represented by a circle 128 cm (or 1.28 m) in diameter. Proportions are as follows in the layers of the atmosphere (given an earth 1.28 m in diameter):

Top of Exosphere	10 cm
Top of Thermosphere	4 cm
Top of Mesosphere	.8 cm (8 mm)
Top of Stratosphere	.5 cm (5 mm)
Top of Troposphere	.25 cm (2.5 mm)

   Cut off a strip of adding machine tape about 2 1/2 meters long. Place a dot at the center of the strip. This represents the center of the earth. Measure out from the dot 64 centimeters in each direction and draw a line at the 64 cm mark. This represents the diameter of the earth. Now, draw lines at the proportional distances given above *from the surface of the earth* and label the atmospheric layers accordingly. The result is an accurate model of the thickness of the earth's atmosphere.

FIGURE 3.24

Models are extremely powerful tools, presenting concrete and visual representations that make lasting impressions. It is vitally important to present models that correctly represent what they are portraying. It is far more difficult to replace an erroneous model with the correct one than it is to provide the correct one in the first place. Check your own feelings about the models of the solar system and the earth's atmosphere presented above to confirm how difficult it is to replace a preconceived model with a new one.

To foster the skill of model-building, children should be encouraged to build their own representations to explain phenomena they observe. Models are not required for everything, of course; for example, there would be no point in constructing a model of the toy truck rolling down the plank—we can see the real thing. Similarly, it would not be necessary to construct a model of the pendulum—we can see the real thing. However, the moon crater activity is, itself, a model, for our investigation closely parallels the conditions found on the moon. Since the rocks caused craters in the flour in a manner similar to what is observed on the moon, the pie tin of flour and rocks represents a good model of the formation of craters on the moon.

Let us look at an activity that involves making a model of the earth's surface. Do you remember using globes that show geographical relief? They show the Himalaya Mountains and other mountain ranges, and some of the large plateaus in raised relief from the surface of the globe. This is a good model for children, showing them that there is substantial relief on the earth. Is it accurate? Here is some information.

DATA ABOUT RELIEF OF THE EARTH'S SURFACE

Height of Tallest Mountain (Mt. Everest):
20,028 feet

Depth of Deepest Trench (Marianas Trench):
36,198 feet

Maximum total relief of earth:
56,226 feet

Diameter of earth:
7926 miles = 41,894,280 feet

CONSTRUCTING YOUR IDEAS 3.23
How Smooth is the Earth?

Using the above information, construct a model showing the total relief of the earth. What can you conclude?

Several model-construction activities are suggested in Constructing Science in the Classroom 3.46 and 3.47.

CONSTRUCTING SCIENCE IN THE CLASSROOM 3.46
How Do Whales Stay Warm in Cold Water?

GRADE

A MODEL-BUILDING ACTIVITY

Objective
The student will develop a model showing the relationship between the fat an animal possesses and its ability to survive in cold water.

Give children small plastic bags to secure over one of their hands with tape. Set up buckets of ice water around the room. Children place their gloved hand in the ice water while a partner times how long it takes before their hand gets too cold to keep in the ice water. Next, they immerse the gloved hand in another bag with shortening in it, squeezing the shortening around the gloved hand until the hand is covered fairly uniformly. They place the hand in the ice water, and their partner again records the time it takes for their hand to get too cold to stay in the ice water. The children are constructing a model of how whales are protected from cold.

Literature connections:
Whales by Gail Gibbons (Holiday House, 1991) is an informational text that includes information about different kinds of whales and how they breathe, swim, stay warm, and bear young.

I Wonder If I'll See a Whale by Frances Ward Weller (Philomel, 1991). A young girl observes whales and their interactions with their environment.

CONSTRUCTING SCIENCE IN THE CLASSROOM 3.47
A Model of Radioactive Decay

GRADE

A MODEL-BUILDING ACTIVITY

Objective
The student will develop a model showing the process of radioactive decay.

Put 100 pinto beans in each of several shoe boxes, and fix a dot to one end on the inside of each shoe box. Instruct children to shake the box for 10 seconds, and then remove all the beans whose black eye is pointing toward the dot on the inside of the box. Children record the number of beans removed and the number left in the box, and repeat this activity until all beans are removed from the box. Students then construct a graph from the data: the number of the box shaking (#1, #2, #3, etc.) vs. the number of beans left in the box. Students are asked to determine the "half-life" of the beans (the number of times the box had to be agitated in order to have 50 beans left in the box—half the number started with). The children are constructing a model of the half-life of radioactive decay.

Literature connections:
The Story of Radioactivity by Ann Stepp (Harvey House, 1971). In a simple to understand format, Stepp contrasts peaceful applications to the devastating power of nuclear energy. A small section of the book explains the concept of radioactive decay which would be useful for building a model of the half life of radium.

The King's Chessboard by David Birch (Dial Books, 1988).

A Grain of Rice by Helena Pittman (Hastings House, 1986). Both stories have similar story lines. Both involve predicting what will happen when a quantity (such as one grain of rice) is continually doubled over time.

The Process-Oriented Objective

In the preface to his book, *Preparing Instructional Objectives*, Robert Mager (1984) relates the fable of a seahorse who cantered out to seek his fortune. After buying an eel's flipper and a sponge's jet-propelled scooter to help speed him on his way, he accepts the offer of a short-cut through a shark's mouth. He zooms into the interior of the shark, never to be heard from again. "The moral of this fable," writes Mager, "is that if you're not sure where you're going, you're liable to end up someplace else" (p. v).

For each of the processes, you have been asked to sketch an activity that could be used by children to investigate that process and gain skill in its use. You also have been asked to write a process-oriented objective in each case. Simply put, the process-oriented objective is an ordinary learning objective where the verb is a process skill. "The student will observe _____." "The student will classify _____." "The student will predict _____." The process-oriented objective serves the same purpose as the instructional objective described by Mager; it is "a description of a performance you want learners to be able to exhibit before you consider them competent" (p. 1). The process-oriented objective enables teachers and children to focus on the development of one or more process skills rather than content as the main outcome of the lesson.

A process-oriented objective might be the following: "The student will develop a hypothesis to explain the formation of craters in mud during a rain storm." The objective focuses attention on hypothesis development. Contrast this with a more traditional objective: "The student will explain why craters form in mud during a rain storm." In this case, the focus is on content. In the former objective, students are to form a hypothesis; in the latter, students are to learn what someone else has discovered, and then explain it. It is strongly encouraged that process-oriented objectives be written for science lessons to ensure that children focus on the processes.

If children are to learn to do science the way scientists do science, if they are to do own their own thinking, if they are to take charge of their own learning, then they must be encouraged in every possible way. The use of the process-oriented focus in science education turns the spotlight away from learning what others have discovered, onto the children and what and how they are investigating.

Conclusion

The process skills, both basic and integrated, are the core of doing science. Children use the processes to recognize problems, ask questions, formulate hypotheses, identify variables, and reach conclusions. They verify these conclusions and use them as starting points for further investigations. Through using the processes to inquire into science, children learn skills that help them think and reason while they are discovering scientific concepts. Through using the process skills, children do science the way scientists do science and begin to acquire scientific literacy.

CHAPTER 3   Additional Questions for Discussion

1.   Develop an activity that includes all twelve processes. Identify each process and show how it is experienced by children in the successful completion of the activity.
2.   There is a certain sentiment in opposition to the use of behavioral objectives in lesson and unit planning. Contrast the process objective with the behavioral objective, and describe advantages and disadvantages of using process objectives in planning elementary science lessons and units.

Notes

1. For detailed treatment and additional information concerning the process skills, refer to McCormack & Yager (1989), Padilla, and Rezba, Sprague, Fiel, & Funk (1995).

2. The activity described in "A Case of Moon Watching" was drawn from Duckworth, E. (1986).

3. The complete Piagetian development assessment tasks are given in Appendix A of Charlesworth, Rosalind & Lind, Karen K. (1995). *Math and Science For Young Children*, Second Edition. Albany, NY: Delmar Publishers.

4. Comets are named after the people who discover them. Halley's comet is named in honor of Edmund Halley who calculated its orbit in the late 1600s and successfully predicted its return in 1758. It was last in the earth's vicinity in 1985, and it returns every 76 years.

5. Actually, we cannot calculate the speed of a pendulum since it is constantly speeding up and slowing down. This is why pendulum investigations center on the *period* on the swing (the time to complete one cycle). The word "speed" is used here to simplify the problem.

References

A First Grade Class (1994).

A Day in the Desert. St. Petersburg, Fla.: Willowisp.

Aliki. (1989). *My Five Senses.* New York: Crowell.

———. (1990). *My Feet.* New York: Crowell.

———. (1993). *Communication.* New York: Greenwillow Books.

Allen, J. (1990). *Mucky Moose.* New York: Macmillan.

Allen, P. (1980). *Mr. Archimedes' Bath.* Sydney: Collins.

Arnosky, J. (1983). *Secrets of a Wildlife Watcher.* New York: Lothrop, Lee & Shepard Books.

———. (1992). *Crinkleroot's Guide to Knowing Trees.* New York: Bradbury Press.

Baker, K. (1990). *Who is the Beast?* San Diego: Harcourt Brace Jovanovich.

Bash, B. (1974). *Desert Giant: The World of the Saguaro Cactus.* San Francisco/ Boston: Sierra Club/Little Brown.

Baylor, B. (1974). *Everybody Needs a Rock.* New York: Macmillan.

Beech, L. (1995). *The Magic School Buus in the Haunted Museum: A Book About Sound.* New York: Scholastic.

Berger, M. (1992). *All About Seeds.* New York: Scholastic.

Birch, D. (1988). *The King's Chessboard.* New York: Dial Books.

Brankley, F. & Vaughn, E. (1956). *Mickey's Magnet.* New York: Scholastic.

Brett, J. (1989). *The Mitten: A Ukrainian Folktale.* New York: G. P. Putnam and Sons.

Bruner, J. S. (1960). *The Process of Education.* Cambridge, MA: Harvard University Press.

Burningham, J. (1970). *Mr. Gumpy's Outing.* New York: Holt, Rinehart and Winston.

Cartwright, S. (1975). *Sand.* New York: Coward, McCann & Geohegan.

Cherry, L. (1992). *A River Ran Wild.* San Diego: Harcourt Brace Jovanovich.

Cleary, B. (1983). *Dear Mr. Henshaw.* Orlando: Harcourt Brace and Company.

Dav (1994). *Dog Breath.* New York: Blue Sky.

Dodd, A. W. (1992). *Footprints and Shadows.* New York: Simon and Schuster Books for Young Readers.

Dorras, A. (1991). *Follow the Water from Brook to Ocean.* New York: Harper Collins.

Duckworth, E. (1986). Teaching as research. *Harvard Educational Review 56*(4), 481–495.

Getz, D. (1994). *The Frozen Man.* New York: Holt and Co.

Gibbons, G. (1991). *Whales.* New York: Holiday House.

Graham, J. B. (1994). *Splish, Splash.* New York: Ticknor and Fields.

Greenblat, R. (1991). *Aunt Ippy's Museum of Junk.* New York: Harper Collins.

Haas, D. (1986). *The Secret Life of Dilly McBean.* New York: Bradbury Press.

Herda, D. J. (1991). *Environmental America.* Brookfield, CT.: Millbrook Press.

Hiscock, B. (1988). *The Big Rock.* New York: Atheneum.

Hoban, T. (1978). *Is It Red? Is It Yellow? Is It Blue? An Adventure in Color.* New York: Greenwillow Books.

———. (1984). *Is It Rough? Is It Smooth? Is It Shiny?* New York: Greenwillow Books.

———. (1985). *Is It Larger? Is It Smaller?* New York: Greenwillow Books.

———. (1990). *Shadows and Reflections.* New York: Greenwillow Books.

Hopkins, L. B. (1987). *Click, Rumble, Roar: Poems About Machines.* New York: Crowell.

Hutchins, P. (1970). *Clocks and More Clocks.* New York: Macmillan.

Jennings, T. (1990). *Junior Science: Magnets.* New York: Gloucester Press.

Kelley, T. (1986) *The Mystery of the Stranger in the Barn.* New York: Dodd, Mead and Co.

Krauss, R. (1945). *The Carrot Seed.* New York: Harper & Row.

Kudlinski, K. (1991). *Animal Tracks and Traces.* New York: Franklin Watts.

Lauber, P. (1990). *Journey to the Planets.* (3rd ed.). New York: Crown.

Lessem, D. (1994). *Iceman.* New York: Crown.

Lobel, A. (1970). *Frog and Toad are Friends.* New York: Harper & Row.

Lyon, G. (1990). *Come a Tide.* New York: Orchard Books.

Macaulay, D. (1990). *Black and White.* Boston: Houghton Mifflin.

Machotka, H. (1992). *Breathtaking Noses.* New York: Morrow Junior Books.

Maestro, B. (1994). *Why Do Leaves Change Color?* New York: Harper Collins.

Maestro, B. & Maestro, G. (1990). *Temperature and You*. New York: Lodestar.

Mager, R. F. (1984). *Preparing Instructional Objectives*. (2nd ed.). Belmont, CA: Davis S. Lake Publishers.

Markle, S. *(1993). Outside and Inside Trees*. New York: Bradbury.

Mathis, S. B. (1986). *The Hundred Penny Box*. New York: Puffin Books.

McCormack, A. J., & Yager, R. E. (1989). Towards a taxonomy for science education. *The Georgia Journal of Science* 19(3), pp. 11–12.

McMillan, B. (1994). *Sense Suspense: A Guessing Game for the Five Senses*. New York: Scholastic.

Merriam, E. (1991). *The Wise Woman and Her Secret*. New York: Simon and Schuster Books for Young Readers.

Moore, K. (1992). *The Weather Classroom*. Atlanta, GA: The Weather Channel.

Morris, W. (1990). *Just Listen*. New York: Atheneum.

Mylar, R. (1962). *How Big is a Foot?* New York: Atheneum.

Padilla, M. J. The science process skills. "Research Matters . . . To the Science Teacher." National Association for Research in Science Teaching.

Parnall, P. (1986). *Winter Barn*. New York: Macmillan.

Pittman, H. (1986). *A Grain of Rice*. New York: Hastings House.

Renner, J. W. & Marek, E. A. (1990). An educational theory base for science teaching. *Journal of Research in Science Teaching* 27(3), p. 243.

Rezba, R. J., Sprague, C., Fiel, D. L., & Funk, H. J. (1995). *Learning and Assessing Science Process Skills*. Dubuque, IA: Kendall/Hunt Publishing Company.

Roop, P. (1985). *Keep the Lights Burning, Abbie*. Minneapolis, Minn.: Carolrhoda Books.

Schwartz, D. (1985). *How Much is a Million?* New York: Lothrop, Lee & Shepard.

Selsam, M. (1959). *Seeds and More Seeds*. New York: Harper & Row.

Selsam, M. (1966). *Benny's Animals and How We Put Them in Order*. New York: Harper Row.

Selsam, M. (1980). *Eat the Fruit, Plant the Seed*. New York: Morrow.

Seuss, Dr. [pseud. for Geisel, T. S.] (1949). *Bartholomew and the Ooblick*. New York: Random House.

Shapp, M. & Shapp, C. (1975). *Let's Find Out About What's Light and What's Heavy*. New York: Franklin Watts.

Showers, P. (1961). *Find Out By Touching*. New York: Thomas Crowell.

Silver, D. M. (1993). *One Small Square Backyard.* New York: Freeman.

Silverstein, S. (1974). *Where the Sidewalk Ends.* New York: Harper & Row.

Simon, S. (1980). *Einstein Anderson Shocks His Friends.* New York: Viking Press.

———. (1987). *Einstein Anderson Tells a Comet's Tale.* New York: Viking Press.

Sloane, E. (1966). *The Sound of Bells.* Garden City, N.J.: Doubleday.

Stepp, A. (1971). *The Story of Radioactivity.* Irvington-on-Hudson, N.Y.: Harvey House.

Stone, H. & Igmanson, D. (1968). *Rocks and Rills—A Look at Geology.* Englewood Cliffs, N.J.: Prentice-Hall.

Taylor, B. (1990). *Bouncing and Bending Light.* New York, London: Watts.

———. (1986). *I'm in Charge of Celebration.* New York: Charles Scribner's Sons.

Thomas, P. (1979). *There Are Rocks in My Socks Said the Ox to the Fox.* New York: Lothrop, Lee & Shepard.

Weller, F. W. (1991). *I Wonder If I'll See a Whale.* New York: Philomel.

Wolkstein, D. (1972). *8,000 Stones: A Chinese Folktale.* Garden City: Doubleday.

Zubrowski, B. (1979). *A Children's Museum Activity Book: Bubbles.* Boston: Little Brown.

CHAPTER 4

Constructivism in Elementary Science Education

In the first three chapters, you explored many activities; in each, you developed your own understanding of the concept involved. For example, you developed your own understanding of how different variables influence the rate of swing of pendulums and you formulated your own ideas about the origin of lunar craters. You also formulated your own ideas about the nature of science, what it means to be scientifically literate, and how scientists do science. You developed your own perception of the goals and objectives of the elementary science program. You investigated the processes of science and came to your own understanding of the nature of the processes, their importance to elementary science education, and how they can be taught by you and learned by children.

153

You constructed your understandings of each of these notions in ways that make sense to you.

Jean Piaget, seeking an answer to the perennial philosophical question, "How do we come to know what we know?" concluded that knowledge cannot be transmitted intact from one person to another; people must construct their own knowledge and their own understandings. Learning does not occur by transmitting information from the teacher or the textbook (or the video or the demonstration) to the child's brain. Instead, each child constructs his or her own meaning by combining prior information with new information such that the new knowledge provides personal meaning to the child (Cobern, 1993).

The notion that people build their own knowledge and their own representations of knowledge from their own experience and thought is called *constructivism*. Each activity that has been suggested thus far, and, indeed, this book itself, is constructivist in orientation. It is the basic premise of this book that learning in science occurs best when approached from a constructivist point of view.

BATTERIES AND ELECTRICITY

Recently, I was asked to teach a lesson on electricity for a fifth grade class. Equipment available consisted of several shoe boxes each containing 1.5-volt batteries, a few pieces of wire, a few bulb holders, some 1.5-volt light bulbs, a knife switch or two, and a 1.5-volt electric motor. The children in the class came from a wide background of prior experiences with electricity. Some had studied electricity previously in school; some had never studied it; others had been exposed to textual material on electricity, but had never experimented with it. I asked the children to divide themselves into small groups, and I gave a box of materials to each group. Because of the wide range of prior experiences, I provided very simple directions: "Using the materials in the box, figure something out you didn't know before."

Some children connected a piece of wire to the bottom and the top of the battery, and felt the wire get hot. It was the first time they had been given the opportunity to try things out with electricity. Other children overcame their fears of electricity by trying a variety of different connections, none of which hurt them or gave them a shock. Others lit the bulbs; some found out that it did not matter which way the wires were connected to the batteries— the bulbs lit anyhow. Others set up elaborate series circuits and parallel circuits, discovering elementary principles of circuitry. One group fashioned a paper propeller and attached it to the motor, making an electric fan.

Does the number of batteries affect how brightly the light burns?

FIGURE 4.1 Investigating batteries and bulbs

Each person learned something he or she had not known before; each person added to his or her store of information about electricity. And each child did it by constructing his or her own conceptualization about electricity, whether the conceptualization was basic or advanced.

Children explored; children connected what they were able to make happen during that class with what they already knew; and children developed their understanding of electricity. They shared their discoveries with each other, often arriving at new ways of conceptualizing their own information as a result of these interactions. They made connections to previously-learned information in ways that were unique and meaningful to them.

Constructivism

For centuries, philosophers have debated the question of what constitutes "reality." The traditional epistemological[1] paradigm holds an *objective* view of reality; reality exists outside the individual, is discovered, and is communicated to learners by language or some other representation. "Teaching Is Telling."

An opposing view holds that individuals construct their own *subjective* reality; reality is that which has been constructed by the individual from his or her own observations, reflections, and logical thought. This reality must be built by each individual for himself or herself.

The constructivist view of learning is grounded in the notion of subjective reality. Far from being a contemporary paradigm, constructivism's basic ideas were proposed as long ago as 1710 by Giambattista Vico. Vico's notions about the nature of reality included the following:

1. "Epistemic agents [people who know] can know nothing but the cognitive structures they themselves have put together."
2. "God alone can know the *real* world, because He knows how and of what He has created it."
3. "In contrast, the human knower can know only what the human knower has constructed," (Von Glasersfeld, 1989).

Ernst Von Glasersfeld, considered by many to be today's foremost scholar of constructivism, says that once a teacher abandons the notion that knowledge is a "commodity" transferable to children, that notion must be replaced with an attempt to discover what actually goes on in children's minds as they learn. He wrote:

> As long as the educator's objective was the generation of more or less specific behaviors in the student, the educator saw no need to ask what, if anything, might be going on in the student's head. Whenever the student could be got to 'emit' the desired behaviors in the situations with which they had been associated, the instructional process was deemed successful. The student did not have to *see* why the particular

actions led to a result that was considered 'correct,' nor did the educator have to worry about how the student achieved it; what mattered was the 'performance,' i.e., that he or she was able to produce such a result.

If, in contrast, the objective is to lead the children or students to some form of *understanding*, the teacher must have some notion of how they think. That is to say, teachers must try to infer, from what they can observe, what the students' concepts are and how they operate with them. Only on the basis of some such hypothesis can teachers devise ways and means to orient, direct, or modify the students' mental operating (Von Glasersfeld, 1991).

The constructivist believes that each learner must construct meaning for himself or herself—that the only learning that can take place is that which is connected to already-existing knowledge, experiences or conceptualizations. What a child learns is not a copy of what he observes in his surroundings, but is the result of his own thinking and processing. As Tobin wrote, "Learners have no option but to use what they already know as a basis for making sense of any experience they have" (Tobin, 1991).

In Chapter One you explored the notion that the same event can be interpreted differently by different people according to their prior experiences. Since no two people internalize the same experiences the same way, it follows that information "imparted" by the teacher is not necessarily "learned." Therefore, it is incumbent upon teachers to learn how each child is constructing information, and then help each individual attach new experiences in ways that are both meaningful and convincing to the child.

In the constructivist approach, the primary job of the teacher is to enable children to find and make their own connections that result in valid internalized meanings unique to the child. The teacher does this by asking questions to see how children may have previously constructed information related to the topic. The teacher leads the children through exploratory activities that enable them to investigate on their own and come to their own conclusions as to what is happening. The teacher interacts with each child to see *how* he or she is constructing the new information, and helps him formulate sound conclusions by aiding the child in reconstructing the information in ways that are both valid and meaningful *to the child*.

Prior Beliefs

Children begin their formal study of science with ideas already in place about the natural world.[2] Some of these ideas are congruent with currently accepted scientific understandings. But, some are not. For example, children "know" that a baseball will fall faster than a marble because it is bigger and heavier.

Though this preconceived notion is not supported by precise investigation, it is believable to the children, and makes sense to them because
of their limited experience with the phenomenon. Since it makes sense to
them, it is difficult to change their beliefs simply by telling them otherwise. Children have to *experience* for themselves occurrences that contradict their currently-held beliefs. Children are not going to understand
that a baseball and a marble fall at the same rate simply by being told.
In fact, many college level pre-service teachers believe the two balls do
not fall at the same rate. In my classes, I have stood on a table to let a
baseball and a marble drop from the same height onto a floor that is not
carpeted so students could hear the sounds made in unison, demonstrating that the balls hit the floor at the same time. Only after several repeated attempts (often done by the students themselves) did these college
seniors begin to successfully reconstruct their prior conception. Yet it is
likely they were exposed to this phenomenon somewhere along the line.
If so, they probably memorized the correct answer for the test, but re-
tained reservations about the truth of the teacher's answer since it was
not reconciled with their own beliefs.

Conceptual Change

In order for conceptual change to occur, children must become dissatis-
fied with their existing conception. Their existing conception, believable
on the surface, must be shown to fail to explain some new observation
satisfactorily. For example, the belief that heavy balls fall faster than light
balls does not account for the baseball and the marble hitting the floor at
the same time when dropped from the same height. The belief that the
speed of a pendulum ought to depend on the weight of the bob is not
supported by experimental evidence.

When experimental evidence fails to provide support for a prior conception, people begin to question the validity of the prior conceptualization.
They become aware of conflict between what they *thought* was true and
what they observe for themselves. Magic tricks and special effects in movies
are good examples of this phenomenon. We hold fast to the notion that it
is impossible for certain things to happen (such as a human body levitat-
ing, or a man flying on his own power). When we see these things happen,
we strive to resolve the conflict between what we observe and our notion
that they *cannot* happen, by suggesting plausible explanations such as "It's
done with mirrors," or "It's done with a computer."

Discrepant events (unusual happenings) are used by constructivist
teachers to spark children's curiosity about the validity of their prior
beliefs. The "Floating Coffin" (Figure 4.2) is a good example of a discrepant event. It can be purchased at novelty shops, and consists of two

round bars of steel in a frame. One of the bars (the "coffin") floats above the other. How can that be? Our experience tells us that steel bars do not float in air. Our experience also tells us there must be a reasonable explanation for what we observe. As we work to reconcile the difference between what we believe and what we see, we become satisfied that magnetism could explain this discrepant event.

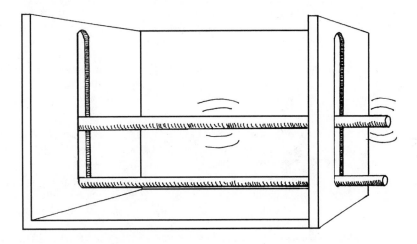

The top steel rod floats freely above the bottom steel rod. How can that be?

FIGURE 4.2   The floating coffin

Cognitive Disequilibration

One's dissatisfaction with what actually *is* happening as contrasted with what *ought* to happen is called, in Piagetian terms, *cognitive disequilibration*, or sometimes, *cognitive dissonance*. Disequilibration begs a solution.

The constructivist teacher seeks to induce cognitive disequilibration by setting up situations that encourage children to question their existing beliefs and ask what is going on. Children attempt to make predictions about the situation based on prior understandings. When these predictions do not work, the children question the prior beliefs. This brings the existing belief to the surface, giving the teacher access to what is in the children's minds, and thus the opportunity to help them reconstruct their beliefs in valid ways that include the new information and make sense to the children.

IN THE SCHOOLS 4.1
Dancing Raisins

A good example of an activity that challenges children's prior beliefs is making raisins dance. First, ask children if they think raisins sink or float. After they have predicted, put a few in a glass of water so children can see them sink. Children believe things either sink or float. Now, fill a plastic jar about 3/4 full of water and mix in about 1/2 cup of white vinegar. Put a handful of raisins in the jar. They sink to the bottom. Then add a tablespoon of baking soda, and watch the raisins rise and sink. Ask children why they think the raisins are dancing. [The reason is that some of the carbon dioxide gas generated by the reaction between the baking soda and vinegar becomes lodged in the crevices of the raisins making them light enough to rise to the surface. When they reach the surface, the gas escapes and they sink.]

Literature connections:

A Wizard of Earthsea by Ursula Le Guin (Parnassus, 1968). This is a fantasy about a novice wizard student who struggles with opposing forces of good and evil within himself.

Elephant by Judy Allen (Candlewick Press, 1993). Receiving an ivory necklace made by her ancestors leaves Hannah uncomfortable as she attempts to reconcile her feelings and values that are different from her ancestors' beliefs.

To aid children in their reconstruction of prior beliefs, the teacher may encourage the children to investigate on their own, or the teacher may introduce minimal understanding of the conceptualization as generally agreed upon by the scientific community. The result is that the child is compelled to relate the new phenomenon, new ideas, and new experiences and observations to existing knowledge in ways that are most appropriate *to the child*.

THE SUN AND THE MOON ON THE ECLIPTIC

I remember a high school junior who was taking a course in general science. On a particular morning, I happened to notice that the sun and the moon were both visible in the sky. Since these celestial bodies can serve as anchor points for the ecliptic (the plane on which all planets in our solar system revolve about the sun), I decided to take the class outside so they could see for themselves. This student was dumbstruck. He asked many questions, and demanded considerable explanation concerning what he was seeing. After listening to him for some time, I realized that the reason he couldn't understand the concept of the ecliptic I was trying to illustrate that morning was that it had never occurred to him that the sun and the moon were two different objects. He had seen them at the same time for the first time in his life, and it was necessary for him to rearrange his conceptualizations to accommodate this new observation.

It is a fundamental principle of the constructivist approach to learning that cognitive disequilibration is a necessary precursor of learning - that learning will not take place unless explanations are sought. If our existing understandings were to explain everything, there would be no need for further understanding.

Validity of Self-Constructed Conceptualizations

If a new conceptualization constructed by the child appears more plausible than the prior notion, it may be accepted by the child as a tentative replacement for the prior notion. For lasting acceptance, the new conceptualization must have both *explanatory* and *predictive* power. It must be able to explain what has been observed, and it must predict accurately what will happen in other occurrences. In other words, it must possess *validity*.

The explanatory and predictive power of the new conceptualization is best tested through hands-on explorations and in small group peer interactions where children share their views and test their predictions with others in their group. We must encourage children to share their conclusions in order for them to demonstrate that the results of their investigations have both predictive and explanatory power. Having children work in groups helps promote this critical sharing. Different people investigate the same question in different ways, and when they share their information, the strengths and weaknesses of each person's thinking become apparent. The collective thinking of a group is more likely to be valid than the isolated thinking of any one individual.

Occasionally the teacher needs to present a view more congruent with currently accepted scientific principles than those the children have come up with. This may be because the concept is unlikely to be discovered by the children without help, or because children are getting stuck. When this happens, the teacher presents this view as just another view for children to discuss, question, test, and explain. Children are provided the opportunity to discuss the pros and cons of all the various views (including the teacher's view), and resolve their differences by discussion and laboratory tests. A conceptualization is valid to the child as long as it explains and predicts more satisfactorily than other conceptualizations.

Inquiry

Cognitive disequilibration not only results from teacher intervention; often children get curious about some phenomenon as a result of a chance observation, a casual remark, or simply wondering about something. In the constructivist classroom, the teacher facilitates children in their personal investigations of these questions. The teacher asks, "How would you find out?" and encourages the children to explore possible ways of answering their question. Since the children do it themselves, they are able to construct the answers to their questions in ways that make sense to them; discussions with the teacher and with classmates help confirm validity or show where additional exploration is needed. Chapter Five is devoted to the inquiry method of teaching.

Constructivism and Science Learning

The learning of science is a process of construction and reconstruction of personal theories previously held. It is a process of continuously refining existing knowledge and constructing concepts in intricate organized networks which are unique to each child and which provide explanatory and predictive power—at least until the next observation that produces disequilibration.

IN THE SCHOOLS 4.2
Cleaning Tarnished Pennies

How can we clean a tarnished penny? A constructivist kindergarten teacher encouraged children to try the various ways they could think of to clean a tarnished penny: washing with different kinds of soaps, washing without soap, brushing, soaking, etc. Of course, none of these methods worked, and so the teacher introduced such unexpected options such as soaking the penny in vinegar, rubbing a lemon on it, and soaking it in a mixture of vinegar and salt. She invited the children to try these new methods. The penny became bright and shiny!

Literature connection:

Water Magic by Carole Mitchener, Virginia Johnson, and Phyllis Adams (Modern Curriculum Press, 1987). Two young children question their dad about how objects appear differently in water and how a tarnished penny can sparkle after placing it in a glass of water and vinegar.

Will soap clean the penny?   Will a lemon clean the penny?

FIGURE 4.3   Cleaning a tarnished penny

What do kindergarten children get out of this activity in addition to experience in the processes of observation, communication, and prediction? There is a fundamental scientific concept at work here: the notion of the physical change versus the chemical change. Without realizing it, children are beginning to construct the underpinnings of this concept—they are beginning to notice that soaking the penny in certain liquids can produce a change. "How can this be?" they wonder. They do not completely understand, but they are now alert to other occurrences that produce changes similar to that produced by soaking a penny in vinegar. A cognitive disequilibration has entered their minds, and they begin trying to resolve it. They are constructing their own understanding of the phenomenon.

IN THE SCHOOLS 4.3
Examining Snowflakes

Do all snowflakes look alike? In a fourth grade class, the teacher set a 10-power binocular microscope and some pieces of black construction paper outdoors on a cold and snowy day. After about fifteen minutes, the paper was cold enough that snowflakes landing on it did not melt. Children captured the snowflakes on the black paper and examined them with the naked eye, with magnifying glasses, and under the microscope, drawing what they saw. Children began to construct the idea that each snowflake is at least slightly different from each other snowflake.

In this activity, children began to construct notions about the infinite variation the orderliness of nature, in addition to the possibility that no two snowflakes are identical.

Piaget, The Constructivist

Jean Piaget was a constructivist (Von Glasersfeld, 1991, p. 16). He is perhaps best remembered by education students for his stages of cognitive development. However, in his later years, he lamented the singular focus given to his stage theory; he felt his work on accommodation and assimilation, and especially the resulting equilibration was far more important than the stages.

Piaget viewed knowledge as a *process* rather than a *state*: knowledge is a relationship between the knower and the known in which the knower constructs his or her own representations of what is known. Children's knowledge changes as their cognitive systems develop and as their experiences are filtered through increasingly mature ways of thinking and ways of constructing representations of knowledge.

Mechanism of Constructing Knowledge

Piaget viewed the mind as a collection of cognitive structures he called *schemata* (singular: *schema*). Schemata are opened, enlarged, divided, and connected in response to the influx of information into a person's mind. Two fundamental processes are at work in this mental activity: assimilation and accommodation. As we go through life, we record new experiences into already-existing schemata, and they get bigger. Taking in new information and fitting it into existing schemata is called *assimilation*. However, there comes a time when either the existing schemata are too filled with information to warrant enlargement, or there are no existing schemata appropriate for certain new pieces of information. In these cases, new schemata are opened. Either brand new schemata can be opened to accommodate exposure to experiences and observations which are new to the individual, or an existing schema can be split into two or more to accommodate a wider range of experience. The opening of new schemata or splitting of existing schemata into new ones is called *accommodation*. The human mind develops through assimilation and accommodation of new information into one or more schemata.

The schemata are linked to each other in ways that are unique to the individual and which represent the unique experiences of the individual and the unique connections the individual has made between and among those experiences. In a sense, schema theory is similar to computer files. Each file is labeled with its appropriate content. You might have separate files for addresses, finances, personal correspondence, business letters, term papers, and so on. You might need to open a new file for personal correspondence if the existing one became too full. If you were assigned to write lesson plans, you might open a new file entitled "Lesson Plans" since you did not already have one. You would assimilate new material where possible, and you would accommodate overloads of new categories with new files. In both cases, you would know the rationale for opening the new files, and you would know how the new ones connect with the old.

The crux of Piaget's theory of cognitive development is the drive for achievement of *equilibration*, a state of mental equilibrium. An example may help clarify the equilibration concept. Suppose you are taking a course in human physiology, and you are given hundreds of new terms to memorize and dozens of intricate processes to understand. Suppose, furthermore, you had never studied the human body in detail. All this new information about physiology comes at you, and you can't make heads or tails of it. What do you do with it? Well, since you have to know it at least until the exams are over, you store it in a mental file called "human physiology." This file (or schema) has no connection whatever with information that currently exists in your mind; it simply is there— as mental storage. As the course progresses, you add information, you expand the physiology schema, you break off new ones, and you try to make sense of the material when it is compared to itself; but you are not able to relate it to anything you have ever experienced. You are developing a whole set of schemata which is unrelated to anything else in your mind. This is disconcerting, and you feel a necessity (often not accomplished) to make some sort of connection to something you already know. You feel a drive to achieve equilibration.

In another example, suppose you are studying a course in elementary science methods. In this course, you attempt to relate new experiences to understandings previously existing in your mind. You assimilate new information by finding the appropriate existing schemata from your prior experiences in which the new material most appropriately belongs. When these schemata get too cumbersome to be able to work with, you split off part of one or more of them and start new ones. The new ones are connected in ways unique to your method of thinking and your prior experiences. You are achieving equilibration relative to connecting the new experiences of this course with your prior experiences.

The same is true of children's thinking. To learn something new, they must be able to connect it to something they already know. They must construct personal meaning of the new material either by assimilating it into existing schemata, or by accommodating it through forming new schemata which are connected to existing ones. In the constructivist approach to learning, children are encouraged to make meaningful connections to previously-existing information so the situation of having to construct schemata in isolation as in the physiology example will not occur. Exposure to new experiences often causes the phenomenon of cognitive disequilibration which we discussed earlier in this chapter. Cognitive disequilibration signifies that the new experience does not readily fit into any other previous experiences the child may have had; the new experience cannot be assimilated into existing schemata (as the concept of "bear" could be assimilated into the schema dealing with "animals.") Therefore, the child must either enlarge an existing schema to assimilate the novel experience, or must open a new one that is somehow connected with existing schemata in order to make sense out of the new experience. In this manner, new information is constructed in terms of understandings which evolve and are reformulated in response to lack of fit between new experiences and previous understandings. Von Glasersfeld explained the phenomenon as follows:

> The learning theory that emerges from Piaget's work can be summarized by saying that cognitive change and *learning* take place when a scheme, instead of producing the expected result, leads to perturbation, and perturbation, in turn, leads to accommodation that establishes a new equilibrium. As a result, the human mind is a complex network of schemata which are intricately connected to each other in patterns completely unique to the individual (Von Glasersfeld, 1989, p. 128).

It is plain to see that, since the development of schemata begins as soon as the mind is capable of processing stimuli, it is to a child's advantage to experience the richest and most widely varied stimuli possible.

Head Start and other pre-school projects are designed to do precisely this. Elementary school science experiences should include the widest breadth of experiences possible in order to provide a rich experiential base for children as they process their disequilibrations through assimilation and accommodation.

Stages of Cognitive Development

Piaget suggested four stages of cognitive development commencing with birth: the sensorimotor stage, the preoperational stage, the concrete operational stage, and the formal operational stage. Although he expressed dissatisfaction with having proposed specific ages to accompany the stages, he believed all people progress through the same four stages in the same unvaried sequence.

Each stage represents more advanced capability for cognitive processing than the previous stage. Much has been written about the characteristics of each stage, so they will not be discussed in detail here. However, it is essential that the elementary science teacher understand the intellectual capabilities and limitations of children at the various stages.

STAGE	CHARACTERISTICS	WAYS TO FOSTER DEVELOPMENT
SENSORIMOTOR	Thought based on sensory input	Opportunity to act on environment
PREOPERATIONAL	Increased use of symbolism and language Limited logic Egocentric Perspective	Language and symbol use
CONCRETE OPERATIONAL	Must see—feel—touch—smell—hear to "know" Thinking is reversible Some classification Some conservation	Hands-on experiences
FORMAL OPERATIONAL	Abstract reasoning	Abstractions in the form of problems, hypotheses, probabilities, correlations, proportions Formal reasoning skills

FIGURE 4.4   The cognitive development stages of Piaget

Sensorimotor Stage

The child's intellectual endeavors in the sensorimotor stage consist of the senses interacting with the child's environment. Children at this stage cannot initiate internal thought; they are building schemata that describe the environment and its effect on the child. It is crucial to the intellectual development of children that they be given the opportunity to act on the environment in unrestricted (but safe) ways in order to start opening up and building these schemata. Such activities as walking unaided up and down stairs, working puzzles with large pieces, playing with push toys, exploring the house and the yard, and going for rides with the family contribute to the development of a rich network of schemata.

Preoperational Stage

The preoperational stage of intellectual development characterizes children from pre-school through first or second grade. The child's world becomes reshaped by developing the realm of mental representation. "The child develops from an almost entirely reflexive organism to one that can intentionally manipulate symbols (Salkind, 1985, p. 201).

The most significant intellectual achievement during the preoperational stage is the ability to represent objects and thoughts symbolically. Language is developed, and the child begins to use the abstractions of language to communicate thought. Imagine the intellectual leap required to move from pointing at something that Daddy gets into when he goes to work, to the use of the three-letter word *car* to represent the concept. Of course, children at this stage often use language literally ("He has grown a foot!") and invent their own spellings and grammatical rules ("He goed to the store"). But they are learning how to represent thoughts abstractly, and, to the extent that other people understand what they are trying to communicate, they have succeeded.

To compound the intellectual difficulties, we ask children to learn to represent these abstract sounds with letters—to write them! The cognitive development required to achieve facility in such abstractions is uncanny. Yet, children do it all the time, and they often do it before they reach kindergarten. To gain an appreciation of what this is like, try learning to read and write a language with non-English characters, such as Arabic or Japanese!

Preoperational children are egocentric in perspective. Logical thought is not widely available to the preoperational child; everything is based on what they see. They cannot assume a perspective different from themselves. For example, they cannot imagine what someone in a different position would see. Thus, the elementary science teacher asks the preoperational child what HE or SHE sees, NOT what he or she thinks someone else would see. We ask the question, "What do you see under this magnifying glass?" not "What do you suppose Mark sees under his magnifying glass?" We ask, "Why did you group the buttons the way you did?" not "Why do you suppose Janie grouped the buttons the way she did?"

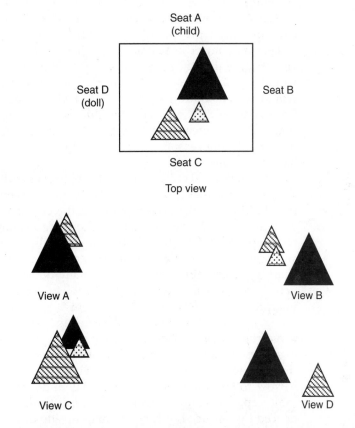

Three pyramid-shaped blocks ("mountains") are placed on a table as shown in the above "bird's-eye" view. A child seated at Position A sees the mountains as shown in View A. The child is asked which view of the mountains on the table would be seen by the doll seated at Position D. The preoperational child indicates the doll would see View A.

From *Theories of Human Development,* Second Edition, by N. J. Salkind, Copyright © 1985, John Wiley & Sons, Inc. Reprinted by permission of John Wiley & Sons, Inc.

FIGURE 4.5 Mountains on the table

Preoperational children cannot reverse operations. They can learn that 2 plus 4 equals 6. But, they cannot yet make the reverse logical inference that if you take 4 from 6 you get what's left (2), or if you take 2 from 6 , you get 4. They can find their way on an illustrated map from the school to the firehouse; but they cannot retrace their steps backward without instruction to get from the firehouse to the school. Elementary science educators must be careful not to expect operations reversal capabilities from preoperational children. For example, a kindergarten teacher may introduce an activity where children add heat to ice cubes and observe that they melt; however, preoperational children normally would not infer from that activity that taking heat away (or, as they would put it, "adding cold") would produce the opposite effect. Or, a first-grade teacher may have the children do an activity to demonstrate that exercise increases one's rate of breathing. The preoperational children would not reason that resting will reduce the breathing rate; they have to try it for themselves.

Preoperational children cannot conserve quantity or mass or volume. This was discussed in Chapter Three in the section on Measurement (p. 89). More detailed descriptions of the classic Piagetian conservation experiments on number (involving the space a certain number of pennies takes up), mass (involving rolling a clay ball into the shape of a cigar), and volume (involving pouring water from a tall, thin container into a short, wide container) are given in many other texts; the interested student is referred to them for the complete experimental paradigm and interpretation of results. (See also note 3, p. 147.)

It is worthwhile to note that adults operate in a preoperational mode to a certain extent. To test this, go to a store that sells aquariums, and ask to see several 20-gallon tanks. It requires a terrific imagination to believe that all the tanks you are shown, which vary in shape from long and narrow to short and wide, pentagonal, and circular in shape, have the same capacity. Adults also experience difficulty in reversing, as is evidenced by our need to turn the map upside down when driving south.

Concrete Operational Stage

The primary characteristic of the concrete operational stage is that the individual must see, hear, feel, touch, smell, taste, or, in some other way, utilize the senses in order to "know." Concrete operational children cannot think abstractly, and they do not wonder about abstract concepts. They are busy learning skills and how to manipulate things they can experience at first hand. Studies show that many children are concrete-bound through the middle grades; indeed, many adults never get out of this stage. Remember that a cognitive stage represents the capability of a level of intellectual development; it does not represent the accomplishment of that level.

The thinking process of concrete operational children can be reversed; they can think backward and reconstruct the original situation. For example, they can think about what would happen if a certain variable had *not* been changed the way it had been.

IN THE SCHOOLS 4.4
Solutions and Crystals

A good example helping children understand reversibility of operations involves experimentation with solutions and crystals. Children add heat to a solution to enable more of a solute (the solid material) to dissolve in the solvent (the liquid part). The more the heat, the more solute will dissolve. Concrete operational children are able to infer what will happen to the solution if heat is taken away (cooled). The solute that dissolved because of the heating will precipitate out of the solution when it cools. In fact, the excess solute precipitates in the form of crystals, and the slower this happens, the larger the crystals will become. See Constructing Science in the classroom 4.1 (p. 172) for details of how to make crystals and ways inquiring into crystal formation.

IN THE SCHOOLS 4.5
Balancing

In a fourth-grade class, children were experimenting with the relationship between weight of objects and distance from a fulcrum on a balance beam. Concrete operational children are able to infer what might happen when weights are moved without necessarily having to *do* it first; they then confirm their predictions by testing them.

The classification capabilities of concrete operational children are extensive (refer to Chapter Three). They can create hierarchies and they can understand relationships within classes (such as plants and animals) and relationships to the class itself, though they are not yet ready to devise complex hierarchical interrelationships and complex classification systems.

Concrete operational individuals can conserve quantity, mass, and volume, though conservation of volume occurs toward the end of the concrete operational stage. For example, concrete operational children understand that the amount of solute dissolved in a solution is the same before and after mixing it with the solvent.

They have the ability to form hypotheses, including the ability to define the term, and they can verbalize hypotheses concerning the relationships between two variables. They have the ability to develop experimental conditions that test the validity of hypotheses, including identifying

CONSTRUCTING SCIENCE IN THE CLASSROOM 4.1
Growing Copper Sulfate Crystals and Sugar Crystals

GRADE

Crystal growing provides an excellent vehicle through which children can hypothesize and experiment. Questions that might be asked include the following:

1. How big can crystals grow?
2. Do crystals of different materials grow bigger than others?
3. Can crystals be grown from all materials?
4. What effect does heat have on the rate of growth of crystals?
5. What effect does rate of evaporation have on the rate of growth of crystals?

To grow crystals, you need to have a saturated solution of some material, and let the liquid evaporate; as the liquid evaporates, the dissolved material is left behind in the form of crystals. Different substances require different treatments for most effective crystal formation. Below are "recipes" for growing sugar crystals and copper sulfate crystals.

SUGAR CRYSTALS (ROCK CANDY)

Home-grown sugar crystals are called rock candy. Well-defined sugar crystals are difficult to grow since sugar tends to become candy-like and non-crystalline when it is dissolved in water, heated, and then cooled.

METHOD 1: Formation on a string

Dissolve $2\frac{1}{2}$ cups sugar in 1 cup water, heating the mixture until the sugar is dissolved. Let cool. Pour the syrup into a glass into which you have previously suspended a weighted string. Let the water evaporate. Rock candy will form on the string in a day or two.

Method 2: Formation without strings

Dissolve $2\frac{1}{2}$ cups sugar in 1 cup water, heating the mixture until the sugar is dissolved. Pour the syrup into a shallow wide-mouth container. Cover tightly with aluminum foil or plastic wrap, and poke three small holes in the covering with a pencil. Let the jar set on a counter without disturbing it for 6 weeks or so. Crystals will form on the bottom of the container.

If desired, you can pour off the fluid, remove the crystals, rinse them off, and set them in a warm, dry place to dry.

Note: In both methods, you can add food coloring to the solution to obtained colored crystals of rock candy.

Inquiry questions to investigate: If you poke more holes in the wrapping, or if you make the holes bigger, or if you leave off the wrapping, what happens to the size of the crystals and to the rate at which they form? What happens if you put the container in a warmer place? A cooler place? (The principle is that the more slowly the liquid evaporates, the larger the crystals grow.)

COPPER SULFATE CRYSTAL GROWTH

Below are the directions for preparing a solution of copper sulfate. When the solution is left to evaporate, the copper sulfate crystallizes into beautiful deep-blue crystals in the shape of parallelograms. The more slowly the liquid evaporates, the larger the crystals grow.

1. Heat 300 ml of tap water to about 100°F—about the temperature of a baby's bottle.
2. Stir in 175 g powdered copper sulfate (cupric sulfate—$CuSO_4 \cdot 5H_2O$). It will *not* all dissolve. Most will dissolve, but there will be a layer of undissolved copper sulfate on the bottom of the container.

3. Let the solution cool, preferably overnight. The copper sulfate that cannot remain dissolved in the solution as it cools will precipitate out; thus you will have a completely saturated* solution at the temperature of the room.

4. Carefully pour (decant) the cool solution into a clean jar, filling it to about 1/3 or 1/4 full; be careful that no undissolved residue gets included. Leave the leftover solution (including the undissolved residue) in the original jar, covered and sealed tightly. This will be the stock solution.

5. Put a piece of paper or plastic wrap over the top of the second jar, and fasten it with a rubber band. Poke two or three small holes into the paper with a pencil. Let it set overnight. Tiny crystals will form on the bottom of the jar because some of the water evaporates.

6. Decant the solution from the second jar into a third container. Look at the crystals left in the bottom of the second jar. Select one well-formed baby crystal, and put it in the bottom of the third container, put on the paper with the holes in it, and let it set overnight. Pour the extra liquid and solid material into the stock solution jar.

7. The next day, use a pair of plastic or stainless steel tweezers to remove the crystal. Wipe it clean and put it back into the jar.

8. Keep doing this as long as you want. Each day or two, remove the growing crystal, wipe it clean, and return it to the jar. Add more solution from the stock solution as you need to. Remove unwanted crystals as they form and add them to the stock. Figure 4.6 shows crystals of copper sulfate after different periods of growth.

Inquiry questions to investigate: Does the rate of evaporation affect the rate of growth of the crystals? Does the temperature of the solution affect the amount of copper sulfate that will dissolve in the water?

---

* In a saturated solution, the maximum amount of solid has been dissolved in the liquid that *can* be dissolved without changing the temperature. Normally the higher the temperature of the liquid, the more the solid that can be dissolved.

FIGURE 4.6   Copper sulfate crystals grown in a science classroom. Left to right: 3 months, 1 month, 2 weeks, 6 days, 1 day.

conspicuous variables and devising means of controlling all identified variables except one. However, in contrast to formal operational individuals, concrete operational people have difficulty discovering less evident variables. For example, they might have difficulty suggesting the effect of air resistance on freely-falling objects; if a light ball and a heavy ball were dropped at the same time, air resistance may slow the light ball's rate of descent, causing the heavy ball to hit the floor before the light ball. Concrete operational children may reason that the heavier ball falls faster because it is heavier, the possible interference of the air not occurring to them. They often have difficulty with testing hypotheses about phenomena when their preconceived theories are strong; in these situations, they tend either to ignore or to distort data that contradict their preconceived beliefs. Part of the potential difficulty with the light ball—heavy ball experiment may be due to prior beliefs. The pendulum activity suggested in Chapter Three is a good example of the opportunity to distort or ignore data; if one believes, for example, the height of the drop influences the rate of swing, one may selectively record data to prove that hypothesis correct.

IN THE SCHOOLS 4.6
Effect of Salt on How Long It Takes to Heat Water

In a fifth-grade class, children gathered data to show the effect of adding salt to water on how long it takes the water to heat. They placed beakers with measured amounts of water in them on hot plates, and then added different amounts of salt to the water. They used thermometers to record the temperature of the water at given intervals. If an individual believes the salt will cause the water to take less time to heat to a certain temperature, he will tend to record those data that support his hypothesis, omit data that refutes it, and interpret fractional parts of data in favor of supporting his hypothesis. (Note: adding salt to water increases the length of time it takes the water to heat, and raises its boiling point to well above 100° Celsius.)

Literature connection:
A Wrinkle In Time by Madeleine L'Engle (Dell, 1962). In the Murry household, many science experiments are performed using ingredients found in the cupboards.

Concrete operational individuals possess improved understanding of space, including geographic locations, and of time, including time lines. Whereas the teacher of preoperational children would not ask them to construct maps of their town or school yard, concrete operational children are quite capable of perceiving the space and size ratios necessary to draw maps. They also are capable of understanding the relationship between time and length of a line in order to construct meaningful time lines.

IN THE SCHOOLS 4.7
A Geologic Time Line

A time line showing the entire period of geologic time from the formation of the earth to the present can be drawn on a length of adding machine tape about 10 feet long. The period of time that represents human inhabitation of the earth is less than 1 mm in length. Concrete operational children can not only construct such a time line, but they can internalize the relative brevity of human life on earth (as well as the relative lengths of other major events in the history of the earth).
(See Figure 12.18 for the Geologic Time Scale.)

Concrete operational children have the capability of understanding elementary probabilities, ratios, proportions, and variations, and can calculate, for example, the ratio between number of boys and girls in the class, the length of lines represented by given periods of time, and the ratios involved in constructing scaled models of the earth and the solar system. (See Constructing Science in the Classroom 3.44, p. 140, and 3.45, p. 141, and Figure 3.24, p. 143.) Elementary science teachers of concrete operational children encourage manipulation of actual materials. Mental manipulations have their place in the mind of the concrete operational child, but, to the extent possible, thinking must be backed up concretely. Thus, questions posed for investigation result from everyday observations.

IN THE SCHOOLS 4.8
Investigating Laundry

Ernst Von Glaserfeld and Jack Lochhead tell of a teacher whose seventh grade class investigated the problem of why underwear seems to get turned inside-out in the dryer. The problem arose from ordinary observations and became the focus of a year-long study. Children devised experimental procedures to test hypotheses they proposed; they counted numbers of right-side-out and inside-out underwear after each different kind of experimental treatment; they calculated probabilities, and the deviations from expected probabilities. They even wrote to relatives in Europe asking them to replicate the experiments to see if continent made a difference. This was a constructivist project, process in orientation, which utilized the full intellectual potential of the concrete operational child.

Formal Operational Stage

The primary difference between the concrete operational and the formal operational stages is that in the formal operational stage, people have the ability to think and reason abstractly without requiring concrete examples. They are not bound by the present and they are not bound by the concrete. Many children in elementary grades are capable of some degree of formal operational thought.

In Piagetian theory, formal operations is the ultimate achievement in human intellectual development. One must have progressed through the preceding three stages in order to arrive at a developmental stage that permits internal abstract thinking. However, mere arrival at that stage does not imply the individual is employing formal operational thinking. These powers of thought must be developed.

Lawson (1978) has identified five aspects of formal operations (abstract thinking): proportional reasoning, isolation and control of variables, probabilistic reasoning, correlational reasoning, and combinatorial reasoning.

Proportions are utilized in comparing the relationships between variables such as distance and mass in balancing weights on a balance beam.

IN THE SCHOOLS 4.9
Proportions of M&M Colors

A teacher passed out bags of M&M plain chocolate candy to groups in a fifth grade class and asked them to count the numbers of each color and calculate the percentage of each. The percentages of each group were compared, and a class average was computed. These percentages were then used to predict the number of each color that would be contained in an unopened bag of the candies.

Information for teachers: On average, a bag of M&M plain chocolate candies contains following percentages:[3]

>   30% brown
>   20% yellow
>   20% red
>   10% orange
>   10% green
>   10% tan or blue

Isolation and control of variables refers to the ability to identify the variables that bear on a given hypothesis, distinguish those that are to be manipulated from those that must be held constant, and devise ways to ensure that the result of the experiment is caused by the manipulated variable, and not by something else. The pendulum investigation (Chapter Three) ia a good example of an activity that requires isolation and control of variables.

IN THE SCHOOLS 4.10
What Keeps Plants Healthy?

Kuhn and Brannock (1977) describe a plant problem. Four plants were displayed on a table, two of which appeared healthy while the other two were obviously in poor condition. Next to each plant were glasses of water, plant food, and bottles of leaf lotion as follows:

Healthy Plant #1: Large glass of water, light-colored plant food

Healthy Plant #2: Small glass of water, light-colored plant food, bottle of leaf lotion

Non-Healthy Plant #1: Large glass of water, dark plant food, bottle of leaf lotion

Non-Healthy Plant #2: Small glass of water, dark plant food

The teacher explained that she had cared for each of the plants with weekly doses of those materials displayed next to each plant. She then asked the children what she ought to use in caring for her plants in the future. Children must be able to isolate the four variables (plant health, amount of water, type of plant food, and use of leaf lotion), and infer which is (are) operative. (In this case, only the type of plant food seemed to operate on the health of the plants.) As an extension of this isolation of variables activity, children can develop their own experimental procedures.

Probabilistic reasoning includes such phenomena as coin tosses, lottery chances, and the like. Interpreting Punnett Squares in Mendelian genetics requires probabilistic reasoning. The Punnett Square represents crossing the male and female of a species, from which the probabilities of offspring possessing certain characteristics can be calculated. (See Figure 4.7.) Children can integrate this concept with mathematics using probabilities to interpret data about offspring from graphs. Environmental studies often include estimating the probability of given occurrences, as, for example, the probability of camouflaged insects being discovered.

PUNNETT SQUARE

		FEMALE	
		T	t
MALE	T	TT	Tt
	t	Tt	tt

Punnett square showing probabilities resulting from crossing two pea plants hybrid for height.

Genes for height: T = Tall; t = short

Tall (T) is dominant over short (t).

RESULTS

75% probability a resulting plant will be tall (TT or Tt)
25% probability a resulting plant will be short (tt)

25% probability a resulting plant will be pure tall (TT)
50% probability a resulting plant will be hybrid tall (Tt)
25% probability a resulting plant will be pure short (tt)

FIGURE 4.7

IN THE SCHOOLS 4.11
Camouflage

A natural camouflage activity that fosters development of probabilistic reasoning involves counting the number of colored toothpicks that can be picked up in a given period of time from a measured area of grass. The teacher measures several adjacent 1-meter squares of grass in the school yard, and outlines them with string. Teams of children work together at each square. One child is designated "It," and turns around while another child scatters a given number of toothpicks of various colors throughout the measured square. (For example, the toothpicks may include 10 each of white, red, blue, green, and orange.) At a signal, "It" turns around and gathers as many toothpicks as possible in, say, one minute. The team then counts the number of each color, and records the results. After each member of the team has had a chance to be "It," the data from the entire team, and, ultimately, from the entire class is combined. The results indicate the probability of a given color of toothpick being selected. This principle carries over to insect camouflage and other natural protection phenomena.

Literature connections:

Alice by Whoopi Goldberg (Bantam, 1992). This is a humorous tale of Alice and her great desire to win the sweepstakes. Entering every contest imaginable, Alice is notified that she won a prize but does not realize it may not be what she had imagined.

Jumanji by Chris Van Allsburg (Houghton Mifflin, 1981). In this wild adventure, two children are trapped playing a board game that comes to life. The only way to save themselves from the volcanic eruption is to roll a pair of sixes with the dice. What are the odds that they can succeed?

Correlation, by definition, is the extent to which changes in one variable are associated with changes in another variable. Correlation does not imply causation; correlation is simply congruence in change. For example, there is a correlation between grade point average in college and amount of study, and there is a correlation between people's vocabulary and the quality of their term papers. Correlations for variables that increase or decrease together are *positive* correlations. However, if one variable increases while the other decreases, the correlation between the two is *negative*. The relationship between exercise and stress is negative; to a point, the greater the exercise, the lower the stress. If there is no relationship between two variables (such as the relationship between amount of money in people's pockets and their height), the correlation is *zero*.

Much scientific experimentation seeks to establish the presence and degree of correlation between two variables. Although one cannot establish a cause and effect from correlation alone, a consistently high positive or negative correlation between two variables suggests the possibility of a cause-and-effect that warrants further investigation. In the inside-out underwear investigation (In The Schools 4.8, p. 175), if it were to be shown that there were a higher incidence of inside-out underwear in the southern hemisphere than in the northern hemisphere (all other variables being equal) one might want to investigate possible cause and effect reasons.

Combinatorial reasoning refers to the statistics of permutations (how many ways one can arrange a given number of items in sequence) and combinations (how many ways one can arrange a given number of items in certain pre-determined combinations). Combinatorial reasoning is used in establishing the number of different causal effects possible from interactions of more than one variable. A good example is the increasing complexity of the moon crater investigation discussed in Chapter Three.

Stage Overlapping

According to Piagetian stage theory, individuals go through all the cognitive development stages in order. However, people function to some extent in all stages preceding and including the one they are in. For instance, children in the concrete operational stage also function to a certain extent at the sensorimotor stage and the preoperational stage. It is important to note that the ages and grades Piaget originally identified with the stages are flexible, and that children once thought to be solely in the preoperational stage may well have the intellectual capacity to function to a certain extent in the concrete operational stage. Many individuals in the concrete operational stage can, and do, function in formal operational ways; these individuals have been stimulated through challenging situations to use increasingly abstract and complex forms of thought. Conversely, many college students function at the concrete operational stage, never having been required to perform successfully at the formal operations level. One of the goals of science education is the development of higher order thinking skills, and the alert teacher will ensure that children are challenged to think for themselves.

Dinosaurs and the Solar System

Many schools encourage the study of dinosaurs and the solar system in kindergarten and first grade when most children are still in the preoperational stage of cognitive development. Can preoperational children comprehend these concepts? Legions of stories tell of children coming home with descriptions of dinosaurs. "How big were they?" asks Mother. "This big," replies the child, holding her thumb and forefinger as far apart as they will go. The child is representing the size of the toy dinosaur she saw in school.

Preoperational children do not have the mental capability to abstract from a model to an actual size in proportional terms. That is to say, given a toy model of a dinosaur, the preoperational child cannot visualize it to be one hundred or one thousand times larger in real life. Preoperational children *must* experience life-sized replicas of dinosaurs. Providing for this is not difficult.

IN THE SCHOOLS 4.12
Size of the Dinosaurs

How big were the dinosaurs? Obtain the dimensions of several dinosaurs. Sketch them out on large sheets of butcher paper and cut them out. You wil probably have to use the gymnasium or the cafeteria in order to have enough room, and you will have to mount the finished product on the gymnasium or cafeteria wall.

IN THE SCHOOLS 4.13
Lengths of Dinosaurs

How long were the dinosaurs? Children obtain essential information about dinosaurs of their choice, and record this information in a booklet about their dinosaur. They may cut out a small model of their dinosaur to show its overall shape. In the hall, the teacher lays out a long strip of wide adding machine tape which has been marked into one-foot segments. Each child, in turn, places his dinosaur cut-out on the foot marker on the adding machine strip that represents how long the animal was. Or, children lay down on the adding machine strip, head to toe, until the entire length of the dinosaur has been filled with children. Then, they count how many children it takes to make one of each kind of dinosaur.

In these activities, the children see the *actual* sizes of dinosaurs. In addition, their concrete operational skills are being developed through comparison and through observation of actual dimensions.

Many excellent pieces of children's literature dealing with dinosaurs are available.

An Alphabet of Dinosaurs by Peter Dodson (Scholastic, 1995) is a book of information about familiar and newly-discovered dinosaurs focusing on they way these creatures lived.

Dinosaur Fun Book by Karen Moore and *Dino Dave's Dinosaur Coloring Book* (Dinocardz, 1994) show realistic outline drawings of dinosaurs in their natural habitats and provide many interesting facts about dinosaurs. The period of time when each dinosaur lived is depicted on a geologic time scale. This company also markets sets of illustrated dinosaur flash cards with many facts on the reverse of each card.

The Dinosaur Who Lived In My Back Yard by B. G. Hennesy (Puffin Books, 1988) compares sizes of dinosaurs with things children are familiar with. "By the time he was 5, he was as big as our car."

Dinosaurs For Every Kid by Janice Van Cleave (John Wiley & Sons, 1994) contains a wealth of information and many activities for learning about dinosaurs.

The Magic School Bus In the Time of Dinosaurs by Joanna Cole (Scholastic, 1994). Children explore the age of dinosaurs and many life forms that thrived during that time. A geologic time scale shows the relative period involved.

Big Book of Science Charts: Dinosaurs (Teacher Created Materials, 1992) contains drawings and facts about nine dinosaurs together with suggested activities and resources of additional material.

How appropriate is studying the earth, the planets, and interplanetary space in the early elementary grades? The preoperational child can compare distances and sizes relative to each other, but cannot be expected to relate a scaled model of the solar system to the actual solar system. The Temperature of the Planets activity (In The Schools 3.21, p. 142) is a good example of this phenomenon. In this activity, children are asked to discover that there is a relationship between how hot something gets and how far away it is from the source of heat. They are also asked to extend their thinking along these lines to the solar system. Most preoperational children will understand the relationship, and will be able to extend their thinking to the solar system, but they will not be able to visualize the distances involved in the solar system. The *only* way the planetary system can be represented is through models, and preoperational children cannot visualize the relationship between models of something they can not see and the real thing. A model of the planetary system is, to the preoperational child, relatively meaningless. The solution for cases of not being able to represent something in its true dimensions is to leave it out of the early childhood curriculum. There is plenty of time to study these topics as the child develops greater ability to reason abstractly. This is not to say that all studies of astronomy should be omitted from the early childhood science program; there are many topics appropriate for investigation by preoperational children, such as phases of the moon, constellations, stars, planets, comets, and other celestial objects that can be viewed through a telescope or can be shown in picture form. What ought *not* to be introduced to preoperational children is material that requires intellectual skills they do not yet have, such as the skill of proportionality in model representation. Perhaps the biggest contribution the study of the solar system can make to the intellectual development of the preoperational child is in the arena of imagination. The activities on the following pages use the magic of the moon, planets, and space to stimulate imagination and develop creativity.

IN THE SCHOOLS 4.14
Let's Make a Constellation

Give children gold or silver stars and black paper. Have them arrange the stars in the shape of a constellation without connecting the stars with lines. Then have other children guess what the constellation they invent is. Finally, the child who made the constellation can reveal what it was supposed to represent, and, if desired, connect the stars. (See Figure 4.8.) Processes fostered: communicating; inferring.

To help children understand actual constellations, trace a set of constellations on a piece of white paper, and poke holes in the stars with a pin—small holes for dim stars and larger holes for bright stars. Project on a screen using the overhead projector. (See Figure 4.9.)

Literature connections:
Tigerella by Kit Wright (Scholastic, 1993). A girl tiger explores the night sky and constellations.

Sky Songs by Myra Cohn Livingston (Holiday House, 1984) is a collection of poetry of the beautiful and mysterious changes in the sky that occur from day to night and with weather conditions. The acrylic paintings are bold and lively.

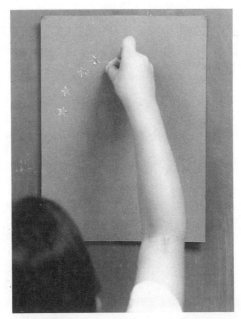

FIGURE 4.8 Constructing constellations

Isn't this
the Big
Dipper?

FIGURE 4.9 Exploring constellations

IN THE SCHOOLS 4.15
Holding a Star-Gazing Session

If children are going to investigate the stars, the best time for them to do this is at night when the stars are out. Constructing Science in the Classroom 4.2 offers details for holding a star-gazing session with young children.

Literature connections:

The Night of the Stars by Maria Oliver and Douglas Guterrez (Kane Miller, 1988). A Native American man did not like the darkness of night so he stood on the mountain top and poked a hole into the dark sky. He continued poking holes until little sparks of light were visible, creating the beginning of our stars and moon.

Boat Ride with Lillian Two Blossom by Patricia Polacco (Philomel Books, 1988). A Native American Lady takes two children on a boat ride in the sky. She explains how the apparance of the sky changes because of magical spirits.

Marcella and the Moon by Laura Jan Coats (Macmillan, 1986). Marcella paints the moon as it goes through its phases.

CONSTRUCTING SCIENCE IN THE CLASSROOM 4.2
How To Hold a Star-Gazing Session

GRADE

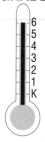

1. WHEN TO HOLD IT

Season: Best viewing is late fall or early winter.

Time: After dark. Allow about 1 hour after sunset for the sky to get dark. Then allow 20 minutes for eyes to get used to the dark. Try to avoid holding it when the full moon is high in the sky. Set an alternate date in case the sky is cloudy. Allow about an hour.

2. WHERE TO HOLD IT

Some place dark—away from buildings and tall trees—away from street lights. An open park or the school yard where the personnel will turn off the lights are ideal places. But, be sure trees and building walls don't get in the way of viewing the lower portion of the sky. *Scope it out first!*

3. WHAT TO BRING

Binoculars—Monoculars—Telescopes

Star maps and star charts

Flashlights. Flashlights should be covered with red cellophane (two or three layers of red cellophane from cheese wrapping is fine). This avoids people being blinded by the lights.

Warm clothing (It gets cold out there at night!)

4. WHAT TO LOOK FOR

A. If the moon is out, you can see craters and other features very well through binoculars. Also, children can speculate on the cause of the moon's current phase—have them visualize where the sun just set.

B. Planets —check local papers or science periodicals for listings of which planets are visible. Show children how to find this information for themselves. Most likely planets are Mars, Jupiter, and Saturn. (You can see Venus in the early morning.) You can see the moons around Jupiter with binoculars; there may be two, three, or four moons lined up around the planet. The rings of Saturn are visible with low-powered telescopes. How can you tell a planet from a star? (1) Planets are brighter than the stars in the area. (2) Planets tend to "glow" rather than "twinkle." (3) Planets are on an imaginary line that connects the position of the moon with the position where the sun set (called the *ecliptic*).

C. Stars—Observe differences in stars—differences in *brightness* and differences in *color* (white, blue-white, blue, yellow, green, red).

D. Constellations in the Northern Sky

Big Dipper (Part of *Ursa Major*)—This is an open cluster of 5 stars. *Mizar* (2nd star in the handle) is a double star. You can see two stars instead of one if you look slightly *away* from the star. The two stars in the bowl of the Big Dipper point toward the North Star.

Little Dipper (*Ursa Minor*)—The last star in its handle is the North Star (also called "Polaris").

Cassiopeia, the Ethiopian Queen, is shaped like a "W."

Cepheus, the Ethiopian King, is the "hat."

E. Prominent Late Autumn and Early Winter Constellations

Orion, the Hunter, is a very prominent constellation. Look for three bright stars lined up in a row and somewhat inclined to the horizon. These are Orion's "belt." One of the shoulders is a red star named *Betelgeuse* (pronounced "beetlejuice") and is a red giant. *Orion* contains the *Great Nebula of Orion*, a cloud of gas in the process of coming together to form a new star. This is the middle "star" in *Orion's* sword—but, this middle star isn't a star at all—it is the Nebula. It is dramatic to look at it with binoculars or a small telescope.

Big Dog (*Canis Major*) follows *Orion* around the sky, and contains **Sirius**, the brightest star in the sky.

F. Other Constellations Visible During Each Season

Autumn:	*Pegasus*	*Ophiuchus*
	Andromeda	*Serpens Caput*
	Aries	*Serpens Cauda*
	Triangulum	*Taurus*
	Perseus	*Pisces*
	Auriga	
Spring:	*Leo*	*Bootes*
	Virgo	*Corona Borealis*
	Cancer	
Summer:	*Cygnus*	*Lyra*
	Sagitta	*Scorpius*
	Hercules	

Conclusion

There is an "emerging consensus among psychologists, science educators, philosophers of science, and others that learners (including scientists) must construct and reconstruct their own meaning about how the world works" (Good, Wandersee & St. Julian, 1993, p. 74). Yager wrote that "Constructivist teaching is now offered by many as a way of reforming science education. Basic to this view of learning is the idea that each learner must construct meaning for him- or herself" (Yager, 1993, p. 146). Teachers of elementary science must encourage children to construct their own meanings of scientific concepts, develop their own understandings of the uses and nature of the processes, and apply science to their lives in ways that are meaningful to them, the children. Teachers of elementary science also must understand the intellectual limitations and advantages available to children as they progress through the stages of cognitive development. Combining intellectual capability with individual construction will ensure a meaningful science program—one that will meet the goals and objectives of science education.

In an address to the Holmes Group, Judith Lanier, then Dean of the College of Education at Michigan State University, said:

> Competent teachers jump into the heads of their students to see how they are constructing information . . . Competent teachers combine content knowledge with a flexible and creative mind, constructing and reconstructing subject matter in multiple ways as they teach the children. They get inside the children's heads. They listen to them. They remain alert to *students'* interpretations and the ways *they* are making sense (Lanier, 1987).

This is the essence of constructivism.

CHAPTER 4   Additional Questions for Discussion

1. Discuss the significance of the quotation that opens this chapter: "The most important factor influencing learning is what the learner already knows."
2. Discuss ways in which your prior beliefs have influenced what you learned or were unable to learn.
3. In Chapter One, the point was made that our beliefs about science and about teaching science, together with our metaphoric perspective of teaching, exert a strong influence on how we approach teaching elementary science. Discuss this proposition in terms of constructivist theory.

Notes

1. Epistemology refers to the study of the nature and grounds of knowledge, especially with reference to its limits and validity.

2. I am indebted to Dr. Russell Yeany, Dean, College of Education, University of Georgia, Athens, GA, for summary material presented at a symposium on constructivist teaching of science at the Georgia Academy of Science annual meeting, April, 1993.

3. These proportions were provided by officials of Mars, Incorporated, makers of M&M Plain Chocolate Candies. A free teacher's packet about chocolate, candy, and M&M's is available from M&M*Mars, High Street, Hackettstown, NJ 07840.

References

Adams, P., Mitchener, C., & Johnson, V. (1987). *Water Magic.* Cleveland: Modern Curriculum Press.

Allen, J. (1993). *Elephant.* Cambridge, Mass.: Candlewick Press.

Ausubel, D. P., Novak, J. D., and Hanesian, H. (1978). *Educational Psychology: A Cognitive View.* Second Ed. New York: Holt, Rinehart and Winston, p. iv.

Big Book of Science Charts: Dinosaurs. (1992). Teacher Created Materials, P.O. Box 1214, Huntington Beach, CA 92647.

Coats, L. J. (1986). *Marcella and the Moon.* New York: Macmillan.

Cobern, W. W. (1993). *Contextual Constructivism: The Impact of Culture on the Learning and Teaching of Science.* In Tobin, K. (Ed.) (1993). *The practice of constructivism in science education.* Hillsdale, NJ: Lawrence Erlbaum Associates, Publishers. 51–69.

Cole, J. (1994). *The Magic School Bus in the Time of the Dinosaurs.* New York: Scholastic.

Dodson, P. (1995). *An Alphabet of Dinosaurs.* New York: Scholastic.

Goldberg, W. (1992). *Alice.* New York: Bantam Books.

Good, R. G., Wandersee, J. H., & St. Julien, J. (1993). *Cautionary notes on the appeal of the new "Ism" (constructivism) in science education,* Chapter 5 in Tobin, K., (Ed.) (1993). *The Practice of Constructivism in Science Education.* Hillsdale, NJ: Lawrence Erlbaum Associates, Publishers.

Gutierrez, D. & Oliver, M. (1988). *The Night of the Stars.* Brooklyn, N.Y.: Kane/Miller Book Publishers.

Hennessy, B. G. (1988). *The Dinosaur Who Lived in My Backyard.* New York: Puffin Books.

Kuhn, D. & Brannock, J. (1977). Development of the isolation of variables scheme in experimental and "natural experiment" contexts. *Developmental Psychology 13*(1), 9–14.

Lanier, J. (1987). From a tape recording of an address to the first Holmes Group conference.

Lawson, A. E. (1978). The development and validation of a classroom test of formal reasoning. *Journal of Research in Science Teaching 15*(1), 11–24.

L'Engle, M. (1962). *A Wrinkle in Time.* New York: Dell Pub. Co.

Le Guin, U. (1968). *A Wizard of Earthsea.* Berkeley, Calif.: Parnassus Press.

Livingston, M. C. (1984). *Sky Songs.* New York: Holiday House.

Moore, K. (1994). *Dino Dave's Dinosaur Coloring Book.* Dinocardz Company, 4339 California Street, San Francisco, CA 94118.

———. (1994). *Dinosaur Fun Book.* Dinocardz Company, 4339 California Street, San Francisco, CA 94118.

Placco, P. (1988). *Boat Ride With Lillian Two Blossom.* New York: Philomel Books.

Salkind, N. J. (1985). *Theories of Human Development.* New York, NY: John Wiley & Sons, p. 201.

Tobin, K. 1991. *Learning How to Teach Science.* Paper presented at annual meeting of Southeastern Association for the Education of Teachers in Science, Stone Mountain, GA, 1991.

Van Allsburg, C. (1981). *Jumanji.* Boston: Houghton Mifflin Co.

Van Cleave, J. (1994). *Dinosaurs for Every Kid.* New York: John Wiley & Sons.

Vico, G. (1710). *De Antiquissima Italorum Sapientia.*

Von Glasersfeld, E. (1989). Cognition, construction of knowledge, and teaching. *Synthese 80*, 121–140.

Von Glasersfeld, E. (1991). *Knowing Without Metaphysics: Aspects of the Radical Constructivist Position.* In Steier, F. *Research and reflexivity.* London: SAGE Publications.

Yager, R. E. (1993). The need for reform in science teacher education. *Journal of Science Teacher Education 4*(4), 144–148.

CHAPTER 5

Inquiry

In the first four chapters, you explored a number of concepts related to teaching science to young children. You examined the concept of scientific products *vs.* scientific processes as the primary goal of elementary science education, and you considered the proposition that there is very little in the way of scientific facts, concepts, generalizations, theories, and laws that *all* elementary children must know. You considered utilizing those products of science that are of interest and relevance to children as vehicles for teaching the processes. You explored the suggestion that it is better for children to understand *how* science is done than to know the results of what has been done by others; that it is better for children to *do* science and to be able to pose and investigate their own questions than to verify the results that have been concluded by others.

You also examined the constructivist viewpoint of learning which suggests children learn only by constructing their own conceptualizations; that they must make their own meaningful connections between what they already know and the new information they encounter. You considered the notion that the responsibility of the teacher is that of a facilitator of learning rather than imparter of information.

Now the question arises as to how to accomplish these goals. In this chapter, you will construct your understanding of the *process-oriented guided inquiry* methodology of science teaching.

The Expository-Discovery Continuum

Many teaching methodologies have been described by various educators. Competent teachers develop an ever-expanding repertoire of teaching techniques which they use as they make decisions about which techniques are most appropriate for the situation at hand. These methodological decisions are based on the nature of the material to be studied, the personality of the teacher, the age, intelligence, interests, and prior experiences of the children, and many other factors. No *single* method meets the needs of *all* children.

Teaching methodologies can be arranged on the basis of the relative amounts of teacher and learner contribution to the learning situation. Consider the continuum in Figure 5.1.

FIGURE 5.1   Expository-discovery continuum of teaching methodologies

This continuum represents a succession of teaching methodologies between a hypothetical totally teacher-dominated *expository* methodology on the left and a hypothetical totally student-dominated *free discovery* methodology on the right. Any given lesson can be located somewhere on this continuum, depending on the relative degree of expository and discovery activities included in the lesson.

At the left end of the continuum (no political analogy implied) is the expository methodology. Expository teaching centers around the teacher as the controller of the class and the imparter of knowledge. The teacher does the work, and the student, who may or may not be engaged in the learning, is supposed to absorb the information. The most characteristic activity of the expository methodology is the lecture.

At the right end of the continuum is the free discovery methodology. Free discovery is characterized by children exploring subjects of their own interest in ways most comfortable to them. The teacher is the facilitator. Students are engaged in a variety of activities such as experimenting, reading, writing, discussing, and other ways of exploring.

Somewhere near the center of the continuum, about half way between the expository and the free discovery modes, is a broad band representing the guided inquiry methodology. In guided inquiry, teachers facilitate children in their investigations of teacher-established topics in ways that are comfortable to the children and which also stimulate children to ask and investigate additional questions suggested by the original explorations.

Expository Methodology

Expository teaching is teacher-dominated. The teacher decides what is to be taught. The teacher lectures, provides notes, shows videos, explains charts, solves sample problems, demonstrates laboratory exercises, reads stories, and so on. All these activities focus on the teacher. What the teacher says is what is to be learned; the teacher is the source and the owner of the knowledge. The students may or may not be involved cognitively; the teacher has no way of knowing except to stop and ask children to summarize as they would when reading a story, and even then, the understandings internalized by the children may not be apparent.

The expository methodology has its place in science education, especially when new information is to be presented to the entire class as background for upcoming studies. Often it is desirable to demonstrate an activity before setting children to work on their own. When giving directions, it is necessary that the teacher have the attention of all the children. Explanations of certain scientific concepts such as nuclear energy, atomic theory, and cellular structure are best handled in an expository mode with the whole class. There are certain scientific procedures best illustrated through demonstration, such as working with certain chemicals or using expensive equipment. Lesson summaries and closures often are best accomplished in an expository mode. Other advantages of expository teaching include efficient dissemination of information, uniformity of presentation, and clear development of the topic.

However, there are serious disadvantages, including the very uncertain degree of attention of the children, lack of tailoring the lesson to the needs of each child, the inability of children to follow the flow of the lesson at the same pace, and the potential lack of relevance of the material to children's lives. Jerome Bruner argued that expository teaching has "two major weaknesses: (1) It makes the learner passive, and (2) the knowledge presented is inert" (Eggen & Kauchak, 1994, p. 411). He cited several disadvantages to expository teaching, including the following:

1. Expository teaching leads to over-dependence on the teacher.
2. Children learn only what the teacher presents.
3. Expository teaching results in reduced ability to use the material and the thinking processes outside the classroom.

Free Discovery Methodology

The free discovery methodology is located at the extreme right on the Expository-Discovery continuum. The following activity is described to help you gain an idea of what free discovery is like.

SAND

My family and I lived for a time in the Kingdom of Saudi Arabia where I taught middle grades science. When we returned to the United States, we brought with us samples of different kinds of sand from different regions of the Saudi Arabian desert. (See map in Figure 5.2.) One sand came from the far reaches of the *Rub' al Khali* (or Empty Quarter). The *Rub' al Khali* occupies the south central portion of the Arabian Peninsula; nearly the size of Texas, it is the largest continuous expanse of sand in the world (Lebkicher, Rentz & Steineke, 1960, p. 275). Sand mountains in the *Rub' al Khali* are several hundred meters high, rising out of salt flats which are nearly at sea level. The temperatures in the *Rub' al Khali* soar to over 140° F. in the daytime in summer, and sink to as low as 25° F at night in winter (Nawwab, Speers & Hoye, 1980, p. 114, 240). The sand from the *Rub' al Khali* is very fine, like the sand in hour glass egg timers, and is reddish-orange in color, like rust or ground cinnamon. This sand is uniform in consistency.

The second kind of sand is ordinary beach sand that comes from the dunes near the beaches on the Arabian Gulf. The dunes were formed from the accumulation of wind-blown sand. This sand is yellowish-white in color, contains a few impurities, and is much coarser than the *Rub' al Khali* sand with grains two to three times larger.

The third kind of sand comes from a region near the Arabian Gulf called *Al-Uqair*. This region is thought to include the remains of the ancient city of *Gerrah* described by Strabo and other ancient Greeks as being at the crossroads of ancient trade in Arabia and containing buildings whose "doors, walls, and roofs are variegated with inlaid ivory, gold, silver, and precious stones" (Bibby, 1970, p. 318). Geoffrey Bibby, a Danish archaeologist, concentrated exploratory efforts for several seasons on locating and identifying this ancient city, and came to the conclusion that circumstantial evidence at *Al-Uqair* (coupled with the lack of evidence at other sites) indicated this site may indeed be the ruins of the ancient city. Nothing remains at the site except assemblages of potsherds and ancient irrigation ditches. The sand that comes from this area is a little deeper yellow than the beach sand and contains very fine dark gray flecks which, curiously, always remain at the top of the sand no matter how thoroughly one tries to stir them in. Its grains are uniform and are about the same size as the beach sand.

In a free discovery activity, groups of elementary science methods students are asked to explore samples of each of the three kinds of sand in any way they wish. After 15–20 minutes, during which time I have circulated and asked questions to help people focus their inquiries, groups are asked to share what they found out. Descriptions of the sand samples are among the first discoveries shared: color, texture, grain size, impurities, and so on. Then groups get into deeper questions, such as, "Why is the red sand red?" "Why does the beach sand look like it has been 'bleached?'" "What are those dark flecks mixed in with the Gerrah sand?" Finally, I pose the question, "If you had sufficient funds, time, and equipment at your disposal, what would your next step in your investigation be?" Some say they would like to subject the sands to chemical analyses to find their origins and the reason for the different colors. Others would like to have large sand boxes of each of the three kinds to see what it is like to walk on it, and to try to find out why camels can walk on sand so easily. Others want to study the history of the ancient town of Gerrah. One group wanted to investigate what it must have been like to have lived in the time Gerrah was inhabited. For these students, the concept of sand sparked an interest in the integrated studies of social studies and the Middle East. Still others wanted to study the geology of the region and correlate it with the origins of the sand. Once in a while a group has the courage to say their next step would involve anything *except* sand!

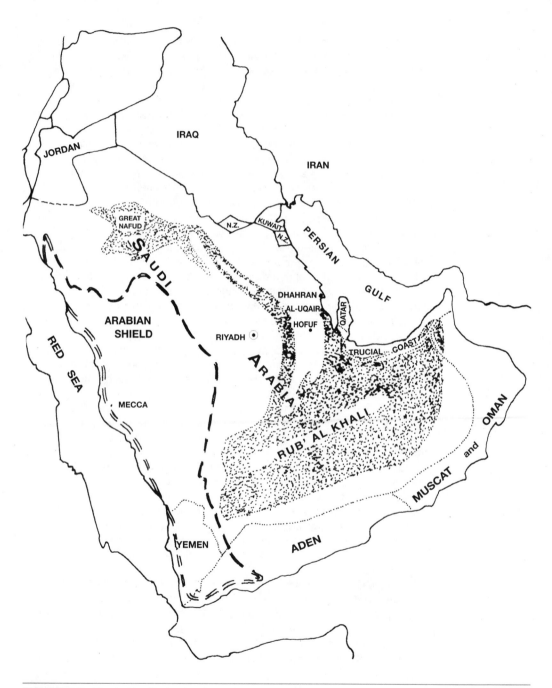

FIGURE 5.2   The Arabian Peninsula

This is an example of a free discovery activity. The only factor keeping it from the extreme right side of the continuum is the fact that the general topic (sand) was suggested by the teacher.

CONSTRUCTING YOUR IDEAS 5.1
Investigating Through Free Discovery

Try this. Find something to investigate on your own, something that is not too complex, something that might capture your interest. Spend about a half hour figuring things out about your topic. Then report back to the class (1) what your study was about, (2) what you found out, and (3) what you would do next if you had adequate funds, time, and equipment. Suggestions might include figuring out something about batteries, shells, clouds, fossils, rocks, recycling, water, the sea, snow, frogs, or flowers. Anything would work. All you have to do is identify something worth figuring something out about, and then do it.

Reflect on how you felt about doing this activity. Did it leave you excited? Interested? Disinterested? Empowered? Free? Frustrated? Confused? Directionless?

Discuss your feelings as a class.

In free discovery, children decide what is important for them to learn; children set up their individual and unique learning activities to explore the topics they have chosen; they devise and explore their own inquiry situations; they go to the references to see what has been learned before. The teacher acts as a resource and co-inquirer. The students are deeply involved cognitively.

Bruner urged involving students as active inquirers in the material they are learning. In discovery, children inquire into scientific phenomena, figuring things out for themselves. This, according to Bruner, is the route to meaningful learning. "Mastery of the fundamental ideas of a field involves not only the grasping of general principles, but also the development of an attitude toward learning and inquiry, toward guessing and hunches, toward the possibility of solving problems on one's own" (Bruner, 1965, p. 20).

The primary advantages of the free discovery teaching methodology include the facilitation of the constructivistic paradigm, the cognitive engagement of all children (for they will not be studying something which does not interest them), the ability to develop process skills, and the meaningfulness of the material learned.

There also are disadvantages to free discovery as a teaching methodology. Chief among the criticisms are that discovery learning does not provide enough structure, can lead to frustration in the beginning as children wean themselves from dependence on the teacher, and reduces the teacher's control of content. Free discovery also may present management problems for when employing this methodology, it is possible for each child in the classroom to be studying something different at the same time. (However, at the pre-kindergarten and kindergarten levels, this is not a significant problem.)

Guided Inquiry Methodology

The guided inquiry methodology is located at the middle of the continuum. Guided inquiry combines the teacher focus of the expository methodology with the child focus of the free discovery methodology. In guided inquiry, the teacher sets the direction, and the children ask questions which, in turn, set new directions. The teacher suggests open-ended activities which the children pursue to find out what they are able to find out, inquire into what they don't understand, and develop their own conclusions as they construct their own conceptualizations. The children check their conclusions against further investigations to see if they possess validity, and they discuss their conclusions with one another and with the teacher to confirm validity or to embark on further investigation to develop revised conclusions and reconstructed conceptualizations. The activities suggested in this text are developed under the constructivist guided inquiry methodological paradigm.

Guided inquiry involves learning by doing. The teacher serves as guide (not director), the resource person, and the co-inquirer. The teacher selects the topic, introduces the unit and the lessons, and provides structure for the investigations. The teacher develops the initial activity, and has a variety of additional activities available. The teacher asks questions, and helps the students in their *own* endeavors, *not* the teacher's. The teacher *listens*—seeking to understand what the student is saying. She probes. She asks more questions, some of which are leading questions, and some of which are intended to help her find out the children's thinking. The classroom is hands-on and laboratory in focus, and typically features small groups of children working together. Students work to construct meanings and discover concepts that are new to them.

In the beginning of a lesson, the teacher may provide a high degree of guidance, but as the lesson proceeds, she works toward reducing the teacher-centered focus and increasing the student-centered focus. She provides both opportunity and fun. She radiates the enthusiasm of a co-inquirer.

The guided inquiry teaching methodology encourages children to construct their own conceptualizations while at the same time exposing them to the content suggested for the grade or level. It allows children to pursue given topics in depth; it permits children to ask and investigate their own questions. Guided inquiry provides enough structure that the feeling of "wandering" children may get in free discovery approaches is eliminated. Children are given the parameters in which to *start* their inquiries, and are given such necessary constraints as time, group size, materials, and so on. The class is manageable, and the content of the curriculum is covered. Guided inquiry utilizes an inquiry constructivist approach in which science content is used as a vehicle for mastery of the processes.

Education students (and, for that matter, all college students) have become accustomed to expository methods of instruction. Therefore, education students need to move a little at a time from their beliefs in the merits of expository teaching to development of understanding of the merits of guided inquiry. This must be done slowly to give time to reconstruct prior conceptualizations about science teaching. Only by testing the waters and finding them safe will the trust be built up that is prerequisite to successful constructivistic approaches to teaching and learning science.

The same is true of children in the elementary grades. They may not be familiar with working and learning within the constructivist approach, and may need to move from expository to inquiry types of activities slowly. Starting children out with a few activities that are between expository and guided inquiry in approach will help provide the children the practice needed to be successful at inquiry approaches, and will gain their trust. The teacher initially sets up the situations and the problems. Later, students set up their own problem situations. In the beginning, the teacher provides a high degree of structure. As the class proceeds, she is able to reduce the structure in the activities. (See Chapter Eight for suggestions on developing a safe classroom environment for guided inquiry.) Ultimately, she poses a question or a problem, and then starts the exploration and questioning technique, letting the children decide the direction of the inquiry. The numerous activities presented in this book give you and the children the opportunity to move safely toward the guided inquiry area of the continuum.

CONSTRUCTING YOUR IDEAS 5.2
Developing Expository, Free Discovery, and Guided Inquiry Lessons

Try this. Divide your class into three groups, and select a scientific topic to be taught at a certain grade level. Then have each group develop a short ten-minute lesson in one of the three styles described above: expository, free discovery, and process-oriented guided inquiry. Present the lesson to the class, and critique the advantages, disadvantages, and feelings you encountered in each style of teaching.

Ausubel's Instructional Model

David Ausubel (1968) suggested that for learning to be meaningful, and therefore lasting, it must fit in with previous information taught in the class. Thus, in all instructional methodologies, the teacher must link new information with the previously-taught information such that children are able to make the proper connections. Ausubel proposed three stages of instruction to ensure the proper connections: *Advance Organizer*, *Progressive Differentiation*, and *Integrative Reconciliation*.

STAGE 1: ADVANCE ORGANIZER

Ausubel proposed that learning is facilitated when students are supplied with an appropriate frame of reference so new information can be related to information the students already possessed. He called this frame of reference the *advance organizer*. Before starting a lesson of any sort (whether it is a new unit, or a new lesson in an on-going unit) the teacher must provide an advance organizer. The advance organizer serves to introduce children to the new unit or to briefly review prior material when continuing an ongoing unit. It provides an overview, shows the children what to expect, and summarizes all aspects of the unit or the lesson in advance. It sets the stage. It provides focus and direction, and it captures children's interest. The advance organizer is to sound teaching what the last chapter in a good mystery is to the novel: it reveals everything. In sound teaching, we want the children to be "with us" all the way through, so we reveal what is going to happen ahead of time.

A typical advance organizer for a new unit might include an initial interest-provoking activity followed by a general discussion of what the unit entails, the unit's goals and objectives, how children will get involved, and so on. For a new lesson in an on-going unit, a typical advance organizer would remind children of previous material and would show how the current lesson is connected to prior information.

As I observe student teachers, one of the biggest difficulties I see is the lack of advance organizers. The student teacher often starts a lesson as though the children knew all along what it was all about. This is natural, for the teacher has been planning and thinking about this lesson for a long time; but, of course, the children do not know what it is all about. So, the teacher has to introduce it. Advance organizers do not have to take very long; they can be as short as a few seconds: "You remember that yesterday we measured the temperature of glasses of water as they sat in the room. Well, today we are going to add ice to the water, and see what happens to the temperature." The advance organizer can be a chart or a concept map portraying the scope of the unit; the teacher can refer to this visual portrayal at the beginning of each lesson, reminding children of prior lessons and showing them how the new lesson fits in with the whole. (See Chapter Eleven for ways of using concept maps as advance organizers.)

THE KALEIDOSCOPE

A student teacher assigned to sixth grade wrote the word "kaleidoscope" on the board, and asked the children to pronounce the word. Without comment on the correctness of their pronunciations, she proceeded to pass out inexpensive toy kaleidoscopes to pairs of children, asking them to look through them and record words that described what they saw. Since there were two different kinds of kaleidoscopes available, after a few minutes she asked the children to trade, and write more of what they saw. She then wrote the responses of all pairs on chart paper in the front of the room. Words like "diamonds," "shapes," "triangles," "brilliant," "jewels," and "crystals" were listed. Next, she read the poem, "Kaleidoscope" from *Small Poems Again* by Valerie Worth (Farrar, Straus and Giroux, 1986) to show that the poem contains many of the same words they had written on their charts, and to show relevance of poetry to daily observations. Though this was an advance organizer for a unit on poetry, it would be ideal to introduce a unit on light, mirrors, and images.

STAGE 2: PROGRESSIVE DIFFERENTIATION

Having set the tone of the lesson or the unit in the advance organizer, the next consideration is to isolate each item of information or skill so it can be connected with information previously learned. This stage is called *progressive differentiation*. The key to effective progressive differentiation is for the lesson to move from the most general to the most specific in a logical manner, making certain that all concepts necessary for understanding are included. The material is progressively differentiated.

Properly differentiated lessons flow smoothly. However, when material is not progressively differentiated properly, confusion and misunderstanding may result. This occurs when the teacher is giving directions for an activity and inadvertently leaves out a key component. For example, she may be explaining to the class how to attach paper feathers to a cutout turkey, but forgets to tell the children to cut out the feathers. This results in confusion and the necessity of stopping the class to provide the missing material. Techniques that help prevent this problem include advance practice, putting yourself in the shoes of the children in your class, and, if necessary, preparing and referring to 3x5 note cards listing all components of the directions (or the lesson).

Often the reason lessons fail is because some necessary component is left out (Okey & Gagne, 1970). Proper attention to the progressive differentiation stage of Ausubel's model in developing lesson plans will help prevent lesson failure due to omission of critical material. Concept mapping is of great assistance in ensuring proper progressive differentiation of lessons. (See Chapter Eleven.)

STAGE 3: INTEGRATIVE RECONCILIATION

Having set the stage and having progressed from the most general to the most specific in a manner which encourages children to make meaningful connections, it is now the responsibility of the teacher to be sure the children have constructed the material correctly. To do this, the teacher helps each child reconcile the new material with material previously taught and the child's own experiential bank. This stage is called *integrative reconciliation*. Integrative reconciliation helps children understand similarities and differences among components of the lesson or the unit. This stage also alerts the teacher to inconsistencies between what children are thinking and the correctness of the lesson's material, enabling the teacher to help the child reconcile these inconsistencies.

The Ausubelian stages often are associated with expository learning. However, for any lesson to be effective, regardless of methodological orientation, it must have an advance organizer, be logically sequenced, possess appropriate content, and encourage children to make valid connections with the material previously taught.

The Expository-Discovery Continuum Revisited

By now you have discovered that lessons do not easily fit a precise location on the expository-discovery continuum. All lessons require a certain amount of expository treatment: directions have to be given, introductions and advance organizers have to be provided, large group discussions may need to be included, lessons have to be concluded, and so on. There is also a certain amount of free discovery inherent in lessons in which children are asked to formulate their own questions and develop their own procedures for obtaining and validating their own conclusions. However, it should not be difficult to assess the relative amount of expository, guided inquiry, and free discovery methodology utilized in the lesson, and, from this reflection and assessment, place a lesson on the continuum. It is to be expected that the beginning elementary science teacher will have many lessons to the left of center, and that as experience and confidence is gained, the lessons will move slowly toward the right until almost all the lessons of the experienced teacher center around the guided inquiry band.

Figure 5.3 provides descriptors of constructivist teaching using the guided inquiry methodology. In the early stages of your lesson preparation and delivery, especially in your field experiences, it is suggested that you use this list to check your own teaching.

DESCRIPTORS OF PERFORMANCE

EVIDENCE OF PLANNING

1. Adequate planning; process-oriented goals are set
2. Relates lesson to *processes* more than products
3. Planning shows logical development of processes and concepts

IMPLEMENTATION

4. Provides for hands-on learning: students handle materials
5. Asks open-ended, inquiry-oriented questions
6. Encourages children to ask questions
7. Encourages children to initiate ideas
8. Encourages children to investigate their own questions and ideas
9. Uses children's questions and responses to develop topic
10. Encourages the use of many sources of information, including printed material, multimedia, and people
11. Avoids supplying answers or explanations
12. Encourages children to suggest causes for what they observe
13. Encourages children to discuss and challenge each other's conceptualizations
14. Encourages children to reflect
15. Responds to individual needs
16. Relates topics to children's lives

OVERALL LOCATION OF LESSON ON EXPOSITORY-FREE DISCOVERY CONTINUUM:

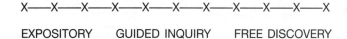

X—X—X—X—X—X—X—X—X—X—X

EXPOSITORY   GUIDED INQUIRY   FREE DISCOVERY

FIGURE 5.3 Constructivist guided inquiry teaching

The Guided Inquiry Lesson Plan

All well developed lessons require planning, and the process-oriented inquiry methodology is no exception. Lesson plans guide the teacher in introducing and developing the lesson, and provide some well thought-out questions and initial direction. Good lesson planning helps the teacher focus on the objectives and intended outcomes of the lesson.

Figure 5.4 shows a recommended format for process-oriented inquiry lesson planning.

LESSON PLAN FORMAT FOR PROCESS-ORIENTED GUIDED INQUIRY ELEMENTARY SCIENCE LESSONS

1. Targeted Grade or Age Level	1. Self-Explanatory
2. Scientific Process(es) Addressed	2. Self-Explanatory
3. Science Topic Addressed	3. That topic (fact or set of facts, generalization, concept, theory, or law) that will be used as the vehicle for exploring the process identified in Item 2
4. Process-Oriented Objective(s)	4. An objective written according to the process-oriented guidelines provided in Chapter Three
5. What Do I Want Children To Discover?	5. The scientific fact(s), generalization, concept, or theory children should be able to articulate as a result of the lesson.
6. Description of Introductory Activity and Discussion	6. Details about how you will introduce the lesson. This should contain the Ausubelian advance organizer as well as details concerning a demonstration or other interest-focusing activity, the initial discussion, directions, and safety and management considerations appropriate for the lesson.
7. Materials Needed	7. The list of materials is an integral part of the lesson plan; it enables you to assemble all necessary materials each time you do the lesson without having to search through the entire lesson plan to figure out what you will need.
8. Description of Activities	8. Details of what the children will do to explore the concept and what you will do to help them in their explorations
9. Typical Discussion Questions	9. Typical questions you will ask of groups to stimulate their thinking toward the objective
10. How Children Will Be Encouraged to Investigate On Their Own In the Classroom	10. What children might do to continue the investigation in greater depth, exploring additional variations, and keeping the explorations going as they investigate the phenomenon fully. These continued explorations can be part of the current lesson, can be held over for the next science class session, or could occur in a science learning center.
11. Expected Conclusions	11. The goals and objectives you want the children to achieve and the conclusions you expect them to formulate as a result of their investigations.
12. Applications to Real Life Situations	12. Answers the question, "So What?" Many times well-meaning teachers ask children to do activities that have little or no application to their daily lives. If an activity or lesson cannot be applied to children's daily lives, the lesson lacks meaning. Thus, this section of the lesson plans ensures meaningfulness of the lesson to the children.

FIGURE 5.4

It is strongly urged that you develop lesson plans for each lesson you teach using the lesson plan format shown in Figure 5.3. One may argue that the process-oriented inquiry methodology encourages children to follow directions suggested by their own interests, and that it is impossible to write plans for every conceivable inquiry, including those that haven't even been thought of. The old phrase, "All roads lead to Rome" comes to mind. In guided inquiry, children begin at a common starting point, and they work to develop self-constructed understandings of common concepts. Individuals may take different paths, but in guided inquiry, they start and end at the same place.

Carefully prepared lesson plans help keep the focus on the objectives, or, if you will, the destination, while concurrently enabling you to follow the thought processes and various inquiry routes of the children. A lesson plan developed according to the above guidelines is shown in Constructing Science in the Classroom 5.1.

CONSTRUCTING SCIENCE IN THE CLASSROOM 5.1
Observing and Classifying States of Matter

GRADE

GUIDED INQUIRY LESSON PLAN

(Thanks to Ms. Kristen Myers-Fox for permission to use this activity prepared for a class assignment while she was an undergraduate preservice teacher.)

1. *Targeted Grade or Age Level*: Second Grade (seven or eight years old)
2. *Scientific Processes Addressed*: Observing and Classifying
3. *Science Topic Addressed*: States of Matter
4. *Process-Oriented Objectives*: (A) The students will observe and identify solids, liquids, and gases. (B) The students will classify materials according to their states.

5. *What Do I Want Children To Discover?*
I want children to discover that materials can be classified into solids, liquids, and gases. Ultimately, I want them to discover that the same material can exist in any of the three states, depending on temperature. The present lesson is an introduction to the concept.

6. *Description of Introductory Activity and Discussion*
To begin, I will have a lava lamp and a small neon sign set up. Children will write in their journals about them, and will infer what they think is inside of each. (We will return to this later.)
I will then ask them what kinds of foods they had for breakfast and I will make a list on the board. Someone will probably say "cereal" (if not, I will), and I will ask what they put in the bowl when they prepare cereal to eat. I will ask how milk is different from the cereal.
Then I will give each child a cup of hot chocolate and some mini-marshmallows. I will ask them to describe what is in the cup, and then I will ask if anyone has heard the term, "liquid." I will ask what it means, or what they think it means, and we will come up with a

definition based on the properties of the milk and the hot chocolate that we have discussed. We will then talk about the marshmallows and discuss how they are different from the liquid. I will present the term, "solid," and we will find and discuss examples of solids around the room. We will form a definition of "solid" based on the properties of the solids observed. Finally, I will ask children to put their hands over the cup of cocoa and describe what they see and/or feel.

We will then talk about air and what it is like. I will present the term, "gas," and we will come up with a definition as we did for the others.

The children can put the marshmallows in the hot chocolate and drink it (providing they are not allergic to it).

7. *Materials Needed*:

Ice in a bowl, butter, a variety of different solids, liquids, and gases (such as blocks, soap for making bubbles, books, lemon juice, cola, helium in a clear balloon, oil, pencils, a blown-up clear balloon, etc.), different shaped containers, paper towels, and other items such as dirt, flour, and jelly that are more challenging to classify.

8. *Description of Activities*:

As children are drinking their hot chocolate, I will again ask them to put their hands over the cup. After a few seconds, I will ask them to look at their hands and tell what they see (moisture). I will ask where they think the moisture came from. After a few responses, if they have not determined that it came from the steam from the hot chocolate, I will ask if maybe the steam had something to do with it, and will guide the discussion that way.

I will pass around pieces of ice and ask if ice is a solid, liquid, or gas. Then I will have some children melt the ice with their hands, or show them what is happening to the ice in my container. I will guide the discussion to help them realize that t..ie solid ice is becoming a liquid, and that the steam is the liquid in the cocoa turning first to a gas, and then back to a liquid on their hands. I will ask how the same material could be in two states, and if maybe it has something to do with the ice being cold and then warming up in their hands, and the steam being hot, then cooling off on their hands. We can explore this however the children want to. I will have butter as another example of a solid turning to a liquid when I put it in the sunny window. I will also have non-examples (for instance, I can chill a wooden block with ice, and put a block in the sunny window and ask why the blocks didn't change.)

Next, I will pass out the different items to each group and let them explore the items. I will tell them to put each item into a group, either solid, liquid, or gas. After they do this we will discuss their groupings, especially the balloons with helium and air (How are they different? What is inside? Can we pop it and find out?) and the soap bubbles (Blow a bubble. Is it a liquid or a gas? Could it be both?) since these represent a combinations of states. If the class seems to have an easy grasp of the concepts, I will bring out items that are harder to classify, such as jelly, dirt, and flour. This could be an extension of the lesson for the whole class, or could be an extension for those interested in pursuing the activities further. I will lead the children in discussions of why they classified these materials the way they did. (Note that flour takes the shape of its container like a liquid. Why is it a solid?) Children will be asked to adjust their definitions as desired.

I will turn their attention back to the lava lamp and the neon sign, and give them the opportunity to revise their inferences as to what is inside them.

9. *Typical Discussion Questions*:

Do all solids change into liquids when you heat them? Why? or Why Not?

What is the state of water at room temperature? Is that its usual state? What about water at the North Pole, or in the winter?

Besides liquid and solid, what state can water be in?

How can you tell if something is a solid, liquid, or gas?

Are all things solids when they are cold?

What happens when you open your freezer? Does "steam" come out?

Other questions will be generated by the children.

10. *How Children Will Be Encouraged To Investigate On Their Own In The Classroom*
     I will ask them to look around the room and the school to see if they can find things of each state of matter. I will ask them to share anything unusual or questionable with the class. I will suggest that they ask if they can have soup for dinner one night and do a "magic trick" for their family—they can put their hand over the soup and it will "magically" be wet; then they can explain to their family what happened.

11. *Expected Conclusions*:
     Matter exists in three states; some matter can exist in different states depending on the temperature. Another conclusion might be that there are different kinds of gases other than just air, and there are different kinds of liquids other than water, and that different solids have different properties.

12. *Applications to Real Life Situations*:
     This lesson relates to the children's lives since the material things a child encounters exist in one of the three material states. This concept forms the building blocks for the study of matter in later years. Children can be encouraged to find pictures depicting the three states of matter and can paste them in their journals or on charts that show the states of matter and their characteristics.

Microteaching

Microteaching involves presenting a short lesson to a small group of colleagues. Microteaching is "a technique that affords both beginning and advanced opportunities to *plan* and *practice* a wide array of new instructional strategies" (Orlich et al., 1990, p. 169). The "micro" in microteaching can refer to the lesson which is considerably reduced in scope and length, and to the student peers who typically are few in number.

Much has been written about the value of microteaching in preparing preservice teachers. Detractors argue that the technique is not sufficiently similar to actual classroom teaching to be valuable. However, research shows microteaching is "an effective way to have students in methods classes plan, teach, and evaluate a lesson presented to a small group of their peers" (Pauline, 1993, p. 9). Students consistently report that microteaching is a valuable component of their methods experiences.

The constructivist paradigm of education and the process-oriented inquiry methodology for teaching elementary science is relatively new to education students. Thus it is strongly urged that you try it out among yourselves. You already have done some peer microteaching when you availed yourselves of the opportunities to teach microlessons centered around the processes of science in Chapter Three. Microteaching utilizing the process-oriented inquiry methodology should involve teaching a short lesson of about 15 minutes in duration to a small group of eight to ten peers. The teaching student prepares the lesson in accordance with the lesson plan format shown in Figure 5.4, and has all the materials available. She teaches the lesson while the "children" take the intellectual role of children of the age and grade of the lesson. At the end, peers critique the lesson. Since peer critique is difficult and is often less than candid, it is suggested that the descriptors in Figure 5.3, p. 201, be used for the critique. Ultimately, the lesson can be located at some point on the expository-free discovery continuum. Some guided inquiry activities are more teacher-guided than open, and they are located toward the left end of the continuum; some are more open than guided, and they are located to the right of center.

In addition to peer critique, it is strongly urged that students video-tape their lesson so they can critique themselves. Studies show that videotaping is extremely valuable in helping teachers refine their techniques.

The personal critique of the teaching of the lesson on solids, liquids, and gases detailed in Constructing Science in the Classroom 5.1 is shown in Constructing Science in the Classroom 5.2.

CONSTRUCTING SCIENCE IN THE CLASSROOM 5.2
Critique of Microteaching Lesson on Observing and Classifying States of Matter

Obviously, I could not do this entire lesson in the time allotted for the microteaching, but I did not want to leave anything out of the written lesson. For the videotaped lesson, I did only the basic activity with the hot chocolate and the classification, and left off the journal, the extra discussion, and the extension activity. My group mates liked the lesson, especially the visual aspect, and they thought the hot chocolate was a great idea to show all three states at the same time. I found that it is harder than I thought to change certain manner-isms. (I always clasp my hands and, although it probably doesn't make a difference, it sometimes looks awkward.) My peers liked the overall lesson, and we had a discussion about the states of matter and how the traditional definition of a liquid (takes the shape of its container) could be confusing because some materials that aren't liquids do take the shape of the container, like sand and flour. I thought that letting the children come up with their own definitions with teacher guidance would be the best way to do it. I felt that giving non-examples was a good idea so that children can compare and contrast.

CONSTRUCTING YOUR IDEAS 5.3
A Guided Inquiry Lesson

Now it's your turn. Prepare a process-oriented guided inquiry lesson that takes about 15 minutes to teach. Write a lesson plan for the lesson in accordance with the format given in Figure 5.4. Teach this lesson to a group of your classmates. Videotape your teaching. After the lesson, ask your classmates to critique your lesson on the basis of the inquiry descriptors presented in Figure 5.3, and ask them to assess where on the expository-free discovery continuum your lesson would be placed *as your taught it*. Then, in private, look at the videotape and reflect on the videotape, the feedback from your group, and your own awareness of what went on during the lesson. From your reflections, develop an honest critique of your lesson. (Remember that a critique contains strengths as well as areas that need additional work.) Finally, re-write the lesson plan to reflect changes you would make as a result of the critique.

Is Learning Taking Place?

The primary goal of all education is for children to learn. Unfortunately, many well-intentioned learning activities do not necessarily produce this result. In this section, the question of whether learning is taking place will be investigated.

Is Hands On Minds On?

We often hear the phrase, "Hands-On-Minds-On." Is it true that hands-on activities ensure that minds are on—that hands-on activities ensure that learning is taking place?

Let us set up a "Hands-On-Minds-On" grid. "Hands On" is the degree of manipulation of materials and equipment; "Minds On" is the degree of cognitive engagement. For purposes of the grid, "hands on" is divided into high and low levels of manipulation, and "minds on" is divided into high and low levels of cognitive engagement. Four cells result.[1]

		Level of Cognitive Engagement	
		HIGH	LOW
Level of Manipulation	HIGH	HANDS-ON MINDS-ON	HANDS-ON MINDS-OFF
	LOW	HANDS-OFF MINDS-ON	HANDS-OFF MINDS-OFF

FIGURE 5.5   Hands-On-Minds-On grid

As can be seen from reading across the top row of the Hands-On-Minds-On grid, "Hands-On" can be associated with either "Minds-On" or "Minds-Off." A high level of manipulation does not necessarily produce a high level of cognitive engagement, as can be the case in driving to school, or in executing certain "cookbook" laboratory activities. Many traditional science activities require the student to verify what someone else has discovered, and students can accomplish this by following directions without the need for much in the way of real thinking. An example of this is the food test activity described in Chapter One, (p. 17).

Conversely, looking down the first column, you can see that "Minds-On" can be associated with either "Hands-On" or "Hands-Off." A high level of manipulation is not necessary to produce a high level of cognitive engagement. "Hands-Off" could produce "Minds-On," as is the case when children are totally engaged in a fascinating story or video, or when the teacher is doing a captivating demonstration.

Since the idea of education is for learning to occur, we must be certain that children have the highest possible degree of cognitive engagement. Hands-on activities must also produce "minds-on" for this to occur. The guided inquiry methodology promotes "minds-on" through "hands-on."

Deductive *vs* Inductive Teaching Styles

Teaching styles can be inductive or deductive. Inductive teaching proceeds from the most specific to the most general. For example, discovering the difficulties encountered in observing a number of different insects against the backgrounds of their natural habitats leads children to form a generalization about camouflage. Deductive teaching is the other way around, proceeding from the most general to the most specific. For example, in deductive teaching, the teacher moves from the general concept of living things through the more specific concept of animals to specific varieties of animals as examples of living things.

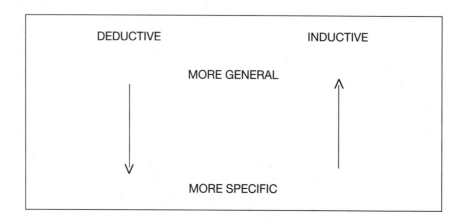

FIGURE 5.6 Deductive vs. inductive teaching styles

This book is written largely in an inductive manner. That is to say, specific details are presented for each situation or phenomenon, and you are encouraged to explore the various details before coming to your own conclusion. Any conclusions suggested in this book are presented after the specific instances have been examined.

In addition, the activities suggested in this book are inductive in nature. They are designed for the learner first to explore individual cases and then form generalizations. For example, in the snowflake activity where children capture snowflakes on a piece of cold black paper and observe them with magnifying glasses and the microscope, children are asked to observe several snowflakes before they make conclusions about the variety of snowflake shapes. (In The Schools 4.3, p. 164) In the pendulum activity suggested in Chapter Three, you were asked to list and explore many variables before coming to a conclusion.

Who Owns the Knowledge?

Constance Kamii observed that "For Piaget, the aim of education was intellectual and moral authority" (1984, p. 410). She continued,

> Unfortunately, teachers do not often encourage children to think autonomously. Instead, they frequently use sanctions to prod children to give "correct" answers . . . As early as first grade, many children have learned to distrust their own thinking. Children who are thus discouraged from thinking autonomously will construct less knowledge than children who are mentally active and confident (p. 413).

Expository teaching tends to be thought of as deductive in nature, and inquiry learning tends to be thought of as inductive. This is not necessarily true. There is a relationship between the expository-discovery continuum and the deductive *vs.* inductive teaching styles, and that relationship lies in the *ownership of knowledge.*

It is possible to construct a grid from the intersections of the expository-discovery continuum and the deductive *vs.* inductive teaching styles. Four quadrants are formed as depicted in Figure 5.7.

The quadrant formed by the deductive-expository intersection is represented by the typical lecture in which the teacher develops and transmits the information from most general to most specific. The task of the student is to acquire this teacher-owned knowledge. The child learns what the teacher decides is to be learned, and, therefore, the teacher is the primary owner of the knowledge.

The quadrant formed by the inductive-expository intersection is represented by television documentaries such as "60 Minutes," where the viewer is led through several specific cases of the situation being

WHO OWNS THE KNOWLEDGE?

	EXPOSITORY	DISCOVERY
DEDUCTIVE	▌Teacher owns ▌Teacher transmits to students ▌Lecture	▌Teacher owns ▌Teacher tires to transfer ownership to children ▌Teacher tells children how to develop ▌Verification ▌CD-ROM Videos
INDUCTIVE	▌Teacher owns ▌Teacher develops ▌"60 Minutes"	▌Children own ▌Teacher ensures integrity of children's constructions ▌Experimentation into curiosities

FIGURE 5.7

examined. Ultimately, the conclusion is suggested by the narrator, who therefore owns the knowledge. This style of teaching in a classroom is often mistaken for true child-owned inquiry. The teacher presents several carefully-selected demonstrations or activities which are intended to lead the learner to the conclusion predetermined by the teacher and which have been tried out ahead of time to be sure they "work." The demonstrations may be followed by textbook reading, teacher-dominated class discussion, or teacher explanation of the phenomenon demonstrated during which generalized conclusions that logically follow the demonstrations or activities are provided. Statements of objectives might read as follows: "The student will be able to name food, light, and water as the three basic requirements for plant growth," or "The student will be able to explain that the further from a fulcrum a weight is placed, the lighter it must be in order to balance a given weight on the other side of the fulcrum." The objectives, themselves, cite the predetermined conclusions to which the children are led by the demonstrations and readings. Both the conclusion and the method of arriving to it are owned by the teacher. The job of the children is to learn what the teacher has decided has to be learned, and, therefore, the teacher owns the knowledge.

The quadrant formed by the deductive-discovery intersection is illustrated by certain "cookbook" laboratory experiences where students perform activities that lead to predetermined conclusions "owned" by the teacher or the textbook author. Pains are taken in writing such activities to limit children's investigations to those that will verify the concept being studied. The activities typically proceed from the most general to the most specific. The teacher attempts to transfer ownership to the children by assigning the investigation to them. However, the teacher (or the text or the lab manual) tells the children how to develop the activity. Therefore, the teacher owns the knowledge. CD-ROM videos and hypermedia technology permit children to select a general topic and then explore specific interesting information related to the topic. Children work in a discovery mode from the most general to more specific. However, the discoveries are limited to what is programmed on the videodisc or the computer. Therefore, ultimately the machine (or the teacher) owns the knowledge.

The quadrant formed by the inductive-discovery intersection is the one most likely to promote student ownership, for students must construct their own meanings and their own conclusions from the evidence they, themselves, examine. The students are the owners of their own constructions. Students pose the situations, suggest the methodology for solving the problems, and do the activities themselves. The teacher ensures student integrity of student constructions. Students own the knowledge. The activities suggested in this text are inductive-discovery in orientation. Fostering children's ownership of their knowledge is critical for the development of their thinking. Constructivistic teaching that combines inductive approaches with process-oriented guided inquiry is the only way to make that happen.

IN THE SCHOOLS 5.1
How Much Space Does Light Illuminate at Different Angles?

In a fifth grade class, children used flashlights and an angle template to find the area illuminated on a sheet of graph paper by the beam of a flashlight. The flashlight was held parallel to the angles inscribed on the template: 90°, 60°, 45°, 30°, and 23 1/2°. Children traced the area of illumination at each angle with different colored pens, and counted the number of squares. They found that the greater the angle from the vertical, the greater the area of illumination. (See Figure 5.8.) As the area of illumination increased, the intensity of the light over that area decreased. Applied to the revolution of the earth about the sun, this phenomenon explains the causes of seasons. As the angle of the earth's axis relative to its plane of revolution changes, any given latitude receives its solar energy at different angles from the sun, resulting in different intensities of solar radiation.

FIGURE 5.8 How much space does light illuminate at different angles?

A Different Kind of Bloom

Benjamin Bloom developed a taxonomy of the cognitive domain which all education students have studied (Bloom et al., 1956). This taxonomy is presented in abbreviated form in Figure 5.9.

How do we foster thinking at the higher levels? If we want children to think at higher levels, we must ask higher level questions. If we want children to develop thinking ability above the levels of recall, knowledge, and comprehension, we have to tell them our expectation. There are several ways we tell children what we expect. We tell them through the language we use in our objectives by selecting verbs that focus on higher levels of Bloom's taxonomy, higher order thinking skills, and processes of science rather than recall of knowledge. For example, the following objective suggests the expectation of higher-level thinking:

The student will devise and execute an experiment to investigate the effect of sunlight on plant growth.

BLOOM'S TAXONOMY OF THE COGNITIVE DOMAIN

I. **KNOWLEDGE**
Recall of facts and specific information
Characterized by recognizing, memorizing, remembering

II. **COMPREHENSION**
Transforming information
Characterized by interpreting, translating, describing in one's own words

III. **APPLICATION**
Using information to solve new problems
Characterized by solving problems

IV. **ANALYSIS**
Separating the whole of an idea into its component parts
Characterized by subdividing, taking apart thoughts and problems

V. **SYNTHESIS**
Combining elements to form *new* and *unique* entities
Characterized by creating something new to the individual

VI. **EVALUATION**
Suggesting well-reasoned decisions on debatable topics
Characterized by resolving differences of opinion

FIGURE 5.9

The following objective suggests the expectation of lower-level thinking:

The student will name three factors required for plant growth.

We also tell children our expectation for higher levels of thinking through the questions we ask. Questioning is an extremely important teaching strategy with potential for stimulating student thinking, understanding what children are thinking, providing clarification, and so on. Questions asked by teachers also reflect the depth of thinking teachers expect of their students. If the nature of the questions involves recall, children will get the idea that recall of factual information is the most important aspect of their learning. On the other hand, if the questions are directed at analysis, synthesis, and evaluation, students will get the idea that their thinking must be at these levels. Open-ended questions encourage a greater diversity of responses and depth of thinking than closed questions for which there is a limited number of acceptable responses.

The question is often asked as to whether young children can deal with the higher levels of learning in science. Following is an example of questions that can be asked of very young children about plant growth.

These questions encompass the full spectrum of Bloom's taxonomy.

1. Name the parts of a plant. (Knowledge)
2. What part of the plant is this? How do you know? (Teacher points to the stem.) (Comprehension)
3. What are the leaves on this plant? (Teacher shows a plant children have not studied, such as an evergreen.) (Application)
4. If a plant were to lose all its roots, would it be able to live? (Analysis)
5a. Suppose you lived on a far-away planet. Draw a plant that would grow on that planet. (Synthesis)
5b. What do plants need in order to live? How would you prove that? (Synthesis)
6a. Do the rest of you agree that this plant would grow on the planet he has described? (Evaluation)
6b. From our experiment, did we prove that plants need food, light and water in order to live? (Evaluation)

If we want our children to think at higher levels, we must also provide wait time. In Chapter One, you were asked to play a game with knowledge-level questioning (Constructing Your Ideas 1.8, p. 24). In that activity, you recognized that it requires students a much longer time to formulate their answers to a higher level question than a lower level one. Wait time must be provided for children to organize their thoughts. It has been estimated that it takes five times longer to respond to a higher level question than to a lower level question. This, naturally, means that the teacher will be able to ask only one-fifth the number of questions. Teachers want to fill silence in a classroom with talking; silence is considered wasteful in elementary classrooms. Quite to the contrary, silence provides the opportunity for children to formulate their thoughts and construct their responses to challenging questions. Practice waiting for children to respond to questions; after asking a question, count fifteen seconds to yourself before you say anything else.

Other suggestions for fostering higher order thinking in the classroom include demonstrating that you value all student responses, and engaging children in interactions among themselves and with the teacher.

Lee Shulman has posited a seventh taxonomic level unique to teachers. To understand this level, we must recognize that Bloom's taxonomic system deals with the *individual*. The *individual* is able to (1) recall knowledge, (2) explain it, (3) apply it to new situations, (4) analyze situations involving it, (5) synthesize new material with it, and (6) evaluate new situations using it relative to some standard suggested by the student or someone else. However, teachers not only must be able to work by themselves within all six levels of the taxonomy as they prepare and teach their lessons, but they must also be able to know how each of their children is constructing his or her own unique knowledge, comprehension, application, analysis, synthesis, and evaluation of the information. No longer is the taxonomy limited to the individual; with teachers, it is expanded to include the children as well as the teacher. In other words, teachers not only know for themselves the information being taught, but also know how the children are constructing it. Teachers must have vicarious understanding of all six levels of processing for each of the children in their classes. This is most assuredly a level above the most advanced level for individual intellectual development. Lee Shulman has dubbed this very empowering concept the *pedagogical* level.

In order for a person to be able to think at higher levels, he must possess the basic information necessary to do the thinking with. He must know the facts, he must understand them, and he must be able to apply them to different and unique situations. Having that ability with a certain collection of facts, he can then proceed to analyze, synthesize, and evaluate with them. This thinking must be fostered in the elementary science classroom through stimulating activities, higher-level questioning, and listening to children to understand how they are thinking and constructing information so they can be helped in their pursuit of learning.

Conclusion

This chapter has dealt with the process-oriented guided inquiry methodology, the agent of constructivist science teaching, and thought to be the most appropriate way of teaching science to elementary children. You have examined the methodology from a number of perspectives, including contrasting it with expository and free discovery methodologies, contrasting inductive and deductive learning, considering the taxonomy of cognitive learning outcomes, and focusing on the primary outcome of ownership of knowledge. The rest is up to you as you construct your own understanding of the methodology.

CHAPTER 5   Additional Questions for Discussion

1. Contrast the expository, guided inquiry, and free discovery methodologies of teaching elementary science with respect to (A) amount of learning likely to occur, and (B) amount of prescribed science content likely to be learned.
2. Explain how the guided inquiry methodology fosters the development of scientific processes and promotes children's constructions and validations of their own conceptualizations.

Note

1. I am indebted to Dr. Mike Hale, professor of mathematics and educational technology at the University of Georgia, Athens, GA, for the ideas involved in the hands-on-minds-on grid.

References

Ausubel, D. P. (1968). *Educational Psychology: A Cognitive View.* New York, NY: Holt, Rinehart & Winston.

Bibby, G. (1970). *Looking for Dilmun.* New York, NY: Alfred A. Knopf.

Bloom, B. S., Englehart, M. D., Furst, E. J., Hill, W. H., & Krathwohl, D. R. (Eds.). (1956). *Taxonomy of Educational Objectives. The Classification of Educational Goals. Handbook I: Cognitive Domain.* New York, N.Y.: McKay.

Bruner, J. S. (1965). *The Process of Education.* Cambridge, MA: Harvard University Press, p. 20. Bruner, J. (1965).

Eggen, P. and Kauchak, D. (1994). *Educational Psychology: Classroom Connections.* New York, NY: Merrill.

Gasset, J. O. Y. (1961). *Meditations on Quixote.* New York: Norton.

Kamii, C. (1984). Autonomy: The aim of education envisioned by Piaget. *Phi Delta Kappan,* February, 1984, 410–415.

Lebkicher, R., Rentz, G., and Steineke, M. (1960). *Aramco Handbook.* Dhahran, Saudi Arabia: Arabian American Oil Company.

Nawwab, I. I., Speers, P. C., & Hoye, P. F. (1980). *Aramco and Its World: Arabia and the Middle East.* Dhahran, Saudi Arabia: Arabian American Oil Company.

Okey, J. R. and Gagné, R. M. (1970). Revision of a science topic using evidence of performance on subordinate skills. *Journal of Research in Science Teaching, 7*(4), 321–325.

Orlich, D. C., Harder, R. J., Callahan, R. C., Kauchak, D. O., Pendergrass, R. A., Keogh, A. J., & Gibson, H. (1990). *Teaching Strategies: A Guide to Better Instruction* (3rd ed.). Lexington, MA: Heath.

Pauline, R. F. (1993). Microteaching: An integral part of a science methods class. *Journal of Science Teacher Education 4*(1), 9–17.

Worth, V. (1986). *Small Poems Again.* New York: Farrar, Straus and Giroux.

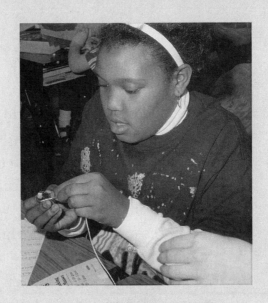

CHAPTER 6

Learner Differences

The most universal quality is diversity.

Michel Eyquem de Montaigne "Of the resemblance of children to their fathers," from *Essays.* (1580–1588)

Children come to our schools with tremendously diverse backgrounds and genetic material, bringing their unique capabilities, strengths and limitations, likes and dislikes, cultural environments, and experiential backgrounds with them to their classes.

The goal of education in general, and science education in particular, is that *all* children learn regardless of their differences—whether academic or cultural. In previous chapters we have suggested the notion that no two people are alike, that no two people perceive, internalize, process, and construct information the same way. We have suggested that inquiry teaching is the means by which *all* children are able to construct processes, products, and attitudes of science in unique and valid ways that result in meaningful and lasting learning.

Children are different in multitudinous ways, some of which can be identified and described, and some of which cannot. Certain of these differences have been shown to have pronounced influences on achievement and understanding in science. In this chapter you will explore the nature of these differences and ways these children learn best. You will refine the inquiry methodology to accommodate these special needs, and you will consider the notion that the process-oriented inquiry methodology method of science instruction solves the problem of how to teach science successfully to *all* children.

Constructivism says that all children learn in different ways. Inquiry provides the means.

Positions of National Organizations

The National Commission on Science Education Standards and Assessment has based its work on the premise that all students can and should learn science. The committee's guiding principle of equity reflects the stand that "All students, regardless of gender, cultural or ethnic background, physical or learning disabilities, aspirations, or interest and motivation in science, should have the opportunity to obtain higher levels of scientific literacy than they do currently" (National Academy of Sciences, 1994). The October, 1993, working paper set the tone:

> We emphatically reject the current situation in science education where members of populations defined by race, ethnicity, economic status, gender, physical or intellectual capacity are discouraged from pursuing science and excluded from opportunities to learn science . . . the commitment to Science for All implies inclusion not only of those who traditionally have received encouragement and opportunity to pursue science, but of women and girls, all racial and ethnic groups, students with disabilities, and those with limited English proficiency. Further, it implies attention to various styles of learning and differing sources of motivation. Every person must be brought into and given access to the ongoing conversation of science (National Research Council, 1993, p. 7).

The National Science Teachers Association emphasizes that science education must enable *all* Americans to achieve scientific literacy, and urges science curriculum developers to "Intensify and expand efforts to develop model science curricula for *all* students, including special populations such as underrepresented groups, talented students, and at risk students" (1990, p. 2). In 1989, the NSTA added the Division of Multicultural Science Education to explore issues and initiate programs relevant to teaching science to students of differing backgrounds (Anderson, 1989, p. 1).

The Goals 2000 program is predicated on "all children" and "every adult" achieving competency.

Some Differences in the Way Children Learn

CONSTRUCTING YOUR IDEAS 6.1
Listing Individual Differences

Try this. In groups, list as many individual differences among children as you can think of in one minute. Consolidate all the lists into one.

How many different items did you list? The differences in your list, plus many more you may not have thought of, characterize learners and the different ways they learn.

Individual learner differences include children's learning styles, their socio-economic status, their cultural background, their facility with the English language, their intelligence in each of several intelligence factors, their physical talents and limitations, their emotional well-being, their prior experiences, their home support, and many more. Indeed, it is safe to observe that there are very few areas of people's lives in which they are not decidedly different from other human beings.

The number of ways in which people differ from each other is enormous. It is not the purpose of this text to present an exhaustive list. Rather, we ask the question, "How can we teach science to *all* children?" For, with the huge number of individual differences, it seems a difficult undertaking to teach science equally meaningfully to *all* children.

Many individual differences have been discussed elsewhere in your teacher preparation program. In this chapter, you will focus on several individual learner differences that have been shown to have particular influence on achievement in science, and you will explore appropriate means of accommodating these differences in elementary science through the use of the process-oriented inquiry methodology.

Learning Styles

People learn more and retain it longer when they learn in a manner which is comfortable to them. But a style of learning comfortable for one individual may be uncomfortable for someone else. To demonstrate this in a physical sense, do the following activity.

CONSTRUCTING YOUR IDEAS 6.2
Which Way Do You Fold Your Hands?

Sit with your body relaxed and your hands folded in your lap or on your desk. Now, unfold them and refold your hands the other way—so the other thumb is on top.

One way was much more comfortable than the other. Yet, about half the class experienced comfort in *each* of the two ways of folding hands. The same can be done for crossing legs, folding arms, and choosing which ear the telephone is brought to. These are personal preferences. Similarly, people have strong personal preferences in the way they learn.

Visual, Auditory, and Kinesthetic Learning Modalities

People take in and process information in three fundamental ways termed modalities: visual, auditory, and kinesthetic. Visual learners learn best by seeing; auditory learners learn best by hearing; and kinesthetic learners learn best by touching and feeling. For each individual, one of these learning modalities is stronger than the other two, though the other modalities also are functional.

One's predominant learning modality is as comfortable to that individual as right- or left-handedness. It has been shown that people function primarily in one of the three main modalities as they learn. It also has been shown that achievement is fostered by being taught in a compatible modality (Dunn, 1988).[1] Thus it is useful for the teacher to understand the way people think in each of the modalities in order to be prepared to provide science experiences in all three modalities.

Characteristics of the Learning Modalities

The right-handed person normally has no idea what it is like to write left-handed. By the same token, people often have little or no idea of what it is like to learn in a modality different from their own. The following activity will allow you to investigate the three learning modalities to gain a better understanding of all three.

CONSTRUCTING YOUR IDEAS 6.3
Exploring Learning Modalities

Divide your class into pairs of students. (If there is an odd number of students, one "pair" will have three students.) Assign the number "1" and the number "2" to the members of the pairs. (If you have a group with three members, two people will be assigned "2's.") Ask the "1's" to leave the room and receive instructions as how to proceed and what data to collect; the "2's" are not given this information. Upon return, the "1's" sit directly across from their partners. Looking into the eyes of the partners, they record the direction (up, down, or to the side) the eyes move when the partner attempts to respond to the following types of reflective questions:

1. "What is the name of your favorite television program?"
2. "What is the name of the movie you saw in the past year you liked the best?"
3. "Who is your favorite relative?"
4. "What is your favorite song or piece of music?"
5. "What is your favorite sport to watch?"
6. "Who is your favorite actor?"
7. "Who is your favorite actress?"

If your partner's eyes move upward as he or she reflects on the proper answer, the individual is probably a predominantly *visual* learner. If the eyes move to one side or the other, the individual is probably a predominantly *auditory* learner. If the eyes move down, the individual is probably a predominantly *kinesthetic* learner. (See Figure 6.1.)

Now, ask the "2's" to describe as accurately as they can what went on in their minds as they decided on the response to each question.

Since the way people recall information is congruent with the way they perceive and process information (they way they learn), these descriptions reveal the ways visual, auditory, and kinesthetic individuals learn. Here are some sample descriptions; the people in your class are bound to supply additional material.

a. Visual learner looks up.

b. Auditory
learner looks
to one side.

c. Kinesthetic learner looks down.

FIGURE 6.1 Eye movement when recalling events indicating primary learning modality

Visual learners construct visual representations of what they are trying to remember. In deciding on their favorite TV show, they "see" the
opening title screen; they "see" scenery of given episodes; they "see" the
faces of the people who play the parts. When recalling their favorite
movie, they "see" the advertisement in the paper; they "see" the title of
the movie on the theater marquis. Visual learners "see" the faces of their

relatives and their favorite actor and actress. They "see" their favorite sports game being played in a stadium they can visualize. They may associate their favorite song or piece of music with the title page of the sheet music or with the faces of the soloists singing the song and the visual impact of the video or the live performance.

Auditory learners construct auditory representations of what they are trying to remember. Auditory learners "hear" the theme music of their favorite television program. They "hear" the voices of the actors and actresses who play the show's parts. In recalling their favorite movie, they "hear" portions of the sound track—the voices, the music, the sound effects. They may recall the discussion they had with someone about selecting the movie to be seen. Auditory learners "hear" the voices of their relatives and favorite actor and actress. They "hear" the announcer describing the play-by-play of their favorite sports event, and they "hear" the action. They "hear" their favorite song or piece of music.

Kinesthetic learners construct images of feeling and muscular tension and movement concerning what they are trying to remember. They "feel" the muscular strain associated with the drama or the humor in their favorite TV show; they "feel" the way they sit in their chair or couch; they "feel" the movement required to tune the program in. When recalling their favorite movie, they "feel" the same muscular movement and strain they exerted when actually watching the movie. They might re-create walking to the movie theater from their car, paying for the ticket, and pocketing the change; they might "feel" the kind of chair they sat in and the stickiness of the floor. Kinesthetic learners "feel" the emotions associated with visiting with their favorite relative and "feel" the emotions associated with seeing their favorite actor and actress perform. They "feel" the action involved in playing their favorite sports game; they "feel" the emotions and physical tensions associated with the win, the defeat, the good play, the poor play, and so on. They associate their favorite song or piece of music with the physical and emotional feelings of hearing it or, perhaps, playing it. Kindergarten children are essentially kinesthetic and tactile in modality. With time and maturity, children's preferences evolve from the kinesthetic to the visual and then to the auditory (Dunn, 1988).

People often process information in two or even all three modalities at the same time. Thus, people in your class may report that two or three modalities were operating at the same time. However, one of the three tends to be stronger—in many cases, much stronger than the others.

The way people reflect on past occurrences is congruent with the way they learn. With this activity, you have begun to understand how people who learn in a modality different from yours perceive and process information. Does the way others learn sound strange to you? Of course! We have a difficult time understanding how people can learn and remember in ways that are different from our own. Hearing about how others learn helps us gain understanding.

Accommodation of Different Learning Modalities

Since people learn and process information in different modalities, and since it is not always possible to tell which modality is the strongest in each child in a given classroom, it follows that we must teach in such a manner that all three modalities are accommodated. This is not difficult to accomplish. Visual learners learn best by utilizing visual stimuli—by *seeing* what they are to learn. Thus, visual learners remember pictures, graphs, charts, and illustrations. They remember where on a page a certain passage of text or a certain illustration occurs. They remember where in the classroom a certain activity was performed, and they remember what they *saw* during that activity. They remember locations, positions, and visual observations.

IN THE SCHOOLS 6.1
Activities For Visual Learners

Activities utilizing the strengths of the visual learner might include observation and classification of pictures showing different seasons, diagramming sound waves, drawing series and parallel circuit schematics, describing characteristics of rocks and minerals, and setting up bulletin boards or displays showing results of experiments with plants.

Auditory learners learn best by utilizing sound stimuli—by *hearing* what they are to learn. They remember the voice of the person who explained something; they remember the tone of voice of the teacher and the members of their group. They remember the sounds that attended an activity and the discussions that accompanied it. They remember what they *heard* during that activity.

IN THE SCHOOLS 6.2
Activities For Auditory Learners

Activities utilizing the strengths of the auditory learner might include engaging children in experimenting with sound, presenting their group's classifications system to the class, engaging in creative writing activities about the sounds of weather, and investigating how animal sounds aid in their adaptation to their environments.

Kinesthetic learners learn best by utilizing feeling stimuli—by *feeling* what they are to learn. They remember the weight of an object hefted in their hand; they remember what it felt like to move around the room and what things feel like. They remember the roughness of rock, the smoothness of polished wood; they remember the feel of sand and water and rice. They remember the act of writing down data for later interpretation. They remember the thrill of discovery.

IN THE SCHOOLS 6.3
Activities For Kinesthetic Learners

Activities utilizing the strengths of the kinesthetic learner might include investigating force, motion, and balancing, classifying objects by texture, presenting a pantomime about the planets in the solar system, and constructing Jell-O models of cells.

All three modalities should be combined in each lesson to the extent possible by ensuring that appropriate stimuli are present. For example, an exploratory lesson on rocks and minerals involves looking (visual stimulus), hefting (kinesthetic stimulus), and listening to discoveries, discussions and explanations (auditory stimulus). In the Mystery Boxes activity suggested in Chapter One, some students focused their inquiry on what the box must look like on the inside, some focused on the sounds made by the objects inside the box, and some focused on the feel of the magnet when it contacted the magnetic objects inside the box. Children in elementary grades tend to know the ways they learn most easily, so it is not necessary to check every child for modality preference. Instead, teachers must include material suitable for all three learning modalities in their lessons. The process-oriented inquiry methodology is the most appropriate vehicle for accommodation of all three learning modalities, for children are able to pursue their explorations in the learning styles which are most comfortable to them. Traditional methodologies emphasize having children look and listen. In inquiry, children also can *do*.

CONSTRUCTING YOUR IDEAS 6.4
Activity That Includes the Three Learning Modalities

Now it's your turn. Select a process-oriented inquiry investigation, and write activities you can include specifically for the visual learner, the auditory learner, and the kinesthetic learner.

Locus of Control

Locus of control is a trait concerned with "whether people attribute responsibility for their own failure or success to internal factors or to external factors" (Slavin, 1994, p. 355). Individuals have either a predominantly *internal* locus of control or a predominantly *external* locus of control. People with an internal locus of control believe their successes or failures are due largely to their own abilities and efforts—their behavior, persistence, inquisitiveness, and intelligence. People with an external locus of control believe their successes or failures are caused largely by external factors—luck, other people's actions, or the difficulty of the situation; they often exhibit learned helplessness.

Like many other factors in education, locus of control can be thought of as a continuum with external locus of control on one end and internal locus of control on the other.

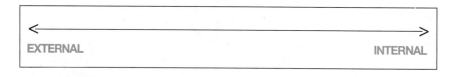

FIGURE 6.2 Locus of control continuum

The attributes discussed above represent extreme ends of the continuum. The placement of an individual's locus of control on the continuum varies with circumstances. Most of the time, an individual is somewhere between the two extremes with both external and internal factors influencing the situation at hand. Nonetheless, one tends to be the dominant factor.

The presence of an internal locus of control is a powerful predictor of academic achievement (Brookover et. al, 1979, p. 355) and has been shown to have a positive relationship to the amount of voluntary investigation which children seek and their willingness to make predictions (Rowe, 1978). Children with an internal locus of control believe they can influence the outcomes of investigations and thus are motivated to make predictions and test them through experimentation. Children with an internal locus of control also demonstrate significantly higher achievement than children with an external locus of control. The reason is that children who believe that their success or failure is due to their own efforts work hard to achieve success (when suitably motivated).

However, children with an external locus of control believe they have little or no control over their performance or achievement, and so attribute whatever success or failure they experience to outside factors and fail to see any point in trying. They are reluctant to expose themselves to the risk of failing to make accurate predictions, and they lack the internal motivation needed to pursue investigations on their own. They are likely to think "What's the use; I can't do anything about it anyhow!"

People with a predominately external locus of control can develop a more internal locus of control if the change is properly fostered. Fostering an enhanced internal locus of control involves encouraging children to become aware of the influence they can exert on various situations and the outcomes that occur as a direct result of their actions. Helping children discover that their efforts affect the results of an activity can aid children in developing a more internal locus of control. To facilitate this, teachers must provide activities children can manipulate and must engage them in dialogue intended to help them see *their* roles. Teachers can ask "no risk" questions where all responses are equally valid. For example, all children should be able to respond to the question, "What do you know about plants?" In this way, children begin to internalize that they already possess relevant information which can be of use to the class. Teachers also can encourage children who are hesitant to write or verbalize to draw pictures of the outcomes of their investigations (Rowe, 1978; Tomlinson, 1987).

In Figure 6.3, teaching strategies that can be used to foster development of a more internal locus of control are suggested.

CLASSROOM STRATEGIES THAT FOSTER THE DEVELOPMENT OF AN INTERNAL LOCUS OF CONTROL

1. Encourage children to evaluate the outcomes of investigations.
2. Encourage children to suggest ways of changing variables.
3. Encourage children to suggest additional ways of investigating a given phenomenon.
4. Encourage children to suggest topics for investigation and to set their own goals.
5. Encourage speculation by asking questions.
6. Teach children to ask questions.
7. Use appropriate wait time in questioning to allow children to formulate well-thought-out responses.
8. Encourage children to evaluate their own progress.
9. Encourage cooperative inquiry.
10. Change cooperative groups when no longer functioning.
11. When possible, assign older children, parents, another teacher, or a paraprofessional to help with the inquiries.

FIGURE 6.3

Any activity described in this book can facilitate the development of a stronger internal locus of control when the teacher explicitly shows children the influence they have in their investigations.

IN THE SCHOOLS 6.4
Activity on Diffusion to Help Foster an Internal Locus of Control

In the activity on diffusion of food coloring in Constructing Science in the Classroom 3.35, p. 120, children are asked to compare rates of diffusion in cold water and in warm water. To help children see that they can influence the results of this activity, the teacher asks the children to decide for themselves how hot and how cold the water should be, and asks them to measure the rates of diffusion. The teacher then shows the children that they were the ones who manipulated the temperature variable, and that they are able to influence the rate of diffusion by what they do. The teacher then asks what else the children can do to change the rate of diffusion, and asks them to try out their ideas, again reinforcing that the children are in control of the investigation.

In the process-oriented inquiry methodology, children develop their own investigations to answer questions they, themselves, raised in response to observations they made. Children take charge of their own investigations and, thus, of their own learning. We referred to "Ownership of Knowledge" in Chapter One and Chapter Five. Children who develop ownership of their knowledge develop a more powerful internal locus of control.

Jungian Learning Style Preferences

People vary tremendously in the ways they perceive and process information. Some people are impeccably logical in their approaches to problems and new situations; some are more creative than logical. You may have encountered a learning situation in which the way the instructor presented the material was completely foreign to your way of thinking. The difficulty did not have anything to do with the material itself; it had to do with the way it was presented. For example, a mathematics instructor may have required that you show every step in your solution to a problem. But you were able to arrive at the correct solution in a completely different way and were not able to write down all the steps. The instructor may have been presenting the information in a style incompatible with your style of learning.

The way a person perceives and processes information exerts a powerful influence on his or her ability to learn. In science activities, some people need to subject their data analyses and conclusions to tests of rigorous logic, while others arrive at the same conclusions more intuitively. Each thinks the other is wrong, and neither understands the other's way of thinking.

You may be familiar with the Myers-Briggs personality profile. Hanson, Silver, and Strong[2] have developed a learning style preference model similar to the Myers-Briggs model.

According to Jungian psychology, the way people learn depends on two factors: the way they take in and perceive information, and the way they process it. People have two basic ways of taking in and perceiving information: predominantly by sensing, or predominantly through intuition. People who perceive by sensing need to see, hear, feel, taste, or smell a stimulus in order for it to be registered in the brain. For example, "Doubting Thomas" was a sensing individual. On the other hand, people who perceive through intuition simply "know" a stimulus is present, registering it without needing sensory verification. People who "know" they are being watched without having to look at the offender are intuitive individuals.

People also have two ways of processing information: predominantly by thinking, or predominantly by feeling. People who process information by thinking employ rules of logic such as "if . . . then" clauses and syllogistic reasoning. People who process information by feeling simply "know" the result of a thought process without having to prove it. For example, in purchasing a new car, the thinking individual needs to evaluate all specifications whereas the "feeler" makes the decision from appearance and general impression.

In the learning style preference model, the Sensing-Intuiting perception functions and the Thinking-Feeling processing functions are placed on continua which are crossed to form four quadrants. (See Figure 6.4.) Each mode is identified with its first letter (except "Intuition" which is identified with the letter "N" because the "I" is used for a different attribute in Jungian psychology). The quadrants are identified by their intersections: Sensing-Thinking (ST), Sensing-Feeling (SF), Intuitive-Thinking (NT), and Intuitive-Feeling (NF). The four quadrants represent astonishingly different ways of learning.

The **Sensing-Thinker (ST)** perceives information through the senses and processes it through logic. The ST is realistic, practical, and matter-of-fact—a "walking computer." The ST is the type of individual who loves to recite facts and bits of information and who always seems to

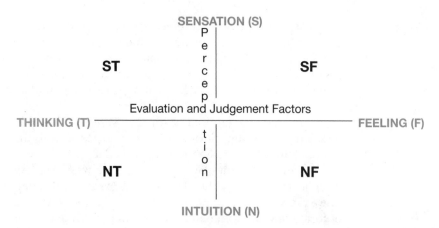

Hanson Silver Strong's Thoughtful Education Model courtesy Hanson Silver Strong &
Associates, Inc., 119 Mt. Laurel Rd., Moorestown, NJ 08057

FIGURE 6.4   Learning style preference grid

challenge other people's logic. The ST learns best in a well-structured,
instructor-directed atmosphere in which he is actively engaged in hands-
on experiences.

The **Sensing-Feeler (SF)** perceives information through the senses
but processes it through personal feelings rather than precise logic. The
SF is sociable, friendly, and interpersonally oriented, sensitive to his own
and others' feelings. The SF is the type of individual who loves stories
and who seems to want to personify and decorate everything. The SF
prefers to learn about feelings rather than facts and theories, and works
best when emotionally involved and able to explore spontaneously and
impulsively.

The **Intuitive-Thinker (NT)** perceives information intuitively but
processes it through logic. The NT is theoretical, intellectually curious,
and knowledge-oriented, approaching problems in a systematic, organized and logical way. The NT wants to know how things work, and is
always taking things apart. He wants to know "why." The NT learns best
when there is freedom to identify his own interests and participate in
selecting his own activities.

The **Intuitive-Feeler (NF)** perceives information intuitively and processes it through personal feelings instead of impeccable logic. The NF is
curious, insightful, imaginative, and creative; the NF dares to dream and
searches for new and unusual ways of approaching problems. The NF is
the inventor. The NF learns best in a flexible and innovative atmosphere
where there are few restrictions and where curiosity and creativity are
valued.

Research has shown that children learn best when they are taught in styles that complement their own learning styles. For example, the ST learns best from the ST style of teaching; conversely the SF has a difficult time adapting to the ST teaching style. However, it is not always possible to tell children's styles of learning. Thus it is necessary to teach in styles congruent with all four learning styles. This means teachers have to find different ways to portray information and teachers need to be receptive to different ways children choose to portray what they have learned.

IN THE SCHOOLS 6.5
Simple Machines Lesson in the Four Learning Styles

A lesson on simple machines can contain four different approaches compatible with each of the learning styles. For the NT, the definition of each simple machine and the appropriate conservation of energy facts and equations can be presented. For the SF, simple machines can be discussed from a society work-saving and energy-conserving point of view. For the NT, several simple machines can be made available for children to take apart, analyze how they work, and put back together. For the NF, the teacher may challenge children to develop their own unique machine that utilizes one or more simple machines. All these options are suggested at the same time during the introductory phase of the lesson, following which children take off in their own directions depending on their preferred styles.

Literature connection:
Dr. De Soto by William Steig (Farrar, Straus and Giroux, 1982). Dr. De Soto, a dentist, reaches the teeth of large animals with a series of pulleys.

Teaching characteristics designed to promote comfortable learning in each of the four learning styles are shown in Figure 6.5.

An example of a unit planned to include activities appropriate for each of the four basic learning styles is shown in Constructing Science in the Classroom 6.1.

The process-oriented inquiry methodology permits the teacher to structure the learning environment so all children can pursue their investigations in styles that are comfortable, challenging, and meaningful.

Field Dependence/Field Independence

Field independence is the ability to recognize camouflaged information easily.

You probably have seen the "hidden figures" puzzles in publications like *Highlights for Children.*

TEACHING IN EACH OF THE FOUR
BASIC LEARNING STYLES

Teaching in the ST Style:

- Provide concise step-by-step directions for activities.
- Set measurable goals and objectives.
- Clearly structure the learning environment.
- Focus on mastery of skills, acquisition of knowledge, and the opportunity to apply the skills and knowledge to real-life situations.
- Reduce emphasis on open-ended or interpretive questions.
- Provide ample opportunity for reading and research.
- Give immediate feed-back.

Teaching in the SF Style:

- Provide a warm, friendly, supportive, and interactive environment where children are encouraged to share their thoughts and feelings with each other.
- Provide group activities and games where everyone participates and no one loses.
- Read stories about people and their feelings.
- Include art and music in activities to allow expression of feelings.

Teaching in the NT Style:

- Challenge children to think critically.
- Provide independent and creative approaches to learning.
- Provide opportunities for discovery and experimentation.
- Ask for children's input concerning meaningful material for study.
- Encourage discussion and argument with others as a way of clarifying ideas.

Teaching in the NF Style:

- Provide an atmosphere with minimum number of restrictions.
- Include a selection of diverse learning activities.
- Encourage self-expression, creativity, and exploration.
- Encourage children to find their own methods of solving problems.
- Encourage independence and non-conforming activities.

FIGURE 6.5

CONSTRUCTING SCIENCE IN THE CLASSROOM 6.1

A Unit on Africa and the Rainforest that Includes Activities Appropriate for Each of the Four Basic Learning Styles

(Thanks to Cynthia Bennett Butler who developed and implemented this strategy while a graduate education student at Kennesaw State College.)

A first-grade teacher planned the following activities for a unit on Africa and the Rain Forest in an effort to present a unit such that all four learning styles were available to her children; the activities are categorized by teaching/learning style.

Sensing-Thinking (ST)

■ Collect and classify leaves.

■ Classify pictures of rain forest animals.

■ Develop a data bank of rain forest animals by choosing a few rain forest animals and charting their size, their color, the way they move, what they eat, the type of home they inhabit, etc.

Sensing-Feeling (SF)

■ Read a story such as *Mufaro's Beautiful Daughters* by John Steptoe (Lothrop, 1987), and discuss the good/evil and kind/unkind acts and the trickery involved.

■ Plant a tree.

■ Keep an African Jungle Journal (which can include anything the child wants to record).

■ Create a bird out of construction paper and buttons using colored chalk, glue, and scrap paper to practice conservation.

■ Create a mural for a door or the hall.

■ Create African masks out of papier mache, balloons, bric-a-brac, glue, and paint.

Intuitive-Thinking (NT)

■ Make bark rubbings to explore different trees and their coverings.

■ Read *The Egyptian Cinderella* by Shirley Climo (Thomas Y. Crowell, 1989) and compare it with *Cinderella* using character maps.

Intuitive-Feeling (NF)

■ Make and observe an ant farm; explore and experiment with it. Take the class on an ant hunt and compare with the ant farm.

■ Investigate factors that influence the rate of plant growth.

There may be, for example, a picture of a house with several common objects hidden in the drawing. The field independent child is able to spot the objects in the picture quickly, much to the consternation of the field dependent child (or adult) who sees the roof, the windows, the door, and the chimney, but little else. The field independent person has the ability to ignore the surrounding camouflaging field, whereas the field dependent person is less able to do so.

A hidden figures drawing is shown in Figure 6.6.

Another example comes from quiz shows such as *Jeopardy*. Many questions include related but unessential information. The field independent person is able to separate what is important from what is not important and bore directly to the core of the question. For example, what is superfluous in this question?

> What is the name of the world's longest river flowing from north to south in an African country known for two of the Seven Wonders of the Ancient World?

HIDDEN FIGURES

FIGURE 6.6 Find the following tools needed for home maintenance: broom, hammer, 2 ladders, pliers, saw, screwdriver, shovel, rake.

Field dependent people have difficulty separating essential information from complex situations, and tend to rely on external factors to achieve solutions to problems. In contrast, field independent people tend to rely on their own internal frames of reference. For example, field dependent persons often have difficulty separating essential from non-essential information in mathematics word problems such as the following:

> A certain room is 12 feet long and 10 feet wide. Its floor is completely covered with a beige carpet 1/2 inches thick costing $12.00 a square yard. The room has 8-foot ceilings, and has a door on each end. What is the floor area of the room?

Studies have shown that persons who are field dependent exhibit lower levels of achievement in science and reduced acquisition of formal reasoning skills than people who are field independent (Lawson, 1985). Thus, it is desirable to encourage field dependent children to operate in a more field independent manner. The methods used to foster a more field independent manner of thinking primarily involve helping children focus on key patterns and issues. Careful observation helps field dependent children learn to spot characteristics closely associated with the background they might otherwise overlook. For example, field dependent children may become so engrossed in examining the "wholeness" of a rock sample that they do not see the texture, the layering, or the variegations in color. Teachers can help such children with their observations by asking questions that lead to discoveries of the unobserved properties. The observation sheet suggested in Figure 3.1 would be an appropriate aid for field dependent children in their observation of rocks and minerals. Classification also often requires identification of properties that may have been overlooked. Teachers can help field dependent children by encouraging them to develop alternate systems of classification.

When children engage in process-oriented investigations in which they try to figure out what caused what, they have to isolate the variables. Variables often are camouflaged by other factors, and field dependent children may encounter difficulties in isolating them. For example, suppose your class was investigating the effect of weather on mood. Many weather variables exist: type of weather, temperature, amount of sunshine, barometric pressure, precipitation, and so on, and they all seem to be rolled up into one variable called "weather." There also are many component variables that make up a person's mood. Helping field dependent children seek and tease out the component variables helps them work in a more field independent manner.

Defining operationally involves deciding how to measure variables. Teachers can help field dependent children find equivalent ways to measure variables that are difficult to measure (such as rate of plant growth) or that cannot be measured directly (such as plant health). This aids the field dependent children in associating variables with something tangible, thus expanding their conception of variables such that they can be measured.

Employing inquiry and discovery learning methodologies help field dependent children move toward more field independent thinking by encouraging them to focus on their own thoughts and giving them the opportunity to figure things out for themselves.

Encouraging children to develop the ability to think in a field independent manner is essential in paving the way for them to develop formal operational skills. This should be done in the elementary science classroom as early as possible. Specific suggestions are provided in Figure 6.7.

STRATEGIES FOR FOSTERING FIELD INDEPENDENCE

■ Emphasize development of the process skills, especially observation, classification, isolation of variables, and defining operationally.

■ Utilize the process-oriented inquiry instructional methodology.

■ Employ constructivist teaching techniques.

■ Play games involving "20 Questions" and other incremental clues.

■ Work puzzles.

■ Play challenging board games.

■ Provide overviews of lessons.

■ Encourage work on computers.

■ Provide concept maps so children can see how each segment of a lesson fits in with the whole. (See Chapter Eleven.)

FIGURE 6.7

Teachers' Learning Styles

Just as children have their own unique styles of learning, teachers also have their personal learning styles. As adults, teachers have developed their styles more completely than children, and have had the opportunity to strengthen areas where they have perceived weaknesses. For example, many adults with a dominant visual learning modality have been able to strengthen the auditory area. Many who have experienced difficulty in tasks and activities which field independent individuals find less challenging have strengthened their field independent thinking skills (even though they may not be aware of doing so) by working puzzles, figuring out computer programs, playing challenging board games, and so on.

Teachers tend to teach in their dominant learning styles. This is advantageous for children with the same learning style as the teacher's, but is disadvantageous for children with opposing learning styles. Thus, it is incumbent on teachers to know their most comfortable learning styles so they can (1) utilize the strengths associated with them in their teaching, and (2) make overt efforts to teach in the less dominant styles so all children can have an equal advantage.

Many factors bear on the abilities of children to learn, and the learning styles discussed in this chapter represent selected examples. Good teachers are aware of the learning that is taking place with their children and constantly search for ways to optimize the learning on the part of *all* children in their classroom.

Gender

CONSTRUCTING YOUR IDEAS 6.5
Characterizing Scientists

Try this:
  Name five scientists.
  List five things scientists have done.
  Name two Nobel prize winners.

Were your responses predominantly male in nature? Were they predominantly female? Or were they equal? If your responses were predominantly male or female, you might want to examine your own belief system about science and gender. (See Figure 6.8.)

Research indicates that "females are getting a significantly poorer science education than males, even when they are in the same classroom (Baker, 1989, p. 7; Becker, 1989). The scientist is stereotyped as an older man with unkempt hair and round glasses. Science textbooks portray males in the more significant scientific roles. Teachers who believe science is difficult and is the realm of males exhibit behaviors and teaching strategies that lead to science avoidance and negative attitudes toward science on the part of females. In a self-perpetuating manner, the message is sent that science is best undertaken by boys and men.

What are your beliefs about women in science?

FIGURE 6.8   A view of science

If girls are to be given the same opportunities to learn science as boys, it is critical that teachers do everything possible to dispel the notion that science is for males. This means involving girls as often as boys as helpers in demonstrations and as laboratory assistants. It means recognizing the in-class and out-of-class science achievements of girls as much as boys. It means talking about women scientists as much as men.[3] And, above all, it means examining your own beliefs to reveal any science gender bias you may have. In Chapter One, the point was made that one's beliefs affect one's behavior. Teachers who believe science is more appropriate for boys than for girls tend to convey that belief in their classroom interactions. Only by recognizing your biases can you begin to change the way you act, and, ultimately, the way you believe.

Some specific strategies for teaching in a gender-neutral manner are suggested in Figure 6.9.[4] Names and contributions of prominent women in science including women who have won the Nobel prize (McGrayne, 1993) are shown in Figure 6.10.

STRATEGIES TO HELP AVOID GENDER BIAS IN ELEMENTARY SCIENCE EDUCATION

1. Call on girls as often as boys.
2. Give girls as much wait time as boys.
3. Give positive non-verbal behavior such as head-nodding and encouraging smiles to girls as much as boys.
4. Watch group dynamics to ensure girls are not given stereotypical roles such as secretary or recorder, and are as active in investigations as boys.
5. Rotate group roles so girls have opportunities to function as team leaders.
6. Consider having same-gender groups so girls are active in all roles.
7. Engage girls as much as boys in actual hands-on classroom experiences.
8. Give attention to the subject of women in science.
9. Bring women scientists and upper level women science teachers to the classroom to talk about their careers.
10. Arrange a "career day" and include women in non-traditional roles such as science.
11. Provide lists of famous scientists that include as many women as possible.
12. Refer to scientists as "he or she."

FIGURE 6.9

WOMEN IN SCIENCE

*(*Denotes a Nobel Prize Winner)*

Maria Agnesi (1718–1799) Mathematician. A professor at the University of Bologna in Italy, she published *Analytical Institutions* which was widely translated and used as a textbook.

Elizabeth Blackwell (1821–1910) Physician. After she became the first woman doctor in the United States, no hospital would admit her. She then bought her own house and established a small dispensary which expanded to become the New York Infirmary for Women and Children.

Mary Bunting (b.1910) Microbiologist. She is known for discoveries on the effect of radiation on bacteria and became the first woman member of the U.S. Atomic Energy Commission.

Eleanor Margaret Burbridge (b.1919) Astronomer. As the first woman astronomer, she directed the Royal Greenwich Observatory in England.

Jocelyn Bell Burnell (b. 1943) Astronomer and Physicist. Credited with the discovery of pulsars, rapidly rotating stars that have completed their life cycles and have contracted into a "thick soup" of neutrons.

Annie Jump Cannon (1863–1941) Astronomer. Called the "census taker of the sky," she classified about 400,000 stellar bodies according to their temperature.

Rachel Carson (1907–1964) Marine Biologist. Her writings brought to public attention the destructive effects of pesticides, resulting in curtailment of their use, and in stronger efforts to develop natural biological controls for harmful insects.

Eugenie Clark (b.1922) Marine Biologist. Through studying the nature and behavior of sharks, she has been able to teach them to choose between targets of different designs and colors.

FIGURE 6.10   (Continues on the next three pages)

Jewel Plummer Cobb (b.1924) Cell Physiologist. Her early research led to new discoveries concerning normal and malignant pigment cells. Interested in helping to solve the puzzle of cancer, she undertook many research projects for the National Cancer Institute. In 1981, she became the first Black woman college president in the 19-college California State University system.

Jacqueline Cochran (1906–1980) Pilot. First woman to break the sound barrier in 1952 while flying a North American Canadair F-86 over Royer's Dry Lake, California, at a speed of 652.337 miles per hour; she was also the first woman to win the Bendix Transcontinental Air Race. During World War II, she directed the Women's Air Force Service Pilots.

Anna Comnena (1083–1148) Physician, Mathematician. Author of a book on gout, she also ran a hospital of 10,000 beds and provided medical services to pilgrims and Crusaders and their camp-followers.

*Gerty Cori (1896–1957) Biochemist, Physician. The first woman to receive the Nobel Prize for Medicine/Physiology (1947), she carried out research into carbohydrate metabolism, the method by which the body uses its fuel supply of starches and sugars, and the relation of this mechanism to certain hormone secretions.

*Marie Curie (1867–1934) Chemist. The first person ever to receive two Nobel awards: Physics in 1903, and Chemistry in 1911, she won the prizes for her discovery of radium and her research into radioactivity.

Amelia Earhart (1898–1937) Aviator. The first woman to fly solo across the Atlantic, she set many aviation records, including long distance ones, such as flying from Hawaii to California.

*Gertrude B. Elion (b.1918) Biochemist. Won the Nobel Prize in Medicine/Physiology in 1988 for demonstrations showing the differences in nucleic acid metabolism between normal cells and disease-causing cancer cells, protozoa, bacteria, and viruses.

Rosiland Franklin (1920–1958) X-ray Crystallographer. Pioneer of the study of molecular structures including DNA. Discovering enough information about the structure of DNA to explain the molecular basis of heredity, her work helped lead to the unravelling of the complete structure of DNA.

Lillian Gilbreth (1878–1972) Industrial Engineer. She charted ways to save energy and human motion in the office, factory, hospital, and home. She also has 12 children.

Jane Goodall (b.1934) Animal Behaviorist. Living for long periods of time in the field, her studies were the first to show that chimpanzees are intelligent, social animals.

Beatrice Hicks (1919–1979) Electrical Engineer. In the 1960s she was the only Black woman engineer at Western Electric. She received the Society of Women Engineers Achievement Award for her theoretician study and analysis of sensing devices under extreme environmental conditions.

Lucy Hobbs (1833–1910) Dentist. The first woman to earn a dental degree in the United States, she developed one of the most extensive practices in Kansas.

*Dorothy Crowfoot Hodgkin (1910–1994) Crystallographer. She was awarded the Nobel Chemistry Prize in 1964 for determining the crystal structure of biomedical compounds, particularly penicillin.

Grace Murray Hopper (1906–1992) U.S. Naval Officer, Inventor. She is the inventor of the computer language COBOL for which she received the 1983 American Association of University Women Educational Foundations Achievement Award.

Hypatia (c.370–415 A.D.) Mathematician. She taught mathematics and philosophy at the University of Alexandria, Egypt, and is credited with the development of the astrolabe and the planesphere, instruments used for studying the stars.

Shirley Jackson (b.1946) Physicist. The first Black woman to graduate in theoretical physics from the Massachusetts Institute of Technology, she works at Bell Laboratories using computers and mathematical formulas to explore physics. She was a visiting scientist at the European Organization for Nuclear Research in Switzerland.

*Irene Joliot-Curie (1897–1956) Physicist. She was awarded the Nobel Chemistry Prize for discovering a technique for making artificial radioactive elements.

Reatha Clark King (b.1938) Research Chemist. One of only two black graduate students at the time, she earned her master and doctorate degrees in chemistry at the University of Chicago, specializing in high temperature chemistry. She later became a college administrator, supporting programs for women and minorities.

*Rita Levi-Montalcini (b.1909) Biochemist. Received the Nobel Prize for medicine/physiology in 1986 for her discovery of NGF (nerve growth factors), a class of molecules that provides a regulatory link between targets in the body and the nerve cells that innervate them.

*Maria Goeppert Mayer (1906–1972) Physicist. She received the Nobel Prize for Physics in 1963; during World War II she worked on isotope separation for the atomic bomb.

*Barbara McClintock (1902–1992) Biochemist. She received the 1983 Nobel Prize for Medicine/Physiology for her discovery that genes can move from one spot to another on the chromosomes of a plant, thus changing future generations of plants.

Elsie Gregory MacGill (b.1905). Aeronautical Engineer. She was the first woman to become chief aeronautical engineer of any company and is known internationally for her work on engineering designs of fighter and transport aircraft.

Margaret Mead (1901–1978) Anthropologist. She was one of the first to do field work in the islands of the southwest Pacific and to bring back eyewitness accounts of the native cultures and peoples of New Guinea, Samoa, and Fiji.

Lise Meitner (1878–1968) Physicist. The first woman to be awarded the Enrico Fermi Award, she worked on splitting the atom, and explained mathematically the fission of the uranium atom.

Maria Mitchell (1818–1899) Astronomer. Self-taught, she discovered a comet that was named for her, and became professor of astronomy at Vassar College.

Emmy Noether (1882–1935) Mathematician. Professor of mathematics at Bryn Mawr, she discovered many methods of great importance to abstract algebra and was also a member of the Institute for Advanced Study at Princeton.

Jennie R. Patrick (b.1949) Chemical Engineer. The first Black woman in the United States to earn a doctoral degree in chemical engineering, she does research on energy conservation and pollution control. As a role model, she encourages young people to develop their own potential and establish their own goals.

Susan Laflesche Picotte (1865–1915) Physician. Born on the Omaha Reservation, this Native American woman attended the Woman's Medical College of Pennsylvania, and returned to serve her people's medical needs. She later became the leader of the Omahas and represented their interests in Washington.

Sally Kristen Ride (b.1951) Astronaut. Graduate of Stanford University with a Ph.D. in physics, she was the first American woman to go into space aboard the space shuttle *Challenger* as flight engineer for nearly six days.

Florence Sabin (1871–1953) Physician. She was one of the first women to enter medical research. She determined the origin of red corpuscles and did important research on tuberculosis.

Margaret Sanger (1883–1966) Public Health Nurse. A pioneer in birth control, she fought for the right of women to have access to birth control and was one of the founders of Planned Parenthood.

Susan Smith McKinney Steward (1847–1918). Physician. She was the first Black woman to receive her M.D. from the New York Medical College for Women. She helped found a hospital for treatment of "indisposed" shop girls.

Ellen Swallow (1842–1911) Chemist. The first woman to graduate from the Massachusetts Institute of Technology, she was the founder of home economics as a science and a profession.

Valentina Tereshkove (b.1937) Cosmonaut. A Russian textile worker, she learned to parachute and eventually entered the space program. She is the first woman to orbit the earth in space.

Adah Belle Thoms (1863–1943) Nurse. She was the first Black person to hold an administrative position at New York City's Lincoln School for Nurses. She played an important role in guiding the progress of Black women in the field of nursing.

Jane C. Wright (b.1919). Cancer Researcher. Motivated by the challenge to find a cure for cancer and to help cancer patients live more comfortable lives, she worked in chemotherapy research. She has received numerous awards and honors for her work.

Chien-Shiung Wu (b.1912) Physicist. She made important contributions to the research of nuclear forces and structures; in particular, she helped to prove the principle of parity unacceptable.

***Rosalyn S. Yalow** (b.1921) Nuclear Physicist. She was awarded the Nobel Prize for Medicine in 1977 for the discovery of radioimmunoassay, a method of measuring minute concentrations of hundreds of substances in body tissues. It is invaluable in determining the differences between diseased and normal states of body tissues.

(Courtesy, Rosemary G. Cameron, College of St. Rose, Albany, NY)

FIGURE 6.10

Multicultural Factors

The U.S. Census Bureau statistics show that in the decade 1980–1990, the population of African Americans in the United States increased by 13.2 percent, the population of Native Americans increased by 37.9 percent, the population of Hispanics increased by 53 percent, and the population of Asians increased by almost 108 percent.

PERCENT OF POPULATION INCREASE OF MAJOR ETHNIC GROUPS IN THE UNITED STATES 1980–1990

(Compiled from *The World Almanac*, 1994)

ETHNIC GROUP	PERCENT INCREASE 1980–1990
White	6.0
Black	13.2
Native American	37.9
Hispanic	53.0
Asian	107.8

FIGURE 6.11

Science magazine predicts that by the year 2006, 675,000 science and engineering jobs will be vacant if we do not enlarge the pool of candidates from which these positions are filled (Malcolm, 1990, p. 112).

Shirley Malcolm, head of the Directorate for Education and Human Resources Programs for the American Association for the Advancement of Science (AAAS), cites the following predictions:

▌ By the year 2010, one-third of 18 year olds will be black or Hispanic, compared with one-fifth in 1985.

▌ Minority children are or soon will be the majority in the public schools of some states.

▌ By the year 2000, minorities, women and immigrants will account for 85 percent of new members of the work force.

Malcolm asks the question, "Who will do science in the 21st century?" and answers it by concluding ". . . there exists a vast and strangely invisible talent pool that remains virtually untapped. Who are these people who would do science if they could? They are Blacks and Hispanics and American Indians, girls and young women of all races, and disabled students of both sexes and all races" (1990, p. 112).

It has never been acceptable to ignore a small segment of the population in school; however, what used to be small segments are rapidly becoming large. This rapid change in cultural and racial demographics requires a closer look at the potentially serious cultural dichotomy between teacher and student.

Ethnic and cultural factors exert powerful influences on the way children learn. From the constructivist perspective, it is clear that children's differing cultural backgrounds have led to differing prior experiences. Children of different cultures have constructed culture-based information in different ways, and thus bring different perceptions and understandings to the classroom.

As indicated earlier in this chapter, teachers tend to teach in a dominant style which consists of multiple factors, including factors related to the teacher's cultural background. When a child's learning style is congruent with the teacher's, the child tends to learn more and retain it longer. However, it is becoming increasingly common for teachers to have children in their classes who come from a variety of different cultural, racial, or ethnic groups whose behaviors, cognitive styles, and other culture-based qualities differ from those of the teacher. The question arises as to how to make these multicultural classrooms responsive to the needs of *all* children.

There are at least three aspects to multicultural considerations: (1) attitude, (2) teaching methodology, and (3) curriculum.

Attitude in Multicultural Education

> Nothing inherent in culture itself, or in other forms of human diversity, creates pedagogical problems . . . It is that attitude of the educator toward diversity that creates problems in the education setting. When educators do not notice diversity, when they give negative notice, or when they lose the opportunity to give positive notice of the natural diversity that is always there, they create a bogus reality for teaching and learning (Hilliard, 1994).

To address the attitude concern, it is suggested that you first acquire general cultural sensitivity. The best way to do this is to examine your own cultural, ethnic, and racial beliefs to disclose to yourself any bias you might have. With this information, you will be able to change the way you act, and, then, the way you believe. By resolving any concerns you have toward multicultural classroom settings, you will be able to make your classroom a warm and receptive environment for all children.

Multicultural Methodology

This book is about teaching in a constructivist approach, utilizing the process-oriented inquiry methodology to facilitate the science education of all children, all of whom are uniquely different from each other in multiple ways. Race, ethnicity, and culture are included among these differences. Thus, from a constructivist perspective, multiculturalism can be considered a special case of individual learning needs.

In a multicultural approach to learning, teachers use a variety of teaching styles consistent with the learning styles of the cultural and ethnic groups represented in their classrooms. This principle is not different from the principle of accommodating the wide variety of learning styles discussed in the first section of this chapter. Different racial, ethnic, and cultural groups have different learning styles and competent teachers provide for these learning styles as well as other special learning needs in multicultural settings.

Many of the unique learning needs associated with individual cultural groups have been identified. A few examples are given below.

- Hispanic students tend to learn best when they have a personal relationship with the teacher and can interact with peers in small groups (Willis, 1993, p. 7).

- African-American students respond best to collaborative hands-on approaches (Willis, 1993, p. 7).

- In Asian and Native American cultures, learning is "circular" rather than "linear" and students learn through active discussion (Willis, 1993, p. 7).

▍ Minority students can analyze science situations better when they are centered around natural topics of life (Anderson, 1994, p. 99).

▍ For many students of color, analogies to familiar phenomena helps make new and unfamiliar information more meaningful (Anderson, 1994, p. 99).

▍ African-American and Hispanic students learn best when cooperative teaching techniques are used (National Council for the Social Studies, 1992).

▍ Mexican-American and African-American students tend to be field dependent in learning style (Cushner, McClelland & Safford, 1992, p. 110).

General characteristics of effective multicultural teaching are essentially the same as general characteristics of constructivist inquiry teaching (see Figure 5.3, p. 201).[5] They include

▍ Encouraging children to share their experiences with each other

▍ Providing activities that meet the needs of individual children

▍ Ensuring that lessons and units are relevant to children's lives

▍ Utilizing hands-on activities

▍ Encouraging children to verbalize their reasoning processes

▍ Guiding children in how to ask questions

▍ Helping children make connections of new information with information they already possess

Specific strategies for effective inclusion of children from foreign countries are suggested in Figure 6.12.

STRATEGIES FOR THE EFFECTIVE INCLUSION OF CHILDREN FROM FOREIGN COUNTRIES

1. Provide a homework folder with clear directions.
2. Assign a "buddy."
3. Ask child to write his or her name on the desk in the native language.
4. Prepare bulletin boards with "Hello" and other common phrases written in native languages of children in the classroom or the school.
5. Display flags of native countries represented.
6. Mark native countries represented on world maps.
7. Ask children to decorate their science folders with drawings of their native country.
8. Invite parents to class to discuss their native country.

FIGURE 6.12

Multicultural Curriculum

In a multicultural approach to learning, teachers not only employ teaching strategies congruent with the learning styles of the children, but they also include content areas representative of other cultural and ethnic groups. It is clear that multiculturalism does *not* mean the occasional inclusion of material on notable people and significant events from minority ethnic and racial groups, such as what often happens during Black History Month. Rather, multiculturalism involves the continuous inclusion of material from other cultures. All children need exposure to other cultures. The only way children will overcome a long history of ignorance of other cultures is to provide lessons that focus on other cultures. Unless everyone learns about all cultures, whether the cultures are present in a particular classroom or not, the ignorance will be perpetuated.

Science education tends to be based on the methodology and products of Western scientists. Limiting science education to this Western view, which is only one way of thinking about science, is "exclusionary of multiple perspectives and is ultimately detrimental to both science education and to science" (Stanley & Brickhouse, 1994, p. 395). "Students should learn how the purposes and nature of science are different in different cultures and different periods of time, thereby grasping the idea that Western science is not universal, inevitable, or unchangeable" (Stanley & Brickhouse, 1994, p. 393). Stanley and Brickhouse cite an example.

> One of the results of imperialism in Africa was the replacement of many indigenous sciences with Western science. Indigenous agriculture was destroyed and replaced with a more "efficient" agricultural process that provided greater profits for the land owners. As a result, today in many parts of Africa, the farmers are unable to grow food for their own families and must live on land that has been perhaps stripped of its usefulness (1994, p. 393).

One way of exposing children to other cultures is through the use of culturally diverse literature. We have already referred to several such pieces; *Mufaro's Beautiful Daughters* and *The Egyptian Cinderella* are cited in Constructing Science in the Classroom 6.1, p. 233. Other pieces of multicultural literature that support process-oriented inquiry science are suggested in Figure 6.13.

Another way of incorporating a multicultural perspective is to utilize an ethnocentric curriculum, wherein units and lessons center around facts, problems, and issues of ethnic significance.

An Afrocentric issue, for example, might center around finding ways to solve the problem of who really discovered America. Several lines of evidence suggest that Africans arrived in the New World before Columbus. Columbus reported the presence of people with Negroid features

SELECTED EXAMPLES OF PROCESS-ORIENTED
MULTICULTURAL CHILDREN'S LITERATURE

Great Black Heroes: Five Brave Explorers by W. Hudson (Scholastic, 1995). Includes a biography of Mae Jennison, the first black woman to explore space. (Fourth–sixth grades) (Occupations)

How the Sun Was Brought Back To the Sky by Mirra Ginsburg (Macmillan Publishing Company, Inc., 1975) is a Slovenian folk tale about how animals restored the sun to its original brilliance after it had been hidden behind the clouds. (Kindergarten) (Astronomy; fantasy)

Ming Lo Moves the Mountain by Arnold Lobel (Greenwillow Books, 1982) is an oriental folk tale of a couple whose house was being destroyed by rocks falling from the mountain. A sage advised them to move the mountain; instead they moved their house. (Second–third grade) (Observing; relativity)

Stone Soup by Marcia Brown (Charles Scribner's Sons, 1975) is an old Irish tale of the successful efforts of hungry soldiers to get the villagers to contribute ingredients for a hearty soup so it would not have to be made of stones. (First–third grade) (Inferring; rocks and minerals)

The Turnip by Pierr Morgan (Philomel Books, 1990) is an old Russian folk tale of many people working together unable to pull a giant turnip from the ground, but when a field mouse helps, it is pulled successfully. (Predicting; inferring) (First–third grade)

An excellent source of multicultural children's literature is *Multiethnic Children's Literature* by G. Ramirez, Jr. and J. L. Ramirez published by Delmar Publishers Inc., Albany, NY (1994). The authors discuss the value of multiethnic children's literature, and describe many books for and about Hispanic, African-American, Asian-American, and Native American cultures. Activities for extending children's experiences with multiethnic literature are provided.

FIGURE 6.13

when he arrived. Archaeologists in Central and South America have excavated stone heads of Negro men dating from 800 to 700 BC. African folklore tells of Abubakare, the African King of Mali, who set out in the year 1311 to sail the Atlantic, reaching the New World by following the strong African-Atlantic oceanic current. Various additional archaeological data, historical correlational data between Africa and Central and South America, and ethnographic data support the notion that Africans may have settled the New World before Columbus. The possible areas of scientific inquiry centering around this theme are numerous, and include oceanography, archaeology, geology, human biology, and meteorology. The processes of science and employment of logical thinking skills can be taught using this case as a basis for study (Van Sertima, 1976).

Cotton indigenous to Africa is grown in Central and South America. Very interesting experiments have been executed in modern laboratories to test the theory that these varieties of cotton entered the New World by the seeds floating on the Atlantic Ocean, carried across by the oceanic currents. The experiments centered around the effects of ocean water, over varying amounts of time, on the germination capability of the seeds. Similar experiments can be designed using locally-available seeds to replicate the cotton seed experiments. From this Afrocentric occurrence, children can be led to process-oriented investigations of their own design. The cotton seed migration base can be used to start studies of such concepts as seed germination, plant growth requirements, ecological communities, species survival, genetics, and life science in general.

An example from ancient Egypt shows the struggle man has had in giving up well-established concepts such as the geocentric nature of the universe. The scarab, sacred to ancient Egyptians, and amply illustrated in the treasures from the tomb of King Tutankhamun, was thought to be the agent which pushed the sun around the sky in the daytime. Everyone knew, of course, how the sun gets from one side of the earth to the other at night: There was a huge boat manned by the gods who put the sun in the boat when it set and rowed it to the other side across the huge lake that lies under the earth. But how did the sun move in the daytime? There is a beetle called the dung beetle, or scarab, which is indigenous to desert environments. This beetle lays its eggs in the nearly spherical droppings of camels, and rolls the dung ball around the sandy floor of the desert all day long. If this happens on earth, why shouldn't it also happen in the sky? So, the explanation emerged: There is a giant scarab in the sky that rolls the sun across the sky just as the dung beetle rolls dung balls. Thus, the scarab became sacred, and is found depicted in many Egyptian tombs and on many items of jewelry. This event, African in nature, is ideal for promoting discussion on the nature of science, the lengths we go to in order to support preconceived notions, our willingness to employ mystification and deification when rational explanations cannot be found, and the difficulties we encounter when we try to change conceptual bases. The behavior of dung beetles also is ideal to stimulate discussions on ecology, adaptation, specialization, reproduction, and preservation of species.

Though culturally diverse topics must be included in the education of all children, a science curriculum in an elementary classroom with high numbers of African-American children which is grounded in self-referencing Afrocentricity, increases the opportunities children have to use relevant prior experiences to make the science investigations meaningful. The Afrocentric occurrence becomes the starting point for the exploration of concepts—the event which provokes children to ask "Why?", "How did that work?", "How could they do that?", "How does that relate to what we know today?" The chosen event becomes the base from which learning experiences which lead to achievement of the desired objectives are constructed.[6]

Teachers must consider cultural and ethnic differences when planning instruction. Instructional programs must be structured to reflect the cultures and learning styles of students from the diverse cultural and ethnic groups in the classroom. Most importantly, we must "stop seeing cultural differences as developmental disturbances and . . . allow competence to be expressed in many different ways. Our thinking about the education of . . . minority children needs to begin not from an assumption of deficiency but from a recognition of cultural competence" (Bowman, 1994, p. 221).

Conclusion

Children exhibit many learning styles and bring the heritage and prior experiences of many cultures to the classroom. Elementary science teachers must examine their cultural literacy and biases and work toward eliminating any negative or intolerant biases. They must design and deliver instruction that achieves maximum possible congruity with the learning styles and cultural factors of the children. Only in this way will all children be able to construct meaning successfully.

CHAPTER 6   Additional Questions for Discussion

1. Asa Hilliard has written, "When educators do not notice diversity, when they give negative notice, or when they lose the opportunity to give positive notice of the natural diversity that is always there, they create a bogus reality for teaching and learning." (See page 244.) Discuss the implications of this statement for the elementary science classroom.
2. How does teaching in an inquiry-oriented constructivist manner promote optimum learning by all children regardless of their differences?

Notes

1. This article also offers many suggestions for teaching in a basically kinesthetic style.

2. Hanson Silver Strong & Associates, Inc., 119 Mt. Laurel Rd., Moorestown, NJ 08057. Note that a short "Learning Style Inventory" is available for teachers to help them identify learning profiles.

3. The Association for Women in Science (AWIS) promotes opportunities for women in science. Regional chapters throughout the United States sponsor a variety of programs aimed at promoting girls and women in science; many maintain lists of women scientists willing to speak at elementary schools. For more information, contact the AWIS, 1522 K Street, NW, Suite 820, Washington, DC 20005.

4. For detailed suggestions for teaching in a gender-neutral manner, refer to Baker, D. (1989).

5. For detailed information about effective teaching strategies in multicultural classrooms, see Anderson, J. A. (1994). Examining teaching styles and student learning styles in science and math classrooms. In Atwater, M. M., Radzik-Marsh, K., & Strutchens, M. (eds). *Multicultural Education: Inclusion of All*. The University of Georgia, Department of Science Education, 212 Aderhold Hall, Athens, GA 30602-7126.

6. For additional information about Afrocentric science topics, see Van Sertima, I. (1988).

References

Anderson, H. O. (1989). Board established the new NSTA Division of multicultural science education. *NSTA Reports!*, September/October, 1989.

Anderson, J. A. (1994). Examining teaching styles and student learning styles in science and math classrooms. In Atwater, M. M., Radzik-Marsh, K., & Strutchens, M. (eds). *Multicultural Education: Inclusion of All*. The University of Georgia, Department of Science Education, 212 Aderhold Hall, Athens, GA 30602-7126, p. 99.

Baker, D. (1989). Teaching for gender differences. *Research Matters . . . To the Science Teacher* in *The Georgia Science Teacher*, 29(2) 7–8, 141–169.

Becker, B. J. (1989). Gender and science achievement: A reanalysis of studies from two meta-analyses. *Journal of Research in Science Teaching*, 26(2), 141–169.

Bowman, B. T. (1994). The challenge of diversity. *Phi Delta Kappan* 76(3), 218–224.

Brookover, W., Beady, C., Flood, P., Schweister, J., & Wisenbaker, J. (1979). *School Social Systems and Student Achievement*. New York, NY: Praeger, cited in Slavin, 1994.

Brown, M. (1975). *Stone Soup: An Old Tale*. New York: Charles Scribner's Sons.

Climo, S. (1989). *The Egyptian Cinderella*. New York: Thomas Y. Crowell.

Cushner, K., McClelland, A., & Safford, P. (1992). *Human Diversity in Education*. New York: McGraw-Hill, Inc.

Dunn, R. (1988). Teaching students through their perceptual strengths or preferences. *Journal of Reading, 31*(4), 304–308.

Ginsburg, M. (1975). *How the Sun Was Brought Back to the Sky.* New York: Macmillan.

Hilliard, A. G. (1994). Foreword to King, E. W., Chipman, M., and Cruz-Janzen, M. *Educating Young Children in a Diverse Society.* Boston, MA: Allyn and Bacon.

Hudson, W. (1995). *Great black heroes: Five Brave Explorers.* New York: Scholastic.

Lawson, A. E. (1985). A review of research on formal reasoning and science teaching. *Journal of Research in Science Teaching, 19*(3), 233–248.

Lobel, A. (1982). *Ming Lo Moves the Mountain.* New York: Greenwillow Books.

Malcolm, S. (1990). Who will do science in the next century? *Scientific American,* February, 1990.

McGrayne, S. B. (1993). *Nobel Prize Women in Science: Their Lives, Struggles, and Momentous Discoveries.* New York, NY: Birch Lane Press.

Morgan, P. (1990). *The Turnip.* New York: Philomel Books.

Montaigne, M. E. (1907). *Essays.* New York and London: G. P. Putnam's Sons.

National Academy of Sciences (1994). *National Science Education Standards—Draft.* Washington, DC: National Academy Press.

National Council for the Social Studies (NCSS) Task Force on Ethnic Studies Curriculum (1992). Curriculum guidelines for multicultural education. *Social Education,* September, 1992, 274–292.

National Research Council, National Committee on Science Education Standards and Assessment. (1993). *National Science Education Standards: An Enhanced Sampler.* National Science Education Standards, 2101 Constitution Avenue, NW HA 486, Washington, DC, 20418.

National Science Teachers Association. (1990). *Science Teachers Speak Out: The NSTA Lead Paper on Science and Technology for the 21st Century.* Washington, DC: National Science Teachers Association.

Ramirez, G. & Ramirez, J. L. (1994). *Multiethnic Children's Literature.* Albany, NY: Delmar Publishers, Inc.

Rowe, M. B. (1978). *Teaching Science as Continuous Inquiry: A Basic* (second edition). New York: McGraw-Hill Book Company.

Slavin, R. E. (1994). *Educational Psychology: Theory and Practice.* Boston, MA: Allyn and Bacon.

Steptoe, J. (1987). *Mufaro's Beautiful Daughters: An African Tale.* New York: Lothrop, Lee & Shepard Books.

Steig, W. (1982). *Dr. DeSoto.* New York: Farrar, Straus and Giroux.

Tomlinson, L. M. (1987). *Locus of Control and Its Affect on Achievement.* ERIC Document Number ED 276 965.

Van Sertima, I. (1988). *Blacks in Science.* New Brunswick, NJ: Transaction Books.

———. (1976). *They Came Before Columbus.* New York: Random House.

Willis, S. (1993). Multicultural teaching: Meeting the challenges that arise in practice. *ASCD Curriculum Update*, September, 1993. Association for Supervision and Curriculum Development, 1250 N. Pitt Street, Alexandria, VA 22314–1453, p. 1–8.

CHAPTER 7

Assessment

The primary goal of assessment in education is to obtain and interpret information about student attainment—what children know and what they can do. To accomplish this, the assessment information obtained must reflect the goals and objectives of the curriculum and must represent student achievement fully, completely, and accurately.

A second, equally important goal of assessment is the evaluation of teacher performance and the program itself.

It is well known that assessment sends clear messages to children about what is valued in the classroom and, thus, what must be done to get good grades. In elementary science, children must be sent the message that the important outcomes of their work are facility and progress in the processes of science and in inquiry—that science is a process and not merely a collection of facts. Sometimes teachers succumb to the notion of teaching what is tested rather than testing what is taught. Since acquisition of factual information is relatively easy to test, tests of factual information tend to dominate, and teachers teach facts so children will do well on the factual tests. This tendency must be replaced with the notion of testing what we teach rather than teaching what we test.

American education is undergoing a paradigm shift in assessment. Testing in traditional pencil-and-paper formats is yielding to more authentic methods such as interviews, observations, portfolios, performance assessment, and human judgement. Furthermore, rather than assessment being limited to specific occasions scheduled at the end of lessons, units, or school terms, it is becoming an integral part of learning, woven directly into the instruction. This new paradigm enables teachers to gather the maximum possible information about the achievement and progress of each child.

In this chapter, you will consider ways in which process-oriented inquiry science teachers can assess the learning of their students. Several authentic assessment models are offered. The question of process *vs.* content as the focus of various assessment plans is considered, and the role of standardized tests in elementary science is examined.

In the quality elementary science program, teacher performance and the science program itself also must be assessed. To this end, you will consider ways to reflect upon the success of the work you do in the classroom and the program you develop.

As is the case throughout this text, no formulas are offered. Rather, you are encouraged to construct your own valid conceptualization about assessing student progress and achievement in elementary science as you begin developing assessment systems congruent with your conceptualization of constructivism and process-oriented inquiry science teaching in the elementary grades.

Authentic Assessment

There are three sides to the education triangle: what to teach, how to teach it, and how to measure the results. Most of the attention in science education has focused on the first two sides: what to teach (curriculum) and how to teach it (methodology). The assessment side has been less prominent.

Since teachers have received little guidance on developing assessment systems, many have relied on textbook tests and standardized achievement tests for much of their elementary science assessment program. These tests, the only assessment instruments readily available, have driven the curriculum, with the result that teachers have taught what is to be tested, and the concept of the test-driven curriculum has been reinforced. Furthermore, similar to the notion that teachers tend to teach the way they were taught, teachers tend to test the way they were tested— largely through paper-and-pencil tests. Unfortunately, typical science tests generally are not "consistent with current science education goals" (Smith, Ryan & Kuhs, 1993, p. 8).

CONSTRUCTING YOUR IDEAS 7.1
What Should Be Assessed?

Try this. In groups, make a list of things you believe should be assessed in elementary science. Then, for each, list one or more ways of assessing that item. Discuss your results as a class.

There is a principle that underlies all assessment: teachers must assess what children are supposed to learn. Assessment in science must be congruent with the goals of science education. Everyone is familiar with the incongruities often encountered between objectives and assessment. There was a teacher who assessed her children's facility in addition and subtraction by presenting complex story problems. When children failed the test, she attributed the poor performance to their not knowing addition and subtraction facts. Then there was a teacher who assigned the children inquiry investigations about the behavior of mealworms under various circumstances, and then gave a test on the external anatomy of the worms.

If children are supposed to accomplish a certain objective, they must be assessed on their achievement of that objective and not on something else. For example, if we want children to learn to classify, we must assess their ability to classify, not their ability to reproduce classification systems devised by someone else. The objectives of elementary science are process and inquiry in orientation. Thus, the focus of the elementary science assessment program must be on student attainment in process and inquiry, areas that are difficult to assess using paper and pencil tests.

Assessment must provide the best possible picture of what children know and how they think. Traditional paper and pencil tests do not always provide clear indications of what children have achieved. Typical multiple-choice and short-answer tests may do a reasonably good job of assessing acquisition of content, but content is not the focus of the elementary science program. This dilemma has provided impetus for shifting to alternative forms of assessment that are congruent with the goals of science education and that enable teachers to find out what the children *really* know.

The notion of assessing what children *really* know in the areas of the program they are being taught is termed *authentic assessment*.

The national science organizations support the shift to authentic assessment. The National Science Teachers Association urges science educators to "Develop and use evaluation and assessment tools that reflect the goals of science education" (National Science Teachers Association, 1990). In the National Science Education Standards, assessment is described as a range of strategies involving the collection and interpretation of educational data (National Research Council, 1996, p. 76).

What is Assessed in Elementary Science Education?

CONSTRUCTING YOUR IDEAS 7.2
Critiquing and Refining the Preliminary Goals Statements

Before you go any further, please review the elementary science education goals you developed in your philosophy statement in Chapter Two (Constructing Your Ideas 2.11, p. 53). Critique these goals in light of the additional information you have considered, and revise them if necessary. Your goals probably will deal with processes, inquiry, attitudes, and, to a lesser extent, content. These are the goals that will be the focus of your assessment program.

In this chapter, you will consider the question of what children can do to show they have accomplished these goals.

Assessment of Process Skills

A primary goal of elementary science is for children to acquire facility in the process skills. Assessment of the process skills involves determining how well children have mastered them. Each of the processes of science can be articulated into several indicators that show degree of proficiency in the process. Process assessment can be based on children's demonstration of these indicators. Figure 7.1 shows some indicators of progress in the process skills.

Of course, the extent to which children actually can demonstrate proficiency in a process depends on the grade level, age, and individual factors of the children as well as the circumstances in which the skill is being applied. The teacher can prepare a check list of those indicators which show proficiency in the processes at the grade being taught, and compare children's actual proficiencies with the indicators. Lists constructed by teachers reflect their own situations and the needs of their children; the indicators shown in Figure 7.1 are provided as a start.

Observation is an excellent technique for assessing children's mastery of the processes. Observation, combined with formal or semi-structured interviewing (discussed below), can yield much information about children's achievement and progress in the process skills.

Informal observation occurs as the teacher watches children do activities while circulating among groups.

SOME INDICATORS OF PROFICIENCY IN THE PROCESSES

Observation
> Identifies objects
> Utilizes more than one sense
> Utilizes all appropriate senses
> Describes properties accurately
> Provides qualitative observations
> Provides quantitative observations
> Describes changes in objects

Classification
> Identifies major properties on which objects can be sorted
> Identifies properties similar to all objects in a collection
> Sorts accurately into two groups
> Sorts accurately in multiple ways
> Forms subgroups
> Establishes own sorting criteria
> Provides sound rationale for classifications
> Develops complex classification systems

Communication
> Describes objects accurately
> Provides descriptions such that others can identify unknown objects
> Transmits information to others accurately in oral and written formats
> Verbalizes thinking

Measurement
> Selects appropriate type of measurement (length, volume, weight, etc)
> Selects appropriate unit of measurement
> Uses measurement instruments properly
> Applies measurement techniques appropriately
> Uses standard and non-standard units

Prediction
> Forms patterns
> Extends patterns
> Performs simple predictions
> Applies the process of prediction in appropriate situations
> Exhibits sound logic in verbalizing reasons for predictions
> Suggests tests to check for accuracy of predictions
> Predicts by interpolation of data
> Predicts by extrapolation of data

Inference
> Describes relationships among objects and events observed
> Utilizes all appropriate information in making inferences
> Does not utilize non-existing information
> Separates appropriate from non-essential information
> Exhibits sound reasoning in verbalizing inferences
> Applies the process of inference in appropriate situations
> Interprets graphs, tables, and other experimental data

FIGURE 7.1   (Continues on next page)

Identifying and Controlling Variables
Identifies factors that will and will not affect the outcome of an experiment
Identifies variables that can be manipulated and those that can be controlled

Formulating Hypotheses
Constructs a hypothesis when given a problem or question
Formulates own hypothesis from own problem

Interpreting Data
Identifies data needed and how to measure it
Collects useable data
Constructs data tables
Constructs and interprets graphs
Makes valid interpretations of data

Defining Operationally
Tells whether a variable can be measured conveniently
Recognizes the need for an operational definition in given situations
Decides how to measure the variable in operational terms
Verbalizes congruence between operational definition and the variable to be measured

Experimenting
Follows directions for an experiment
Develops alternative ways to investigate a question
Manipulates materials
Performs trial-and-error investigations
Identifies testable questions
Designs own investigative procedure
Formulates valid conclusions

Constructing Models
Differentiates between model and real thing
Identifies appropriate needs for models
Interprets models in terms of the real thing
Develops own accurate and appropriate models

FIGURE 7.1

This informal observation gives the teacher a general idea about what the children are doing, whether they are on the right track, and whether they are sequencing operations in a logical and appropriate manner.

Formal and structured observations can be set up in several ways. The teacher can prepare a list of specific behaviors indicative of achievement of the objective or objectives (such as those shown in Figure 7.1), and, as she circulates throughout the room, can check off those behaviors she sees exhibited by each child. (Figure 7.2.)

FIGURE 7.2   A station where children demonstrate proficiency in the skill of observation

For a qualitative assessment, the teacher checks off the indicators as the child demonstrates them; when all indicators are checked off, the child is considered to have achieved mastery of the process at that age and grade level.

For a quantitative determination, check-lists can be used to derive quantitative scores by assigning numerical values of 1–4 for each indicator and calculating the sum or the average. The average of the averages would be the total process score of the child.

The checklist system of assessment is subjective in that the teacher makes a personal judgement about proficiency in each process; however, it is objective in that each process is broken into several indicators which can be assessed and evaluated quantitatively.[1]

As with everything else, you need to prepare your *own* lists to reflect the particular needs of the children in *your* classes.

Special hands-on (or performance-based) assessment activities can test children's proficiency in the process skills (Ostlund, 1992). The technique involves setting up several stations, each of which requires the children to perform some activity that indicates proficiency in a process skill (Smith, Ryan & Kuhs, 1993, p. 9). Children rotate from station to station, either individually or in groups, and perform the required activities. Figure 7.3 shows an example of a practical process skill assessment for early elementary children. Teachers must design their own hands-on practical assessment tasks to reflect their expectations of their children and the activities done in class.

In the lower elementary grades, the teacher records each child's response to the task; in the upper elementary grades, a sheet may be provided on which children record their responses. Children's performance on each task can be scored on the basis of 1 to 4, where "1" means the skill was not seen, "2" means it was done satisfactorily, "3" means it was done well, and "4" means it was done in an outstanding and advanced manner. (See Figure 7.4.) An example of this system that includes reasons for each score is provided in Figure 7.5.

SAMPLE PRACTICAL PROCESS SKILL ASSESSMENT FOR EARLY ELEMENTARY CHILDREN

Station 1: Three or four different vegetables
  Activity: Describe the characteristics of each vegetable. Tell what senses you used.
  Process skill assessed: Observing

Station 2: A collection of 10-15 seeds
  Activity: Group the seeds into two groups, and name each group.
  Process skill assessed: Classifying

Station 3: An object in a paper bag
  Activity: Describe the object to a partner such that the partner can identify it correctly.
  Process skill assessed: Communicating

Station 4: A wooden block and a ruler
  Activity: Measure the length of the block.
  Process skill assessed: Measuring

Station 5: A tub of water with several objects beside it
  Activity: Predict whether each object will sink or float.
  Process skill assessed: Predicting

Station 6: Three opaque canisters with different things in them
  Activity: Tell what's in the canisters.
  Process skill assessed: Inferring

Station 7: Two clear soda bottles, each filled to a different level with water; wooden stick
  Activity: Tell which will make the higher sound when hit with the stick.
  Process skill assessed: Predicting

Station 8: Three different rocks
  Activity: Describe the characteristics of each rock. Tell the similarities and differences among them.
  Process skill assessed: Observing

Station 9: A collection of 10–12 shells
  Activity: Group the shells and name each group.
  Process skill assessed: Classifying

Station 10: Two wooden blocks and a simple 2-pan balance
  Activity: Tell which is heavier; tell how you know.
  Process skill assessed: Measuring

Station 11: Picture of an outdoors scene with long shadows
  Activity: Tell where the sun is.
  Process skill assessed: Inferring

FIGURE 7.3

SCORING SYSTEM FOR
PRACTICAL PROCESS SKILLS ASSESSMENT SHOWN IN FIGURE 7.3

Score	Criterion
1	Not Seen
2	Performed Satisfactorily
3	Performed Well
4	Performed in an Outstanding and Advanced Manner

Station	Process Skill	Score
1	Observing	_____
2	Classifying	_____
3	Communicating	_____
4	Measuring	_____
5	Predicting	_____
6	Inferring	_____
7	Predicting	_____
8	Observing	_____
9	Classifying	_____
10	Measuring	_____
11	Inferring	_____
	TOTAL	_____

Divide by Maximum Total of 44 = Percentage

PERCENTAGE   _____

FIGURE 7.4

SAMPLE OF SCORING FOR A CHILD DOING
PRACTICAL PROCESS SKILL ASSESSMENT
SHOWN IN FIGURE 7.3

Station	Process	Score	Reason For Score
1	Observing	2	Child did not use sense of smell.
2	Classifying	4	Child formed two mutually exclusive groups.
3	Communicating	1	Child was able only to identify object—not describe it.
4	Measuring	3	Child measured whole units; did not round increments to nearest whole.
5	Predicting	4	Child made accurate predictions and tested each.
6	Inferring	2	Child used limited investigation.
7	Predicting	4	Child made accurate predictions and tested each.
8	Observing	3	Child described properties; did not tell similarities and differences.
9	Classifying	3	Child formed only two groups, but they were mutually exclusive.
10	Measuring	4	Child operated balance properly.
11	Inferring	2	Child said "sun is in the sky;" did not give location.
	TOTAL SCORE	32	
	PERCENTAGE	$32 \div 44 = 73\%$	

FIGURE 7.5

There are several advantages to the hands-on activities method of assessment. You can see what the children can do under relatively controlled and constant conditions, and you can obtain quantitative data comparable for all the children in your class. Children's performance on the activities is representative of their proficiency in the process skills. The cultural bias and the emphasis on verbal skills often inherent in other assessment methods is reduced, and different learning styles can be accommodated. The disadvantage is that the atmosphere can be test-like, and children may bring the anxieties and fears to this situation that they bring to any testing situation.

Assessment of Inquiry

A second major goal in elementary science education is proficiency in inquiry. Inquiry implies a penchant for investigating, a curiosity, a personal necessity to resolve cognitive disequilibrations, and the desire to pursue questions to satisfactory solutions. In process-oriented inquiry science, the teacher suggests open-ended activities. Children pursue these activities to construct initial understandings, and inquire in greater depth into what they do not readily understand. They investigate additional questions suggested by their explorations, and develop their own tentative conclusions. They discuss their conclusions with one another and with the teacher to confirm validity or to plan further investigations to develop revised conclusions. The role of the teacher is to develop the rationale, goals, and objectives for the lesson or unit, prepare the initial activity, have additional activities available, ask questions, help children ask their own questions, and, especially, *listen* to gain understanding of what the children are saying. Inquiry is the agent of constructivist teaching.

Children's facility with inquiry is a major component of their progress in science. Thus assessment of children's inquiry skills is an integral component of the elementary science assessment program. Figure 7.6 shows some indicators of inquiry learning which can be considered when assessing inquiry are suggested.[2]

Each teacher or team or school must develop their own list of indicators that reflect their particular program and the expectations of their particular children. The indicators provided are intended to help you get started.

As in the process check-lists, several options are available to the teacher in using the inquiry check-list. In a qualitative approach, it can be used as a guide for an overall, subjective assessment of the child's inquiry. In a quantitative approach, each indicator can be rated on a 1 to 4 basis (with "1" = not seen, "2" = performed satisfactorily, "3" = performed well, and "4" = performed in an outstanding and advanced manner), with the average equalling the inquiry grade.

SOME INDICATORS OF STUDENT PROFICIENCY IN INQUIRY

▮ Selects and applies processes appropriately
▮ Asks appropriate questions about phenomena under investigation
▮ Initiates own ideas for investigation
▮ Investigates own questions and ideas
▮ Utilizes a variety of information sources, including printed material, multi-media, and people
▮ Relates investigations to prior experiences
▮ Suggests causes for what is observed
▮ Explains thinking process in a rational and logical way
▮ Presents ideas and conceptualizations to others for their input
▮ Discusses and challenges the ideas and conceptualizations of others
▮ Analyses conclusions and reformulates them in light of new evidence, new experiences, and input from others
▮ Subjects conclusions to tests of explanatory power and predictive power
▮ Seeks opportunities to continue explorations
▮ Exhibits realistic self-appraisal
▮ Relates learning to out-of-school situations

FIGURE 7.6

An example of the use of the inquiry check list is shown in Figure 7.7. The scores from the process and inquiry check lists can be coupled with other assessment methods to enable the teacher to arrive at an authentic assessment of the child's progress and achievement in science. Once again, it is best if you get together with your team members and develop your own checklists that are tailored to meet the needs of the children in your classes.

Assessment of Attitude

A third major goal of elementary science education is the development of positive attitudes toward science and scientists. Positive attitudes center around valuing scientific reasoning, scientific accomplishments, and the benefits to society of advancing science and technology. To a certain extent, attitudinal factors are incorporated in the inquiry indicator list. Factors such as collaboration, reflection, curiosity, and extension of learning to out-of-school situations represent positive attitudes toward science. In Figure 7.8, some indicators of positive science attitudes are suggested.

You are certain to observe additional indicators of positive science attitudes. It is useful to add these to the list so you maintain as complete

INQUIRY CHECK LIST REPORT

Score	Criterion
1	Not Seen
2	Performed Satisfactorily
3	Performed Well
4	Performed In An Outstanding and Advanced Manner

1. Selects and applies processes appropriately   _____
2. Asks appropriate questions about phenomena under investigation   _____
3. Initiates own ideas for investigation   _____
4. Investigates own questions and ideas   _____
5. Utilizes a variety of information sources, including printed material, multimedia, and people _____
6. Relates investigations to prior experiences   _____
7. Suggests causes for what is observed   _____
8. Explains thinking process in a rational and logical way   _____
9. Presents ideas and conceptualizations to others for their input   _____
10. Discusses and challenges the ideas and conceptualizations of others _____
11. Analyses conclusions and reformulates them in light of new evidence, new experiences, and input from others _____
12. Subjects conclusions to tests of explanatory power and predictive power _____
13. Seeks opportunities to continue explorations   _____
14. Exhibits realistic self-appraisal   _____
15. Relates learning to out-of-school situations   _____

TOTAL _____

PERCENTAGE (= TOTAL ÷ 60) _____

FIGURE 7.7

SOME INDICATORS OF POSITIVE ATTITUDES TOWARD SCIENCE

▌ Uses extra time for science investigations
▌ Perceives science as fun and interesting
▌ Verbalizes curiosity
▌ Extends science to out-of-school situations
▌ Voluntarily participates in out-of-school science activities
▌ Visits museums, planetariums, botanical gardens, and other public attractions of science orientation
▌ Inquires into scientific occupations and careers
▌ Seeks additional work in science
▌ Volunteers to assist in set-up and clean-up of science activities
▌ Takes an active role in maintaining the science center and live plants and animals in the classroom
▌ Chooses science-oriented television programs to watch

FIGURE 7.8

a list of attitudinal indicators as possible. Of course, the exact nature of the list will depend on your unique situation, the availability of science-oriented resources in the community, the characteristics of your class, and the needs and prior attitudes of the children.

Attitudinal questionnaires often can provide a means of assessing children's feelings about science. Figure 7.9 shows a survey designed to assess children's attitudes about their science program; it was adapted from an attitudinal questionnaire developed for fourth, fifth, and sixth grade children in one school district.

SCIENCE CLASS ATTITUDE SURVEY

Directions to student: Please answer each of the following items as honestly as possible.

1. Do you wish you had more time for science in school?
   A. yes   B. no   C. I don't know.

2. Do you have fun in science class?
   A. yes   B. no   C. I don't know.

3. Is your science class interesting?
   A. yes   B. no   C. I don't know.

4. Is your science class exciting?
   A. yes   B. no   C. I don't know.

5. Do you feel comfortable in your science class?
   A. yes   B. no   C. I don't know.

6. Do you feel successful in science?
   A. yes   B. no   C. I don't know.

7. Does your science class make you feel curious?
   A. yes   B. no   C. I don't know.

8. Does your teacher ask you questions about science?
   A. yes   B. no   C. I don't know.

9. Do you like to ask questions about science?
   A. yes   B. no   C. I don't know.

10. Do you like keeping a science portfolio?
    A. yes   B. no   C. I don't know.

11. Are the things you learn in science useful to you when you are not in school?
    A. yes   B. no   C. I don't know.

12. Do you think that knowing a lot about science will help you in the future?
    A. yes   B. no   C. I don't know.

13. Do you feel that the science you study is generally useful to you?
    A. yes   B. no   C. I don't know.

14. Do you think that being a scientist would be fun?
    A. yes   B. no   C. I don't know.

15. Do you think that being a scientist would make you feel important?
    A. yes   B. no   C. I don't know.

Courtesy: Larry Small, Science/Health Coordinator, School District 54, Schaumburg, IL 60194

FIGURE 7.9

Assessment of Content

The emphasis in this text is process-oriented inquiry where children construct their own conceptualizations. Scientific facts, concepts, generalizations, theories, and laws are used as vehicles for inquiry and process skill development and are discovered and constructed by children through their process-oriented inquiries.

Since the emphasis is on *doing* science rather than on learning about science, it is obvious that the assessment should deal with how children are *doing* science rather than with the science they learn about.

Nevertheless, there is a certain public sentiment favoring the acquisition of science content by children. Since educators are accountable to the public, it is probable that you will need to assess achievement in scientific content in addition to processes and inquiry.

One of the basic premises of the process-oriented inquiry approach to elementary science is that children will learn the content selected to be the vehicles through which the processes are mastered, will learn it more thoroughly, and will retain it longer than through other methodologies because children are constructing their own meaning. If you believe this, then student acquisition of content should pose no particular concern. In situations where content assessment is required, there generally is a listing of content children are expected to acquire. This content can be selected for use as the vehicles for process attainment and can form the basis of inquiry investigations. However, bear in mind that in inquiry it is desirable to let children explore in directions their own thinking takes them. To restrict the content used for process and inquiry vehicles is to limit the explorations of children.

Using the content required by the district as the basis for the process and inquiry activities enables children to learn both content and process. For example, if the district requires that kindergarten children learn about magnets, you can use magnets and magnetism as the vehicle through which children observe, classify, communicate, measure, predict, and infer. You can develop inquiry activities that use magnets and magnetism. If necessary or desirable, you may choose to give occasional content oriented tests to demonstrate content achievement. Tests provided by textbook publishers normally contain suggestions for content-oriented tests.

Assessment of content achievement should be considered simply another aspect of the total assessment program rather than its focus; the focus is on processes and inquiry and how well children are learning how to *do* science.

Authentic Assessment Techniques

In the constructivist methodology, children construct their own valid meanings. In assessing what children have learned and how they think, it is necessary to discover the meanings children have constructed. Paper-and-pencil tests are inadequate for accomplishing this goal.

We have already suggested several authentic methods of assessing process skills and inquiry. Several additional alternative forms of assessment enable teachers to probe deeper into children's thinking than is permitted by traditional methods of assessment.

Interviewing

In keeping with the constructivist view, one of the best ways to find out how much children have learned and how well they understand what they have learned is to ask them about it. Open-ended and partially-structured interviews with individual children accomplish this goal and are truly authentic ways of obtaining information about children's achievement and their thinking (Seda, 1991, p. 24).

The open-ended interview is a free-flowing conversation between teacher and child in which the teacher asks questions relating to the objectives of the lessons and follows up on the responses. The teacher probes, asks additional questions, and, in general, attempts to discover how the child has arrived at the responses given. Eleanor Duckworth describes the kinds of questioning that helps teachers understand children's thinking (1987, p. 97).

What do you mean?

How did you do that?

How does that fit in with what she just said?

Could you give me an example?

How did you figure that?

The open-ended interview is, perhaps, the ideal way to "jump into the children's heads to see how they are constructing information," as Judith Lanier said (See Chapter Four, p. 186). The primary advantage of the open-ended interview technique is that, given enough time, the teacher ultimately can gain a depth of understanding of what the children are thinking. However, it takes time, and time usually is a constraint. Furthermore, the teacher's understandings are subjective in nature and cannot easily be translated into marks.

In the partially-structured interview, the teacher prepares the questions and the guidelines for the interview to be certain the same questions are asked of all children. The line of questioning was somewhat predetermined as the lesson plans were developed (Item 9 "Typical Discussion Questions" of the lesson plan format suggested in Figure 5.4, p. 202); the teacher follows up on the children's responses to obtain clarification. For example, in a class of children working on the lesson, "Observing and Classifying States of Matter," shown in Constructing Science in the Classroom 5.1 (p. 203), the teacher circulates among groups and uses the "Typical Discussion Questions" to gain information about children's understandings:

What is the state of water at room temperature?

Is that its usual state?

What about water in winter?

Besides liquid and solid, what other state can water be in?

How can you tell if something is a solid, a liquid, or a gas?

Do all solids change into liquids when you heat them?

Can you give an example of solids that do not melt?

As the teacher asks the questions, she engages the children in discussion and she probes so she understands what the children are thinking; in addition, children's thinking is clarified and taken a step further because of the interchange.

This method provides opportunity for children to talk and teachers to listen, but since the questions are predetermined, the conversation does not reach as deeply into children's thinking as the open-ended interview. The opportunity for children to explain something that is not on the list of questions is limited.

Good teachers conduct open-ended and partially-structured interviews continuously as their children work on their investigations. They move from group to group, asking salient questions about what children observe, what they concluded, and why they concluded it.

The interview should become a routine part of the assessment program in elementary science education. It is only by asking children questions and listening to their responses—probing until the *teacher* understands what the *children* understand—that the teacher will know what the children know and how they think.[3]

Notes of informal interviews can be made throughout the day. In addition, at the end of an activity, an experiment, or an area of inquiry, the teacher should engage the children (individually or in groups) in discussions of what they did, what they concluded, what they learned, and what their thought processes were. Such discussions provide much information concerning achievement and construction of ideas and concepts.

Questioning techniques have been discussed throughout this book. In Chapter One, it was suggested that constructivist teachers frame questions to find out what children are thinking rather than to find out if they know facts. In Chapter Three, you asked questions of peers as you did the various process activities. In Chapter Five, it was suggested that for children to think at higher levels, we have to ask them higher level questions. Throughout this text, questioning has been suggested as the only way teachers can jump into children's heads to see how they are constructing information.

The "Think-Aloud" is a questioning technique that aids the teacher in informal assessment. Children are asked to describe their thinking as they do activities, make decisions in an experiment, or work through problems. In this manner, the teacher can obtain information about how the child is constructing meaning. We engage in think-alouds when we talk out loud to ourselves about the next move in a game of chess or when we discuss unit planning with members of our team.

The directions for employing the think-aloud technique are simple: the teacher asks the child to talk his way through the situation, and then follows up with open questions as necessary about why he did this or that. Indirect questions are used so as not to suggest "correct" responses to the children. Examples of such questioning are as follows:

"Tell me what you are thinking."

"Talk me through this."

"Can you tell us more?"

"Why?"

"And, so . . ." (asking the child to end the comment)

Think-alouds have been shown to foster teacher understanding of children's thinking in reading (Wade, 1990), and are excellent tools to assess children's understanding of science. In addition, think-alouds help children clarify their own thinking.

Note that the primary purpose of oral assessment techniques is to listen to the children so you can find out what they are thinking. It is *not* to find out if they are right or wrong. Remember the concept of "no wrong answers." Sometimes children put information together in invalid ways, and oral assessment gives the teacher the opportunity to help correct the problem. Sometimes the children's thinking it is valid but something the teacher never thought of; oral assessment gives the teacher the opportunity to help the child assume ownership.

Journals

Many teachers ask their children to keep journals in which to record a variety of information, some of which is assigned (such as weather information and information on special events or happenings), and some of which is unassigned (such as spontaneous reflections). Children's science journals can contain a plethora of information about their activities, their experiments, questions they have asked, answers they have found, their feelings, and their reflections. Science journals also can serve as a dialog between the child and the teacher. Entries can help the teacher "jump into the children's heads." Read the entries regularly, and write comments back to the children. Act on concerns shared. Help correct invalid thinking. Help children find meaningful ways to construct information as the need is revealed in the journals.

Journals can be formal, with the teacher prescribing what children are to enter, or they can be informal collections of children's thoughts. It is well to involve the children in the decision about what is to be included in the science journal.

Portfolios

A portfolio is "a container of evidence of someone's knowledge, skills, and dispositions" (Lawrenz, 1991, p. 15). The chief purposes of portfolio assessment are:

1. To enable the teacher to assess the *whole* child rather than just the child's test scores

2. To encourage children to reflect on their own work and engage in self-assessment rather than relying solely on test scores for their personal views of their accomplishments

3. To foster increased communication between teacher and student, teacher and parent, and teacher and other professionals in the school concerning the child's achievement, progress, and growth

4. To enable the teacher to evaluate the instructional program

Unlike tests which show achievement at a particular point in time, a portfolio provides evidence about a child's progress over the entire school year. Unlike tests which assess factual knowledge and information largely at the lower taxonomic levels, a portfolio provides evidence of a child's overall understandings. Unlike tests which contain selected items about what the *teacher* wants children to know, the portfolio provides complete evidence of what the child has accomplished. Unlike tests which limit communication, the portfolio is a collaborative communication effort between teacher and child.

In assessing achievement through portfolios, *all* facets of a child's progress and growth can be considered. Through the portfolio, a picture of the whole child emerges, including attitudes, interests, ideas, learning styles, and cognitive development, as well as skill with the processes, facility in inquiry, and acquisition of content.

The portfolio system of assessment must be designed carefully before it is implemented so the end product is manageable and provides the needed information. Elements of design include the purpose and uses of the portfolio, how it will be assessed, how it will be used in establishing course marks, how often it will be reviewed, the nature of the evidence that goes into the portfolio, who determines which evidence should be included, how much evidence will be included, the physical nature of the portfolio, and where it will be kept (Collins, 1992).[4]

Evidence of achievement appropriate for elementary science portfolios may include the following:

- Summaries of activities
- Experiment write-ups with hypothesis, method, data, and conclusion
- The student's own version of an experiment
- Raw data and measurements made during investigations
- Lists of observations made in activities
- Classification systems devised
- Charts and graphs
- Individual and group reports
- Written class work and homework assignments
- Tests
- Evidence of out-of-class science activities (Scout work, museum visits, planetarium visits, etc.)
- Evidence of the child's recognition and application of science in daily life
- Anecdotal records
- Check lists
- Results of observation and practical tests

Evidence may be presented in any of the following forms:

- Written material
- Video tapes

- Audio tapes
- Photographs
- Computer printouts
- Drawings, diagrams, and other art work
- Any other form children decide would show their accomplishments fairly and completely

FIGURE 7.10 Recording experimental data for inclusion in portfolio

Since the primary purpose of portfolio assessment is to understand the whole child and how he or she is constructing information, you might consider having children include reflections, "portfolio paragraphs," or "memos to portfolios." These devices allow the children to communicate their feelings and understandings in a non-threatening way. You might also consider including notes of informal observations conferences, which, for younger children, would include records of discussions and interviews you held with them about their science work.

The question of who determines what goes into the portfolio is answered from a collaborative perspective. The constructivist viewpoint suggests that the children themselves have the best idea of what is in their heads, and are best able to decide how to portray this. Thus, children need to help decide what to include. In the lower grades, children need assistance in making these decisions; teachers should ask why the child wants to include something and can encourage children to include items of particular significance. In the upper elementary grades, children are given more freedom in making their selections. Children should write (or communicate in some other way) the reason they selected what they did so the teacher will know what to look for. For example, a child may want to include a creative writing story about dinosaurs because it shows he knows the names of many dinosaurs, or, alternatively, because it shows he has a good grasp of the ecosystems in which dinosaurs lived. The teacher would review the evidence differently, depending on the reason for its inclusion.

It is a good idea to solicit the input of parents since the portfolios ultimately go to them. Parents can help in deciding what is most helpful and meaningful to them as they help their children. This practice also has the advantage that the parents know what to look for and praise when the portfolio comes home.

The teacher may require the inclusion of certain items that are indicative of student achievement and progress or that will enable grades to be determined fairly and efficiently. Teachers should explain why they have chosen items they require to be in the portfolio.

Should only the *best* work be included? This depends on the purpose of the portfolio. It may be desirable to include examples of less excellent work to demonstrate growth. It may also be desirable to include early drafts of experimental work and investigations to show development of thinking and increased sophistication in applying process skills.

What does a portfolio look like? The product should be carefully planned. What you do not want is a huge folder filled with a potpourri of children's work that you have to sift through and try to make sense out of when the term ends. Experienced portfolio users suggest having a "working" portfolio and a "permanent" portfolio (Lambdin & Walker, 1994, p. 319). The working portfolio is an accordion-style folder easily accessible to children into which they drop items they may want eventually to include in the permanent portfolio. Much of this material will be discarded or taken home as children select what is most representative of their efforts and thinking for inclusion in the permanent portfolio.

The permanent" portfolio, is also an accordion-style folder but of a different color, and is kept in a secure place. It includes specific items that the child, parents, and teacher have jointly agreed will make up the portfolio. Each item the child includes in the portfolio should be labeled and the reason for its inclusion should be written so the teacher will know what to look for.

To be effective as an assessment tool the portfolios must receive continuous attention and be accessible to children. The whole idea is for the permanent portfolio eventually to contain the best possible evidence of each child's science work. Do not wait until the end of the marking period and then have everyone, including yourself, hustle to create gradable portfolios. Have children keep them up to date on a daily basis as they grow, improve, and accomplish.

Older children should include a table of contents, a paragraph describing the contents and what the items show, and a self-evaluation paragraph when it is time to assess the portfolio.

How many items should be in the permanent portfolio? That depends on many factors, not the least of which is the time you have available. Most users of portfolios urge limiting the number of items to the minimum necessary to get a complete picture; many suggest that five or six carefully selected items often are sufficient for assessing a child's progress during a grading period. These, of course, are in addition to the items the teacher chooses to include.

There are two elements to be evaluated in a portfolio: the child's contribution and the teacher's requirement.

Since the child's contribution includes the products the child feels are most indicative of his best work, keenest interests, and most pronounced progress, this portion of the portfolio is assessed relative to the evidence presented. The child's contribution is *not* assessed relative to some external standard such as percent correct or progress according to some standard. Rather, it is assessed according to such criteria as the following:

1. **Selection**. Did the child select examples that show what he wanted to show? Were the examples indicative of the child's best thinking and best work? Did the examples show progress and growth?
2. **Reflection**. Were the explanations logical? Did they show what they were intended to show? Did the child's evidence and explanations showcase strengths and exhibit progress in weaker areas? Overall, does the child indicate an accurate grasp of the quality of his work? Does the evidence show he understands what is going on? Does it show he has worked effectively to gain understanding in weaker areas?
3. **Mechanics**. Is there a Table of Contents? Are all exhibits properly labeled and explained? Is the agreed-upon format followed?

The child's contribution can be assessed on a scale of 1 to 3 for each criterion, and an overall mark of "excellent," "satisfactory," or "needs improvement" can be assigned for the child's contribution. Personal comments on the portfolio are critical; some teachers require children to include a blank sheet for teacher comments.

The teacher's contribution is likely to be more objective in nature, including such items as

- Process skill assessments
- Inquiry assessments
- Content assessments
- Interview notes

■ Observation notes
■ Results of hands-on process skill activity tests
■ Check lists
■ Test scores
■ Activity evaluations
■ Homework and class work grades

When assessing children through the portfolio method, the child's contribution should be compared with the teacher's contribution to establish the complete picture. For example, if a child's daily grades are low, the portfolio may demonstrate excellence in achieving the objectives even though the grades may not have reflected it. Term grades can be derived from the combination of the child's and the teacher's contributions. As the child grows older, teacher-student collaborations can be invoked in establishing how the portfolio will be assessed. In addition, some schools may have school-wide evaluation guidelines for portfolio assessment.

The portfolio system of assessment provides the opportunity for information to be presented that best shows each child's abilities and understandings.

Assessment Techniques for Children with Special Needs

In Chapter Six you explored some individual differences which affect children's performance in science. Different people have different styles of learning. Teaching to an individual's strength is important for achievement; assessing their achievement through their strengths is equally important. Therefore, different individuals must be assessed in different ways so they are comfortable in the assessment process and can produce their best work. For example, it would yield false assessment data if an auditory learner were taught in an auditory manner and then required to take a written test to demonstrate achievement. Assessment must be customized to learning style.

Several customized assessment suggestions for what children can do to demonstrate competence and achievement are offered in Figure 7.11.

Report Cards

One of the functions of the assessment process is to formulate marks to be communicated to parents and shared with other professionals in the school using report cards or progress reports, in conferences, or by means of other communication devices.[5] The most authentic reporting system is

ASSESSMENT TECHNIQUES CUSTOMIZED TO LEARNING STYLES

- Devise a "visual essay" such as a collage, poster, slide presentation, or overhead transparency presentation depicting main ideas (visual learner)
- Illustrate concept with diagrams (visual learner)
- Tape record responses (auditory learner)
- Do taped interviews similar to TV interviews; formulate conclusions on tape (auditory learner)
- Prepare a scrapbook or collection of articles, pictures, and other artifacts to portray main ideas (kinesthetic learner)
- Write a musical theme, operetta, play (auditory and kinesthetic learners)
- Devise games to challenge others on their understandings, thereby demonstrating their own understandings (field dependent learners)
- Write or recite definitions (Sensing-Thinking learners)
- Compare two or more phenomena to illustrate understanding (Intuitive-Thinking learners)
- Describe feelings relating to discovery and understanding of concept (Sensing-Feeling learners)
- Design and execute an experiment to demonstrate understanding (Intuitive-Feeling learners)
- Encourage both boys and girls to portray their understandings in comfortable ways (gender differences)
- Ask children to decide for themselves the best way to present their understandings (learners with an external locus of control)
- Give children a choice of short-answer questions, essays, or multiple-choice questions

FIGURE 7.11

one which consists of narratives and/or parent conferences. In this case, the data collected from checklists, observations, and portfolios provides everything needed for reporting progress, together with back-up documents and data.

As you doubtless have inferred, the establishment of marks is artificial, for marks cannot represent the totality of what a child has achieved. Furthermore, they do not always represent the same criteria across the country, within a school, or even from subject to subject with the same teacher. Much as it would be desirable to replace quantitative marking systems with narrative progress reports, marks are inherent in the accountability system of education.

Thus the question arises as to how to translate the assessment data into marks. Indeed, the type of assessment data you collect is a direct function of the way the data will be used to establish report card marks. If the marking system is broad (such as **E** for "excellent," **S** for "satisfactory," and **N** for "needs improvement") you will need less quantitative data than you will need if the marking system is quantitative (**A, B, C, D**, and **F** or percentages).

For quantitative marking systems, the first task is to establish the factors that go into the mark and the percentage or weight of each factor. *All* factors that go into determination of the mark for science should deal with science achievement, and not such factors as behavior and performance in other areas such as reading, writing, spelling, and mathematics except as they play significant roles in the science program.

Factors to be considered when calculating the science mark could include the following:

- Interviews. If necessary, children can be assigned grades for the project or activity or area of inquiry partly on the basis of the interview and partly on their actual execution of the activity.
- Scores on process check-lists and/or practical tests
- Scores on inquiry check-lists
- Scores on tests of content
- Portfolio scores. Portfolios can be scored using a point system in which points are assigned for each item in the portfolio, including child's contribution. Total points are calculated and proportioned to a percentage score. This score is then compared with what the child has offered in the portfolio, and is adjusted up or down based on the evidence submitted by the child.
- Extra activities that exhibit positive or improving science attitudes
- Quizzes, unit tests, major tests, and final exams
- Homework
- Class work
- Projects, reports, and presentations. In grading major activities such as reports and presentations, you might consider basing half of the grade on the planning, preparation, execution, and completion of the activity, and half on the child's understandings as revealed through interviews.
- Participation

Journals should *not* be used for grading if they are considered private documents shared between teacher and child.

The final mark should be calculated in accordance with a weighted system which has been pre-established and, especially in the case of upper elementary children, shared with the children. Either the point system or the percentage system can be employed.

A typical plan for establishing marks might look like this:

Process Skill Achievement	30%
Inquiry Achievement	30%
Portfolio	20%
Other Activities	20%

You will notice there is no provision for content achievement. Considering its secondary place in the scheme of elementary science education, the content achievement factor, if included at all in the marking system, should be small.

Many states and individual school districts are working to establish criteria for report cards. Often this work is done in committees composed of teachers, administrators, and parents. You can bring an authentic assessment perspective to such committee work.

Marks are difficult to assign in process-oriented inquiry science, for it is difficult to establish measurable criteria that can be administered uniformly with all children. However, the suggestions provided in this chapter for quantifying assessment information and preparing marks should help you grade your children fairly and consistently.

CONSTRUCTING YOUR IDEAS 7.3
Constructing Your Assessment System

Now it's your turn. Construct a system for determining final marks in science in the grade you plan to teach. First, in a paragraph, summarize your rationale for your system and the philosophy of grading which guided you. Then, indicate whether you will establish marks on the point system or the percentage system. Show all categories you plan to include and how much weight each category will carry in the final mark, and describe how you will obtain the needed data. Be sure to include flexibility to accommodate unknown elements (for example, different numbers of homework and class assignments than originally anticipated, extra opportunities that present themselves, etc.). Also show how you plan to treat extra credit, effort, behavior, and so on.

Standardized Achievement Tests

School districts often require specific content preparation for specific standardized achievement tests, the results of which are used to highlight areas of strength and diagnose specific weaknesses. However, the standardized percentile ranks, grade equivalents, and stanines that are reported often overshadow the diagnostic potential of the tests, and are used to compare individual children or groups of children (such as classes, schools, or school districts) with each other and with national norms. Standardized tests also are administered to assess the state of scientific knowledge among America's youth, to assess annual progress of the nation's students in science, and to compare America's children with children of other nations, all of which are needed to meausre progress in the Goals 2000 program. Standardized achievement tests normally are content in focus, and "cannot assess a student's ability to conduct science investigations and a student's growth in science knowledge and performance" (Smith, Ryan & Kuhs, 1993, p. 9).

Much rhetoric is devoted to the notion that, since tests drive instruction, it is necessary to change the tests if there is to be permanent change in instruction. This is especially true in the science education area where tests must be revised to focus on processes and inquiry skills—quite different material from content, much more difficult to assess objectively, and extremely difficult to norm on a national basis. Then, too, there is the constructivist notion that children often understand scientific content in forms that are different from those presumed by the question writers, and so cannot demonstrate their understandings on standardized tests.

However, the current focus on standardized tests cannot be ignored, and though the tests may not assess the processes and inquiry skills and specific items of content that have been explored in a particular classroom, they are here to stay and we have to help children do their best on them.

To this end, it is suggested that you devote a small amount of time reviewing, reinforcing, and presenting areas of content that are prescribed for the standardized tests. It is also suggested that you assist children in developing their test-taking skills such as how to bubble in chosen responses, how to eliminate unlikely responses in multiple choice questions, how to use other test items to help in answering more difficult items, and how to manage time. Having children take one or two practice tests in the same format as the standardized test helps identify test-taking difficulties that need attention. Helping children develop sound test-taking skills helps ensure that test results reflect competence in subject matter and not lack of test-taking skills.

The authentic assessment methodology you use in your classroom should be shown to parents in an open-house format or by letter. Often it is the parents who are reluctant to give up standardized methods of testing. Take time to explain the methods of assessment—their nature and what they show.

A word of caution is in order. Though a compromise solution to the standardized test dilemma has been suggested, this is in no way meant to imply that the process-oriented inquiry teaching methodology should become secondary to preparation for achievement tests. It is far better to teach in the style and methodology known to be effective, while concurrently working for the replacement of content-oriented standardized tests with tests that measure what is taught.

Assessment of the Elementary Science Teacher and Program

In his article on knowledge and teaching, Shulman suggests six aspects to pedagogical reasoning (Shulman, 1987):

1. *Comprehension* of the material to be taught
2. *Transformation* of the material into forms that meet the needs of the children
3. *Instruction* of the material in the classroom
4. *Evaluation* of children's understandings and one's own performance
5. *Reflection* on one's own performance and that of the class
6. *New comprehensions* of the material, the children, and one's teaching

This is a cyclical model in which the new comprehensions (Step 6) result in new original comprehensions (Step 1) as the cycle begins again.

Competent teachers continuously evaluate their understandings, their performance, and their teaching effectiveness while they are teaching in the classroom. Competent teachers also engage in reflection (alone or with other professionals), looking backwards to capture the strengths of previous work and identify areas which need improvement. Teachers also must reflect whether the curriculum is appropriate for the children in their classes and on their own changing attitudes toward science and science teaching.

Introspective reflection is supported in the literature (Sparks-Langer & Colton, 1991) and is a powerful vehicle for enabling teachers to recreate science lessons that are meaningful to children and which better reflect the individual differences and varying prior constructions children bring to the class. Introspective reflection also enables teachers to check their own skill in urging children to inquire, to come up with their own ideas, and to develop their own plans to investigate their own ideas.

It is suggested that teachers keep their own reflective journals. Journals, portfolios, learning cohorts, and attendance at professional seminars all assist the teacher in introspective reflection. You commenced this practice of self-appraisal when you critiqued your microteaching lessons. You are urged to continue this vital reflection process throughout your teaching careers to reconcile your actions with your beliefs, your teaching practices with your education, and the outcomes of your teaching with your intents. The indicators of constructivist approaches and inquiry teaching provided in Figure 5.3 (p. 201) are suggestions you may wish to use to aid in your reflection and self-assessment process.

No lesson, unit, or school term is complete until the teacher has examined the class's response and her own performance, and has reflected upon both in order to construct for herself increasingly accurate understandings of her effectiveness as a teacher.

Conclusion

In this chapter, you have considered multiple aspects of the question of assessment, and you have begun to design your own authentic assessment programs that are congruent with your conceptualizations of process-oriented inquiry science teaching. You have explored the nature, advantages, and disadvantages of a number of methods of assessment. You have tackled the issue of how to turn assessment indicators into course marks. Your constructions and conceptualizations of assessment will become more solidified with time and experience. However, you must continue to search for new ideas and better ways for assessment that truly indicate what children have gained in their science education.

CHAPTER 7   Additional Questions for Discussion

1. Contrast traditional assessment methods with authentic assessment methods relative to advantages and disadvantages.
2. How can a teacher justify giving class grades when employing authentic assessment and constructivist teaching and learning methodologies?

Notes

1. Refer to Hart, D. (1994) for additional details concerning rubrics that can be used to quantify authentic assessment techniques.

2. For additional detail about indicators of constructivist teaching and learning, refer to Yager, 1991.

3. For a detailed discussion on questioning techniques in inquiry science, the reader is referred to Rowe, M. B. (1978).

4. A reference list for more information on portfolios is provided on p. 28 of the March, 1992 issue of *Science Scope*.

5. The entire October, 1994 issue of *Educational Leadership* 52(2) is devoted to methods of reporting what students learn.

References

Collins, A. (1992). Portfolios: Questions for design. *Science Scope, March, 1992,* 25–27.

Duckworth, E. (1987). *"The Having of Wonderful Ideas" and Other Essays on Teaching and Learning.* New York, NY: Teachers College Press.

Hart, D. (1994). *Authentic Assessment: A Handbook for Educators.* Menlo Park, CA: Addison-Wesley Publishing Company.

Lambdin, D. A. and Walker, V. L. (1994). Planning for classroom portfolio assessment. *Arithmetic Teacher,* February, 1994, p. 318–324.

Lawrenz, F. (1991). Authentic assessment. *Research Matters . . . To the Science Teacher.* National Association for Research in Science Teaching, June, 1991, No. 26.

National Research Council (1996). *National Science Education Standards.* Washington, DC: National Academy Press.

National Science Teachers Association (1990). *The NSTA Lead Paper on Science and Technology Education for the 21st Century.* Washington, DC: National Science Teachers Association.

Ostlund, K. L. (1992). *Science Process Skills: Assessing Hands-On Student Performance.*

Rowe, M. B. (1978). *Teaching Science as Continuous Inquiry: A Basic* (Second edition). New York: McGraw Hill Book Company, Chapter 12: "Inquisition Versus Inquiry."

Seda, I. (1991). Interviews to assess learners' outcomes. *Reading Research and Instruction, 31*(1), 22–32.

Shulman, L. S. (1987). Knowledge and teaching: Foundations of the new reform. *Harvard Educational Review 57*(1), 1–22.

Smith, L. H., Ryan, J. M., & Kuhs, T. M. (1993). *Assessment of Student Learning in Science.* Columbia, SC: The South Carolina Center for Excellence in the Assessment of Student Learning, College of Education, University of South Carolina. ERIC Document ED 358–160.

Sparks-Langer, G. and Colton, A. (1991). Synthesis of research on teachers' reflective thinking. *Educational Leadership, 48,* 37–44.

Wade, S. (1990). Using think alouds to assess comprehension. *The Reading Teacher,* March, 1990, 442–451.

Yager, R. E. (1991). The constructivist learning model. *The Science Teacher,* September, 1991, 52–57.

CHAPTER 8

The Elementary Science Classroom

"The time has come," the Walrus said, "To talk of many things:"
Lewis Carroll, *The Walrus and the Carpenter*, st. II

You have been constructing your own conceptualization about how and what to teach in the elementary science program, how to assess children's growth and achievement and how to assess your own performance. This chapter is devoted to practical suggestions pertaining to implementing your constructivist process-oriented inquiry science program in your elementary classroom.

Strategies for Successful Science Activities

Science activities in the constructivist elementary classroom involve children devising and executing their own investigations to answer their own questions that arise from observations they make. Nonetheless, it is prudent for teachers to exercise some measures to ensure the activities achieve maximum productivity with minimum disruption. The following are some factors you may wish to keep in mind.

To the Student

1. There's no such thing as "it didn't work."
2. There's no such thing as a dumb question.
3. There are no wrong answers.
4. Question everything!

To the Teacher

1. Try it yourself first.
2. Discuss the activity in class before the children start work.
3. Show connections with prior lessons.
4. Demonstrate in class first if necessary.
5. Be very specific and very structured if necessary.
6. Be sure your directions are clear and complete. Practice giving the directions ahead of time, and use notes on 3x5 cards or on an overhead transparency if you are afraid you might forget to include something.
7. Have all materials ready, counted out and packaged so all the materials needed by each group are together.
8. Do not pass materials out until you have completed all introductory work and have given the directions. Children will start to fool with the materials as soon as they get them—no matter what you say to the contrary.

Time Management

Science in the elementary schools often is allocated less time in the daily schedule than is desirable or necessary to permit children to inquire openly. There are several ways you can schedule science. One is to hold it daily for short periods of time. Another is to hold it two or three times weekly for proportionately longer periods of time; this has the advantage of providing enough time for children to complete their explorations. Many teachers adjust schedules from week to week to provide the needed time. In addition, state and national Science Olympiad competition preparation and local science enrichment programs can be held after school to provide supervised time for children to explore areas of inquiry.

Student laboratory assistants can save a great deal of time in setting up for science activities. You may select the lab assistant on the basis of interest, achievement, or other appropriate criteria. Lab assistants can be given the responsibility for setting up before science activities, obtaining additional materials as needed during the activities, and cleaning up afterward. Teach them where things are, and show them what they are supposed to do. Some teachers elect to have several lab assistants at the same time, in case one is absent. Some teachers rotate the lab assistant position throughout the school year so everyone gets to be lab assistant at least once. It may be possible to invite older children to serve as laboratory assistants; such service strengthens their understanding of science and helps the younger children in the same way cooperative learning groups aid all participants.

Classroom Organization

As was discussed in Chapter Four, constructivist science is facilitated by children working in groups. To this end, it is recommended that you arrange the desks in your classroom in clusters to accommodate groups. Occasionally it may be desirable to re-arrange the desks to provide for individual work or to clear a large floor space. The constructivist classroom has "maximum flexibility of space and movement," and "can accommodate individual, small group, and large group learning experiences each day at varying levels of difficulty" (Wood, 1990, p. i).

Science centers in the classroom are appropriate for all grade levels. They should be easily accessible to all children, and should contain equipment and materials children can use to continue investigations started in class or to pursue investigations they themselves have developed. Make it a habit to suggest to children that they use free time in the science center.

In addition to the classroom science center, kindergarten and first-grade teachers will want to include science centers in their daily learning centers activities so children can pursue their investigations and inquiries in small groups under teacher guidance. Groups of children rotate to the science center just as they rotate to the other centers in the room.

Outdoor classrooms are excellent ways to extend science beyond school walls. Outdoor classrooms can be as simple as designated areas of the school campus; in urban settings, children can observe grass growing through the cement, and can do measurement activities outdoors. Or outdoor classrooms can be as complex as outdoor learning facilities complete with nature trails, butterfly and hummingbird gardens, vegetable gardens, and amphitheaters. When planning an outdoor learning center, be sure to establish goals and objectives for its use, and be sure to involve all interested faculty and administrators. Soliciting the involvement of parents, the parent-teacher organization, and local businesses may aid you in your planning, and often in financing the project.

Paraprofessionals, parents, personnel from local businesses, and preservice teachers may be willing to assist in other ways. Such help can range from assisting children in performing their activities and preparing the needed materials, to helping plan special facilities, giving special presentations, and providing financial assistance.

Equipment and Materials

To the extent possible, it is recommended that you utilize equipment and materials available from familiar sources such as grocery stores, hardware stores, and drug stores. These materials are safe, inexpensive, and easy to obtain, can be duplicated for independent storage of materials for different activities, and can be obtained by children who are interested in doing science at home. It is a good idea to reserve a separate storage area for science equipment and materials. Many teachers put the non-expendable materials for an activity in a unit in a small box appropriately labeled, not to be touched except when children are doing those activities. Though this may mean duplicating some materials, the time saved from having to hunt, assemble, and replace materials every time you have children do that activity is worth the minor extra expense. Shoe boxes make excellent storage containers for the materials for individual activities, as do the inexpensive plastic boxes and containers available in many shops. Be sure to label containers of materials available for children's use, and show them where these materials are so they can get them themselves.

Occasionally you may want to order science equipment from a science supply house. Since there are many varieties of most items, it is strongly recommended that you check with someone knowledgeable about science materials and equipment prior to purchasing. For example, there are dozens of kinds of thermometers, plastic laboratory ware, and microscopes. It is better to check with someone knowledgeable about what you are proposing to order than to purchase something you cannot use.

Parent Involvement

With the current stress on parent involvement in their children's education, parents, guardians, and caretakers are becoming increasingly comfortable in working with the schools toward common goals for their children. Many parents, despite busy work schedules, are able to donate an hour or two a week to school activities. Parents can serve as lab assistants during science, and they can be enlisted to help set up for science activities. Parent assistance can be solicited in writing a weekly science newsletter that includes descriptions of the class's current emphasis in science, suggests home activities to accompany an "experiment of the week," and asks for assistance and materials as needed. Parents can be asked to donate materials required for science activities. Parents may be willing to serve on committees to determine criteria for portfolios, or to help establish guidelines for authentic systems of reporting children's achievement and progress.

Another way to involve parents in science is to prepare parent modules to be taken home by children and returned within a few days. These modules can consist of inexpensive materials, a book, and clear and simple directions for one or more activities for the child and parent to do together at home. Parent modules are particularly successful in second-language homes where parents may be hesitant to come to school for various reasons, such as limited English language proficiency.

To spark parent interest, you might invite parents to the classroom for an evening of science activities where you explain the science program and involve them as co-inquirers with their children in one or two science investigations; this way they will be doing science the way their children do science in the classroom.

The National Science Teachers Association has published a position statement, *Parent Involvement in Science Education*, in which it is affirmed that "Parents play an essential role in the success of students in schools. Parents who encourage the daily use of science concepts and process skills enhance their child's ability to learn the skills necessary for success" (1994, p. 5).

Animals and Plants in the Classroom

You should consider having one or two class pets in your classroom. Class pets provide a way of teaching children responsibility as well as teaching them how to take care of animals humanely. Animals commonly found as classroom pets include the following:

> Goldfish
> Birds
> Gerbils
> Hamsters
> Guinea Pigs
> Salamanders
> Lizards
> Chameleons
> Iguanas
> Tropical Fish
> Rabbits
> Crickets

Pet stores and the local or school libraries can provide material on how to care for the animals you have in your classroom. Be sure children take a certain amount of the responsibility (depending on their age) for feeding and watering the animals, cleaning the cages, and doing other chores that have to be done. Be sure to make adequate provisions for weekend and vacation care of the animals. Be sure the living space for the animal is large enough and replicates its natural environment to the extent possible. Include a lesson on the humane treatment of animals.[1]

Plants can be grown in the classroom, and children can observe their characteristics and measure their rates of growth. Terrariums (containers with small plants, ferns, and mosses planted in a shallow layer of soil and pebbles) can be started by the children and can be maintained throughout the school year.

Cooperative Teaching and Cooperative Learning

Several models of cooperative teaching are appropriate for elementary science education. One model suggests that one or two teachers in a team who have particular interest and expertise in science assume responsibility for all the science education of children in the team. In another model, subject specialists are responsible for teaching their subject to all children in a grade level. These models have the advantage that science is taught by instructors with knowledge and expertise; however, curriculum integration is difficult to achieve.

In a third model, all teachers in a grade level cooperate in the teaching of science by rotating responsibility for lessons in a jointly-planned unit. One teacher assumes responsibility for a certain lesson, and sets up all the needed materials. Each class rotates into that teacher's room for their science lesson during the day. A different teacher assumes responsibility for the next lesson, and so on. Rotating assignments provides coordination of lessons across the curriculum in all sections of the grade level, enables teachers to provide increased depth since they do not have to do everything, and provides different viewpoints to stimulate children's thinking. This system also saves teachers valuable preparation time, for they only have to prepare certain lessons out of the total prepared by the team.

It has been established that cooperative learning fosters achievement. Achievement in science is no exception. Indeed, in the constructivist approach, children must discuss their thinking and their conclusions with one another to establish validity and logical deductions. Discussing their thoughts among themselves often leads to new insights and new ways of constructing concepts that increase meaningfulness.

The traditional system of cooperative learning calls for division of labor wherein one child is responsible for performing the activity and the others are assigned such roles as materials manager, recorder, and communicator. This is to be avoided in science, for the emphasis in constructivist learning is that all children should do all the activities and formulate their own ideas as a result of having done them. Each child must do the activities, each child must record observations, and each child must feel free to interact with the teacher. Only by becoming totally involved in the process of doing science will each child develop the process and inquiry skills needed to construct sound conceptualizations. Thus, it is recommended that children work in unstructured groups in their science activities; groups should include most knowledgeable and least knowledgeable children.

Group size in science should be varied in accordance with the needs of the instruction, and can include whole group instruction, whole group activities, small group activities, individual projects, and specific science centers.

LARGE GROUP ACTIVITY

FIGURE 8.1 First grade children discuss the results of their seed sprouting activity.

Safety in the Elementary Science Classroom

It is of paramount importance that elementary science teachers take appropriate safety precautions in science activities. As teacher and role model, you are expected to display good safety habits at all times and set sound safety expectations for your children.

Before you assign children to work on any activity, it is absolutely essential that you discuss safety precautions with them, and that you assure yourself that they understand the precautions. It also is essential that you be on the lookout for unsafe practices as the children explore.

It is a good idea to discuss science safety in general terms with children at the beginning of the school year. Focus on the following:

1. **Cooperation** between you and the children and among each other on safety matters ensures they will act in a safe manner.
2. **Orderly behavior** reduces the likelihood of accidents.
3. **Listening** for your voice as they do their activities enables them to hear additional instructions.
4. **Common sense** must be invoked at all times when dealing with science activities.

A fun multiple-choice Science Activities Inventory which children in the upper elementary grades can take as an introduction to the discussion on safety is presented in In The Schools 8.1. The inventory is intended to facilitate the safety discussion by highlighting frequently encountered safety and behavior problems as well as providing "correct" choices for various laboratory situations. Included in the discussion should be a thorough review of all safety features available in the classroom, such as a sink, running water, location of fire extinguisher, location of trash cans, and so on.

A Science Activities Safety Contract is shown in In The Schools 8.2. This contract, adapted from NSTA materials, is intended to impress children with the importance of following instructions for science activities. Experience has shown that asking children to sign a contract such as this reinforces the importance of following safety and behavior rules. It also demonstrates that the teacher has stressed safety, thereby providing a degree of legal protection. After the teacher makes a copy for the records, children should include it in their portfolio or science journal.

IN THE SCHOOLS 8.1
Science Activities Safety Inventory

(Adapted from Materials Provided by the National Science Teachers Association)

1. When the teacher is giving instructions about a science activity, you should
   a. listen carefully.
   b. ignore the teacher.
   c. sleep.
   d. figure that the instructions apply to everybody else, but not to you.

2. If you see something during a science activity that is dangerous, what should you do?
   a. Tell the teacher when you have time.
   b. Tell the teacher at once.
   c. Tell the teacher during clean-up time.
   d. Tell the teacher after school.

3. Spills can cause injuries and additional accidents. When should you clean them up?
   a. At once
   b. During clean-up time
   c. When you have time
   d. At the end of the science class

4. When you work with chemicals or hot plates, what should you do with *long hair*?
   a. Cut it off.
   b. Hold on to it with both hands.
   c. Keep it out of the way by wearing a band, barrettes, etc., or pulling it into a "pony tail."
   d. Keep it combed nicely.

5. When you are working on science activities, what should you do with long chains, loose bracelets, loose rings, etc.?
   a. Leave them on.
   b. Remove them and put them on the work table.
   c. Remove them and put them in your pocket or purse.
   d. Leave them at your desk.

6. If you are hurt (cut, burned, etc.), what should you do?
   a. Tell the principal at once.
   b. Tell the teacher at once.
   c. Announce it to the class.
   d. See the doctor after school.

7. If you think there is something wrong with a piece of equipment you are using, you should stop, turn it off (if necessary), and
   a. tell your best friend.
   b. tell the teacher.
   c. tell another student.
   d. tell the custodian.

8. If you accidentally break a piece of equipment, you should
   a. tell the teacher at once.
   b. clean it up with your hands.
   c. hide it so no one finds out.
   d. blame someone else.

9. How do you move around the room during science time?
   a. Run
   b. Skip
   c. Hop
   d. Walk

10. Helping clean up after a science activity is the job of
    a. new students.
    b. old students.
    c. each student.
    d. the teacher.

11. When you use science equipment and/or chemicals, you should give the activity all of your
    a. interest.
    b. attention.
    c. effort.
    d. interest, attention, and effort.

12. Chemicals, small parts, and glassware are *not* to be
    a. treated with respect and care.
    b. put into your mouth.
    c. used properly.
    d. stored properly.

13. To prevent accidents during science activities involving equipment or chemicals, you should
    a. use shortcuts.
    b. follow your teacher's directions.
    c. hurry ahead of the other students.
    d. ask someone else to do the work.

14. *Playing* instead of *working*, or bothering other people during science activities is
    a. always against the rules.
    b. all right.
    c. not dangerous.
    d. okay after you have finished your project.

15. If you see a fire in a piece of apparatus you are using during a science activity, what should you do?
    a. Throw water on it.
    b. Grab your stuff and run.
    c. Tell your teacher immediately.
    d. Open a window.

16. In case of fire during a science activity, notify the teacher *at once* and then
    a. follow the teacher's directions.
    b. open the windows.
    c. yell.
    d. run.

17. Before you touch an electrical switch, plug, or outlet,
    a. your hands must be dry.
    b. your hands must be clean.
    c. you should ask the custodian.
    d. you should check with the nurse.

18. How should you remove an electrical plug from the outlet?
    a. Pull on the plug.
    b. Pull on the cord.
    c. Pull on the appliance it is connected to.
    d. Get your teacher to do it.

19. Why must you wear eye protection during science activities?
    a. To protect your eyes
    b. To prevent nearsightedness
    c. To prevent farsightedness
    d. To look cool

20. You should wear eye protection during science activities even though you wear regular glasses or contact lenses.
    a. True
    b. False

21. Cabinet drawers and doors that are left open cause a hazard. You should
    a. walk around them.
    b. close them.
    c. leave them alone.
    d. wait for the teacher to close them.

22. If chemicals get on your skin or your clothes, what should you do?
    a. Wash at once with vinegar.
    b. Soak the clothes or your skin with milk.
    c. Wash with soap.
    d. Run plenty of water onto the area.

23. Disturbing other students while they are working on science activities is
    a. helpful.
    b. welcome by the teacher.
    c. dangerous.
    d. the quickest way to do a job.

24. Materials and equipment which are already set up for a science activity when you arrive should be left where they are.
    a. True
    b. False

25. Who gets out the materials and equipment for science activities?
   a. The teacher
   b. The laboratory assistant
   c. Either the teacher or the lab assistant
   d. The principal

SCIENCE ACTIVITIES SAFETY INVENTORY
SUGGESTED "CORRECT" RESPONSES

1. a	10. c	18. a
2. b	11. d	19. a
3. a	12. b	20. a
4. c	13. b	21. b
5. c	14. a	22. d
6. b	15. c	23. c
7. b	16. a	24. a
8. a	17. a	25. c
9. d		

IN THE SCHOOLS 8.2
Science Activities Contract

SCIENCE ACTIVITIES CONTRACT

I will:

Follow all instructions given by the teacher.

Protect my eyes and my body during science activities by wearing safety goggles and lab smocks.

Carry out good safety and housekeeping practices.

Know where to get help.

Conduct myself in a responsible manner at all times.

I, _____, have read, and agree to abide by the science activity rules set forth above. I also agree to abide by any additional printed instructions provided by the teacher or the school. I also agree to follow all other written and vebal instructions given in class.

_____   _____
          Date   Signature

Safety goggles should be worn by children during all science activities which have any potential for liquids or solids accidentally getting into eyes. This includes all activities involving water, chemicals, and rocks and minerals. It is a good idea to have children wear their goggles for every science activity. Also be sure children know the locations of fire exits and fire extinguishers.

It is suggested that children bring an old, long-sleeved shirt to use as a laboratory coat. As with the goggles, it is a good idea to have children wear their smocks for every science activity.

It is recommended that, in general, you use plastic instead of glass. Clear plastic containers are available that do everything glass can do except shatter.

Be sure to tell children *never* to taste or eat anything unless you specifically tell them otherwise.

Chemicals must be treated with respect. You will not be using dangerous chemicals in elementary science. All activities suggested in this book use materials that are safe for children to handle and that can be stored without special consideration. Nonetheless, the materials you do use must be handled and stored safely. Factors include the following:

1. The strongest acid you will use is vinegar, which is a dilute acetic acid. You should not use any acids stronger than vinegar in the elementary grades.

2. OSHA (Occupational Safety and Health Administration) has established the degrees of hazard of all chemicals to inform consumers of the best way to store them. Five categories are normally identified:
   a. General
   b. Corrosive
   c. Flammable
   d. Oxidizer
   e. Poisonous

   When considering whether chemicals are safe, look in the science supply catalogs for the OSHA rating. If the chemical is rated "general," it is safe to use in the elementary school classroom, and it can be stored anywhere. Do not use chemicals with any of the other four ratings. It is a good idea to check with a science supervisor or an upper grades science teacher if you are in doubt.

3. Most rocks and minerals are safe. However, there are a few that fall under the "poisonous" category. These include galena (lead sulfide), cinnabar (mercury sulfide), asbestos, and arsenopyrite, realgar, and orpiment (all minerals of arsenic). Do not include these in your mineral collections. If they are already present, dispose of them.

Trust

Many researchers have come to the conclusion that the trust students have in their teachers is established in the early grades. It is redundant to the awesome array of literature to say that the relationship between teacher and child frequently is based on the teacher being the repository of knowledge; that the child is required to absorb the knowledge the teacher imparts and demonstrate this possession through tests of one form or another; that the teacher has the "right" answers, and it is the job of the child to figure out what they are. Even when the teacher doesn't seem to have the right answers, it is assumed that correct answers exist. The impression is given that in discussions, in activities, and in all other types of science class activities, the goal of the child is to obtain or achieve the "right" answers or the "right" conclusions. This has been the case since the earliest grades, and children are extremely adept, through a huge variety of subtle actions, at figuring out and supplying the correct responses. In addition, grades are omnipotent, and no one wants to take the chance of getting a bad grade. So children play the game, which often consists largely of figuring out what the teacher considers to be the correct responses.

It is no wonder that children are suspicious when a teacher encourages them to investigate their own conclusions and form their own unique constructions of information. The *trust* factor is missing.

What can we constructivist teachers do about this situation? First, we must act to develop trust with our children. We need to become authentic human beings in our classrooms, complete with good days and bad days, right, wrong, and missing information, strengths and weaknesses. Do we really believe the thinking of children is important? Do we really believe children are interested in learning what is meaningful to them? Do we really believe children can behave with integrity, both socially and academically? If so, we need to let our beliefs show.

Do we have that penchant so necessary to investigate unfamiliar territory? If so, we need to show we have it by participating actively in the investigations of our children, helping them formulate their own questions and come to their own conclusions. We need to let our children know we also are still learning and discovering—that we are, and always will be, students.

Do we really believe children are capable of investigating situations on their own? Do we really believe they have brains and are capable of using them? If so, we need to let our children know we believe it.

The development of this trust in young children "depends greatly on children's sense that they are understood, respected, and accepted. The disposition to trust teachers—a disposition that may set a pattern for all subsequent responses to school—can be strengthened or undermined during the early years of school" (Katz, 1994, p. 201).

We do all this not by talking about it, but by *acting* on our beliefs. We present ourselves as co-inquirers, as honest and sincere and dependable individuals, as concerned leaders of children. We demonstrate our genuine concern for children as cognitive beings through *all* our actions, verbal and non-verbal. We treat children like people, and we do this all the time. In short, we demonstrate throughout the day that children are important—as individuals, as social beings, and as inquirers.

Secondly, we must start slowly in encouraging children to explore in a constructivist mode, remembering that change comes slowly and some discouragement is apt to occur. Since children are used to expository methods, we need to move them a little at a time toward constructivist learning and guided inquiry. Only when children find that the inquiry method of doing science is safe will the trust be built that is prerequisite to successful constructivist approaches to teaching and learning science.

I suggest you start children out with two or three activities that are somewhere between expository and guided inquiry in nature. It is critical to get children thinking for themselves, and to demonstrate that we truly regard their own constructions of information as valuable as our own. Constructing Science in the Classroom 8.1–8.5 show somewhat structured inquiry oriented science activities children can do to get started on developing confidence in their own thought processes and gaining trust that their thoughts are valuable to the teacher.

CONSTRUCTING SCIENCE IN THE CLASSROOM 8.1
Grouping Common Objects

GRADE

6
5
4
3
2
1
K

Objective
The student will observe and classify common items.

Materials
Items in children's desks—at least 10 items per child

Activity
Introduce the activity by asking children how things are alike and how they are different and modelling the grouping of similar objects in the teacher's own desk. The idea is for children to group the various items in their desks according to properties that are similar for all items in any one group but different for the items in the other groups. Have them give names to each group that describe the major characteristics of the groups.

Then have each child select an object from their own assemblage, bring it to another child, and ask that other child to tell where it would fit into *his* classification scheme, and why. If the other child can fit the new object into the scheme, this means they have done an adequate job of devising their scheme. Otherwise, they might have to rethink their grouping system to accommodate the new object.

CONSTRUCTING SCIENCE IN THE CLASSROOM 8.2
How Can You Tell That Air Takes Up Space?

GRADE

6
5
4
3
2
1
K

Objective

The student will infer why paper in the bottom of a transparent glass remains dry when the glass is inverted and submerged into a pail of water.

Materials

Transparent plastic cup, paper towel, pail partly filled with water

Activity

The children wad up a paper towel and stuff it into the bottom of the transparent plastic cup. They then turn the cup upside down, and submerge it into the pail of water.

Ask them to explain what they observe. Ask them how the result of this activity (the paper towel remains dry) can lead them to the conclusion that air takes up space.

Now, ask children to devise variations on this activity, trying other materials in the jar, using different temperatures of water, and so on. The main reason for this is to encourage children to come up with their *own* ideas.

Literature Connections:

Hot-Air Henry by Mary Calhoun (Mulberry Books, 1981). Henry the cat takes a solo flight in a hot air balloon.

Gilberto and the Wind by Marie Hall Ets (The Viking Press, Inc., 1963). Gilberto has many adventures with the wind, his constant companion.

CONSTRUCTING SCIENCE IN THE CLASSROOM 8.3
Evaporation

GRADE

6
5
4
3
2
1
K

Objective

The student will predict what will happen to water sprayed onto a surface after setting for a short time, and will predict the effect of moving air on evaporation.

Materials

Mini-chalkboards or other smooth surface, water, water spray-bottles

Activity

Ask children to predict what would happen if they were to spray the chalk board with the water bottle. Where do you think the water would go? Allow children to take turns spraying small amounts of water on the chalkboard. Children observe what happens, and record their findings. Discuss reasons for the happening in a large-group discussion.

Next, children predict which hand will dry faster if sprayed with water: one that is held still or one that is waved in the air. They then do the activity and compare their results with their predictions. Discuss results and inferences in a whole-class setting.

CONSTRUCTING SCIENCE IN THE CLASSROOM 8.4
How Does Water Affect Different Materials?

GRADE

6
5
4
3
2
1
K

Objective

The student will predict the effect of water on various materials.

Materials

Cups of water; samples of sugar, salt, baking soda, pepper, flour, rice, oil, vinegar, paper clips, cardboard, chips, noodles, macaroni, etc. It may also be a good idea to have a data sheet available for children to record their predictions and their observations of what happens to the material in water.

Activity

For each item, children predict what happens to it when water is added. Then they add the water, observe what happens, and record their observations. In large group, discuss the processes of prediction, observation (before and after), and classification.

CONSTRUCTING SCIENCE IN THE CLASSROOM 8.5
Gathering Weather Data

GRADE

6
5
4
3
2
1
K

Several items of weather data can be observed and recorded by children each day. These items include (1) temperature, (2) barometric pressure, (3) wind speed and wind direction, (4) rain fall, and (5) type of cloud cover. Using a data collection sheet similar to the one on page 302, children record weather information each day, and plot graphs of the data to interpret.

Temperature should be taken at the same time of day in a shady spot. Pressure can be read from a barometer. Wind speed requires an anemometer (wind speed gauge) which either can be home-made or purchased from science supply firms. Rainfall requires a rain gauge which can be home-made or purchased from science supply firms. Type of cloud cover requires comparing clouds with charts that name the clouds and indicate the type of weather with which they normally are associated. Show children how to read weather charts in newspapers so they can compare their data with that reported officially. Many meteorologists from local television stations are willing to discuss weather forecasting with elementary school children; it is an excellent idea to make use of these resource people.

Literature Connections:

The Cloud Book by Tomie De Paola (Holiday House, 1975) describes specific clouds and the weather that comes from them.

The Weather Classroom by Karen W. Moore (The Weather Channel, 1992) is an upper elementary and middle grades book on weather that suggests many activities for children to do to explore weather.

HOME-MADE RAIN GAUGE

A rain gauge is a vessel that collects rain water. The depth of the water in the vessel after it rains is equal to the amount of rainfall. Use a coffee can or other straight-sided container. Put it outdoors so it can collect the rain as it falls. Use a ruler to measure the depth of the water. The depth equals the number of inches of rain. (Be sure to empty the vessel after each time the rainfall is measured.)

HOME-MADE ANEMOMETER

1. Cut two 16-inch pieces of thin wooden strips, and cross them at their centers at right angles to each other. Drill a hole through both pieces of wood at the center, large enough for the glass or plastic part of a medicine dropper to fit through snugly.

2. Glue a very small paper cup on the end of each of the four wooden vanes, making sure all cups face the same direction. Paint one cup a different color.

3. Construct a base of two pieces of wood. Use electrical tape to attach a long nail to one side of the support.

4. Place the medicine dropper of the wooden vane apparatus over the nail, and adjust the whole thing so the apparatus spins freely.

5. To measure wind speed, count the number of turns the anemometer makes in one minute; the colored cup helps keep track of the rotations. To convert the number of turns per minute to wind speed, count the number of turns it makes per minute in a wind of known speed as reported by an area weather station. Divide this number by the speed of the wind to find the number of turns the anemometer makes per mph of wind speed.

CHART OF DAILY WEATHER OBSERVATIONS

Date and Time	Temperature	Pressure	Wind Speed	Rain Fall	Type of Cloud Cover

HOME-MADE ANEMOMETER

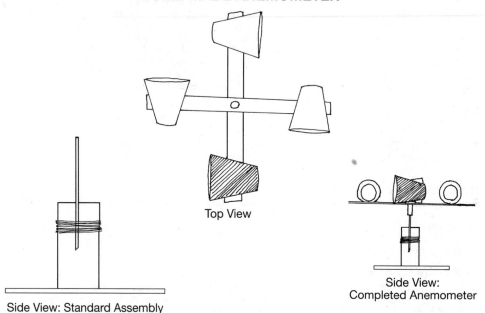

Top View

Side View: Standard Assembly

Side View:
Completed Anemometer

The numbers of turns the anemometer
makes in one minute tells wind speed.

Reading amount of rainfall

Outdoor temperature
recorded in a shady place

Classroom Management

Professor Herbert Kliebard of the University of Wisconsin has observed
that good teaching often is perceived as keeping good classroom order.
So teachers teach in ways that ensure good order: recitation, teacher-
dominated questions and answers, worksheets, choral reading, etc. Teaching in discovery and inquiry modes runs the risk of disorder, and only
the most courageous teachers are willing to take that risk.

In a constructivist approach to science teaching, the order kept in the classroom is of a different type than Kliebard was talking about. Children talk with each other; they try out different things; they argue; they pursue their positions; and they often appear to be "off-task." I get disturbed when I hear the phrase "on-task," for in the constructivist approach to science education, every child conceivably could need to pursue a given problem or situation from a different angle. Therefore, they may be seen as being off-task by observers who believe children should be doing essentially the same thing at the same time. On-task in a constructivist science classroom means children are pursuing their investigations in ways that are meaningful to them. These ways may range from slight divergence from the main task to radical departure from the primary activity as a child pursues something which will help him construct his own meanings of the situation. Children who are interested in what they are doing *are* on-task! Therefore, classroom management is different from setting down rules and requiring obedience.

The primary rule in a constructivist classroom is that every child has the right to learn and the teacher has the right to facilitate this learning. This is an extremely open rule, for it precludes the use of regulatory rules and prescribed punishment for given infractions of rules. However, children are accustomed to having rules to follow, and when we let them have too much freedom, we fear they will take advantage of the situation and bedlam will erupt. Therefore, I offer a few suggestions for successful classroom management in a constructivist science classroom.

1. No matter how committed we are to constructivist teaching and learning, we all use the expository mode in our classes to some extent. Rules of behavior appropriate for expository settings should be enforced.

2. Teachers should move slowly from the expository mode to which children have become accustomed toward guided inquiry approaches.

3. As children are introduced to more inquiry-oriented activities, the teacher might demonstrate the activity before turning it over to the children. While demonstrating it, the teacher should explain ways in which children can explore on their own. During this demonstration, the teacher should discuss behavior expectations and safety precautions to be taken during the activity.

4. While children are working on their own activities, a high degree of interaction exists between teacher and individuals and small groups. (This is exhausting and demanding!) Opportunities continually exist for private encouragement of students to exhibit appropriate behavior and for private correction of inappropriate behavior.

5. Let your building administrators know what you are doing, what your goals are, and what to look for in your classroom. This will keep them

informed, and may help you achieve your goals through their input (which you have solicited). Invite your building administrator to your class when your are doing an activity. Support for the child-centered constructivist approach to teaching and learning must come from within the school; inviting parents, colleagues, and administrators to your class-room to observe children at work helps secure the needed support.

In a constructivist classroom, behavior management problems are minimal because (1) children aren't bored, (2) children are treated with dignity, (3) children's explorations and constructions are valued, (4) children have a say as to what they do during the science class, (5) children are building positive self-concepts while they are performing the activities, and (6) children have power to work out their own activities in the way they best see fit.

If children want to "play" instead of work, you may wish to use a quasi-contractual approach in which child and teacher are equal contributors. A plan of study is agreed upon which includes the activities the child will do, a method of reporting daily progress (such as a log or a journal), the method of evaluation, and a time table. As long as the child is working within the parameters of the agreed-upon plan of study, there should be no need for concern about the child not devoting all attention to science.

Teachers also might profit from using the principle of self-referencing behavior management: "You are doing a great job today... much less fooling around than yesterday." This is to be contrasted with rule-referencing behavior management: "You broke the rule, and now you have to pay the price." Constructivist teachers effectively eliminate the reward-punishment system of classroom management.

Teachers also might profit from the 1-2-3 method of correcting undesirable actions: (1) name the individual; (2) state the specific action to be stopped; (3) state the reason why. ("James, stop talking out of turn; children cannot hear what others are saying.") Say this quietly and in close proximity to the offending child so as not to call widespread attention to the child or the problem. This encourages self-referencing behavior, eliminates confusion and ambiguities, and treats each individual with dignity. Others have written that treating children with dignity is key to successful classroom management. I have found this to be true.

If we want to teach in a constructivist mode, we, ourselves, must recognize that we also are constructing information out of our own experiences. The only way we can change our discipline road map is to try a different approach, begin developing different teacher-child interactions, and evaluate the results. Success in these new interactions will aid in our cognitive and physical construction of the more complete

constructivist classroom. Changing our expectations that children con-
form to a set of rules, and changing our conceptualization of how children solve problems and construct their own information are good first
steps. Most importantly, we must change the outlook that effective teaching is synonymous with good order in the classroom.

Conclusion

The effective elementary science teacher focuses on teaching children
more than on teaching science, leading children to their development of
process and inquiry skills and to a deep belief that they can do science
and that the science they do is valuable. The effective elementary science
teacher varies instructional methodologies and curriculum to meet the
needs of all children in the class. The effective elementary science teacher
encourages children to construct their own conceptualizations, and provides ownership of knowledge and thinking to the children. The effective elementary science teacher *listens* to children.

In the first chapter, you were asked to decide on a metaphor for
elementary science teaching. Now is the time to examine your metaphor
to see if it accurately portrays your beliefs about elementary science
teaching.

> *Discovery consists of seeing what everybody has seen and thinking
> what nobody has thought.*
>
> Albert Szent-Grorgi von Nagyrapott, from J. I Good, ed.
> *The Scientist Speculates* (1962)

> *Every great advance in science has issued from a new audacity of
> imagination.*
>
> John Dewey, *The Quest for Certainty* (1929), Chapter Eleven

> *The whole of science is nothing more than a refinement of everyday
> thinking.*
>
> Albert Einstein: *Out Of My Later Years* (1950)

CHAPTER 8   Additional Questions for Discussion

1. Describe ways of securing support from the school district and community for a constructivist process-oriented inquiry science program.
2. Describe how a constructivist teacher might start a process-oriented inquiry science program in a class of children who have not previously undertaken their own investigations.

Note

1. Note that federal regulations prohibit experimenting with any vertebrate animal. All experimentation should be done with non-vertebrate animals such as worms, insects, and bugs. This means that fish, hamsters, and lizards should not be subjected to experimental procedures.

References

Calhoun, M. (1981). *Hot-Air Henry*. New York: Mulberry Books.

Carroll, L. (1938). *The Walrus and the Carpenter*. Berkeley, CA: Archetype Press.

DePaola, T. (1975). *The Cloud Book*. New York: Holiday House.

Dewey, J. (1929). *The Quest for Certainty*. Carbondale, IL: Southern Illinois University Press.

Einstein, A. (1950). *Out of My Later Years*. New York: Philosophical Library.

Ets, M. H. (1963). *Gilberto and the Wind*. New York: The Viking Press, Inc.

Good, J. I. (1962). *The Scientist Speculates: An Anthology of Partly-Baked Ideas*. London: Heinemann.

Katz, L. G. (1994). Perspectives on the quality of early childhood programs. *Phi Delta Kappan, 76*(3), 200–205.

Moore, K. W. (1992). *The Weather Classroom*. Atlanta, GA: The Weather Channel.

National Science Teachers Association. (1994). *An NSTA Position Statement: Parent Involvement in Science Education. NSTA Reports!*. Washington, DC: National Science Teachers Association, October/November, 1994.

Wood, J. (1990). Implementing developmentally appropriate classrooms. Paper presented at the 41st annual conference of the Southern Association on Children Under Six, Dallas, TX, March 29–April 1, 1990. ERIC Number Ed 332 789.

PART II

Beyond the Science Classroom

CHAPTER 9

Reading, Writing, and Interdisciplinary Aspects

The sole substitute for an experience which we have not ourselves lived through is art and literature.

Alexander Isayevich Solzhenitsyn—Nobel Lecture, 1972.

The means by which we live have outdistanced the ends for which we live. Our scientific power has outrun our spiritual power. We have guided missiles and misguided men.

Martin Luther King, Jr. The Strength to Love (1963), 7.3.

Having constructed solid notions about the methodology most effective in elementary science education, you are now ready to consider additional topics that contribute to program excellence.

No subject can be studied in isolation. This includes science, an interdisciplinary study which is inextricably intertwined with technology and social issues, requires mathematics for interpretation of data, and requires language for communication of findings and discoveries.

Even the traditional boundaries within science itself—the life sciences, physical sciences, and earth and space sciences—erode in the face of their mutual interdependence. One cannot study, for example, the nature of life, a life science topic, without also studying the chemical makeup of living things, a physical science topic, and the relationship of living things to the environment, an earth science topic. Nor can one discuss the weathering and erosion of landforms, an earth science topic, without also discussing the contributions of living organisms to the erosion process, a life science topic, and the laws of motion, inertia, and friction that cause the breakup of rocky material, physical science topics.

In this chapter, you will extend your conceptualization of the process-oriented inquiry science methodology by considering the role of reading, writing, and literature, models of interdisciplinary study, and the science-technology-society thrust. In each, you will examine advantages, disadvantages, and arguments for and against as you deepen your views of the quality elementary science program.

Reading, Writing, and Literature

Science without language is like a ship without a compass. Reading is critical to discovering what others have learned, and writing is critical for children to communicate what they have discovered.

Literature enhances the study of science in a variety of ways. Many activities suggested in this book refer to one or more "literature connections." What is the best way to use these materials? This depends on the nature of the activity, the nature of the piece of literature, the objectives for the activity, and your personally constructed vision of quality elementary science education. The overriding principle is that literature is used to *enhance* children's inquiries and promote their own thinking.

CONSTRUCTING YOUR IDEAS 9.1
Two Bad Ants

Obtain a copy of *Two Bad Ants* by Chris Van Allsburg (Houghton Mifflin, 1988), and ask someone in your class to read it aloud.

Did you notice that several processes of science can be fostered with this book? Many opportunities exist for children to infer, as illustrated in the following questions:

▮ What are the crystals? What makes you think so? How could you be sure?
▮ What is the "boiling brown lake?" What makes you think so? How could you be sure?

Opportunities also exist for children to predict, as illustrated in the following questions:

▮ What do you suppose will happen to the ants after they fall asleep amidst the crystals? Why do you think so?
▮ What do you suppose will happen to the ants after they fall into the "boiling brown lake?" Why do you think so?
▮ Do you suppose the ants will go back to their homes? Do you think they *want* to go back home? Why?

The process of careful observation of the illustrations is a necessary precursor for making inferences and predictions.

Let us consider the question of what the crystals are. To gain additional information, children can examine regular sugar crystals with magnifying glasses or a low-power microscope, observing their shapes carefully and comparing the shape of the real sugar crystals with the shape of the crystals depicted in the book. (See Figure 9.1.) Children will notice that the real sugar is box-like in shape, whereas the crystals in the book's illustrations are more complex. This seems to contradict the idea that the crystals in the story are sugar. Making a list of evidence, children find there are several reasons for believing the crystals are sugar: (1) they are sweet, (2) the Queen likes them, and (3) they are in a bowl labeled "... GAR." The preponderance of evidence in the book suggests that the crystals are sugar. The only thing wrong is the shape of the crystals. This may prompt one to wonder, "Do *all* crystals of sugar look the same?"

Sugar crystals seen through a 20-power microscope projected onto a TV screen using a small video camera

Single sugar crystal (Courtesy The Sugar Association, Inc., 1101 15th Street, N.W., Suite 600, Washington, DC 20005)

FIGURE 9.1 Crystals of sugar

IN THE SCHOOLS 9.1
Growing Sugar Crystals

To investigate the question of what the crystals are in *Two Bad Ants*, children can grow their own sugar crystals in the form of rock candy. (See the crystal-making activities in Constructing Science in the Classroom 4.1, p. 172). Comparing the shapes of the home-made crystals with the shape of the crystals of granulated sugar, they are prepared to form the tentative generalization that sugar crystals always are box-like in shape.

Why, then, are they depicted in a different shape in the story? What would the pictures look like if the crystals were box-like in shape? Children can draw a number of box-shaped crystals and overlay their drawing on the illustration to see the effect. What does this tell us about how illustrations capture readers' attention?

This book also is an ideal introduction to inquiries involving crystal solutions and crystal formation as suggested in the crystal-making activities (In The Schools 4.4, p. 171). Such questions as the following can be investigated:

■ Are all crystals of a certain substance the same shape?
■ How can you make large crystals?
■ What is the relationship between temperature and the amount of a solid that will dissolve in water?
■ What is the relationship between rate of evaporation of the solvent and the size of crystals?

Integrating Children's Literature and Science

The activity with *Two Bad Ants* illustrates how children's literature can be used for continued process development and as an introduction to science inquiry activities. Children's literature can be integrated into science in a variety of ways. Following are ideas and suggestions from actual lessons and units. These are but a few examples; you are encouraged to devise your own.

Introducing Lessons

Literature can be used as an introduction to a lesson—to establish interest, promote questioning, present an area of inquiry, or provide introductory information. *Two Bad Ants* was used to promote questioning which led to an inquiry into the characteristics of crystals and crystal formation. The poem, *Kaleidoscope*, used in the advance organizer described in Chapter Five (p. 199), provided a bridge from actual observations of kaleidoscopic images to poetic descriptions. *Jack and the Beanstalk* as told by L. B. Cauley (Putnam, 1983) is useful to introduce inquiries on plants, requirements for plant growth, and conditions that would promote the tallest and most rapid growth of bean plants.

The poem, "What's In The Sack?" in *Where the Sidewalk Ends* by Shel Silverstein (Harper and Row, 1974) can be used as an introduction to the activity, "What's In The Bag?" (Constructing Science in the Classroom 3.2, p. 65). After reading this poem, the teacher can ask children to guess what's in the man's sack, asking for reasons for each guess, and then have children do the activity.

Miss Rumphius by Barbara Cooney (Viking Press, 1982) is a story of a lady who has followed her grandfather's wish to make the world a more beautiful place, but who becomes too ill to tend to the flower bed she has planted. The following spring, she finds that the wind and the birds have done a magnificent job of re-seeding the land and bringing color to the hills. This book can be used to introduce questions about seed dispersion, propagation, growth requirements, and elements of ecosystems, and is appropriate for fostering development of the affective domain.

Agatha's Feather Bed: Not Just Another Wild Goose Story by Carmen Agra Deedy (Peachtree, 1994) can be used as a springboard for inquiries into natural resources and their uses. The story focuses on Agatha who has purchased a feather bed, and the plight of naked geese whose feathers were used to stuff the bed. Agatha s

ves the dilemma by making coats for the geese out of her hair. This delightful story is filled with puns, word play, and illustrations of various natural materials used to make common products.

The Last Basselope: One Ferocious Story by Berkley Breathed (Little Brown, 1992) can be used to introduce the concept of endangered and extinct species. The story is about an expedition to find the last remaining basselope, a fictitious animal. Members of the party use the processes of observation, inference, and prediction as their search leads them through a trail made by the creature. This story shows how the processes of science are used in investigations of endangered and extinct species. As an extension, ask children to draw and describe a fictitious animal of their own invention. (See also "Exploring Ecosystems Through Writing Imaginary Narratives: Stories of "Creepy Critters," p. 336.)

The Sun, the Wind, and the Rain by Lisa W. Peters (H. Holt, 1988) is the story of a girl who builds a sand mountain on a beach and compares it to a mountain she sees in the distance. The story describes the rapid reshaping of the sand mountain by rain and wind, the same forces that took eons of time to reshape the real mountain. The story can be used to set the stage for children's inquiries into weathering of the earth's surface structures by water and wind. A complete lesson using this story as the introduction is shown in Constructing Science in the Classroom 9.1.

CONSTRUCTING SCIENCE IN THE CLASSROOM 9.1
How Does Weathering By Water Change Mountains?

GRADE

6
5
4
3
2
1
K

Scientific Processes Addressed
Observing, formulating hypotheses, experimenting

Science Topic Addressed
Weathering and erosion

Process-Oriented Objectives
1. The student will observe changes in sand mountains caused by water.
2. The student will hypothesize the relationship between water volume and rate of water flow and the weathering of the sand mountain.
3. The student will experiment to discover the relationship between water volume and rate of water flow and the rate of weathering of the sand mountain.

What Do I Want Children To Discover?
The mountains on the earth's surface are constantly being changed by water.

Description of Introductory Activity and Discussion
Read the story, *The Sun, the Wind, and the Rain* by Lisa W. Peters. Ask questions such as, "Why does the sand mountain wear down?" "Why does the real mountain wear down?" "Do you suppose the same forces cause both?"

Materials Needed
The Sun, the Wind, and the Rain by Lisa W. Peters (H. Holt, 1988), chart paper, markers, sand, large solid plastic storage bins, sticks, pebbles, buckets, shovels, watering cans (one with fine holes and one with large holes), water

Description of Activities
Working in pairs or small groups, children build a sand mountain in their plastic storage bin, complete with sticks to represent trees and pebbles to represent animals, just like Elizabeth did in the story. Next, children decide who will be the rain pourer and who will be the recorder. The rain pourer pours two cups of water slowly from the fine-holed watering can onto one side of the mountain to represent gentle rain. The recorder records the results. Children compare their results with what they see in the book. Next, the pourer pours two cups of water from the large-holed watering can onto the other side of the mountain, representing a heavy rainfall. Again, the recorder records the results, and children compare their results with what they see in the book. Each group records their data on a central chart, and the whole class discusses the patterns seen between force of the water poured and the amount of weathering each side of the mountain received. The next step is to vary the *amount* of water.

Typical Discussion Questions
▮ What happens to the sand mountain when you sprinkle water on it lightly? What happens when you pour water on it more heavily? Why is there a difference?

▮ Do you suppose the same thing happens to the rocks that make up mountains? Why?

▮ Does the volume of water have anything to do with how fast the sand mountain wears away? How about the force of the water?

How Children Will Be Encouraged To Investigate On Their Own In The Classroom
Children will be asked to vary the volume of water, the force of the water, the structure of the sand mountain, and anything else they can think of that might influence how fast the sand mountain weathers.

Expected Conclusions
Children will probably conclude that the rate of weathering of the sand mountain depends on the force of the water and the volume of water poured on it. They may or may not see the relationship between the sand mountain and real mountains, for weathering of real mountains proceeds too slowly to be discernable to children.

Applications to Real Life Situations
Weathering occurs all around us: garden soils, lawns, beaches, overhanging rock structures, and so on. Heavy rainstorms and hurricanes cause mud slides and other damage. Children can be encouraged to bring in newspaper and magazine articles and pictures dealing with hurricanes, severe thunderstorms, mud slides, and other severe weather occurrences that cause weathering.

Additional Literature Connection
McCrephy's Field by Christopher and Lynne Myers (Houghton Mifflin, 1991). Joe McCrephy abandons his Ohio farm to begin a new venture with his brother in Wyoming. The story details the changes that occur to the farm and the land over the next 50 years.

Analyzing Conclusions

Children's literature can be used as a springboard for comparing the conclusions children have formed as a result of their investigations with the science presented in the book. Science in literature often is exaggerated and inaccurate (see the investigation into crystal shapes in *Two Bad Ants*, p. 313–314). Comparing their conclusions with similar phenomena described in literature stimulates children to ask who is right as they compare the predictive and explanatory power of their conclusions with those presented in the book. Many children accept what is written as fact, and through this type of comparison, they begin to question the accuracy of the written word. On the other hand, seeing the same conclusions they derived discussed in a book helps empower children to own their own knowledge and thought processes.

IN THE SCHOOLS 9.2
Investigating Mixing Colors

In a kindergarten class, the teacher provides cups of water colored with red, yellow, and blue food coloring. Children mix the colored water in a cup, observe the resulting colors, and record them on a chart. The teacher then reads *Mouse Paint* by Ellen Stoll Walsh (Harcourt Brace, 1989), a story about mice who walk into red, yellow, and blue paint. As they walk from color to color, they mix the paints, forming new colors. This story, used after children perform their own investigations, may help them validate their conclusions or may stimulate them to pursue further investigations if their conclusions are not congruent with those presented in the story.

My Five Senses by Aliki (Harper Collins Children's Books, 1991) can be used after children have investigated the sense of touch using such activities as "What's In The Sock?" (Constructing Science in the Classroom 3.1, p. 64).

From Seed to Plant by Gail Gibbons (Holiday, 1991) explains how seeds grow into plants, and illustrates the parts of both seeds and plants. It can be used after children explore the nature of seeds to verify their findings (Constructing Science in the Classroom 3.3, p. 65). Children first observe the outsides of lima bean seeds and discuss how they look and feel. Then they guess what they will find on the inside of the seeds and compare their guesses with pre-cut seeds. They can compare their observations with those depicted in the book. Children then plant their seeds.

They may choose to plant whole seeds or halves, and they may choose to remove parts of the seed to investigate whether it will grow with missing parts. The growth of the seed is compared with the descriptions and illustrations in the book to provide verification of children's conclusions.

IN THE SCHOOLS 9.3
Investigating Simple Machines

In a third grade investigation of simple machines, children investigate levers, wedges, wheel-and-axle assemblies, and other simple machines provided by the teacher. They are asked to look around the classroom and the school to find additional examples of these simple machines. Then the story, *The Berenstain Bears' Science Fair* by Jan and Stan Berenstain (Random House, 1977), is read to help children crystallize their thoughts. This book provides information, examples, and demonstrations for the lever, the wedge, and the wheel and axle. Children can be encouraged to bring in toys that illustrate these simple machines.

Providing Factual Information

Digging Up Dinosaurs by Aliki (Harper Collins Children's Books, 1988) can be used as an introduction to various types of dinosaurs whose skeletons and reconstructions are seen in museums. The book explains how scientists uncover, preserve, and study fossilized dinosaur bones.

IN THE SCHOOLS 9.4
Investigating the Metamorphosis of Caterpillars

The Very Hungry Caterpillar by Eric Carle (Philomel, 1987) describes a caterpillar's preparation for metamorphosis into a beautiful butterfly. Children can collect caterpillars and put them in jars or a terrarium to see for themselves. The book will help children decide what to put in the jars for caterpillar food, and will help them make predictions as to what will happen with their own caterpillars. Children record their predictions, make daily observations, and record what happens. The book provides factual material against which children can compare their discoveries.

The Icky Bug Alphabet Book by Jerry Pallotta (Charlesbridge Publishers, 1986) contains factual information about many kinds of bugs. *The Bird Alphabet Book*, also by Jerry Pallotta (Charlesbridge Publishers, 1989) contains a wealth of factual information about birds. For example, "Y is for Yellow-Bellied Sapsucker. The Yellow-Bellied Sapsucker is a woodpecker that got its name because it drinks sap out of its favorite trees. It has a tongue with a brush-like tip."

The Very Busy Spider by Eric Carle (Philomel, 1985) can serve to introduce very young children to the characteristics of spiders, or can be used to help children verify characteristics children have observed.

The Lady and the Spider by Faith McNulty (Harper & Row, 1986), a story of a spider that has made its home in a head of lettuce, provides brief general descriptions of the spider. The main idea of the story is that *all* life is valuable. *A First Look at Spiders* by Millicent E. Selsam (Walker, 1983) classifies spiders according to several characteristics, including eyes, leg positions, webs, jaws, size, and habitat. The book is an excellent guide for field studies of spiders. Note that wildlife experts in the local area often are willing to provide assistance to teachers and children in identifying wildlife and in discussing their habitats.

CAUTIONARY NOTE: All spiders can bite, and people exhibit differing sensitivities to spider bites. Certain species such as the black widow spider and the brown recluse spider are very poisonous. Therefore, caution children not to touch or handle spiders.

The Forces Be With You! by Tom Johnston (Gareth Stevens, 1988) contains detailed information about the forces of inertia, friction, and gravity presented as cartoon captions of children demonstrating and talking about the principles.

After investigating the differences between birds and mammals, groups compare their findings. Then the teacher reads *Stellaluna* by Jannell Cannon (Harcourt Brace, 1993), a story about a mother fruit bat (mammal) who is attacked by an owl, dropping her baby. The baby, Stellaluna, has to live with a family of birds to survive. The story looks at the differences and similarities between the bat, a specific mammal, and birds.

Providing Practical Examples

Literature can provide practical examples of investigations children are pursuing. For instance, *Thunder Cake* by Patricia Polacco (Philomel, 1990) is a story of a little girl who fears the sound of thunder. Her grandmother shows her how to estimate the distance of a storm by counting the seconds between the lightning flash and the thunder crash, and shows her how to calm her fears by making a "thunder cake." The process of measurement together with factual material about thunderstorms are included in the book. The story can be used in conjunction with inquiries into the difference between the speed of light and the speed of sound. (A complete lesson using this story is shown in Constructing Science in the Classroom 9.2.)

CONSTRUCTING SCIENCE IN THE CLASSROOM 9.2
How Does the Speed of Sound Compare with the Speed of Light?

GRADE

6
5
4
3
2
1
K

Scientific Processes Addressed
Observation, interpretation of data

Science Topic Addressed
Speed of sound

Process-Oriented Objective
The student will observe the time difference between seeing an object struck and hearing its sound.

What Do I Want Children To Discover?
Children will discover that sound travels slower than light.

Description of Introductory Activity and Discussion
Ask children if they have observed that there often is a time delay between seeing lightning and hearing the thunder clap in a thunderstorm. Engage children in a discussion of what this tells us about how far away the lightning is and about how fast sound travels compared with the speed of light.

Materials Needed
Hollow pail such as a garbage pail or garbage can cover; wooden mallet or bat

Description of Activities
Take children outdoors to the playground or some other fairly large area. Divide the class into two groups, and place one group at each end of the field. One child hits the garbage pail with the mallet or the bat (or makes some other loud sound that children at the other end of the field can both see and hear). Children observe that sound travels slower than light. Read the story, *Thunder Cake* by Patricia Polacco (Philomel, 1990) to show how this activity enables a person to calculate how far away thunderstorms are.

Typical Discussion Questions
■ Does the loudness of the sound change its speed?
■ The speed of sound is approximately 1088 feet per second (or 740 miles per hour) at normal temperatures. Why is the speed of sound specified "at normal temperature?" What do you suppose happens to the speed of sound if the air is warmer? Cooler? What happens to the speed of sound if the air pressure is higher? Lower? How would we find out?
■ How can you use the speed of sound to calculate distances?

How children will be encouraged to investigate on their own in the classroom
Children will be encouraged to try the same activity when the air is warmer and cooler, and when the barometric pressure is higher and lower.

Expected Conclusions
Children will conclude that sound travels slower than light.

Applications to Real-Life Situations
The distance of a thunderstorm can be calculated from the time difference between seeing the lightning and hearing the thunder; the less the time, the closer the storm. (A thunderstorm is one mile away for every five seconds of delay between seeing the lightning and hearing the thunder. Thus, if there is a 15 second delay between lightning and thunder, the storm is 3 miles away.) Be sure to review with children the safety procedures to be taken in severe thunderstorms. (Note: The Weather Channel provides much information on severe weather phenomena and safety precautions to be taken; see Appendix A for address.)

Children can collect newspaper and magazine articles and pictures on thunderstorms.

IN THE SCHOOLS 9.5
Investigating the Reaction of Materials with Vinegar

In a fourth-grade class, groups of children were provided with pieces of limestone, marble, sandstone, and shale, some baking soda, baking powder, sugar, and salt, a plastic plate, and some vinegar. They were asked to predict which of the materials would fizz when vinegar was dropped on them, and then try each material one at a time and record their results. (The limestone, marble, baking soda and baking powder all fizz in the presence of vinegar.) To show practical examples of this phenomenon, the teacher read *The Magic School Bus Gets Baked In a Cake: A Book About Kitchen Chemistry* based on an episode from the animated TV series (Scholastic, 1995) which portrays children exploring the chemistry involved in baking, especially the production of gas from baking soda mixed with vinegar.

Developing Process Skills

Children's literature can be an integral component of a science lesson designed to help children develop process skills.

IN THE SCHOOLS 9.6
Daytime Sky Watching

In a lesson on observing, children go outside and observe the sky, writing down what they see in as much detail as possible. While still outside, the teacher reads *The Sky* by Arlane Dewey (Green Tiger Press, 1993), pausing after each page to ask the children to compare what they observed with what was described on that page. The lesson culminates in a creative writing activity, such as Haiku or other poetry. The discussion can be carried into a multicultural dimension by discussing the symbolism, significance, and explanations different cultures have for what can be seen—and not seen—in the sky.

CAUTIONARY NOTE: Never allow children to look directly at the sun. The lens in the human eye acts as a magnifying glass, concentrating the sun's rays on the retina and burning the retina much as a magnifying glass can be focused to burn a leaf. However, the retina does not contain nerves sensitive to pain, so people cannot feel the burn. Since children want to look at the sun, it is necessary to provide them with an alternative to looking at it directly. A pin-hole camera apparatus would work. Perhaps the best way is to focus the sun through binoculars onto a piece of paper. Hold the binoculars such that the wide lens (objective) is facing the sun and the eyepiece is aimed toward a piece of white paper. Move it around until you get the sun's image focused onto the paper. The binoculars will not become hot because they reflect all the sun's energy through mirrors or prisms from the objective lens to the ocular. (See Figure 9.2.)

Mysteries provide an excellent source of practice in the processes of observing, predicting, classifying, inferring, communicating, measuring, and forming hypotheses. The book, *Encyclopedia Brown Takes the Cake* by Donald J. Sobol (Scholastic, 1984) contains a series of short mysteries the readers must solve by utilizing the processes as they read the story.

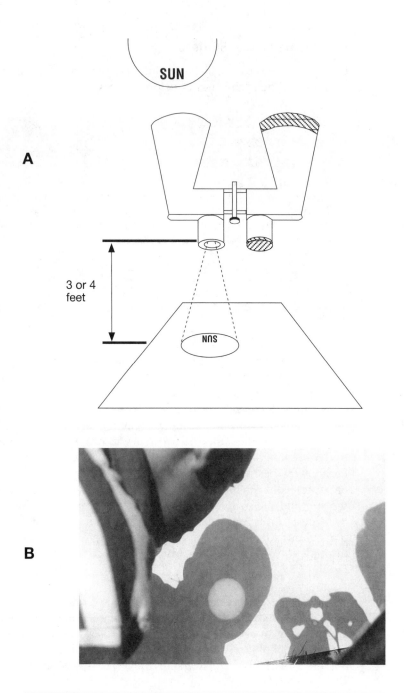

FIGURE 9.2 (A) Using binoculars to observe the sun's image. (B) Using binoculars to project the image of the sun onto the shadow on a white posterboard.

Another mystery, *The Million Dollar Potato* by Louis Phillips (Simon and Schuster, 1991) tells the story of a little boy who inherits a million dollars on condition that he spend it in twenty-four hours. Children participate in solving the mystery as they read the book. *The Westing Game* by Ellen Raskin (Dutton, 1978) is a murder mystery which can be solved before the end of the book. In *Science Mini Mysteries* by Sandra Markle (Athenium, 1988), the author uses a unique format of a short story mystery which the reader must solve using the scientific processes. Procedures and materials necessary for the experiments are listed.

The Mystery of the Stranger In the Barn by True Kelley (Dodd, Mead and Co., 1986) is a good story to demonstrate the difference between evidence and inference. Items seem to be disappearing from a barn, but a hat was left behind. Is there a mysterious stranger hiding in the barn?

Providing Vicarious Experiences

Literature can be used to provide experiences the children would not otherwise be able to have when they are needed. For example, several pieces of children's literature can be used to provide mental experiences for kindergarten children exploring rain. In *Bringing the Rain to Kapiti Plain* by Verna Aardema (Dial, 1981), children can see that clouds are the source of rain. In *Thunder Cake* by Patricia Polacco (Putnam, 1990), the rain comes in the form of a thunderstorm (see Constructing Science in the Classroom 9.2, p. 321). In the poem, *Listen To the Rain* by Bill Martin, Jr. and John Archenbault (H. Holt, 1988), children can "hear" different sounds rain makes through the poet's use of alliteration.

Providing Interdisciplinary Bridges

Children's literature can lead children from activities in science into activities associated with other areas. For example, *Out and About* by Shirley Hughes (Lothrup, Lee & Shepard Books, 1988) is a compilation of poetry about various weather occurrences. The poems can follow children's exploration of such phenomena as rainbows and wind, serving as an inspiration for them to compose their own poetry or other creative writing or artistic expressions.

Guidelines for Selecting Children's Literature

There is a plethora of children's literature available from which you can select both fiction and non-fiction. We have listed only a few of the many fine pieces available. Sources of children's literature titles appropriate for science are shown in Figure 9.3. In deciding what to use in your classes, you may wish to apply the criteria listed in Figure 9.4.

SELECTED SOURCES OF CHILDREN'S LITERATURE TITLES
APPROPRIATE FOR ELEMENTARY SCIENCE

Brainard, A. & Wrubel, D. H. (1993). *Literature-Based Science Activities: An Integrated Approach, Grades K-3*. New York, NY: Scholastic Professional Books.

Butzow, C. M. & Butzow, J. W. (1989). *Science Through Children's Literature: An Integrated Approach*. Englewood, CO: Teacher Idea Press.

Lima, C. W. & Lima, J. A. (eds.) (1993). *A to Zoo—Subject Access to Children's Picture Books*. (4th Edition). New Providence, N.J.: R. R. Bowker.

Moore, J. E. & Evans, J. (1991) *Exploring Science Through Literature, Level A, Grades K–1*. Monterey, CA: Evan-Moor Corp.

Moore, J. E. & Evans, J. (1991) *Exploring Science Through Literature, Level B, Grades 2–3*. Monterey, CA: Evan-Moor Corp.

Moore, J. E. & Evans, J. (1991) *Exploring Science Through Literature, Level C, Grades 4–6*. Monterey, CA: Evan-Moor Corp.

Ramirez, G., Jr., & Ramirez, J. L. (1994). *Multiethnic Children's Literature*. Albany, NY: Delmar Publishers, Inc.

The Association of Childhood Education International in Washington, D.C. publishes *Bibliography of Books for Children* which is revised every three years.

Science and Children, published by the National Science Teachers Association, includes an annotated bibliography of children's science trade books (non-fiction books dealing with scientific information) each year in the March issue. The list is compiled in conjunction with the Children's Book Council, and includes all science fields and biography. Books in Spanish also are listed.

Many public libraries have extensive collections of children's literature—both fiction and non-fiction.

FIGURE 9.3

CRITERIA FOR SELECTING CHILDREN'S LITERATURE
FOR USE IN SCIENCE CLASSES

1. Does the book foster the development of processes?
2. Does the book provide the opportunity for children to ask and answer their own questions?
3. Does the book encourage children to think for themselves?
4. Is the science topic addressed appropriate to the lesson?
5. Is the content based on sound scientific principles? Is it accurate?
6. Are the illustrations clear and accurate? Do they accomplish the purpose you have in mind?
7. Is the book written at the level of your children?
8. Is there a multicultural component? Is it free of stereotyping?
9. Is it free of gender bias?
10. Does the book show the close association between science and other disciplines?

FIGURE 9.4

CONSTRUCTING YOUR IDEAS 9.2
Using Literature in Elementary Science

Now it's your turn. Briefly describe one way literature can be incorporated into elementary science education. Then, to illustrate, sketch out one process-oriented inquiry science activity, the specific literature you would use to accompany it, and how you would use it.

Science Textbooks

Many school districts provide basic textbook series for the study of science. The temptation is to let the text determine the science program. There are several reasons for this. Elementary teachers may feel unprepared to teach science and want the guidance provided by the textbook. Teachers may prefer to have a structured program of the sort provided by textbooks. Teachers may look to texts for instructional resources, avenues of questioning and discussion, and directions for demonstrations and children's activities (Armbruster, 1993).

In the extreme, some teachers may limit their science program to the textbook. Their typical lesson begins with the children reading out of the text. The teacher then may do a demonstration, show a video, or hold a question-and-answer discussion in an effort to get children involved and to increase meaningfulness. Occasionally the children may participate in an activity. The text then is used to close the lesson, and the questions at the end of the section serve as class work or homework. It should be obvious that such use of the text replaces inquiry with knowledge acquisition and verification activities. Children read about science instead of doing science. They do not have the opportunity to make and test predictions, and they do not have the opportunity to verify their conclusions, because the investigations are written out in the text. They do not have the opportunity to develop facility in the processes of science. The text provides all the needed information, and children are discouraged from "actively making meaningful connections to their existing knowledge" (Ulerick, 1989). This is the anthesis of constructivism.

Textbooks, by their very nature, ignore the individual needs of individual children and assume all children have the same prior knowledge. Given this characterization of science textbooks, the reactionary response has been an inclination to throw away the texts. However, textbooks have several advantages:

1. Textbooks are excellent sources of information for children.
2. Teacher's guides are excellent resources for teachers.
3. A textbook series provides scope and sequence to ensure continuity from grade to grade and consistency within grade levels.
4. Topics included in textbooks generally are appropriate for the age/grade levels of the children.
5. Topics in textbooks are developed thoroughly, with prerequisite information introduced in proper sequence.

Constructivist Uses of Elementary Science Textbooks

Much as we constructivists like to espouse getting rid of textbooks in elementary science, it is incumbent on us to see how we can utilize them to good advantage. The premise of constructivistic learning is that children discover new concepts for themselves and internalize these concepts by constructing valid connections to prior information. It may be desirable to have several copies of each of a number of different texts available in the classroom to aid children in their investigations.

Textbooks also can serve well in the validation role. The elementary science textbook typically provides a discussion and explanation of a scientific concept, followed by activities children can do to verify the textual material. For a constructivist approach, the teacher can use the text in reverse, having the children do the activities first, and then using the text for validation (Barnam, 1992).

For example, a recent edition of a third grade textbook contains a section on friction. Friction is defined, several examples are cited, and ways of reducing friction are listed. The constructivist teacher wishing to use this text might first engage children in an exploratory activity concerning friction. Such an activity is shown in Constructing Science in the Classroom 9.3. After children have done the activity, they can read in the text to confirm what they have already discovered for themselves. Furthermore, the text may spark additional questions children may wish to investigate on their own.

Another use of textbooks involves utilizing them for information that is required in the curriculum but which does not lend itself well to inquiry. If content coverage is an issue in your school, you might consider dividing the topics to be studied into two categories—those that can be mastered through inquiry, and those that do not lend themselves to hands-on inquiry methods. The textbook is an excellent resource for studying those topics that cannot be explored directly by children.

CONSTRUCTING SCIENCE IN THE CLASSROOM 9.3
An Investigation Into Friction

GRADE

Scientific Processes Addressed
Observing, measuring, predicting, inferring

Science Topic Addressed
Friction

Process-Oriented Objectives
1. The student will observe the effect of various surfaces on the force necessary to move a solid object.
2. The student will predict the relative force required to move the solid object across different surfaces.
3. The student will measure and compare the forces required to move a solid object across various surfaces.
4. The student will infer reasons for the differing forces required to move a solid object across different surfaces.

What Do I Want Children to Discover?
Children will discover the concept of friction and the effects of various surfaces on friction.

Description of Introductory Activity and Discussion
Put a book on a smooth surface such as a tile floor or a smooth table top, and give it a sharp push. Observe how far it goes. Then put the book on a carpet and do the same thing, again observing how far it goes. Ask questions such as, "Why does the book go farther on the smooth surface?" "Does the nature of the surface have anything to do with how far the book goes?" "How could we find out?"

Materials Needed
Book, pieces of wood with hooks in one end; waxed paper; coarse sandpaper; fine sandpaper; piece of carpet, piece of plywood; wooded dowels or round pencils; spring balance or equivalent*

Description of Activities
Provide the materials for each group, and ask them to predict the effect each surface will have on the amount of force necessary to move the block of wood across it. Children hook the spring balance into the hook in the piece of wood, and, holding the spring balance parallel to the surface, drag the block of wood along each of the various surfaces available. They feel the amount of force it takes to move the block of wood, and record the reading from the scale. (Note: if the block of wood is light, children may weigh it down with a book.)

Typical Discussion Questions
▮ Which material takes the most force to move the block? The least force?
▮ Why does it take different amounts of force to move the block across different kinds of materials?
▮ How can you reduce the force needed to move the block?
▮ What other materials would you like to try?

How Children Will Be Encouraged To Investigate On Their Own In The Classroom
Children can reproduce the same activity using different surfaces. They can use oil, wax, and soap. They can vary the bottom surface of the block. They can use wooden dowels or rollers to compare rolling friction with sliding friction. Children may observe that it takes

more force to get the block started than it takes to keep it going once it is in motion. [This is because of inertia—see Newton's First Law of Motion, Chapter Twelve.]

Expected Conclusions
I expect children will conclude that the smoother the surface, the less force is required to keep the block moving. They will form conceptual understanding of friction, though they may not use the proper terminology.

Applications to Real-Life Situations
Friction is present every time two surfaces are in contact with each other. It is desirable to reduce friction in order to reduce the force it takes to move something. Wheels, rollers, oiled surfaces, polished surfaces, etc. are desirable energy-saving aids.

* A rubber band spring scale can substitute for the spring balance. See illustration below.

RUBBER BAND SCALE

SCIENCE IS A SNAP!
Snappy Spring Scales
Tape a rubber band to the zero end of a ruler. Attach an opened paper clip to the other end of the rubber band to act as a hook. Hang small objects on the hook. Observe how far the rubber band is stretched. The amount of stretch is an indication of the relative weight of the object. Relate weight to earth-pull on the object.

Snappy Investigations
Have students investigate to find out:
▌ How does thickness of a rubber band affect its strength?
▌ What effect does temperature have on rubber band stretch?
▌ Does the thickness of a rubber band affect its pitch when plucked?

Write for free catalog:
© Idea Factory, Inc. 1988   10710 Dixon Dr., Riverview, FL 33569

Reprinted with permission: Idea Factory, Inc.

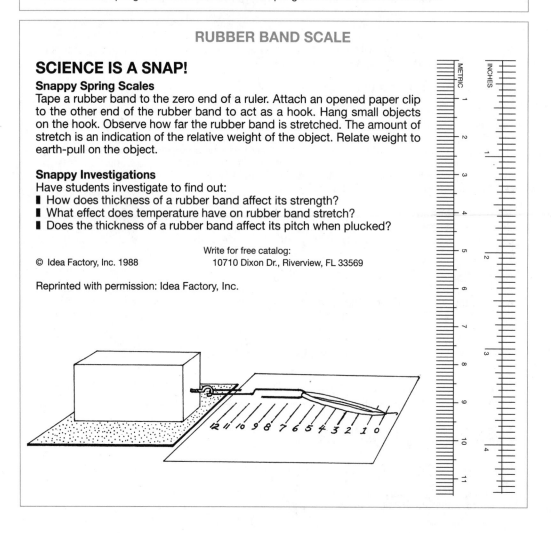

Examples might include learning the names of the planets, learning the names of cloud types, learning how nuclear reactors work, and studying plate tectonics.

Textbooks also provide assistance in the area of career explorations. Many texts describe the nature of various careers in science and what scientists do in those careers. Textbooks also frequently include biographies of famous scientists.

Commercially Available Hands-On Materials

In response to the desire of teachers to implement hands-on science programs, many publishers are providing materials in the form of investigative kits and project-oriented units that support constructivist approaches to elementary science education. Assuming these materials are selected with the input of the teachers who will use them, that they are understood by teachers, and that teachers are given both time and resources to implement these materials, they are excellent alternatives to texts. Several hands-on investigative elementary science programs are described in Figure 9.5.

SELECTED ELEMENTARY SCIENCE MATERIALS THAT UTILIZE CONSTRUCTIVIST APPROACHES

AIMS (Activities for Integrating Mathematics and Science) uses a hands-on, inquiry-oriented approach that integrates mathematics, science, and other disciplines. AIMS materials include nearly 40 volumes of guided inquiry student investigations involving a wide variety of topics at all grade levels, K–12. AIMS also has available complete laboratory kits, manipulatives, equipment, data organizers and charts, a newsletter, and a magazine showing new activities and evaluation results. The activities are inquiry in orientation and are constructivist in nature. The AIMS activities are probably the best inquiry-oriented constructivist activities that have been developed for science education in recent years.

For complete information, contact
    AIMS   Education   Foundation
    P.O. Box 8120
    Fresno, CA 93747-8120

ESS (Elementary Science Study) is among the original discovery approaches to elementary science education. Its developers came from the scientific and the teaching fields. Units detailed in teacher's guides are designed to help children develop the fundamental skills necessary for organized scientific thought. Over 40 units deal with common scientific phenomena from ant farms to "whistles and strings." Each unit suggests many open-ended, hands-on, inquiry-oriented activities children can investigate as they form and validate personal conceptualizations of the phenomena. Equipment kits are available.

For details, contact
    Delta Education, Inc.
    P.O. Box 915
    Hudson, NH 03051-0915

FIGURE 9.5 (Continues on next page)

Full Option Science System (FOSS), developed at the Lawrence Hall of Science under a grant from the National Science Foundation, is an elementary science program that is process-oriented and guided inquiry in nature. Activities are designed to match children's cognitive abilities at their different levels of development. The program focuses on children aged 9–12 (grades 3–6), and is divided into four themes (scientific reasoning, physical science, life science, and earth science). Each theme contains modules that focus on single science concepts and suggest several activities. All materials, including teacher's guides, are available in kit form.

> For complete information, contact
> Encyclopaedia Britannica Educational Corporation
> 310 South Michigan Avenue
> Chicago, IL 60604

Insights (1992) is a hands-on inquiry-based elementary science curriculum designed to meet the needs of all children in grades K–6. Specifically addressing urban children, the program integrates science with language arts and mathematics in a science-technology-society setting. Seventeen six- to eight-week modules are available, each including a comprehensive teacher's guide and a set of materials.

> For further information, contact
> Education Development Center, Inc.
> 55 Chapel Street
> Newton, MA 02160

MacMillan/McGraw-Hill Science (1993) is a series of 42 topical units for Grades K–8. Lessons are based on a cycle of "engage—explore—develop—extend/apply." Each lesson begins with an activity designed to engage children in the topic, such as a discussion, a piece of literature, photographs, or a hands-on activity. This is followed with a hands-on exploration activity, after which textual material and additional hands-on activities help children develop the concept. The lesson closes with applications, and the cycle begins again with a new lesson.

Scholastic Science Place (1993 and 1994) is reminiscent of the highly successful programs of the 1950s and 1960s in its focus on hands-on activities. The series contains 42 topical units of study for grades K–6, with a heavy emphasis on literature, each packaged in a case that contains all materials and equipment needed for the investigations suggested in the lessons. A teacher's manual and a wide assortment of textual material is supplied to help children master the concept. One should weigh the cost of the kits versus the cost of providing one's own materials where 100% of the materials will be used.

FIGURE 9.5

Textbook Review

It is critically important that teachers become involved in the selection of materials they will use in their classrooms. Many teachers serve on textbook adoption committees. To facilitate the text review process, the chart in Figure 9.6 is offered as a generic aid to the textbook evaluation review process. Of course, each school district develops their own textbook review form to meet their unique needs; the form in Figure 9.6 suggests important elements supportive of a constructivistic approach to science.

SCIENCE TEXTBOOK EVALUATION REVIEW FORM

TITLE _____

AUTHOR(S) _____

PUBLISHER _____

COPYRIGHT DATE _____ LEVEL(S) _____

Rate each of the following from 1 (lowest) to 10 (highest)

_____ Process-oriented
_____ Fosters inquiry
_____ Suggests inquiry activities
_____ Inductive in presentation
_____ Encourages children to explore on their own
_____ Suggests extended activities
_____ Suggests remedial activities
_____ Contains appropriate content
_____ Content accurate
_____ Illustrations clear and accurate
_____ Reading level appropriate
_____ Treats men and women in science equally
_____ Contains multicultural component without stereotyping
_____ Reflects interdisciplinary approaches
_____ Interdisciplinary problems are relevant and issue-oriented
_____ Suggests literature connections
_____ Special treatment for children with special needs
_____ Contains information on scientific careers
_____ Includes technology
_____ Attractive
_____ Material well organized
_____ Ancillary materials available
_____ Physical characteristics of student texts
_____ Cost value
_____ Teacher's Edition contains activities and resources
_____ Teacher's Edition rich in supplemental materials
_____ Total Points

Comments _____
_____
_____
_____

Overall Recommendation: Strongly Recommend   _____
                           Recommend   _____
                           Questionable   _____
                           Do Not Recommend   _____

Reviewer's Name _____ Date_____

FIGURE 9.6

There are pros and cons to using textbooks in elementary science; textbooks can serve many different functions. As always, you have to make up your own mind.

The Role of Reading and Writing in Elementary Science

Reading and writing skills are essential areas of development for children. On the other hand, through process-oriented inquiry, science is one area that can be investigated successfully by children independent of reading and writing. This gives rise to the question of the role of reading, writing, and literature in quality science education and the extent to which reading and writing should be an integral part of the science program.

There are opposing views to the issue of incorporating reading and writing in the elementary science program. One argument suggests that reading and writing should have a *limited* role in elementary science. Some children learn to read and write faster than others, some have greater facility than others, and some enjoy reading and writing more than others. Science is a field that can be studied *without* having to read or write. Children who experience difficulty with language can succeed in science by doing activities, experimenting, engaging logic, and discussing with others. For example, children can classify shells without having to read about their characteristics; their success can be assessed by talking with them about their classification system rather than through a written description. It is entirely possible to experiment successfully with the effects of different surfaces on the force needed to move a block of wood without reading about the concept of friction or writing one's findings.

Children's success in the science arena can serve as a catalyst to develop the self confidence needed for more successful language experiences. The most powerful reading strategy teachers can implement is to enable children to provide themselves with meaningful purposes for reading. Science can provide purposes for reading and writing through children's own desire to pursue interesting areas of science inquiry in greater depth. Children will come to want to read to obtain background information or explanatory information, to find out what has already been discovered, to challenge their ideas with new viewpoints, and to confirm or validate their conclusions.

An argument in opposition to the notion of limiting reading and writing in science suggests that reading and writing must be an integral part of every aspect of the elementary curriculum, including science. All children are capable of recording their observations by picture or by writing simple statements in journals. Children's literature and writing activities can enhance science learning by improving vocabulary, refining auditory and visual skills, and fostering creativity. A good example of this is the poetry writing suggested in conjunction with the poems on weather in *Out and About* by Shirley Hughes (see p. 325). Reading and doing science also foster development of process skills such as observing, formulating hypotheses, inferring, predicting, and interpreting data. Reading requires children to engage prior knowledge. "Because of the reciprocal relationship between science and reading, teaching them together can be mutually beneficial" (Armbruster, 1993).

Reading and writing also may stimulate greater interest in science on the part of children who are not interested in science.

Many strategies for reading and writing in science have been suggested (Glynn & Muth, 1994), and are summarized in Figure 9.7 .

SOME STRATEGIES FOR READING AND WRITING IN ELEMENTARY SCIENCE EDUCATION

Reading (Lower Elementary Grades)
- Children's literature dealing with science topics
- Children's non-fiction books on a variety of topics
- Different textbooks
- Magazines such as *Highlights for Children, Ladybug, Chickadee,* and *Your Big Backyard,* that contain scientific and science-related materials

Writing (Lower Elementary Grades)
- Recording observations and experimental data
- Writing in science journals
- Developing class books on science topics
- Preparing individual books on science topics
- Keeping daily class newspaper on current science events
- Labeling drawings and graphs

Reading (Upper Elementary Grades)
- Newspaper stories about new developments in science and technology
- Magazines such as *National Geographic World, Owl, Kids Discover, 3-2-1 Contact, Ranger Rick, Zoobooks, Odyssey,* and other popular magazines
- Non-fiction books on a variety of topics
- Different textbooks to compare explanations and discussions
- Biographies of scientists, especially those from groups that have traditionally been underrepresented in science
- Science fiction works such as those by Isaac Asimov and Arthur C. Clarke

Writing (Upper Elementary Grades)
- Essays in which students describe their understanding of complex science concepts in depth
- Field trip notes in which children record their observations and reactions
- Lab logs in which children record their observations, hypotheses, methods, findings, interpretations, and (especially) their mistakes
- Science journals or diaries in which children describe their participation in science activities and reflect on their experiences
- Environmental action letters to politicians, newspaper editors, etc.
- Newspaper articles or accounts in which children write stories on science and technology topics for the school paper or the local paper
- Publishing class science newsletters

FIGURE 9.7

The ambivalence toward reading and writing in science education is bolstered by powerful arguments on each side. You will have to decide for yourself the extent to which reading and writing will be incorporated in your science program. We do not take sides on this issue. However, we stress once again that children must learn science by *doing* science, not by reading *about* science.

Exploring Ecosystems through Writing Imaginary Narratives: Stories of "Creepy Critters"

A Case Study
By Dr. Jonelle Pool and Dr. Jean Ketter

Following is an account of an interdisciplinary activity integrating science and language arts through imaginative narratives.

LEAP (Learning Enrichment Activity Program) was a voluntary after-school program for fourth and fifth grade children which was designed to enhance interest in science and mathematics. Thirty-one children participated in the "Creepy Critters" project for two hours a week during a four week period.

The purpose of the project was to integrate science with language arts through imaginative narratives. Children investigated the complexities of ecosystems through the creation of an imaginary animal in one of four environments: desert, rain forest, ocean, or the arctic. Through modeling a continuing drama about discovering a species and investigating its characteristics, we incorporated affective outcomes such as curiosity about and appreciation for the practice of science.

Specific student learning objectives for the project were as follows:

1. To demonstrate knowledge about the interaction of habitat and species adaptation
2. To observe the process of scientific inquiry and to apply it through questioning and problem-solving
3. To demonstrate analysis of the interaction of habitat and species by describing an imaginary animal
4. To create an anthology of narratives describing "newly discovered species" and their habitats for publication

Description of the Project

Class One: The project began with our presentation of a short skit in which a "reporter" interviewed a "scientist" about a new tropical rain forest species she had recently discovered. (Refer to script below.) To set the mood, we collected a few props including binoculars, compass, bush hat, and field vest for the scientist to use. We also had a "photograph" of the new species, the aero-reptilian, *jonelliad*, named after the scientist (Jonelle) who "discovered" it in a rain forest. We continued the skit over the course of the four weeks, using it to introduce each class session. Each segment of the skit modeled the developmental process necessary for scientific inquiry and was designed to scaffold children's knowledge as well as to tap their creative thinking.

After the skit on Day One, we led children on a short nature walk behind the school to encourage them to explore a natural environment and to promote questioning about their observations. We also hoped to foster a sense of the personal discovery associated with scientific inquiry. After the nature walk, we distributed note cards, each identifying one of four specific habitats. The class brainstormed characteristics of each habitat and explored how such characteristics would affect animal adaptation. Children were assigned to groups according to the habitat on their note cards and began analyzing the habitat features that would impact animal survival.

Class Two: The skit segment (see below) for this class period modeled several questions the scientist was pondering about the new species she had discovered. (What sex is the animal? How does it reproduce? What does it eat? Where does it live? What predators does it have?) In their groups, children identified appropriate questions that a scientist would need to address and proposed methods for discovering answers to the questions. They then began the process of creating an imaginary animal that would be able to live in the environment they were assigned. Initially, we gave them scrap paper and encouraged them to make drafts of their drawings so the final drawings would be of high quality.

Class Three: The skit segment for this class built in some of the child-generated methods for species identification and revealed the answers these methods produced. We served a "rain forest" snack and played a video, "The Rain Forest Rap," to enhance factual knowledge of the rain forest habitat. Children continued to refine their illustrations and began drafting accompanying narratives.

Class Four: The final skit portrayed the scientist as completing the investigation and sharing her theoretical results. Within the skit, the scientist shared the story of her discovery of the aero-reptilian *jonelliad* and hypothesized possible theoretical explanations for her findings. We finished the skit with further questions generated by the explanations to emphasize the value of generating questions rather than finding definitive answers. Children completed their illustrations and edited narratives for their anthology, *Creepy Critters*, which they presented to the school media center at the honors day assembly. One child's work is shown in Figure 9.8.

FIGURE 9.8

The Needle-Winged Topper

One day, while walking in the rain forest on one of my expeditions, I saw this strange, colorful, little creature waddle out right in front of me into a bush. It looked interesting, so I decided to follow it. I took out my notepad so I could take notes. Soon, I saw the creature again, but this time in a tree. I stood still and kept quiet so I could see it clearly. I was amazed at what I saw. This creature didn't look like an animal at all. It was all different colors and had feet that sort of looked like pink and blue tennis shoes! It had no legs and the strangest little tail. Plus, it had fluorescent orange wings that really caught my eye. The wings also had little pointy, black spikes, which probably were poisonous. The animal was probably five or six inches tall, maybe shorter. There were other strange qualities, too. One of them was its eyes, which stick out of its head. You can tell if it's male or female by the color of its eyes. If they are blue, then it is a female. If it is a male, then the eyes are brown. The Needle-Winged Topper's eyelids are the same color of its wings, which are fluorescent orange. Around its eyelids, it has rings. Coming out of the top of the eyes, there are little yellow lightning bolts. Right in the middle under the eyes, there is a little yellow nose. Here was another identification of the animal. It was the mouth. The mouth is rather large and is full of white teeth. I have two more identifications left. One of them was the arms. The arms are rather unusual because they are shaped like wavy rectangular prisms. I don't know why they are shaped like that, maybe to warn off predators. The last identification is the color of the body. The Needle-Winged Topper is half pink and half blue. Each side has a triangle of the opposite color. The arms, by the way, are light yellow with darker yellow stripes and the tail looks like little overlapping circles. Every other circle is pink and the rest are blue. In case you are wondering, I was standing right under the tree so that is how I made out all the details.

A week has passed since I last wrote the description. I haven't been writing because I wanted to find out more about the animal. You have probably been wondering why I gave the new animal its name. I named it the Needle-Winged Topper because of its spikey wings and because its body is shaped like a top. I have found out what the animal eats by watching it go and gather food and then bring it back to its lair. The Needle-Winged Topper eats mainly the grasses and flowers, but sometimes he'll eat snakes and insects. This animal is a mammal. Its body is covered with light fur. Its wings are feathers, though. This animal is used to a pretty hot temperature. He just wouldn't survive anywhere except the rain forests. The Needle-Winged Topper is mainly found in the rain forests of Africa. This animal may look completely harmless. Surprisingly, it does have a way to defend itself. It is the wings. As you know, the wings have poisonous "needles" on them. If an animal frightens or alarms the Needle-Winged Topper, he just sticks the spikes into the animal's body. The animal either gets really sick or it dies.

Later in the week, I looked for more information about the Needle-Winged Topper. I found out more about the mating ritual. The Needle-Winged Topper mates twice a year, in the fall and spring. It lays eggs, even though it is a mammal. The eggs are striped blue and white. They hatch after three weeks. The mother and family stay with them all their lives, so they are sort of a herd. The Needle-Winged Toppers are very unusual creatures. But I have only seen them in the rain forests, which are being destroyed. So if we want to save them, we'll have to really try hard to save the tropical rain forests!

By Kristen C.

FIGURE 9.8

Extensions and Evaluation

The final products demonstrated a genuine excitement about the discovery process in scientific inquiry. We were impressed both with their questions and their suggested methods for problem solving. By asking children to participate in the experience of inventing an imaginary animal, we encouraged creativity and schema building through discovery learning. We were surprised by the children's considerable involvement in the skits. Children often sought verification of the "facts" we were presenting; apparently they were willing to believe in the story we told and enthusiastically told their own stories. Children commented on the first day that their science textbooks were boring and emotionless. They recognized that science books reported facts but not the process of discovering those facts. We theorized that the story of the discovery process might be more interesting and create more meaningful elaborations of content for children. Successful incorporation of this unit into a science classroom would require careful attention to factual information about habitats and species adaptation. Children need time to internalize the content and concepts before being asked to apply these complex notions to a creative story.

Scripts for Skits Presented by Teachers
(Jonelle and Jean)

Day One

Jonelle enters in "biologist" garb. She is carrying a briefcase and tools of the trade.

Jonelle: Jean, I am here to share with the class an exciting new discovery. I think I found a new species of animal!

Jean: Where?

Jonelle: I was out backpacking in the Belizian rain forest, and I was, of course, closely observing the environment around me. You know, scientists believe there are thousands of undiscovered species in the tropical rain forest. I was listening carefully for bird sounds and looking in the shadows for camouflaged animals, but at first I saw and heard nothing. Then, out of the corner of my eye, I saw some bright yellow. I thought it was just an orchid flower, but then I saw it move!

Jean: Was it a butterfly?

Jonelle: No. I thought it might be, but it wasn't. It did not have the segmented body or the segmented legs of a butterfly. In fact, it had no legs at all. The best way I can describe it is a small snake with wings.

Jean: A snake with wings?? I've never heard of such a thing! Are you sure?

Jonelle: Yes, I am. I even drew a picture of it so you could see what I mean. (Here, Jonelle takes out a large drawing of her new species and holds it up for the whole class to see.) Look! It has four yellow wings with a black dot in the center of two of them. It also has a yellow snake-like body. Its eyes appear to be at the ends of these feeler-like protuberances. Look! See how the eyes can move around so it can see behind itself? And the yellow orchid it was resting on had a small nick out of it. I think that particular orchid is its food.

Jean: Jonelle, I think you've really found something here. What will you call the species?

Jonelle: Well, I was thinking of *Poolius jonelliad*. What do you think?

Jean: That sounds fair, since you discovered it. Did you notice anything else unusual about this new species?

Jonelle: (Takes off her jacket and fans her face) It's rather warm in here. Yes, I did. When I placed this new animal on the ground, it gradually started to turn brown. And it appears to be able to turn almost any shade of red, orange, or yellow.

Jean: This is an amazing discovery! You're going to be famous!

Day Two

Jean: Hey, Jonelle! I hear you had a very busy time in Belize. I guess you have been working very hard this last month researching some of the questions this group helped you with last time.

Jonelle: On the expert advice of our class consultants, I went back to the rainforest and I took a videocamera with me in hopes of catching the *jonelliad* in its natural habitat. And I caught her on film!

Jean: You mean you discovered what gender this animal was? How did you figure that out?

Jonelle: I couldn't get close enough to see this until I had the camera. I zoomed in on her and I saw some small white sacs. I was right: those sacs were eggs.

Jean: How did you find that out?

Jonelle: Well, I was picking my way through the brush to the spot where I first saw the *jonelliad*, when suddenly I heard a strange and wonderful sound. I couldn't really tell what direction it was coming from. But, as I paused to listen, I realized it was coming from right above me. "Cheep, Cheep, Sssss—Cheep, Cheep, Sssss." When I looked up, the canopy was so thick I could hardly focus, and the sun barely penetrated to the dark forest floor. As my eyes adjusted to the gloom, I glimpsed a bright flash of yellow with black spotted wings. The *jonelliad*, I thought. It's right above me.

Jean: So you found another one!

Jonelle: Yes. I had never heard the *jonelliad's* song before. Let me tell you what happened. I was so glad I had brought my video camera so I could capture this animal's song and its behavior. I hurried to remove the lens cap and set up the tripod in a well-camouflaged area so as not to scare it. I was trying to be quiet so I wouldn't disturb the *jonelliad*, but sometimes when you try to be quiet, it backfires. Searching for a level place to set up the camera, I backed up and tripped over a large root system housing several surprised snakes! The camera clattered to the ground and I jumped back in surprise, a silent scream leaping from my throat. The noise startled the *jonelliad*, and it began screeching. Suddenly, another larger and darker version of the *jonelliad* swooped down at me, joining its mate in the piercing cry, probably meant to scare off its predators.

I quickly reassembled the camera and loaded and rolled the tape to capture the scene that was unfolding above me. The male (at least I assumed the larger *jonelliad* was male) had dropped several small seeds when he uttered his cry — seeds he appeared to be bringing his mate for food. I decided to go away and let the camera do its work — to document and discover the habits of the *jonelliad*. After several hours, near sunset, I returned to get the camera and the tape. Everything was quiet and daylight was fading, but on the forest floor, the night had already arrived. I packed up the camera and hurried back to camp.

Back at my field office, I watched in wonder as the *jonelliad* revealed her secrets. I saw that she was nesting on a white egg sac, just as I had hypothesized. She appeared to be reluctant to leave the nest even when threatened, so I concluded she was using her body heat to keep the eggs warm. There appeared to be specific roles for the male and female *jonelliad*. The male, both protector and provider, defended the nest and brought the seeds, plentiful in the forest, to the female. Both appeared to swallow the seeds whole. Because the female nests on or near brightly colored orchids, her bright coloration was protective. The male's more muted colors helped him forage for seeds near the forest floor more safely. His wings when spread had the coloration of the shady leaves in which he searches for food. The camera even caught the male *jonelliad* sipping water from the surface of a leaf.

It was a great day for answers but it also was a great day for questions. For every question I answered, several more remained unanswered. My work with the *jonelliad* is just beginning, and I know many more fascinating mysteries await me in the rainforest of Belize.

Interdisciplinary Aspects

The prevailing approach to curriculum in elementary schools involves separating learning into discrete components of individual subjects, each with its own time slot, its own text, and its own program of study. This "fractionalized" approach to learning sends the powerful message to children that each subject has its own domain and is independent of the others.

> The reform movement of the 1990s calls for an integration of school subjects: a conceptual convergence of the natural sciences, mathematics, and technology with the social and behavioral sciences and the humanities into a coherent whole. A unity of knowledge will make it possible for students to take learning from different fields of study and use it to view human problems in their fullness from several perspectives (Hurd, 1991, p. 35).

There is an emerging paradigm shift from the compartmentalized approach to an integrated, olistic approach to learning, providing children the opportunity to confront problems that require multiple and overlapping solutions and to apply their knowledge to real life situations. This emerging paradigm is known as integrated curriculum or interdisciplinarianism. In the preceding section, you explored one example: ways of integrating reading and writing within the science program.

Interdisciplinarianism involves including more than one discipline in an area of study. As we have previously observed, no subject can be studied in isolation. To attempt to do so is futile—it simply cannot be done. For example, it is impossible to teach science without some use of language. Mathematics is essential for obtaining measurements, calculating data trends, constructing graphs, and interpreting experimental results. Social studies provides the essential link between the idealism of science and its usefulness to society; indeed, science derives its meaning, in large measure, from social contexts.

Interdisciplinary learning is the natural way people learn. People constantly cross disciplines in daily life. For example, to run for office, one needs to have positions on many issues (social studies, science, economics, political science), manage campaign finances (mathematics), tabulate the number of votes required (mathematics), put together speeches and slogans (communications and language arts), choreograph campaign appearances (drama and physical education), refine political strategies (political science), choose thematic and background music (music), know the constituency one represents (social studies), and so on. Teachers integrate into their daily work such areas as psychology, sociology, mathematics, economics, nutrition, safety, communication, drama, music, and the scientific method of discovery—all in addition to their instructional responsibilities.

Two Interdisciplinary Models

One approach to interdisciplinary studies can be characterized by a *daisy model*. In the daisy model, the major area of study is represented by the center of the flower, with the other areas of study added as petals to the daisy. Each subject retains its own distinctive characteristics, and each subject is readily identified by teacher and children alike. For example, let us suppose the topic of friction is to be used as the main focus of study. Mathematics can be included through calculating speed from distance and time; reading can be incorporated with books that explain friction; writing can be incorporated by having children write their views about what a frictionless world would be like; in music, children can learn songs about runaway bicycles; in physical education, children can run on surfaces with varying degrees of slipperiness. In this approach, each subject is treated independently, though it is related to the central topic. Mathematics is still taught as mathematics; reading is still taught as reading; writing is still taught as writing. The primary difference between this approach and the discipline-centered approach is the thematic nature of the material. The mathematics instruction uses friction for the problems; reading and writing focus on friction for their subjects.

THE DAISY MODEL
Main subject is in the
center; other subjects
are attached as petals.

THE ROSE MODEL
All subjects are
intertwined.

FIGURE 9.9   Models of interdisciplinary studies

Interdisciplinary centers are used effectively in all grades, and often follow the daisy model. The following describes the centers approach used by one kindergarten teacher.

Science objectives are met through discovery at all centers, including science-specific centers. Children learn about mixing colors at the Art Center. At the Block Center, basic physics principles such as rolling or catapulting are daily experiments. The Library Center includes magazines and books. Children get to see how pressure and/or heat can change the shape of objects during cooking. Children investigate funnels and volume at the Rice Center. At the Sand Center and Water Table they make comparisons and observe how various substances react to water. I have a Pulley Center where children hoist classroom materials, and we are adopting a class pet, a rabbit. Parents help out with the centers daily, and I send suggestions for activities children can do at home.

Though the daisy model approach falls short of a truly interdisciplinary approach where the lines of subject demarcation cease to exist, it nonetheless is a good beginning. You can start by combining one other content area with science as you did when you investigated ways of integrating literature with science. With experience, you can integrate more completely (Figure 9.10.)

A first grade child records the results of a plant growth investigation in chart form, integrating mathematics principles with science.

FIGURE 9.10   Charting plant growth

An alternative to the daisy model is a *rose model* of interdisciplinary studies. In this model, the subject areas lose their distinctive subject matter delineations. (See Figure 9.9.) Unlike the daisy where each petal is separate and distinctly visible, in the rose, all the petals are closely intertwined. In the daisy, one sees each petal; in the rose, one sees the whole flower without regard to individual petals. In the rose model, learning focuses on a particular problem or situation meaningful and of interest to children, and the children study whatever is necessary to bring about personal understanding.

Zais uses the term, "problem-centered," referring to the organization of studies around "problems of living, both individual and social" (Zais, 1976, p. 43). He cited Hilda Taba who wrote, "organizing the curriculum around the activities of mankind will not only bring about a needed unification of knowledge but will also permit such a curriculum to be of maximum value to students' day-by-day life, as well as to prepare them for participation in a culture" (Taba, 1962, p. 396). The class might study, for example, the impact of soft drinks on society. To do this, they would have to consider many concepts, including how different brands of soft drinks are different from each other, how marketing trends and needs are assessed, profit and loss factors, and many other factors involving sociology, politics, science, finance, and so on. Children bring in newspaper advertisements on different kinds of soft drinks. They conduct class surveys and graph the results to see which soft drink is most popular. The study is put together in such a way that the children study each of the subject areas normally included in the curriculum, but without the isolation of each discipline. The account below of a student teacher whose second grade class produced a video about their school is a good example of the rose model of interdisciplinary studies.

THE VIDEO

I once supervised a student teacher who was assigned to second grade. This teacher had previously studied the communications field, and had mastered the technique of producing documentary videos. When the principal learned this, she asked the student teacher to engage the class in producing a ten-minute video about their school to be used to familiarize new faculty, staff, and parents with the school. The student teacher discussed the project with his class, and together they decided on the contents of the video. He divided the children into several groups, each with responsibility for one or more distinct phases of the video. In groups, children drew the story boards and wrote the script for each segment. The student teacher taught the children how to operate the camcorder, and the children shot the video footage. When this was done, the children refined the script, and read it into a tape recorder. The only thing the student teacher did by himself was combine the script with the video footage and edit the production.

During the course of this project, which lasted several weeks, the student teacher lamented that, although he was perfectly willing to engage the children in this project, and though he was certain they were having a lot of fun, he was becoming increasingly frustrated over the time spent where "no teaching was going on." He felt the prescribed curriculum had been set aside during this production, and he was not fulfilling his responsibilities as a teacher for he had not covered the topics required for this period of time. I suggested that he list the topics that were supposed to be covered, and indicate those which children had learned through the video project. He did so, and returned the list to me, dumbfounded that the children had, in fact, covered more of the prescribed curriculum than they would have if he had taught it in the traditional manner. The production of the video had enabled the children to learn more than they otherwise would have learned.

This student teacher was engaging in a totally integrated rose model approach to learning. In addition, the children were involved in all aspects of Bloom's cognitive taxonomy, from factual material (what is in the school) to analysis of the strands that should be depicted on the video, synthesis of the video itself, and evaluation of the video and its component parts.

Science, Technology, and Society

One of the greatest difficulties with school science seems to be the belief that there is essential information found in curriculum guides and texts that teachers must cover. The applications suggested often are artificial and have limited application to children's lives. An alternative is to provide situations and problems for study that are real to the children— situations and problems children encounter in their daily lives. For example, studying how a mountain bicycle is designed for its specific function might be more real to fifth and sixth grade children than studying the principles of simple machines.

Science-Technology-Society (STS) is a project-centered approach to science education that embodies the interdisciplinary goals inherent in the rose model. STS involves teaching and learning science in the context of human experience. The experiences selected for investigation are identified by the children who are "full partners in planning and carrying out their own science lessons" (Yager, 1994, p. 34).

As Naisbitt and Aburdene wrote in *Megatrends 2000*:

When we think of the 21st century, we think technology: space travel, biotechnology, robots. But the face of the future is more complex than the technology we use to envision it.

The most exciting breakthroughs of the 21st century will occur not because of technology but because of an expanding concept of what it means to be human (1990, p. 16).

The goal of STS is the "production of an informed citizenry capable of making crucial decisions about current problems and issues and taking personal actions as a result of these decisions" (Yager, 1991, p. 94). In the STS approach, children identify problems, questions, or unknowns, and participate in deciding what they need to do and need to know as they research answers and explanations. STS projects can involve any problem children care to investigate. Problems can be global (energy resources, population explosion, poverty), national (health care, land use, endangered species), local (waste disposal, recycling, traffic patterns), or personal (science fiction, stopped-up toilets, mountain bicycles, power failures at home). STS projects center around real-world issues that children bring up. Local problems such as recycling, trash removal, and pollution control are often used as the basis for STS projects. Projects may begin with a situation at school, such as cleaning up a playground and keeping it clean. Teacher and children collaborate in deciding what should be studied, how to proceed, and how children will get involved. Many new questions and problems are encountered along the way that suggest new inquiries and new avenues of investigation. Teacher and children are co-inquirers into investigations that are inquiry in orientation.

STS is grounded in the constructivist learning model. Children come to understand the concepts and processes because they are useful to them, can be applied to their own lives, and surface from their daily living situations. Children learn through their involvement with real-world problems and issues.

Suddenly the program's major objectives are realized—merely by allowing students to identify questions, propose solutions and explanations, and employ tests for the validity of these items. Such basic ingredients of science are rarely experienced in traditional science education (Yager, 1991, p. 94).

STS gives children an understanding of what science and technology are and the role they play in our lives. In addition, science anxiety is reduced because, in the STS approach, children are studying about familiar phenomena.

The incorporation of children's literature into the science program is one of the easiest ways to embark on an STS approach, and, as we have seen, can begin as early as kindergarten. The book, *Mike Mulligan and His Steam Shovel* by Virginia Lee Burton (Houghton Mifflin, 1939) presents the problem of people having to change to adapt to rapidly changing science and technology. In the story, an old fashioned steam shovel becomes outdated by more modern equipment. This problem of adapting to technological change can be explored by children from a variety of viewpoints, including the nature of simple machines and compound machines, building novel machines, providing directions for their operation, and citing reasons why people should buy them, competing for highest ratings of novel machines, and exploring the societal issues of equipment aging and obsolescence. Children will develop their own questions, problems, and avenues of exploration.

Many topics are appropriate for STS studies. Energy is a major concern in today's world. An STS project centering on energy can take many directions: history of energy use, energy resources, comparisons of energy uses between the United States and other countries, supply-demand-cost factors, consumption and consumers, efficiency of different energy sources, fossil fuel issues, newly-developed energy resources, and conservation of energy. Children can evaluate energy consumption at the personal, family, school, and community levels.

Environmental issues also are of major concern. STS problems can center on how to live in a constantly changing environment, improve personal lifestyles to exert positive influences on environmental factors, the role of government in environmental protection, and so on.

Waste management is an issue that directly impacts children's lives. Recycling, conservation, and landfill problems are appropriate STS topics. As an introductory activity, children can collect trash for one day, put it in a paper bag, and bury it in the school yard. If this is done at the beginning of the school year, it can be dug up every two or three months to see what is happening. Variations on this activity abound, and children are sure to come up with their own.

Investigations into social and political technology issues can center around such problem situations as the one below.

> As part of a technology assessment and trial development project, remote farming villages in India once received information via television beamed from a satellite. The majority of the peasants in these villages were subsistence farmers using practices not very different from those used two thousand years ago. Should the western world interfere? How? Why? Why Not?

Other topics that can be used for STS investigations include

Air Pollution
Communications
Conservation
Endangered Species
Food
Health
Leisure
Medical Issues
Newsworthy Happenings including current newspaper articles
    on science
Ozone Depletion
The Rainforest
Water Pollution
Weather
Work

Personal Bias in STS Projects

To what extent should teachers introduce their personal biases when a class is pursuing a project? We all have personal (and sometimes emotional) feelings about many of the STS topics children bring up, from population explosion issues to conservation, recycling, and preservation of endangered species. A major goal of education is for children to learn to think for themselves. This means children must come to their own informed conclusions based on their own evaluation and validation of evidence.

There are many reasons for teachers to encourage children to come to their own conclusions. One involves promoting children's ownership of their own thinking. When teachers allow their personal biases to set the direction of an investigation, children are denied the opportunity to think freely for themselves. For example, a teacher may slant a study of recycling such that children get the idea that they are supposed to come up with supportive evidence. In an open investigation, children would be asked to consider both positive and negative factors influencing recycling, and come to their *own* decisions on whether recycling is useful. There is a story of a teacher who tried to get her second grade children to embrace the principles of recycling. She asked all children to come to class with descriptions of how their parents recycle materials. Several of the children's parents did not recycle and, in fact, thought recycling a waste of time. This put the children in the untenable position of choosing between parents and teacher.

Another reason for keeping teachers' personal biases out of STS investigations involves the constantly changing nature of scientific knowledge. (See Chapter Two.) Facts which were once considered supportive of certain STS positions may be shown to be erroneous later on. For example, people once were very concerned about atmospheric warming, and much discussion occurred over how to prevent this from happening. Data show, however, that the warming trends predicted did not materialize. On average, the actual global warming from 1979 to 1994 was less than one-third the forecast rise.[2]

Still another reason involves the potential for children to slant data to support a given position. It is incumbent on us as teachers to require children to interpret data objectively and to search for hidden variables. For example, the notion that recycling is good is based, in part on conservation of energy resources. Recycling efforts often involve curbside waste management programs that require more collection trucks which means more fuel consumption and increased air pollution. Some recycling programs require considerable resources just to transport the materials to the recycling plants. These factors are part of the overall situation and should be considered by children as they study recycling.

STS represents an ultimate amalgamation of constructivism, science, and interdisciplinary investigations. It is to be hoped that every elementary science teacher will explore STS possibilities for their own classes.

Science Beyond the Classroom

The classroom is only one of many places where science can be learned by children. The outdoor classroom gives children the opportunity of observing and studying natural phenomena at first hand. In addition, there are many non-traditional settings where science learning can be enhanced, such as museums, planetariums, and science and technology centers. Furthermore, field trips taken away from the school setting can open channels of learning not otherwise available.

Non-Traditional Science Settings

Museums, science centers, nature centers, zoos, planetariums, arboretums, botanical gardens, and parks all provide informal science education from an interdisciplinary science-technology-society perspective[1]. Teachers can take advantage of these learning environments through trips to the facilities as well as through travelling exhibits where museum personnel visit schools. In addition, children and their parents can be encouraged to visit these facilities.

The meaningful displays and interactive exhibits found in museums and other centers of informal science learning provide rich opportunities for discovery learning. Children can give their attention to exhibits that interest them. Museums provide concrete learning experiences, and they facilitate inquiry by providing examples of principles previously investigated by children. Museums also provide the opportunities to investigate discrepant events. An example of such a discrepant event is the exhibit of two concave reflectors that look like satellite dishes, facing each other at opposite ends of a hall some 100 feet long. A child whispers into one of the dishes and another child, listening inside the other dish, can hear the whisper clearly. This gives rise to the question of why the sound can be heard so clearly across such a large distance. Children are encouraged to explore a variety of reasons for the phenomenon, eventually discovering that the concave surfaces focus the sound, thereby concentrating it.

Visits to museums and other informal science attractions also help provide positive attitudes about science. Teachers are encouraged to let children find their own areas of interest in trips to these facilities and explore them as they see fit. This is the constructivist approach to museum visits.

There is much to be learned in museums, and much to be experienced. Museums and other informal science learning facilities abound throughout the United States; there are over 350 such facilities designed specifically for children. Taking advantage of these resources is a "must" in quality elementary science education.

Yet museums do not have to be housed in special buildings. The schoolyard, children's backyards, and local parks are living museums. Children can observe animals and plants, describing the habits of the animals, and inferring the elements of the ecosystems they find. What do the animals eat? How do they get their food? How do they keep warm? Why are they here instead of some place else? Daily or weekly visits to the same sites enable children to observe and chart changes. The school building itself is filled with phenomena worthy of observation and study such as pipes, water pressure, heating and ventilation systems, and so on.

Field Trips

THE FOSSIL FIELD TRIP

When I was science curriculum coordinator in Saudi Arabia, a team of third-fourth grade classes was studying a unit on dinosaurs which included a brief section on fossils. Most of the rocks in the local area were sedimentary, and most contained fossils. Some of the children brought their fossil collections to school. That's where I came in. The teachers wanted to know if I could develop some sort of special experience to capitalize upon the children's demonstrated interests in fossils. I suggested a field trip to a couple of areas I knew to be especially rich in fossils.

The teachers told the children of the possibility of the trip, and instructed them to work in small groups to come up with a list of goals for their trip. It was obvious that some of the children were more interested in fossils than others; but it was equally obvious that all were intensely interested in going on the trip.

In small groups, the children did their own planning of the trip's objectives. The teachers worked with the groups to help them think things through, but no teacher imposed pre-conceived notions of what should be learned. The objectives the children fashioned were somewhat diverse, including "learn about fossils," "collect fossils," "eat lunch," "see the desert," and "get away from school for a whole day." (This latter goal was not actually said, but we could tell that for some children getting away from school for a whole day was a major objective.)

Shortly after we got rolling on the bus, we passed out maps with the trip route marked, and we told the children they could follow the maps if they wanted to. With very few exceptions, every one of the children diligently followed the route on the map, pointing out roadside features throughout the trip.

Now, on an all-day trip with a bus full of eight- and nine-year-olds, it is desirable (and essential) to have fun time as well as work time. So our first stop was at a roadside sand dune. The children climbed the dune, and had the time of their lives rolling down the steeply-inclined slip face. Some of the children asked about the dune's shape, sparking a discussion of prevailing winds and how sand dunes form.

As we drove through one of the local villages, the children noticed the contrast between rustic and modern housing, and asked many questions about that phenomenon. They noticed sand beginning to encroach on the village, and asked more questions. We responded to their questions, and made either written or mental notes of them.

At the first fossil bed, the children inquired about the tomb they saw in the distance. Though some had heard of the Jawa'an Tomb, which had recently been excavated, very few had actually visited it. So, we walked over to it and told them a little about it, including how it was thought to have been the burial place for a nobleman and his servants. They examined the tomb's structure, inside and out. At least one child was more interested in bugs, for he concentrated on finding and examining the beetles that were scurrying around the sandy floor of the tomb. Others noticed the tomb was built of fossil-bearing rocks.

We returned to the fossil site, and, in small groups, we set to work chipping out fossils from two main areas, one higher than the other, each bearing a different type of fossil. All the time, we were responding to the children's questions, noting what it was they were curious about.

After lunch, we set out for our second fossil area where children collected and examined more fossils. At the end of the field trip, we held a rap session at the local swimming pool. (Recall that children had said they did not want to get back to school until the whole day had been used up.) Children were asked to tell the most important thing they had learned on the trip. Their responses included the following:

■ What a fossil looks like
■ How to tell lizard tracks and camel tracks
■ How to tell different fossils apart
■ How to tell old fossils from newer ones
■ How fossils were formed
■ How to tell whether fossils formed in shallow or deep water
■ How sand dunes form
■ What it feels like to run down a slip face
■ That local people have rustic and modern houses

From what the children said they had learned, we made a list of suggestions for follow-up study. Some children grouped fossils. Others compared those from one location with those from the other. Still others worked out an elementary stratigraphy (layering) to correlate the two sites which were some 50 miles apart, inferring which invasion of the seas occurred earlier at each site. But some of the children left their fossils at home, and started investigating why the local people have two kinds of houses. Others worked out a chronological log of the trip. Still others engaged in creative-writing experiences about the tomb and about sliding down slip faces of sand dunes.

This one-day field trip opened up many doors of learning to many children. The learning was not limited to science. Children who previously had thought they could never be successful at science followed up the trip's experiences with fossil studies. So-called troublemakers were no trouble at all; they were too enthusiastic and were learning too much to have to dream up ways of getting attention. The children gained an idea of their most comfortable learning styles. They had a chance to be creative. All this and science too! They *did* learn about fossils. They *did* learn how to group them. And they *did* utilize the processes of science.

Before we went, one of the teachers said to me, "But we have to tell those kids what it is they are supposed to learn." Can we? And expect it will be learned?

As you can tell from the experience described above, field trips are truly interdisciplinary, closely aligned with the rose model where the topic or project is the trip itself.

The constructivist approach to field trips involves children deciding what they are going to learn—and this decision is not likely to be made in advance. This is not to suggest planning is unimportant; careful planning is vital to the success of any field trip. The teacher first "scouts" the trip, and discusses with the children what they are most likely to see and experience. The teacher sets guiding goals for the trip based on the outcomes desired and the means available for children to attain these outcomes. When the actual trip occurs, teachers continue in the constructivist inquiry learning mode. Children are going to learn, and they are going to learn what they learn very well. All we have to do is not interfere.

Elements of planning for field trips are shown in Figure 9.11.

> ## ELEMENTS OF FIELD TRIP PLANNING
>
> ▌ Decide on the destination.
> ▌ **TAKE THE TRIP YOURSELF!!!**
> ▌ Note features likely to engage children's interests.
> ▌ Determine cost and how the trip will be funded.
> ▌ Determine how many adults should accompany the children.
> ▌ Decide whether to bring or buy lunch.
> ▌ Secure appropriate administrative permission.
> ▌ Secure parental permission by writing a letter to parents explaining the trip, the goals of the trip, and what the children will do. Attach the required permission blank.
> ▌ Outline the trip to the children.
> ▌ Ask children to decide what they want to focus on.
> ▌ Establish behavior expectations.
> ▌ Take the trip.
> ▌ Help children crystallize their questions and their thoughts during the trip.
> ▌ Help children figure out answers to their questions in an inquiry manner.
> ▌ Consider preparing a short field trip guide of features children can look for during the trip.
> ▌ Point out interesting features children may have missed.
> ▌ On return, ask children the most important or significant thing they learned during the trip.
> ▌ Suggest follow-up work as appropriate, based on demonstrated interest of children and goals of the trip.

FIGURE 9.11

Conclusion

To be scientifically literate, people must know how to *do* science. And they must know how science and all other areas of study are interrelated. Studying science in isolation is impossible. Identifying science as a separate intellectual endeavor sends the message that science is elite, difficult, and esoteric.

There are many ways of integrating science and the rest of the curriculum. Integrating literature (both fiction and non-fiction) with science helps provide relevance of studies to children's lives and opens avenues of inquiry that include the thoughts of others. Other disciplines can be included as adjuncts to the science program to show interrelationships.

Alternatively, the science program can center on a totally integrated investigation of topics of interest and value to children. The Science-Technology-Society approach allows children to study science in the context of the totality of human experience. Non-traditional science learning settings and field trips provide valuable and relevant hands-on learning experiences.

For maximum learning to occur, science must be integrated with all other disciplines and be approached as one of many aspects of understanding the complexities of the world and the people who inhabit it.

CHAPTER 9   Additional Questions for Discussion

1. Contrast the subject-centered approach of teaching science with an interdisciplinary approach relative to content exposure and meaningful learning.
2. What advice would you give to a person who claims that science can be taught adequately through a literature-centered approach?

Note

1. The entire March, 1995 issue of *Science Scope* is devoted to "Science in Nontraditional Settings."

2. Source: World Climate Review, University of Virginia. Forecast figures based on a computer model developed at Geophysical Fluid Dynamics Laboratory, Princeton, NJ. Actual figures measured by NASA satellites.

References

Aardema, V. (1981). *Bringing the Rain to Kapiti Plain: A Nandi Tale.* New York: Dial.

Aliki. (1988). *Digging Up Dinosaurs.* New York: Harper Collins Children's Books.

———. (1981). *My Five Senses.* New York: Harper Collins Children's Books.

Armbruster, B. B. (1993). Reading to learn. *The Reading Teacher, 46*(4), 346–347.

Barnam, C. R. (1992). An evaluation of the use of a technique designed to assist prospective elementary teachers use the learning cycle with science textbooks. *School Science and Mathematics 92*(2), 59–63.

Berenstain, J. & Berenstain, S. (1977). *The Berenstain Bears' Science Fair.* New York: Random House.

Brainard, A. & Wrubel, D. H. (1993). *Literature-based Science Activities: An Integrated Approach, Grades K–3.* New York: Scholastic Professional Books.

Breathed, B. (1992). *The Last Basselope: One Ferocious Story.* Boston: Little Brown.

Burton, V. L. (1939). *Mike Mulligan and His Steam Shovel.* Boston: Houghton Mifflin.

Butzow, C. M. & Butzow, J. W. (1989). *Science Through Children's Literature: An Integrated Approach.* Englewood, CO: Teacher Idea Press.

Cannon, J. (1993). *Stellaluna.* San Diego: Harcourt Brace.

Carle, E. (1985). *The Very Busy Spider.* New York: Philomel.

———. (1987). *The Very Hungry Caterpillar.* New York: Philomel.

Cauley, L. B. (1983). *Jack and the Beanstalk.* New York: Putnam.

Cooney, B. (1982). *Miss Rumphius.* New York: Viking Press.

Deedy, C. A. (1994). *Agatha's Feather Bed: Not Just Another Wild Goose Story.* Atlanta, GA: Peachtree.

Dewey, A. (1993). *The Sky.* New York: Green Tiger Press.

Gibbons, G. (1991). *From Seed to Plant.* New York: Holiday House.

Glynn, S. M. and Muth, K. D. (1994). Reading and writing to learn in science: Achieving scientific literacy. *Journal of Research in Science Teaching, 31*(9), 1057–1073.

Hughes, S. (1988). *Out and About.* New York: Lothrop, Lee & Shepard.

Hurd, P. D. (1991). Why we must transform science education. *Educational Leadership* October, 1991, p. 33–35.

Johnston, T. (1988). *The Forces Be With You!* Milwaukee, WI: Gareth Stevens.

Kelley, T. (1986). *The Mystery of the Stranger in the Barn.* New York: Dodd, Mead and Co.

King, M. L. (1963). *The Strength to Love.* Cleveland, OH: Fount Books.

Lima, C. W. & Lima, J. A. (1993). *A to Zoo—Subject Access to Children's Picture Books.* (4th edition). New Providence, NJ: Bowker.

Markle, S. (1988). *Science Mini Mysteries.* New York: Athenium.

Martin, B. & Archenbault, J. (1988). *Listen to the Rain.* New York: H. Holt.

McNulty, F. (1986). *The Lady and the Spider.* New York: Harper & Row.

Moore, J. E. & Evans, J. (1991). *Exploring Science Through Literature, Level A, Grades K–1.* Monterey, CA: Evan-Moor Corp.

———. (1991). *Exploring Science Through Literature, Level B, Grades 2–3.* Monterey, CA: Evan-Moor Corp.

————. (1991). *Exploring Science Through Literature, Level C, Grades 4–6.* Monterey, CA: Evan-Moor Corp.

Naisbitt, J. and Aburdene, P. (1990). *Megatrends 2000: Ten New Directions for the 1990's.* New York, NY: Morrow, p. 16.

Pallotta, J. (1986). *The Icky Bug Alphabet Book.* Watertown, MA: Charlesbridge Publishers.

————. (1989). *The Bird Alphabet Book.* Watertown, MA: Charlesbridge Publishers.

Peters, W. (1988). *The Sun, the Wind, and the Rain.* New York: H. Holt.

Phillips, L. (1991). *The Million Dollar Potato.* New York: Simon and Schuster.

Polacco, P. (1990). *Thunder Cake.* New York: Philomel.

Ramirez, G. & Ramirez, J. L. (1994). *Multiethnic Children's Literature.* Albany, NY: Delmar Publishers, Inc.

Raskin, E. (1978). *The Westing Game.* New York: Dutton.

Selsam, M. (1983). *A First Look at Spiders.* New York: Walker.

Silverstein, S. (1974). *Where the Sidewalk Ends.* New York: Harper and Row.

Sobol, D. (1984). *Encyclopedia Brown Takes the Cake.* New York: Scholastic.

Taba, H. (1962). *Curriculum Development: Theory and Practice.* New York: Harcourt Brace & World, Inc.

The Magic School Bus Gets Baked in a Cake: A Book About Kitchen Chemistry. (1995). New York: Scholastic.

Ulerick, S. L. (1989). Using textbooks for meaningful learning in science. *Research Matters . . . To the Science Teacher.* National Association for Research in Science Teaching *Newsletter,* April, 1989.

Van Allensburg, C. (1988). *Two Bad Ants.* Boston: Houghton Mifflin.

Walsh, E. S. (1989). *Mouse Paint.* San Diego: Harcourt Brace.

Yager, R. E. (1991). Science/Technology/Society as a major reform in science education: Its importance for teacher education. *Teaching Education 3*(2), 91–100.

————. (1994). Assessment results with the science/technology/society approach. *Science and Children 32*(2).

Zais, R. S. (1976). *Curriculum: Principles and Foundations.* New York: Harper & Row, Publishers, Inc.

CHAPTER 10

Technology in Elementary Science

We live in an age of technology where children in our schools often know more about technology than their teachers. Most teachers did not grow up with the technology that has become part of the every-day lives of today's children. Only in the last few years have talking on cellular phones, playing video games, and surfing the television channels become common-place activities.

Nonetheless, education has utilized technol-ogy for many years. Films, videos, and filmstrips have become staple supplements to the curricu-lum. Models, charts, and displays continue to pro-vide enrichment and depth to programs. Audio tapes continue to have uses in song and dance. Overhead projectors are used to show transparen-cies, manipulatives, money, clocks, color tiles, pattern blocks, the spectrum of visible light, and even magnetic fields by sprinkling iron filings onto a piece of acetate that has been placed over a magnet on the projector glass. Calculators continue to be used to help young children in both mathematics and science.

Computers have been used in education since the late 1950s; the early focus was on computer-assisted instruction (CAI) involving tutorials, drill-and-practice formats, and the mechanics of computer hardware and programming techniques. The 1960s brought computers solidly into the field of education through computerized applications of programmed instruction.

However, it is the emergence of the personal computer in the mid-1970s that has expanded the educational use of computers to include word processing, spreadsheets, databases, graphing, laboratory computer interfacing systems, distance learning, and a multitude of increasingly sophisticated applications. Computers can provide practice, create realistic simulations, gather experimental data previously impossible to obtain, process experimental data rapidly and accurately so valid conclusions can be reached, provide instant access to huge amounts of information, and enable children and their teachers to communicate with peers and experts throughout the world.

It is imperative that teachers become sufficiently familiar with current technology that they can use technology comfortably with their children. In this chapter, you will examine a variety of technological advances and ways they can be used to foster the process-oriented inquiry elementary science program.[1]

Why Use Advanced Technology in Elementary Science Education?

There are many reasons for using advanced technology in the constructivist elementary science program; these reasons range from the near universality of technology in today's society to technology's enormous potential for aiding children in their inquiries.

Nearly every American business, from banks and brokerage firms to warehouses and fast food restaurants, requires some knowledge of computers. Nearly every manufacturing facility utilizes computers and computer-based advanced technology. It has been estimated that in 1995, almost forty percent of homes in America have personal computers, a quarter of which are fitted with CD-ROM capability. As many as fifty percent of American homes are expected to have a computer modem by the year 2000 (Alter, 1995). These statistics suggest one reason for employing computers and advanced technology in our schools: *they are used everywhere.*

A second reason for using technology in the elementary science classroom is that many children are accustomed to using it at home in the form of videos, pre-programmed television shows, camcorders, video games, computer games, and on-line information services such as Prodigy and CompuServe. Just as educational films sought to teach children through media familiar to children, today's educational technology seeks to provide a comfortable atmosphere for children used to technology.

Third, in elementary science, technology is used to gain access to amounts and types of information previously unavailable to children. For example, using laserdisks, children can witness experimental procedures too dangerous or too expensive for the classroom; they can see photographs and action scenes and hear explanations and information presentations on just about any topic of interest, from animal habitats to aviation, from plate tectonics and volcanoes to nuclear reactors. Entire encyclopedias are available on CD-ROM discs from which children can obtain desired information in a matter of seconds. Distance learning, Internet, e-mail, and fax facilities enable children and teachers to access specialized information anywhere in the world.

Fourth, technology in elementary science provides speed, accuracy, and convenience in inquiry investigations. With technology, children spend less time on data collection tasks and mathematical manipulation, and more time processing and interpreting experimental data, thus achieving greater accuracy in data collection, mathematical operations, and experimental results. Probes and sensors that accompany laboratory computer interfacing systems enable children to measure force, temperature, light intensity, barometric pressure, and even heart rate with a degree of accuracy, sensitivity, and speed not otherwise available. For example, temperature probes can be used to compare the difference in air temperature between the floor and the ceiling in the classroom. Motion sensors can be used to record the continuously increasing speed of a cart rolling down an inclined plane.

Spreadsheets can be programmed to do complex mathematical calculations on raw data entered by children to provide desired information. For example, children can enter the number of swings a pendulum makes in 15 seconds into a spreadsheet, and the pre-programmed equations calculate the average period (length of time for one swing).

Graphics programs are used to generate instant graphic portrayal of data collected by children, such as daily outdoor temperature or rate of plant growth.

Database programs can be used to store a variety of information children (or the teacher) have researched on a topic; this information then can be sorted in different ways to help children answer their questions. For example, children who are investigating dinosaurs can research facts about a number of different dinosaurs. These facts can be entered into a "Dinosaur Database," and commonalities among dinosaurs can be searched, such as which dinosaurs were plant-eaters, how many dinosaurs were less than ten feet long, and where the most dinosaur bones have been found.

Fifth, technology can be used to provide learning experiences suitable for individual needs of children. For the visual learner, the array of video material available is virtually unlimited, ranging from pre-programmed shows that air on commercial and public television channels to videos on specialized topics prepared specifically for educational uses. With proper technology, children can access bits of information about a chosen topic from a variety of sources, and can produce their own video on that topic.

Technology has been shown to provide a stimulus to foster the internal locus of control (Steinberg, 1989). Using suitable technologies, children are encouraged to pursue their own strategies to solving problems, thus demonstrating that they are in control of their own learning. Technology has been used to stimulate the field independent mode of cognitive operations on the part of field dependent children. Computer programs were created to increase children's ability to recognize differences in randomly-shown paired pictures, rows of shapes, and grids of patterns and shapes, thereby decreasing their dependence on surrounding details for figure recognition and helping foster higher levels of field independence and, ultimately, critical thinking (Collings, 1985). The operation of computer programs is, itself, an aid for developing a more field independent style, for children must focus on the details of the programmed material rather than on the global aspects of the program.

The use of computers is an aid to children with other learning handicaps, children whose primary language is not English, and physically handicapped children.

Finally, perhaps the most compelling reason for using technology in elementary science education is that *scientists use it*. One of the premises underlying elementary science education is that children should *do* science, not just read about science, and that children should do science the way scientists do science. This means using technology. The National Science Teachers Association adopted this posture in their position statement, "The Use of Computers in Science Education:"

> Just as computers play a central role in developing and applying scientific knowledge, they can also facilitate the learning of science. It is, therefore, the position of the National Science Teachers Association that computers should have a major role in the teaching and learning of science (1993).

Types of Technology

There are many different types of technology ranging from videos, overhead projectors, and simple calculators to computers, one-way and two-way audio-video systems, distance learning, and complex computer-video interaction systems. Some are simple to use, and some are complicated. Some are inexpensive, and some require substantial financial investment. Some have been used in education for years, and some are newcomers.

It is necessary to get past the glitz of technological advances when assessing technology's potential for helping children to learn. Exploring science through fancy and expensive equipment is exciting, but basic hardware and inexpensive software can do the job just as well in encouraging higher-order thinking, helping children solve problems, and permitting extensive and accurate independent exploration of child-generated problems.

Computers in the Elementary Science Classroom

The development of the personal computer and the rich array of educational software and related technologies now available has virtually reformed the use of technology in the classroom. In 1990, 97.3 percent of the public elementary schools in the United States reported using computers; this is contrasted with 11.1 percent which reported using computers in 1981 (World Almanac, 1994, p. 196).

The first general-purpose electronic computer was developed in 1946. Called ENIAC (Electronic Numerical Integrator and Calculator), it weighed 30 tons, had 18,000 vacuum tubes, and occupied 3000 cubic feet of space. ENIAC was used largely for military operations, and generally burned out one or more of its vacuum tubes every few minutes. Grace Hopper, a young Naval officer, was one of the early computer operations experts. One day, while she was trying to find the cause of a problem, she discovered that a bug caught between two electrical terminals was preventing the flow of electricity. She solved the problem by removing the bug, giving rise to the term, "debugging" for the act of looking for program errors. Hopper later became an Admiral, and is one of the American pioneers of computer use.

Today one can purchase personal computers that are smaller than brief cases, and that can process information thousands of times faster than ENIAC.

Computer Specifications

There are three basic types of computer systems: the IBM (or DOS) system, the Apple system, and the McIntosh system. In order for a computer to operate, it must have an operating system (a system that tells it how to respond) and something to operate. The operating systems are different in DOS, Apple, and McIntosh computers, and, generally, the systems cannot be used interchangeably. The "something to operate" is called a *program*; types of programs include games, word processing programs, spreadsheets, databases, and thousands of specific programs designed for specific applications. Each program is written so it will operate on one of the three main operational systems; a program written for one system cannot normally be used on either of the other two. So, when you purchase software, you must be sure to select programs that will work on the kind of computer you have.

To be functional, a computer system must contain three hardware components: the computer itself (called the CPU, or central processing unit), an input device such as a keyboard (often with a mouse), and an output device such as a monitor and a printer. The computer itself is housed in a metal box and contains the operating system, one or more drives for the programs it operates, and a memory facility. Computer memory may be RAM (random-access memory) which allows the operator to work with the stored information as in word processing or database manipulations, or it may be ROM (read-only memory) which allows only access to stored information, as with CD-ROM's. Memories are stored on the hard drive, floppy disks, or compact disks. External drives may accommodate $5^1/_4$-inch floppy disks or $3^1/_2$ inch disks (also called "floppy disks" even though they are rigid). When buying programs, you must be sure to purchase the type of disk your computer can receive. Many computers also have a small drawer that looks like a CD player that enables use of CD-ROM disks.

Inside the computer there may be an additional drive (called the "C" drive) which can hold programs permanently. The "C" drive is available with different memory capacities; normally one would want the largest capacity that one can afford to purchase.

Keyboards are all about the same, and resemble typewriter keyboards.

Monitors come in color and black-and-white, and vary in degree of resolution available. Since the monitor is one of the primary sources of output, one should get a color monitor with a sufficiently high resolution to accommodate graphics and drawings.

Printers may be dot-matrix or laser. The dot-matrix printer can be used for letters, graphs, and other non-drawing applications, but they are slow and the quality of intricate print is poor. Their best application is for text. Laser printers are much more expensive, but they are fast and they produce high quality work, including art work.

Computers come in a variety of sizes and shapes. Current trends are toward reducing size, and desktop and lap top computers the size of a small briefcase, fully portable, and powered by rechargeable batteries are becoming increasingly common. The desktop and laptop computers do everything the larger PCs do. Another current trend is to increase the speed with which computers process information. Yet another trend is to develop software that is compatible with any of the operating systems.

Before you purchase a computer for home or school use, you should review the above information and discuss options with someone knowledgeable. Since computer technology is changing rapidly, be prepared for rapid obsolescence of whatever equipment you purchase.

A Technology Inquiry Continuum

You will recall that, in Chapter Five, we suggested a methodology continuum ranging from teacher-centered expository methodologies to child-centered free discovery. (See Figure 5.1.) The position a particular lesson occupies on the continuum depends on the extent to which children are free to explore on their own.

A similar continuum can be constructed for the wide array of computer technology applications available. (See Figure 10.1.)

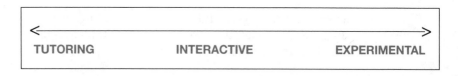

FIGURE 10.1 A technology continuum

Tutorial applications are expository in nature. They dispense information. They teach something to the child. Tutorial applications include such programs as drill-and-practice, tutorials, course reviews, remediation, and testing.

Interactive applications are those that allow children to interact with the computer in some fashion, and include word processing programs, spread sheet programs, database programs, graphic programs, simulation programs, CD-ROM, on-line databases, hypermedia programs, and animation programs.

Experimential applications are those that allow children to use technology as an adjunct to their own experimental procedures. Laboratory computer interface systems permit data gathering that would not otherwise be possible, especially long-term data (such as overnight effects), short-term data (such as increase of speed of a cart rolling down an inclined plane), and hard-to-obtain data (such as temperature differences between the floor and the ceiling).

Tutorial Uses of Computers

A tremendous array of science tutorial computer software exists and is growing rapidly.

Tutorial programs are utilized as dispensers of information and testers of children's mastery of the information. Typically a piece of information is presented on the screen, and the child is asked to key a response to a question about this information. The computer gives a "yes" or a "no" response. The "yes" response may be in the form of points awarded, or distances along an animated path, or height up a mountain, or some other system of portraying success. The "no" response typically refers the child to additional screens which "teach" the material, after which the child tries a similar question. The tutorial programs provide immediate positive reinforcement of children's responses, and are similar to the programmed texts of the 1960s and 1970s; in a sense, they are a newer generation of programmed texts. Programs range from simple to relatively complex, and should be selected on the basis of the age, grade, and sophistication of children, and their intended uses. Computer tutorials often include the basic elements of quality expository teaching: gaining attention, overviewing the lesson, providing objectives, reviewing prerequisite information, delivering new information, providing guidance, giving items for response, and providing feedback. A good example of such programs are the tutorials that accompany most word processing programs; you may have used one yourself to help you master a word processing program.

Tutorial programs can be used for follow-up on a topic the teacher has introduced, or for review of material, or as part of an advance organizer or initial introduction. They can be used to reinforce concepts explored in class from different perspectives. They can be used to enable children to learn about something that has captured their interest or to review material they may have missed due to absence. Tutorials are also extremely useful in helping teachers study scientific material where they may feel the need.

Drill-and-practice programs are designed to help children memorize; they are valuable where mastering factual knowledge and building vocabulary are necessary. Remedial programs present basic knowledge of topics covered and can help children acquire information prerequisite to the study of a topic.

Computerized tutoring has been shown to exert a small but positive effect on learning (Hancock & Betts, 1994). However, all these programs are designed to lead the child to correct responses, and, as such, are clearly expository in nature. There is no room in these programs for children to interact or to apply their own thinking. The computer owns the knowledge, and it is the job of the child to discover "truths."

Interactive Uses of Computers

Interactive uses of computers permit children to use computers as tools to aid them in their inquiries. Though limited in scope by the material written into the programs, these applications allow some degree of mental manipulations directed by children.

Word processing programs are used for written reports, essays, descriptions, and the like. Features such as spell-check and grammar analysis permit attention to the substance of the material without having to worry unduly about mechanics. It has been shown that children who regularly use word processors for their writing exhibit higher quality and greater quantity of writing (Hancock & Betts, 1994). Word processing programs can be used for children to record experimental data; however, data cannot be manipulated using word processing programs.

Desktop publishing programs are word processing applications that allow children to put together newsletters and information pamphlets with a quasi-professional look. How better to show the community what is happening in your science classroom than to distribute a professional-looking periodic newsletter? (A class could start by distributing newsletters to other classrooms in their school.) Programs such as *Print Shop* are available for producing signs and banners. Children can make banners to advertise special classroom science events such as "Science Day" or to welcome guest speakers. They can make signs to label where various kinds of equipment are stored.

Spreadsheet programs are used to record quantitative data and to provide rapid and accurate calculations by using mathematical formulas to process the data. Figure 10.2 shows a spreadsheet used to calculate average period of a pendulum from raw data. (See Constructing Your Ideas 3.14, p. 113, for a complete description of the pendulum inquiry.) Children first input the number of washers they used, the length of the string, and the distance of the pull. They then count the number of swings in 15 seconds for each of three trials, and enter the result in the appropriate blank after each trial. Each time a variable is changed, new values are entered and the results of each of the three trials of swing counting are entered. The spreadsheet is programmed to calculate the average of the three trials, the average number of swings *per minute*, and the average *period* of the pendulum (length of time for one swing). Formulas are shown in the figure. By using the spreadsheet, children can interpret the results of their explorations from accurately calculated averages. Spreadsheets can be used to calculate the rate of growth of each of several plants; children input periodic height measurements, and the spreadsheet is programmed to calculate averages. Spreadsheets have many other uses where calculations from raw data are needed to interpret experimental results. Spreadsheets aid children in their development of the processes of prediction, inference, and interpreting data.

Database programs are used to help children sort and analyze large amounts of data about related phenomena. After entry of many items of information about each of many examples of a set, children can sort the information in different ways to answer questions. For instance, one could develop a database of characteristics of birds. Such characteristics as length, male-female resemblance, habitat, song, and nesting habits might be included. Children might be assigned responsibility for researching the agreed-upon information about one or two birds each. This information is recorded in the labeled sections of each database cell, one cell per bird. The information also can be presented in tabular form. Once the information has been entered, children use the sorting function to discover similarities among birds, such as which birds are located in certain areas, in which birds the male and female look alike, and the most common nesting habits. (See Figure 10.5.) Databases can be developed for just about any topic from

THE PENDLULUM

COLUMNS	C	E	G	I	K	M	O	Q	S
ROWS	NO. WASHERS	STRING LENGT (cm)	PULL DIST (cm)	SWINGS IN 15 SEC #1	#2	#3	AVERAG SWINGS IN 15 SEC	AVG SWINGS PER MIN	AVERAGE PERIOD
10	3	30	10	12	12	13	12.33	49.33	1.22
12	4	30	10	12.5	11.5	12	12.00	48.00	1.25
14	5	30	10	12	12	12.5	12.17	48.67	1.23
16	6	30	10	13	11.5	12.5	12.33	49.33	1.22

FORMULA   COLUMN O—AVERAGE SWINGS IN 15 :   (I11+K11+M11)/3
COLUMN Q—AVG SWINGS PER MIN.:   O11*4
COLUMN S—AVERAGE PERIOD: 1/(Q11/60)

Spread sheet application from Microsoft Works

FIGURE 10.2   Spreadsheet used for pendulum inquiry

DATABASE CELL

Name: Red Head Woodpecker
Length: 21–24
Male-Female Res: Similar
Habitat: Groves
Song: Churr
Nest: Hollows in Trees

Database application from Microsoft Works

FIGURE 10.3

BIRDS DATABASE IN TABULAR FORM

Name	Length	Male-Female Res	Habitat	Song	Nest
Red Head Woodpecker	21–24	Similar	Groves	Churr	Hollows in Trees
Bluebird	18	Sl. Different	Open Country	Musical	Natural Cavities
Oriole	18–20	Similar	Open Woods	Whistle	Lower Tree Branches
Starling	19–21	Similar	Cities	Whistles; Clicks	Builds Nest
Sparrow	15	Different	Cities	Chips	Builds Nest
Nuthatch	11	Similar	Open Pine Woods	Twitter	Nests in Cavities
Chickadee	11	Similar	Woods	Whistle	Nests in Cavities
Cardinal	19–23	Different	Woodland Edges	Whistle; Chirp	Shrubbery
Titmouse	15	Similar	Woodlands	Whistle	Nests
Red-Winged Blackbird	18–24	Different	Marshes	Gurgle	Nests: Water Shrubs
Robin	23–28	Different	Cities	Caroling	Lower Tree Branches

Database application from Microsoft Works

FIGURE 10.4

NAMES OF BIRDS IN WHICH MALE AND FEMALE LOOK ALIKE

Name	Length	Habitat	Song	Nest
Red Head Woodpecker	21–24	Groves	Churr	Hollows in Trees
Oriole	18–20	Open Woods	Whistle	Lower Tree Branches
Starling	19–21	Cities	Whistles; Clicks	Builds Nest
Nuthatch	11	Open Pine Woods	Twitter	Nests in Cavities
Chickadee	11	Woods	Whistle	Nests in Cavities
Titmouse	15	Woodlands	Whistle	Nests

Database application from Microsoft Works

FIGURE 10.5

dinosaurs to populations, animals to planets. Many databases are available commercially; however, if children prepare their own they derive maximum benefit.

A good way to introduce children to the concept of databases is to have them write the data on cards and then sort the cards by common characteristics. For example children would record the information about each different kind of bird on a different card labeled with the name of the bird. They would then flip through the cards to find similar characteristics, such as which birds live in cities. The electronic database is the next logical step, and has the advantage that it can manipulate large amounts of information quickly, and can sort by numerical parameters such as finding birds longer than 15 inches, between 15 and 20 inches in length, or up to 18 inches long. Having done these tasks manually, children develop understanding of how database programs work, and they understand the power of electronic databases programs. Database programs aid children in the processes of classification and interpretation of data.

Graphic programs use the computer to construct any of a variety of graphs from data entered by children. Options for graph construction normally include pie graphs, line graphs, and bar graphs drawn either to pre-determined specifications or to the child's specifications. Line graph and bar graph programs typically ask for identification of units and labels for the horizontal axis and the vertical axis, after which data can be entered. Graphic programs are extremely useful in helping children visualize the impact of their data and interpret the meaning of the data. A graphic program was used to portray the depths and diameters of simulated moon craters formed by dropping marbles from different heights (Figures 3.20 and 3.21, p. 132 and 133). Graphic programs can be used as early as kindergarten to chart plant growth, daily temperatures, times of sunrise and sunset, and the like. Teachers will need to provide the axis set-up, but children can input the data. Figure 10.6 shows the data table and resulting graph of a kindergarten activity involving measuring noontime temperatures.

Graphic programs can show percentages and frequencies (quantities) of non-numeric variables in the form of pie graphs and bar charts. These

DATA TABLE

Row Number	Series Number	Date (Dates)	Temperature (Degrees F)
1	1	21.0	74.0
2	1	22.0	74.0
3	1	23.0	82.0
4	1	24.0	81.0
5	1	25.0	91.0
6	1	26.0	77.0
7	1	27.0	86.0

LINE GRAPH

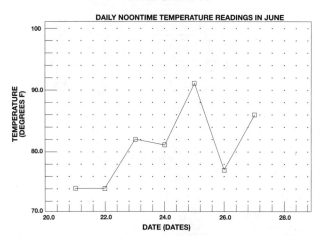

BAR GRAPH

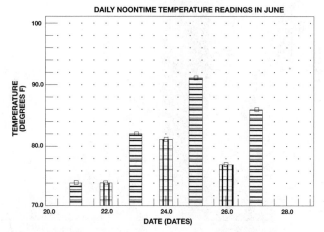

Graphical Analysis program courtesy of Vernier Software, 8565 SW Beaverton-Hillsdale Hwy, Portland, OR 97225-2429

FIGURE 10.6   Daily noontime temperatures in June—data table, line graph, and bar graph

programs are appropriate for charting data that are partially qualitative, such as percentages of basic food groups consumed during a day, numbers of children with certain hair color or eye color, numbers of days with given weather conditions, and the like. Figure 10.7 shows two graphs that portray numbers of children in a third grade class with brown, blue, green, and hazel eyes.

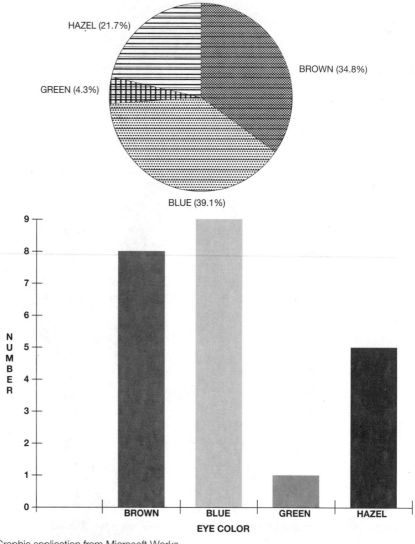

Graphic application from Microsoft Works

FIGURE 10.7 Pie graph and bar graph of eye color

Graphic programs can be purchased individually; however, they often are included in integrated software packages that contain word processing, spreadsheet, database, and graphic programs in the same package.

Simulation programs are programs in which the child inputs a series of inquiries and actions about realistic or hypothetical problems, and receives graphic information about the effect of the actions. For example, an upper elementary grades program called *SimCity*, by Brøderbund Software, invites children to inquire into urban ecosystems. A city plan is presented and children are asked to respond to hypothetical community changes, such as sudden population changes, natural disasters, and poor planning, by suggesting redesigns of the city. Effects of the newly input designs are shown so children can see the results of their planning. Simulation programs are used to train pilots and astronauts and to pose clinical problems for medical students. In elementary science education, simulation software is most often used to explore concepts that require expensive or hazardous materials or procedures (such as nuclear reactions and experiments involving strong acids or highly reactive chemicals), levels of skill not yet attained by children (such as activities involving micromeasurement, vacuum treatment, or super-cooling), or more time than is possible in a classroom situation (such as population growth simulations).

CD-ROM information bases enable children to isolate desired facts and other information through search-and-sort mechanisms. A CD-ROM is a compact disk that has the capability of storing huge amounts of information. The "ROM" in the term means "read-only memory," because you cannot add anything to the CD. A single CD-ROM disk has the capacity to store 550,000 pages of print information; many are multimedia in nature, and provide sound, pictures, and even moving pictures in addition to textual material. For example, illustrated encyclopedias, talking dictionaries, and maps with databases showing facts about major cities and geographic features are available on CD-ROM. The CD-ROM normally has a menu built into the program, enabling children to access the desired information by category quickly. Library catalogs and the ERIC, PSYCHLIT and other reference databases in your college or university library are probably provided on CD-ROM.

CD-ROMs are available for a multitude of scientific topics, and can take the form of databases, providers of multimedia information, simulation programs, or combinations. Though CD-ROMs cannot save children's work, they can provide exciting information presentations and interactive simulations.

Online databases such as *Prodigy* and *CompuServe* enable children to access huge amounts of continuously updated information. One must subscribe to the service and have a modem on the computer to receive the signals over telephone lines. The information children can access through online databases is virtually unlimited; the only computer skill necessary is the ability to select the proper options from the menu screens and limit the options until the amount of information available is manageable.

Hypermedia systems are menu-driven programs that integrate audio, video, and computer functions. They allow children to research information on various topics or different aspects of the same topic, save what is pertinent to their project, and synthesize the parts into a whole that can be stored as a computer file or videotape. Some hypermedia systems combine videodiscs with computers to provide enormous amounts of information.

Animation programs portray processes such as acceleration, cell division, and mountain formation. Programs range in content sophistication from very simple (such as blood coursing through the body) to very complex (such as forces acting on space vehicles). They are designed to enable children to see models of phenomena that otherwise cannot be seen, and to allow children to manipulate given variables to see what happens, thus encouraging children in their development of the process skill of model making.

Interactive computer applications permit children to manipulate data and research vast quantities of information. However, access is limited to what the programmer has written, and children cannot explore beyond the limits of the pre-programmed capability.

Experimental Uses of Computers

Microcomputer-Based Laboratories (MBLs) and *Personal Science Laboratories (PSLs)*, examples of laboratory computer interfacing systems, are computer-operated programs that include software plus probes designed to collect data. The sensors and probes allow children to explore beyond the range normally available in the classroom. An MBL or PSL is a computer-operated program that includes software plus a probe designed to collect data. The probes can extend observation capabilities by detecting very small differences in data (such as tenths of degrees in temperature readings), and sensory input to which humans are not sensitive (such as ultraviolet and infrared radiation and inaudible sounds). They can provide data points at very frequent intervals (such as the speed of a falling object at 1/100-second intervals). They can record observations over very long periods of time (such as the temperature of the classroom every ten minutes for 24 hours).

Accompanying the probes and sensors are programs that provide read-outs of the data, graph the data according to the experimenter's specifications, and perform mathematical manipulations of the data to meet the experimenter's needs (such as averaging trials and calculating acceleration from change in velocity).

Though children are limited in their investigations by the capacity of the program and sensitivity of the probe or sensor, MBLs and PSLs greatly expand the range of inquiry available. The use of MBLs and PSLs supports the constructivist approach to elementary science teaching and learning.

MBLs and PSLs are available for a wide variety of experimental purposes. The temperature probe is an electronic thermometer that detects and records temperatures from below freezing to above 100° Celsius. Temperatures can be read to the nearest tenth of a degree, and readings can be taken at any interval (long or short) over any block of time (long or short). Systems with two temperature probes can gather data from two sources simultaneously and compare them. For example, a child may wonder if warm water cools at the same rate that cool water warms. Using the dual temperature probe system provides data to answer the question. Figure 10.8 shows the raw data and the resulting graphs of temperatures of two cups of the same volume of water which were left in the room for 30 minutes; one was filled with cold water and the other was filled with hot water. Temperature readings were recorded every six minutes and the result was graphed.

The temperature probe also can be used to record outdoor temperatures, monitor aquarium temperatures, and record the conversion of light energy to heat energy.

The light sensor is a photoelectric cell used to detect and record light intensity. Children experimenting with the effect of distance on intensity of illumination can use the light sensor to obtain measurements of actual amount of light received from a light source as the distance is changed. The light sensor can be used to provide visual portrayal of the effects of the tilt of the earth's axis on amount of radiant energy received at various latitudes on a globe. Using a flashlight to simulate the sun, children focus the light beam onto various latitudes of a globe or balloon which simulates the earth to investigate the effect of tilt of the earth in its revolution about the sun on concentration of radiant energy. (See also Figure 12.16, p. 444.)

Motion detectors allow children to gather data on the motion of objects. Similar to the automatic range finders on Polaroid cameras, they send ultrasonic pulses at high frequency and record the time each pulse takes to make one round trip from the device to the moving object and back to the device. From the time for each round trip, the time interval between pulses, and the speed of sound, the accompanying computer program can calculate distance, velocity, and acceleration of a moving object. The motion detector is ideal for measuring the rate of acceleration of a cart rolling down an inclined plane, rate of deceleration of an object rolled down a hall floor, or rate of acceleration of freely falling objects.

CHANGES IN WATER TEMPERATURE
LINE GRAPH

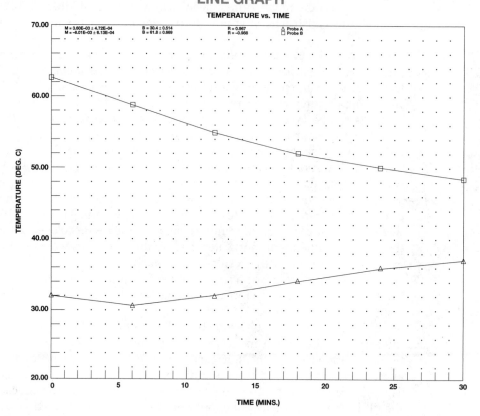

DATA TABLE

Row Number	Time (MM:SS)	Temperature (Deg. C) Probe A	Probe B
1	00:00	31.33	62.78
2	06:01	30.77	58.65
3	11:59	32.50	55.17
4	18:00	34.17	52.30
5	24:01	35.73	50.07
6	29:59	37.08	48.33

Statistics

Readings:		6	6
Mean:		33.60	54.55
Std Dev:		2.50	5.45
Minimum:		30.77	48.33
Maximum:		37.08	62.78

Graphical Analysis program courtesy of Vernier Software, 8565 SW Beaverton-Hillsdale Hwy, Portland, OR 97225-2429

FIGURE 10.8 Graph and data table of changes in water temperature

The results can be displayed in terms of actual data, reductions to velocity, acceleration, or distance, and graphically.

The barometer sensor is an electronic version of the aneroid barometer, and records and displays air pressure data over time.

Heart rate monitors are similar to those found on exercise equipment. The sensor clips to the ear or slips onto a finger and measures pulse rate which is recorded over time. This sensor is ideal to help children explore the effects of exercise and rest on heart rate. (See In The Schools 2.4, p. 41.)

Other kinds of probes and sensors currently available include the following:

Force sensors measure amount of push or pull on objects. These sensors do the same job that a spring balance does, but are far more sensitive.

pH electrodes measure the pH of solutions to establish whether they are acidic, basic, or neutral, and how acidic or basic they are.

Magnetic field sensors measure the strength of magnetic fields surrounding magnets.

Sound frequency sensors, similar to oscilloscopes, graph simple and complex sound waves and are used to investigate the physics of sound.

To use the MBL and PSL probes, a small additional circuit board normally must be added to the computer. The board can be installed by anyone familiar with the insides of computers in a matter of minutes.

Evaluating Computer Software

As you have seen, there is a tremendous amount of computer software available. Some is free; some costs only the price of the disk plus postage; some is expensive. Some require additional items of apparatus. As you also have seen, computer programs vary enormously as to degree of children's inquiry they can support.

Before investing in computer software for use by children, it is essential that you know what you are getting. Does it foster inquiry? It is user friendly? Has it been de-bugged? Is the content appropriate? Can it be networked so many children can use it simultaneously in a computer lab? Is it affordable?

The Software Evaluation Profile shown in Figure 10.9 is provided to help you evaluate software. The profile asks for *boilerplate* information above a double line; this information is obtainable from distributors. The essence of the evaluation is contained in the items below the double line which require you to preview the program. The rating score system suggested is subjective; the Overall Recommendation is the result of the entire review.

SOFTWARE EVALUATION PROFILE

Evaluator _____

Title and Version _____

Subject Area _____

Cost _____ Cost for: Site License _____

Network Version _____

Grade Level:

		Type:	
High School	____	Informational	____
Middle School	____	Drill and Practice	____
Upper Elementary	____	Tutorial	____
Lower Elementary	____	Game	____
Kindergarten	____	Simulation	____
Preschool	____	Lab Assistance	____
Teacher	____	Lab Activities	____
		Teacher Support:	
		Organizational	____
		Teacher Utility	____
		Teacher Support	____
		Other _____	

Amount of Effort/Supervision Required For Students to Learn Program:

Much ____

Some ____

Little ____

Hardware Requirements:

Type of Computer _____

Hard Disk? ____ Capacity_____

Black & White Monitor_____

Color Monitor _____

Game Card _____

Sound Card _____

Mouse _____

Printer Type _____

Special Hardware:_____

===

Rating Scores (10 Points Each):		**OVERALL RECOMMENDATION**	
Documentation & Instructions	____	Strongly Recommended	____
General Design	____	Recommended	____
Content	____	Questionable	____
Technical Quality	____	Do Not Recommend	____
Ease of Program Use	____		
Ease of Installation	____		
TOTAL (60 MAX)	====		

COMMENTS _____
_____
_____

FIGURE 10.9

Many journals and magazines such as *Educational Technology* and *Journal of Computers in Mathematics and Science Teaching* contain software review columns; these will keep you apprised of new software and will aid in the evaluation process. *NSTA Reports!*, published by the National Science Teachers Association, also contains periodic listings of computer software which have been reviewed and assessed. The Association for Supervision and Curriculum Development (ASCD) also publishes annual reviews of computer software. *Only The Best* is the ASCD's annual guide to the highest-rated educational software and multimedia offerings. *Brown's Directory of Instructional Programs*, published annually, provides descriptions of nearly all commercially published teaching materials and programs, including basal, supplementary, and multimedia programs. There is a *Brown's Directory* for each discipline.

In all cases, you should give special consideration to the degree to which a particular technology or technological application supports the process-oriented inquiry method of science instruction and the degree to which it enables children to explore on their own.

Electronic Communications in the Elementary Science Classroom

No longer are teachers limited to the four walls of their classroom (or building or district) for instructional resources. Technology permits teachers to bring the world into the classroom. All it takes is a modem, some inexpensive software, and a desire to reach out. A few examples follow:

- Using Internet, children can "travel" with bald eagles, monarch butterflies, sea turtles, songbirds, peregrine falcons, caribou, and loons during their annual migrations. Migrations of certain species are tracked by satellite from transmitters fixed to the animals; data can be transmitted to classrooms via Internet (Internet Project, 1995).
- K-12 science teachers can access a 24-inch research-grade telescope located in the California mountains for astronomy projects. After reserving a block of time, the telescope can be controlled by the computer in the teacher's classroom and directed to move across the sky to a certain object. The object is photographed and the image is sent back to the computer where it is downloaded. Children can repeat the process to obtain additional images and thus study change (Classes View, 1995).
- Children in an elementary school in Georgia have an on-going relationship with children in an elementary school in Russia and communicate regularly by computer-generated e-mail.

▌ Children working on a project in their school in the United States who desire information, experiment replication, or feedback from children elsewhere can make the request through the Internet which connects them with schools throughout the United States and the world.

▌ Using closed-circuit video, children in American schools have communicated with astronauts in space, deep sea divers, and archaeologists, asking questions, receiving answers, and being shown first-hand demonstrations of operations and responses to their questions.

▌ Children can communicate with astronauts in orbit via e-mail transmitted by satellite to ascertain the current status of experiments they, themselves, designed to be carried out in space.

Does this sound like futuristic science fiction? It is not. Every one of these has been carried out through e-mail and the Internet.

E-mail involves typing messages on a computer and sending them through designated telephone lines. The Internet is a world-wide network of e-mail facilities that connects over 15 million computers in over 134 countries, with new connections being made daily. These communications systems are expensive to install and are expensive to operate. But they exist, and they can extend children's inquiries throughout the world—and beyond. Not only are e-mail and the Internet useful in science investigations, they are an excellent tool for implementing the interdisciplinary model of teaching and learning. For example, children can exchange information about climate, industry, politics, and food with their counterparts in other countries.

In an innovative application of telecommunications, the *National Geographic Kids Network* provides hands-on telecommunications-based science units.[2] The school buys the software package which includes the needed software, a teacher's guide, student activity sheets, and the equipment needed to perform the suggested activities. Children work the problems and do the investigations, recording their data in the computer. This data from many schools is sent via modem to a professional research team headed by a scientist, which analyzes the children's data and provides feedback by modem.

Recall that, in Chapter Four (In The Schools 4.8, p. 175), we told of a project wherein children wanted to find out why underwear turns inside-out in the drier. One child wondered if the same thing would happen in Australia, since it is in the southern hemisphere. E-mail and the Internet would enable the child to ask the question and enlist Australian children in pursuing the same project.

Distance learning is a system that utilizes video cameras and satellite receivers or phone lines to transmit specific lessons prepared and delivered by experts at one location. Though expository in nature, this exposes children to experiences they might not otherwise be able to have. However, two-way and multiple interactive distance learning systems permit interaction among all sites, including the central site. Discussions and question-and-response sessions can be held, explanations can be restructured to meet unanticipated needs, and, in general, the experience is similar to a regular classroom experience. The only difference is that people at the other sites are shown as television images. Two-way and multiple interactive distance learning systems are expensive, requiring video cameras, receivers and control panels at all sites in addition to central control panels. The key to justifying the expense is interaction with experts.

Video In the Elementary Science Classroom

Much advance has been made in the field of video. Commercial and public television stations offer carefully-designed instructional videos which are telecast at times schools are in session so schools can receive them and pipe them into appropriate classrooms. For example, PBS (Public Broadcasting System) regularly broadcasts programs on science and nature. The Learning Channel airs programs on scientific topics suitable for elementary children. The Weather Channel broadcasts daily 10-minute explanations of weather phenomena and offers documentary videos for use in schools. Most educational television material is copyright-cleared and free of commercials. The publication *Cable In The Classroom*[3] monitors and publicizes educational telecasts; this monthly publication also provides detailed schedules of upcoming educational programs.

Children can produce their own videos. Recall the student teacher whose second grade children prepared a 10-minute documentary video of their school (page 346). All it takes is a little know-how (or the assistance of the media specialist) and a desire to let children expand their horizons.

Laser videodiscs contain gargantuan amounts of information about given topics; the information is presented in the form of text material, photos, frame-freezable videos, maps, and the like, and includes lectures, interviews, discussions, demonstrations, explanations, experimental procedures, mini-documentaries, computer animations, and so on. Many laserdiscs offer a choice of English or Spanish as the primary language. Laserdiscs can be used to supplement and illustrate lessons, and they can be made available to children who are investigating a phenomenon on their own.

A laserdisc requires a special disc player and a barcode reader which, when used with the manual accompanying the laserdisc, instantly locates the desired segment. Commercial laserdiscs come with directories which include the barcodes to provide ready access to the desired segments. Many textbook publishers now provide laserdiscs as supplemental material; barcodes in the teacher's editions enable teachers to select segments appropriate for their lessons.

In a more interactive application, laserdiscs can be connected to computers to allow children to access information and images and create their own presentations. Built-in menus permit children to do their own explorations. This application requires a laser videodisc player, a barcode reader, and a computer in addition to the laserdiscs themselves.

Technology for Teachers

Not only is technology advantageous for children's learning, it also can be a tremendous help to teachers in keeping records, generating tests, and communicating with parents and others. Word processing programs make it possible for teachers to store, edit, and update written documents. Letters to parents written on a word processing program can be updated periodically. Using the mail-merge feature available in most word processing programs, letters can be customized for individual recipients, and individual mailing labels can be generated, eliminating the need to spend hours writing addresses by hand.

Spreadsheets significantly reduce the time teachers need to spend calculating grades, and guarantee accuracy. In the spreadsheet, rows are labeled with children's names, and columns represent the various numerical grades. The teacher writes simple formulas for grade calculations, and enters these formulas to appropriate summary columns. As each set of grades is recorded, the computer automatically calculates averages; at the end of the marking period, the grades are ready for transfer to periodic reports. Statistics such as mean and standard deviation are obtained easily by entering pre-programmed formula symbols. Many commercial "Gradebook" programs are available. However, before investing in one, be sure it meets the needs of your class.

Database programs are ideal for keeping track of student data. On a single database, you can record children's names, addresses, phone numbers, their parents' names, the buses they take, medical problems, learning styles, interests, hobbies, and other pertinent information. You can sort to obtain collective information such as names of children who take a certain bus, common medical problems, all children with the same first name, and children with similar learning styles, interests, or hobbies for purposes of group formation.

Generating tests using test-generating software saves huge amounts of time. Once the initial test is written, items can be added, deleted, or changed, the order of questions can be varied, certain items or categories of items can be selected, and all-new tests can be generated from the original test, including several forms of the same test. If children use optical reader marking forms, such as SCANTRON forms, for their answers, automatic rapid scoring is available that provides number and percentage right, number wrong, individual items right or wrong, and the correct answer. With an additional program, you can obtain statistics and a computer-generated item analysis. To adopt a constructivist approach in computer-generated and computer-scored tests, you might invite children to explain their response to any item which was marked "incorrect" by the computer. In this way, you save the time of hand-grading the tests while concurrently encouraging children to offer their individual explanations on an exception-only basis.

Many school districts have adopted computerized systems for one or more administrative tasks. These often can be interfaced with the teacher's individual classroom systems.

Getting Started

The array of technology available to support process-oriented inquiry science programs is dazzling. However, terminology often is indecipherable, choices are seemingly infinite, and hardware can be expensive.

The question arises, "How do I get started?"

If you already are familiar with computers and other technological techniques, you may feel ready to jump right in and enrich your classes with a wide array of computer applications. However, if you are uncomfortable with technology, it is suggested that you start slowly.

It is strongly urged that every teacher learn how to use at least a word processing program, a spreadsheet program, a database program, and a graphic program. You might consider signing up for a computer course or two; many are offered at colleges and universities, local school districts in the form of in-service training, and through commercial firms. Courses range from entry level (starting with how to turn a computer on) to very sophisticated training.

The short time invested in becoming familiar with basic programs will save you countless hours in your professional role, and will enable you to utilize computer technology effectively in your classroom.

In your classroom, try one or two applications that seem to have some merit, such as using a word processing program to write letters and reports, or using a spreadsheet to keep track of grades or attendance, or using a Printshop program to create signs and banners. Do not be dismayed by initial difficulties; we all experience them at first. Keep working with the programs you choose, and you will be amazed at how rapidly you achieve proficiency. You also will be amazed at how much work and time you save.

Then, try a scientific application, perhaps a program that presents a unit you are teaching. Children can run through this program as an additional activity or as a review activity. Many teachers allow children to include computer work in their free time choices. Perhaps a game or two might be appropriate, or a program on some topic that is interesting to your children but that you will not be able to include in your curriculum.

When you decide it is time to use an experimental application, you may wish to demonstrate it first using an LCD panel. This is a panel that fits on top of the overhead projector and, when connected to the computer, projects whatever is on the computer monitor onto the projection screen.

When the time comes for you to provide input into the district's or the school's budget, be prepared to discuss the virtues of technology; your voice and your expertise may help put your school on the cybernetic information highway. You can serve on your local school committee for software evaluation and you can help develop a five-year plan for technology in your school. You can request that your school subscribe to technology magazines.

As you progress in your quest to use modern technology in your classroom, your excitement will mount from day to day. Keep adding to your store of information, expertise, and software, and you will find you are helping your children open doors to inquiry never before available. With technology, there is no limit to children's inquiries.

Conclusion

In this chapter, you have examined a variety of advances in educational technology from the constructivist point of view. A continuum suggesting levels of technology use was presented to help you decide the types of technology you would plan to use in your science program. A hierarchy of uses ranges from tutorial and simulation applications, through interactive uses such as word processing, spreadsheets, databases, and graphing programs, to experimental uses represented by laboratory computer interfacing systems. Most available technology is pre-programmed to some degree, thus limiting student inquiry; however, some applications can aid children in conducting their own inquiries. As an elementary science educator, you are urged to consider the extent to which a given program or application aids children in investigating their own questions. The future is here, and advances in technology provide unlimited access to learning opportunities never before even imagined. It is worth the effort it takes to become technologically current.

CHAPTER 10 Additional Questions for Discussion

1. Max Frisch is quoted as having said that technology is "... the knack of so arranging the world that we don't have to experience it." Discuss how today's educational technology applications can help children experience the world.
2. What advice would you give to an individual who claims that technology is too expensive to be included in schools—that children can learn just as well without it?

Notes

1. The entire October, 1995 issue of *Educational Leadership* is devoted to educational technology and ways technology is transforming teaching.

2. National Geographic Kids Network, P.O. Box 98018, Washington, DC 20090-8018.

3. *Cable In The Classroom* Magazine, 80 Elm Street, Peterborough, NH 03458.

References

Alter, J. (1995). The couch potato vote. *Newsweek*. February 27, 1995, p. 34.

Classes view telescope via computer. (1995). *NSTA Reports!*, February/March, 1995.

Collings, J. N. (1985). Scientific thinking through the development of formal operations: training in the cognitive restructuring aspect of field-independence. *Research in Science & Technology Education*, 3(2), 145–152.

Frisch, M. (1957). *Homo Faber*. Frankfurt a.m.: Suhrkamp Verlag.

Hancock, V. and Betts, F. (1994). From the lagging to the leading edge. *Educational Leadership*, 51(7), 24–29.

Internet project lets students migrate north with wildlife. (1995). *NSTA Reports!*, February/March, 1995.

National Science Teachers Association. (1993). An NSTA position statement on computers in science education. *NSTA Reports!*. National Science Teachers Association, 1742 Connecticut Ave, NW, Washington, DC 20009. December 1992/January 1993.

Steinberg, E. R. (1989). Cognition and learner control: A literature review, 1977–1988. *Journal of Computer-Based Instruction. 16*(4), 117–121.

World Almanac. (1994). Mahwah, NJ: Funk and Wagnall's Corporation.

CHAPTER 11

Concept Mapping in Elementary Science

Natural science always involves three things: the sequence of phenomena on which the science is based; the abstract concepts which call these pheomena to mind; and the words in which the concepts are expressed.

Antoine Laurent Lavoisier: *Traité Elémentaire de Chimie* (1789)

The concept map is an extremely valuable tool in constructivist science education. It fosters achievement, provides relevance of material, and enables teachers to see how children are constructing information.

A concept map is a graphic representation of the way a person relates given concepts. Concepts appear hierarchically on the map from the most inclusive at the top to the least inclusive at the bottom. Lines connecting the concepts and labeled with linking words indicate the relationships among the concepts. Analogous to geographic maps which portray land features and connecting roads and highways, concept maps show arrangement and connections of knowledge.

Concept mapping is used as planning, learning, and assessment aids at all levels of education, from kindergarten through college. This device has been shown to foster increased achievement in science, and thus has become increasingly popular in the field of science education. Concept maps are included in many student science texts, teacher's editions, and reference materials.

The purpose of this chapter is to show what concept maps are, how the technique can be taught, and how concept maps can be used to enhance the effectiveness of your elementary science program. As is true throughout this text, you will construct your own notions about concept mapping, and, ultimately, you will decide the extent to which you feel the device can be useful to you and the children in your classes.

Exploring Concept Mapping

This section contains three activities that will enable you to learn how to construct concept maps. Please do all three.

First, please do the following activity as a class to gain familiarity with what a concept map is.

CONSTRUCTING YOUR IDEAS 11.1
Flowers Concept Map

Cut 3x5 cards to obtain 13 smaller cards. Write the following thirteen words on the cards—one to a card:

FLOWERS	VALENTINE'S DAY	GIFTS
DAFFODIL	COLORS	YELLOW
HOLIDAYS	THORNS	RED
NAMES	EASTER	BIRTHDAYS
ROSE		

Arrange these cards on a table or desk in two-dimensional hierarchical order so that

1. the most important topic or topics are at the top;
2. less important topics are underneath;
3. examples are at the bottom; and
4. equally important topics are at the same level.

It is very important that you do your *own* work in this exercise, for it is highly likely that different students will come up with different arrays. There is no "correct" way of arranging these words, and there are no "incorrect" ways. The way you arrange them represents the way *you* think about them.

> When you have completed your arrangement to your own satisfaction, copy the array you have made onto a sheet of blank paper, putting an oval or a circle around each word to separate it from the others as the cards were separated.

There are two reasons for committing your moveable array to paper. One is to create something that will not blow around easily. The other is to encourage you to take ownership of your view of how these topics relate to each other.

Now, look at Figure 11.1. This is what *I* did with these words. Figure 11.1 is only one person's interpretation. This does not make it "right," nor does it make it "wrong." It simply makes it *mine*. Compare your array with the one in Figure 11.1 Is it similar? Does it have "FLOWERS" at the top? Perhaps yours looks more like one of those shown in Figure 11.2. Regardless of how you constructed your array, it is "right," for it represents the way you perceive the relationships.

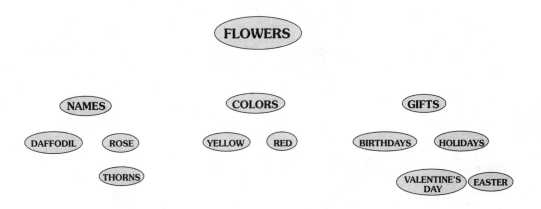

FIGURE 11.1   One arrangement of "flowers" concepts

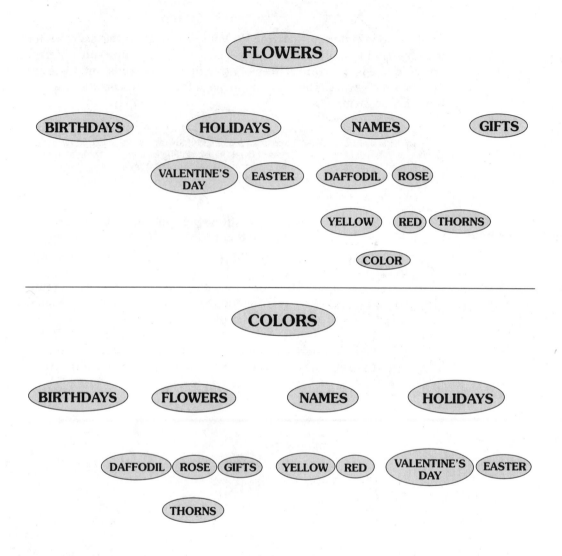

FIGURE 11.2 Alternative arrangements of "flowers" concepts

Take a minute or two and share your constructions with the rest of your class. Explain why you did what you did. A good way of doing this is to "talk your way" through the map.

For example, I could describe Figure 11.1 as follows:

Flowers have names, come in different colors, and are used as gifts. Names include "daffodil" and "rose," which has thorns. "Yellow" and "red" are examples of flower colors. Flowers are used as gifts on birthdays, Valentine's Day, holidays, and Easter.

During your sharing, take special note of the unique ways people visualized how these same thirteen words relate to each other. Recall that constructivism suggests that people put notions together in ways that make sense to *them*, and that these ways are based on each person's prior experiences. One of the values of concept mapping is that you can literally *see* how people perceive and construct information from the ways they arrange key words.

Each word in this exercise represents a *concept*. A concept is a word used to mean some kind of object, some kind of event, or some kind of condition. For example, the words "dog," "grass," and "chair" represent *object* concepts, the words "drive," "sew," and "hop" represent *event* concepts, and the words "hot," "soft" and "green" represent *condition* concepts. Concept words bring pictures to mind. Figure 11.3 provides an activity for you to tell the difference between words that represent concepts and words that do not.

CONCEPTS

Which of these words represents concepts?

among	eating	loud
tree	air	truth
dog	swimming	group
soft	the	land
has	bright	shape
cat	when	thought
table	talking	question
metallic	may	color
yellow	be	deep
train	will	where

FIGURE 11.3

The next step is to draw linking lines between the concepts on your diagram that relate to each other and write one or two words on each line to describe the relationship. These words are termed *linking words*.

Linking words are words that show the relationship between two concepts. For example, the linking words are italicized in the following statements that show connections between two concepts:

Sky *is* blue.
Vegetables *include* peas.
Halloween *uses* pumpkins.
Vegetables *for* health
Animals *such as* cows
Classified *by* color

Figure 11.4 contains an activity to help you gain familiarity in identifying linking words.

LINKING WORDS

Complete the following concept sentences with appropriate linking words.

1. Turkey _____ Thanksgiving.
2. Grass _____ green.
3. Fish _____ water.
4. Eagles _____ fly.
5. Dinner _____ desert.
6. Student _____ teacher.
7. Birds _____ wings.
8. Music _____ loud.
9. Plants _____ tall.
10. Sun _____ moon.
11. Sun _____ energy.
12. Behavior _____ talking.
13. Window _____ square.
14. Teacher _____ questions.
15. Leading _____ group.
16. Triangle _____ shape.
17. Dogs _____ ducks.
18. Parents _____ children.
19. Clock _____ time.
20. Star _____ light.

Adapted from Lucy, E. C. and Martin, D. J. (1994). *Get Your Hands on Concept Mapping.* Workshop presented at Georgia Academy of Science Annual Meeting, Kennesaw, GA, April 29, 1994.

FIGURE 11.4

Concepts can be linked up, down, or sideways. If they are linked vertically or quasi-vertically, it is assumed the linking lines aim from the upper word to the lower word. If they go sideways, arrows may be used to show the direction of the relationship. In Figure 11.1, "FLOWERS" can be linked vertically with "NAMES" with the word "have." "DAFFO-DILS" can be linked with "YELLOW" with the word "are."

Now, take a few minutes and add the lines with a linking word on each line.

Compare what you did with what I did as shown in Figure 11.5. This figure is the same as that shown in Figure 11.1, except that it also shows the relationships. Having done this, you now have completed your first concept map. Congratulations!

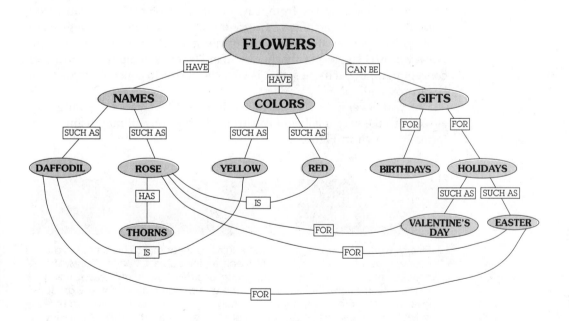

FIGURE 11.5 A completed "flowers" concept map

CONSTRUCTING YOUR IDEAS 11.2
Principles of Curriculum Concept Map

To gain additional experience, construct a concept map using concepts related to principles of curriculum. Work in groups to develop a map with lines and linking words for the following set of sixteen concepts:

Education	Goals
Learners	Learner Differences
Learning Domains	Individuals
Knowledge	Comprehension
Application	Curriculum
Cognitive	Affective
Psychomotor	Feelings
Teachers	Instructional Strategies

As an alternative, you may wish to create your own list of concepts. You can do this in several ways. (1) You can obtain a text on curriculum and extract key concepts from, say, the first chapter. (2) You can *brainstorm* the topic, "Principles of Curriculum," writing concepts suggested by class members on the board, and creating the concept map from them. However, it is suggested that fewer than 20 concepts be used for initial concept mapping activities; that is why the above 16 concept words have been provided.

As you develop this concept map, be sure all members of your group agree with the way it is being constructed. One concept map using these terms is shown in Figure 11.6.

CONSTRUCTING YOUR IDEAS 11.3
Concept Map for a Unit on Water

Finally, work in groups to construct a third concept map. This time, build a concept map for a unit you might teach on the subject, "Water." Draw the concept map of one lesson your group decides they might teach, using ten to fifteen concepts identified by the group. You may select any grade level and any emphasis. Once the map has been drawn to the group's collective satisfaction, copy the map to a blank overhead transparency acetate, and present your lesson concept map to the class.

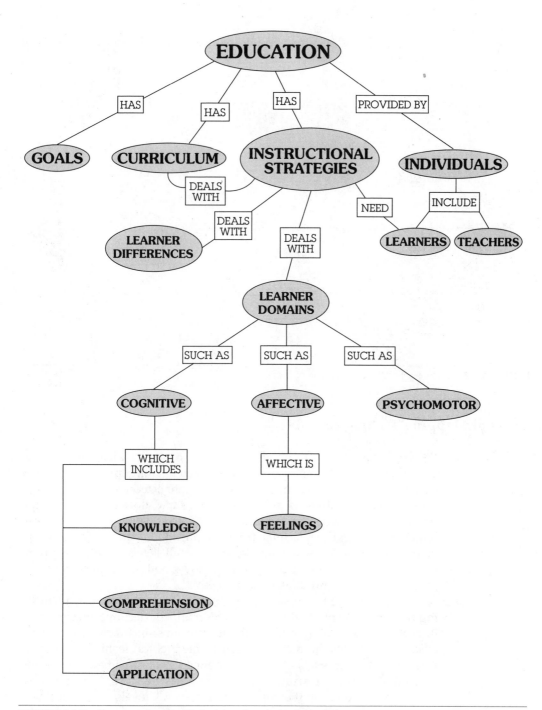

FIGURE 11.6   One arrangement of "principles of curriculum" concept map

Figure 11.7 shows the "Water" concept map drawn by a group of students in one class.

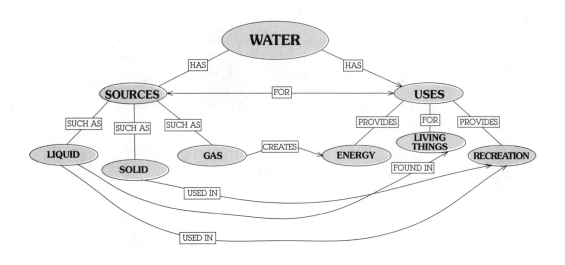

FIGURE 11.7   Student-generated concept map of "water"

Concept Mapping Technique

You have now drawn and interpreted three concept maps. As you probably have observed, concept maps are different from outlining and flow charting in that concept maps show interconnectedness of concepts at similar hierarchical levels, whereas outlines and flow charts are linear, progressing from one point to another without showing linkage between branches. Concept maps differ from classification charts in that concept maps show interconnected relationships at all levels. They differ from semantic webbing in that concept maps show both hierarchical arrangement and meaningful interconnectedness.

The procedure for constructing concept maps involves first identifying the key concepts of the lesson to be mapped, deciding their relative importance, and finally ranking them from most inclusive to most specific. The concepts are then arranged in hierarchical fashion with those that are at similar levels of inclusion aligned at approximately the same horizontal levels. The array flows in Christmas tree form from the most inclusive concepts at the top through several levels of subordinate concepts, each increasing in specificity. Examples of the most specific concepts often appear at the bottom of each branch.

Though by now you probably have developed your own notions of how to construct concept maps, the following list may help clarify the technique, or provide validity to the ideas you have already formulated.

---

1. Select a topic.
2. Pick out the main concept and generate a set of concepts associated with the main concept or topic.
3. Rank the concepts hierarchically from most general (or most inclusive) to most specific (or least inclusive). Group concepts that are related.
4. Draw the concept map with the concepts in ovals.
   ▌ Most general concepts at the top
   ▌ Intermediate concepts below
   ▌ Most specific concepts at the bottom
   ▌ More general concepts normally connected to two or more specific concepts
5. Draw the lines connecting the concepts.
6. Write in the words describing the relationships.
7. Draw in the linking lines.
8. Write in the linking words.
9. REVISE! REVISE! REVISE!

(Adapted from E. C. Lucy, Georgia State University, personal communication, February, 1990)

Uses of Concept Maps in Elementary Science Education

Concept maps have been used successfully in a wide variety of teaching and learning situations. Most commonly, teachers use them as aids for planning, instructing, reviewing, and assessing. Children in elementary grades use concept maps to help them organize material they are studying and to express the organization of their thoughts.

You have seen that concept maps provide visual representation of the way people relate given concepts. This is one of the primary benefits of utilizing concept maps. Children's maps provide a vehicle by which we can look into their heads and see how *they* are constructing information.

Sometimes a concept map constructed by a child shows misconceptions. For example the "FLOWERS" concept map shown in Figure 11.8 contains indications of several possible misconceptions. Try to find them.

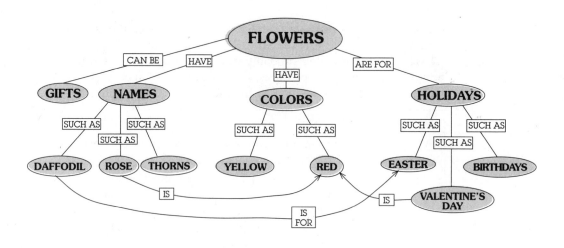

FIGURE 11.8 "Flowers" concept map showing misconceptions

Though it may be that the child simply made errors in constructing the map, the presence of misconceptions in the product alerts the teacher to potential problems, and she can ask questions to see if there really are misconceptions. If so, the teacher can act to correct them. Sharing concept maps in small groups and comparing each others' portrayals may also alert children to their own uncertainties and misconceptions.

Using Concept Maps for Lesson Planning

Ralph Tyler listed three major criteria to be met in lesson planning: (1) continuity, (2) sequencing, and (3) integration (1949). Thirty-five years later, Novak and Gowin suggested using concept mapping to aid teachers in achieving these criteria (1984). Concept maps suggest possible sequencing for lessons in the form of hierarchies of ideas that imply meaningful and valid sequences of lesson development. They show continuity within lessons by visual portrayal of the relationships between concepts. They show integration with their networks of cross links.

Concept maps can help teachers organize their lessons. Suppose, for example, you had decided to teach a lesson on flowers to your kindergarten children that involved names of flowers, colors of flowers, and the ways they can be used as gifts. Please refer to Figure 11.5. One way of organizing the lesson is to divide it into three parts corresponding to the three main sections of the map: one each on names, colors, and gifts. But, by doing this, the cross relationships among the three parts are lost (except, perhaps, as examples or afterthoughts). Often, we teachers teach one of the branches of a topic, then the next one, then the next one, and so on sequentially, relating the parts to each other at the end of the unit, sometimes as an afterthought. The concept map shows that the interconnectedness of concepts throughout the entire scope of the topic is as important as those within each major section. Using the concept map as a basis for organizing the lesson, the teacher can ensure that the topic is treated in an integrated fashion.

A number of researchers have used concept mapping to help teachers develop elementary science curriculum. They found that concept mapping resulted in more cohesive and integrated elementary science curriculum (Starr & Krajckik, 1990), and provides teachers with guidance in showing the relationships among key ideas (Willerman & MacHarg, 1991). Martin (1994) reported that concept mapping helped preservice teachers develop lesson plans which exhibit continuity, which are well-integrated, and which are logically sequenced. Furthermore, though using concept maps to develop lesson plans required that students learn the concept mapping technique and expend extra effort and time, the device was well accepted by students and was used by many students in their full professional capacities.

The technique for using concept maps to develop lesson plans involves first developing a concept map of the main ideas to be included. Hierarchical and cross-linked relationships are shown. It is a good idea, once the initial map is drafted, to share it with peers where you must convincingly "talk your way" through the map; peer review and critique is used to help revise the map. From this revised map, lesson plans are written that include properly scoped and logically sequenced learning objectives, teaching and learning activities for each objective, materials, and methods of assessment.

Instruction is linear in form, and concept maps are two-dimensional showing interrelationships as well as hierarchies. Thus, the concept map can suggest a variety of integrated approaches and teaching sequences, and can help the teacher tailor the material to the needs and interests of the children.

Concept maps are extremely useful in developing a process-oriented elementary science curriculum. The technique is simple: merely key one or more processes to the links. For example, in the FLOWERS concept map, you might key the process "observation" with the link between "FLOWERS" and "COLORS." This suggests the following process-oriented objective:

"The child will observe colors of flowers."

CONSTRUCTING YOUR IDEAS 11.4
*Using a Concept Map to Design a Process-Oriented
Inquiry Lesson*

Demonstrate for yourself the power of concept maps in influencing the design
of lessons and units. Use the concept map you prepared for the lesson on
"Water," and key a process to each of the lines connecting the concepts.
Then, write process-oriented objectives for each, combining similar objectives
as appropriate. Sequence the objectives, and sketch the lesson plan.

Figure 11.9 shows a concept map of a unit on ecology with processes
keyed to the links. Some of the resulting process-oriented objectives ex-
tracted from the concept map are shown below the map.

Using Concept Maps in Instruction

Concept maps can be used in the actual instructional phase before, during, and after lessons and units. Concept maps can be used as advance
organizers to set the stage for units on new material or for individual
lessons. As was mentioned in Chapter Five, advance organizers for
new units inform children of the basic scope and sequence of the
material—what will be studied, and in what order. Advance organizers
used at the beginning of individual lessons show children how the upcoming lesson relates to the main body of the study. Concept maps have
been used successfully for this purpose. In one application, the teacher
presents a concept map of the unit in conjunction with the introductory
material, and leaves the map posted in a prominent place so children can
refer to it as they progress through the unit. In another application, the
teacher gives each child a copy of the overall unit concept map, and
children augment it as they progress through the lesson. Alternatively,
augmentation of the introductory concept map can be done by the class
as a whole, with children building a map of the material studied that
looks like a bowl of spaghetti by the end of the unit. It makes perfect
sense to the children but not to outsiders.

In another introductory application, children build their own map of
their ideas about what to study in a unit, and this map is used to guide
the overall direction the unit takes.

In all these applications, the concept map aids children in internal-
izing the scope of the material and, more importantly, in seeing the ways
different aspects of the material connect to form an integrated whole.

Concept maps can be used for review. In one application, the teacher
presents a concept map showing the scope and interrelationships of the
material that has been included in a unit of study. In another application,
the teacher uses the concept map prepared for the introduction for the
review. Perhaps the most satisfactory application is for children to aug-

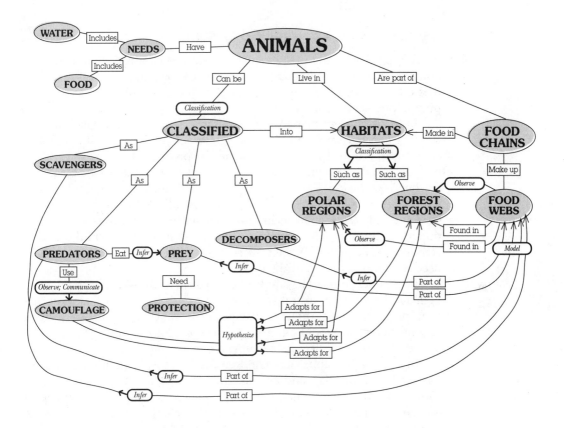

SELECTED PROCESS-ORIENTED OBJECTIVES

1. The student will infer predator-prey relationships between animals in polar and forest habitats.
2. The student will classify habitats into polar and forest.
3. The student will hypothesize how animals adapt to polar and forest environments.
4. The student will observe and communicate ways in which animals use camouflage in their environments.
5. The student will infer the animals that are predators, prey, decomposers, and scavengers in polar and forest habitats.
6. The student will create a model of food webs in polar and forest environments.

FIGURE 11.9   "Ecology" concept map showing processes keyed to links and selected process-oriented objectives derived from the map

ment the introductory concept map as they progress through the unit and then help build a final concept map showing salient points and their interrelationships. If the class has kept up a running concept map, the end result (bowl of spaghetti) can serve as the review.

Using Concept Maps for Assessment

In Chapter Seven, the position was taken that children should demonstrate their understandings and masteries in ways that are authentic and that are comfortable to them. Experience has shown that concept mapping is one such vehicle.

In using concept mapping for assessment, children are asked to construct a concept map showing the scope and interrelationships of key concepts of the study. The concepts may be provided to them, or children may be asked to provide their own concepts. On a one-to-one basis, the teacher asks the child to explain the map. This technique is similar to an interview, except that the child has already gathered his thoughts about the material. Using this technique, the teacher can probe for deeper understandings and can obtain a true assessment of the child's understanding of the material. The results of the concept map interview can be used as the basis for future studies.

In another approach, children are asked to draw concept maps as their final activity in a unit; these maps as graded for inclusion of key concepts, correctness of hierarchy, and inclusion of key cross links much as an essay exam would be graded. The completed concept map can be included in the child's science journal or portfolio.

In yet another approach, children are given specific topics, such as "frog metamorphosis," and are asked to write essay-type responses that show what they know about the topic. These responses are converted into concept maps by trained assessors. The map is then compared to an "ideal" map prepared by the examiners, and children are scored according to the number of concepts included in the map and the number of valid connections made between concepts as compared with the ideal map (Smith et al., 1993, p. 13).

Uses of Concept Maps by Children

Concept maps have been used by children at all grade levels, from kindergarten onward. Children have used them to illustrate main points in a piece of literature, to develop the plan for a piece of creative writing, to isolate variables for an experiment, to develop a plan for investigating a topic, and to write the report of an experimental procedure. Children use concept maps to keep track of where they have been, where they are now, and where they are going in a course of study.

Concept mapping has been shown to aid children with weak academic backgrounds in their understanding of new material (Stice & Alvarez, 1987). It has been proposed as an effective teaching and learning aid for children with learning disabilities (Crank & Bulgren, 1993), and it has been shown to assist field dependent students in science comprehension and achievement (Martin, 1991).

Of course, in order for children to use concept maps, they first must learn how to construct them. Children as young as kindergarteners can be taught to construct concept maps. The technique is similar to that presented in the first section of this chapter. Have the children draw concept maps of familiar topics using four or five concepts, and gradually increase their complexity. Have children "talk their way" through their maps with each other, and provide both peer and teacher critique. Making it a class project to develop a continuous concept map that shows the progression of learning in a unit will help children in their technique and will show them the significance of concept mapping. It usually takes children several months of regular practice to learn to construct good concept maps. But, the time is well spent, and children are provided with a tool they can use for the rest of their lives.

Joseph Novak, the developer of the concept map heuristic, writes

> My experience has been that when students are required to construct their own personal concept maps for topics they are studying, they find new meanings in the subject and new ways to relate what they already know to the new things they are learning. In short, concept maps constructed by students help them to learn meaningfully (Novak, 1991, p. 48).

Conclusion

Concept mapping has been in use since the late 1970s, and has been shown to have positive influences on children's learning, especially in the field of science. Advantages of using concept maps include increased meaning of cognitive material for both teachers and children, ownership of material by teachers and children, increased ability to integrate concepts, increased thoroughness and efficiency in lesson planning, increased capacity to meet children's individual needs in a variety of ways through understanding how children are constructing the material, and increased capacity of teachers to construct conceptual meaning in multiple ways for their children.

Concept mapping helps teachers understand the nature of the science topics being taught, and helps teachers design and implement units of study that are meaningful, relevant, pedagogically sound, and interesting to children. There is merit in the use of concept mapping. You will have to decide the extent to which you feel this device is useful to you and the children in your classes.

CHAPTER 11   Additional Questions for Discussion

1. Describe how the use of concept mapping can help promote children's development of process skills and facility in inquiry investigations.
2. Contrast concept mapping with other diagrammatic techniques such as outlines, flow charts, and semantic webbing with respect to the constructivist teaching and learning.

References

Crank, J. N. & Bulgren, J. A. (1993). Visual depictions as information organizers for enhancing achievement of students with learning disabilities. *Learning Disabilities Research*, 8(3), 140–147.

Lavoisier, A. L. (1789). *Traité Elémentaire de Chimie*. Paris: Cuchet.

Lucy, E. C. and Martin, D. J. (1994). *Get your hands on concept mapping*. Workshop presented at Georgia Academy of Science Annual Meeting, Kennesaw, GA, April 29, 1994.

Martin, D. J. (1991). *The effect of concept mapping on biology achievement of field dependent students*. Unpublished dissertation, Georgia State University.

Martin, D. J. (1994). Concept mapping as an aid to lesson planning: A longitudinal study. *Journal of Elementary Science Education, 6*(2), 11–30.

Novak, J. D. & Gowin, D. B. (1984). *Learning how to learn*. New York, NY: Cambridge University Press.

Novak, J. D. (1991). Clarify with concept maps. *The Science Teacher*, October, 1991, 44–49.

Smith, L. H., Ryan, J. M., & Kuhs, T. M. (1993). *Assessment of Student Learning in Science*. Columbia, SC: South Carolina Center for Excellence in the Assessment of Student Learning, College of Education, University of South Carolina (ERIC Document No. ED 358–160).

Starr, M. L. & Krajcik, J. S. (1990). Concept maps as a heuristic for science curriculum development: Toward improvement in process and product. *Journal of Research in Science Teaching, 17*(10), 987–1000.

Stice, C. F. & Alvarez, M. C. (1987). Hierarchical concept mapping in the early grades. *Childhood Education*, December, 1987, 86–96.

Tyler, R. W. (1949). *Basic principles of curriculum and instruction*. Chicago, IL: The University of Chicago Press.

Willerman, M. & Mac Harg, R. A. (1991). The concept map as an advance organizer. *Journal of Research in Science Teaching, 28*(8), 705–711.

CHAPTER 12

Basic Concepts and Principles for the Elementary Science Program

Science is built of facts the way a house is built of bricks; but an accumulation of facts is no more science than a pile of bricks is a house.

Henri Poincaré, *La Science et l'hypothèse* (1902)

The recurrent theme in this text is that it is more important for children to learn how to do science than to learn about science. It is urged that the focus of elementary science teaching be on processes more than on content, with the concepts and principles of science employed as the vehicles through which children explore the scientific processes and thereby do science.

In this chapter, many of the conceptual and content elements of science appropriate for elementary science programs are summarized. The intent is to provide information about scientific principles to aid you in your own understanding so you can develop sound lesson plans to guide children in their investigations. The material is provided only for your reference. As was stated in Chapter One, teachers do not need to know a great deal of science to be effective elementary science teachers; rather, they must be able to function as co-inquirers with their children. The material included in this chapter is *not* meant to be presented to children, nor is it meant to enable you to guide children toward "correct" conclusions. It is included solely to help you understand currently accepted principles of science. Strategies for process-oriented inquiry investigations using these concepts and principles as vehicles are described throughout this text. Cross-references are found in Appendix A.

The chapter is organized around the three traditional branches of science—physical science, life science, and earth and space science.

Physical Science Principles

The physical sciences are concerned with the nature of matter and energy. Physical science traditionally contains seven distinct fields: (1) force and motion, (2) heat energy and states of matter, (3) sound, (4) light, (5) electricity and magnetism, (6) nuclear energy, and (7) matter and chemical energy.

Force and Motion

Sir Isaac Newton developed three laws of motion that undergird studies of force and motion. *Newton's First Law of Motion* states that an object at rest remains at rest and an object in motion remains in motion in a straight line and at a constant speed unless acted upon by an external unbalanced force. In other words, objects at rest remain at rest unless we act on them with a force, and it takes a force of some sort to slow a moving object down, speed it up, or change its direction.

The tendency of an object to remain at rest or in the same state of motion is termed *inertia*. For example if you put a coin on a card, lay the card on the open top of a glass, and then quickly snap the card away, the coin drops into the glass. This happens because the coin did not receive the external force—only the card did. When a car stops suddenly, passengers are thrown forward because they tend to stay in the same forward motion even though the car has stopped. When the car makes a sharp turn, the passengers are thrown in the opposite direction of the turn, since they tend to keep moving in the original direction when the car turns. This is the reason for seat belts and air bags as safety devices in cars. If a child pulls on a wagon suddenly, the passenger is thrown backward because the passenger tends to remain at rest while the forward force is being applied to the wagon.

Forces that cause changes in the motion of objects include gravity, friction, air resistance, pushing, pulling, throwing, and a number of other more subtle forces.

Gravity causes acceleration of objects toward the center of the earth. The force of gravity is caused by the tremendous mass of the earth. When a toy cart rolls down an inclined plane, the force of gravity causes it to increase speed as it rolls. An object falling freely in the air is acted upon by a force of gravity that causes it to accelerate. This is true regardless of the mass of the object. Thus, when dropping two objects from the same height—a heavy one and a light one—if air does not exert a significant influence, they will hit the ground at the same time. This is because the heavier object has a greater force of gravity acting on it, but it also has greater mass, resulting in the same acceleration as the lighter object.

Another common force influencing the motion of objects is friction. Friction is found between any two objects that come into contact with each other when they move; it is impossible to eliminate all the friction between a moving object and its surroundings. Blocks of wood encounter friction with the surfaces they are being pulled on. Parachutes encounter friction with the air. Bicycle wheels encounter friction with the ground, and the gears and sprocket encounter friction with each other. When a ball is rolled down the smooth hall floor, it slows down because of the opposing force of friction.

Newton's Second Law states that the acceleration of an object is directly proportional to the force applied, and is inversely proportional to the object's mass. Thus, when a force is applied continuously to an object, it will move faster and faster in the direction of the force. The greater its mass, the less it will accelerate under a given force, or, conversely, the more force is needed to produce a certain acceleration. For example, it takes much more force to get a train moving at 60 miles per hour than it takes to accelerate a car to that speed.

Newton's Third Law states that for every force there is an equal and opposite force. This is the familiar "action-reaction" system, and governs the movement of rockets and jet airplanes. Balloons blown up in the classroom and let go respond in accordance with Newton's Third Law.

The universe is made of energy and matter. The *Law of Conservation of Energy* says that energy can neither be created nor destroyed. However, energy can change forms. Energy can be potential or kinetic, and these are interchangeable. Potential energy is energy that could do work if it were released; a toy car on the top of a steep incline is in a potential energy position. Kinetic energy is energy that is happening; when the toy car is released, it converts its potential energy to kinetic energy continuously until it reaches the bottom of the track and there is no more potential energy left. At this point, all its energy is kinetic.

Forms of energy traditionally have been categorized into seven fundamental forms corresponding to the seven subdivisions of physical science. They are mechanical energy, heat energy, sound energy, light energy, magnetic and electric energy, nuclear energy, and chemical energy. All forms can be transformed into any of the other forms of energy without loss of energy. For example, mechanical energy can be transformed into sound energy through playing musical instruments. Heat can be converted to mechanical energy by turbines, and the mechanical energy, in turn, can be converted to electric energy through generators. Sound energy that seems to disappear is converted to heat energy. Chemical energy is converted to heat energy when things burn. When energy seems to be destroyed, careful searching will reveal that it has transformed into a different kind of energy; often it has transformed into heat, as happens with friction.

The *Law of Conservation of Matter* says that matter can neither be created nor destroyed. When chemical reactions occur, the amount of matter after the reaction is precisely the same as the amount before (except for a very small change in mass due to the energy involved—a change in mass too small to be measured).

The Law of Conservation of Energy and the Law of Conservation of Matter were considered inviolate for a long time. However, Albert Einstein developed his theories of relativity which theorized that matter may change to energy and energy may change to matter under certain circumstances. The formula Einstein developed to show this relationship between energy and matter is given by the famous formula **e=mc²**, where **e** is the amount of energy, **m** is the amount of mass, and **c** is the speed of light, 300,000 kilometers per second. When the mechanism of radioactivity was discovered, it was learned that small amounts of matter found in the nuclei of atoms convert to energy during reactions that emit radiation. It was further learned, through experiments with high-powered particle accelerators, that if particles of matter can be caused to go fast enough, they will gain in mass. These discoveries seemed to invalidate the traditional laws of conservation and resulted in the *Law of Conservation of Matter and Energy*, which states that the *sum* of the matter and the energy in the universe remains constant.

Energy is needed to do *work*. In order for *work* to be done in the scientific sense, an object must be moved through a distance in response to some force; energy must be transferred from one object to another. Pushing on a brick wall with all your might produces no work if the wall does not move. Work is defined as force times distance. *Power* is the rate of doing work, and is measured in watts and horsepower.

Simple machines allow people to gain maximum benefit from the work put into the machine. There are six basic types of simple machines: (1) lever, (2) inclined plane, (3) wedge, (4) pulley, (5) wheel and axle, and (6) screw. (See Figure 12.1.) Simple machines are used to magnify force, to increase speed, or to change direction.

The lever allows a person to magnify force, increase speed, or change direction. The inclined plane provides magnification of force at the expense of distance; you can move a piano up a ramp, but you have to move it further than if you were hoisting it straight up. The wedge permits magnification of force in such situations as log splitting. The pulley reduces the force needed to move an object, but the amount of rope needed to be pulled out is increased in order to achieve the reduction of force. For example, a double two-wheel block-and-tackle pulley requires you to pull four times the amount of rope as the distance you are moving the object, but you only have to use one-fourth the force. (See Figure 12.2.) The wheel and axle is used largely to increase speed. As with bicycle pedals, a force is applied to a large wheel (the pedals) which transfers the force to a small wheel (the rear sprocket) by means of a chain. The small wheel makes several complete turns for every turn of the large wheel, increasing the speed. Gear systems are a special case of the wheel and axle where the component parts are interlocked by means of gear teeth. Gear boxes show children that gears can be used to change both direction and speed. The smaller the affected gear is relative to the gear that is moved, the faster the affected gear moves. One can count the number of teeth in each of two interlocking gears; if the teeth are the same size, the ratio between the number of teeth equals the magnification of the speed. For example, if a larger gear has twice as many teeth as a smaller interlocking gear, the smaller gear will rotate twice for each rotation of the larger gear, thus turning twice as fast. (See Figure 12.3.)

THE LEVER

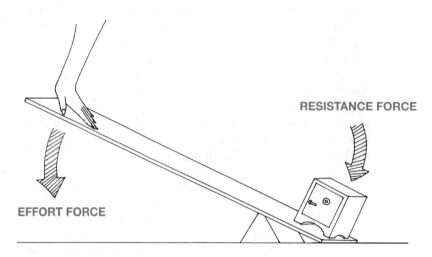

THE INCLINED PLANE

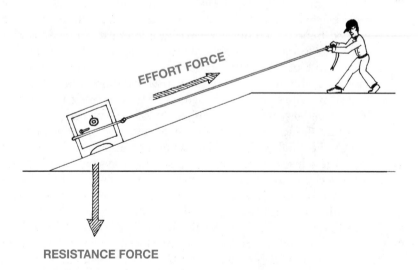

FIGURE 12.1 The six simple machines (Continues on next two pages)

THE WEDGE

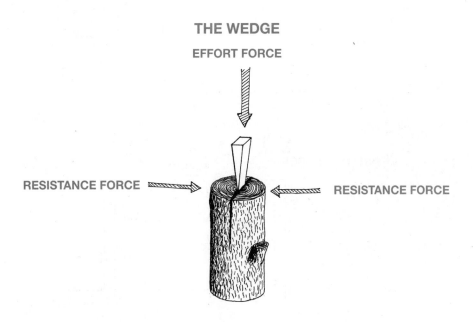

EFFORT FORCE

RESISTANCE FORCE ⇒ ⇐ **RESISTANCE FORCE**

THE PULLEY

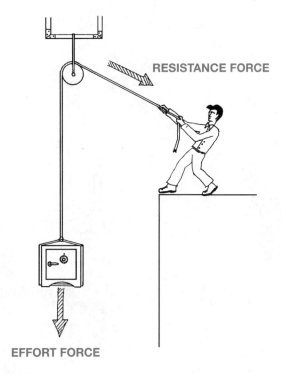

RESISTANCE FORCE

EFFORT FORCE

THE WHEEL AND AXLE

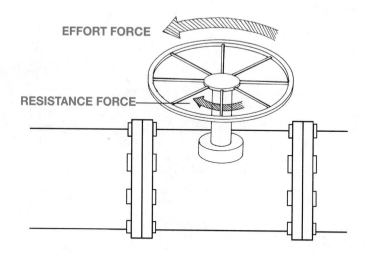

EFFORT FORCE

RESISTANCE FORCE

THE SCREW

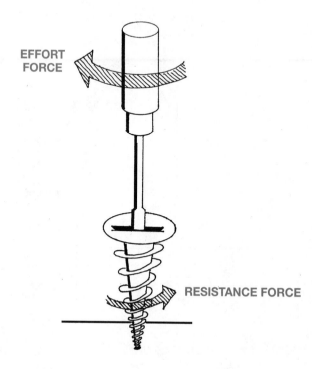

EFFORT
FORCE

RESISTANCE FORCE

PULLEY SYSTEMS

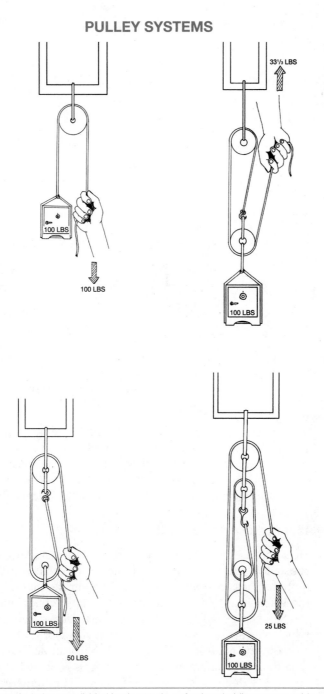

FIGURE 12.2   Effort equals resistance divided by the number of strings holding up moveable pulley

GEAR SYSTEMS

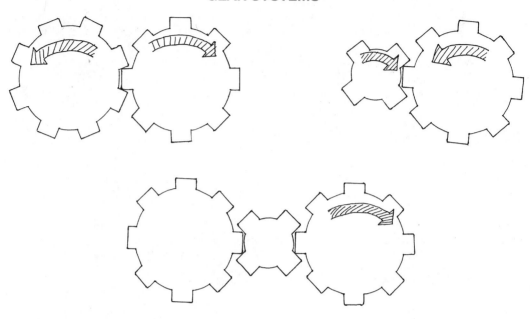

FIGURE 12.3   How many revolutions does the gear on the left make for each turn of the gear on the right?

The screw permits magnification of force by increasing distance; it is essentially an inclined plane wrapped around a central rod.

The *Law of Simple Machines* states that the force you put into a machine (effort force) times the distance the effort moves equals the output force from the machine (resistance) times the distance the resistance moves.

Heat Energy and States of Matter

Heat is caused by the motion of the particles making up a substance. All substances are made of atoms and/or molecules which are in constant motion. The cooler an object is, the slower the motion of its particles, and the warmer an object gets, the faster its particles move.

Solids are made of particles that are packed very closely together and which vibrate. As solids get cooler, the vibration of the particles decreases. The coldest temperature a solid can achieve is the temperature where all molecular motion ceases; this is called *Absolute Zero*, and is about 273 degrees below zero Celsius. This temperature has been approached, but never achieved in laboratory conditions.

As solids get hotter, the vibration gets more vigorous, and a point is reached when the vibration of its particles is so rapid that they escape their solid boundaries and start to move more freely. This is called *melting*, and the resulting state of matter is a liquid. In liquids, particles move freely, as can be seen when a drop of food coloring is put into a glass of water; the food coloring eventually disperses throughout the water because of the movement of the molecules. The warmer the liquid gets, the faster the particles move.

When the particles of a liquid move so rapidly they cannot be contained within the liquid boundaries, they escape as a gas. This is called *vaporization*, or *evaporation*, and the resulting state of matter is a gas. Molecules of gases move very rapidly, darting from one position to another at random. This can be demonstrated by opening a bottle of perfume at one end of a room; within minutes, the perfume vapors are detected throughout the entire room. In fact, if you have children raise their hands when they smell the perfume, they can observe that the gas moves from its original source in a spherical pattern, showing that the gas diffuses regularly from the area of higher concentration to areas of lower concentration.

Diffusion is the movement of particles from areas of high concentration to areas of low concentration. In any system, diffusion occurs until the concentrations of all particles is the same in all regions. This is called a state of equilibrium. Particle motion continues as before, but the concentrations remain the same. This is what occurs with food coloring in water and perfume in air.

There are three states of matter: solids, liquids, and gases. A solid has a definite shape and a definite volume. A liquid takes the shape of its container and has a definite volume. A gas expands to fill all space available to it, and has neither a definite shape nor a definite volume unless it is contained. There is a fourth state of matter—the *plasma* state—which is half-way between liquid and gas. The plasma state is formed when materials become so energized they ought to turn into a gas, but where very strong forces keep the particles together as a liquid. The sun is in the plasma state. Cold and low pressure plasmas also are common. For example, the gas in a fluorescent tube, lower in pressure than the surrounding atmosphere, is in a plasma state when in operation.

Most solids, liquids, and gases expand when heated due to the increased motion of the particles; and most solids, liquids and gases contract when cooled due to decreased motion of the particles. For example telephone wires expand and sag when the air is warm; when the air is cool, they shrink and become more taut. Tire pressure increases during a trip because the heat of friction between the tires and the road causes the air in the tires to heat and expand. When the car is left in the shade, the tires often look under-inflated because of contraction of the air in them when it is cool.

An exception to this phenomenon is ice. As water freezes, it expands. This is caused by the molecules of water arranging themselves into a crystalline matrix as they turn into ice; the crystalline matrix occupies more volume than the liquid water at the freezing point.

Molecular motion cannot be seen directly except with specialized equipment; however, it can be inferred in liquids and gases through the behavior of added materials introduced into the system such as food coloring into water and perfume into air. Molecular motion in solids can be inferred largely through the expansion of the solids as they heat, which is a result of the increased motion of the particles.

Heat is produced in many ways, all of which act to increase the motion of the particles making up a substance. Mechanical energy can be transformed into heat through rubbing, hitting, grinding, and so on. Sound energy turns into heat when the energy of the sound waves causes the particles of the surrounding gases and solids to vibrate more rapidly; this is why rooms get warmer when they are noisy. Electricity produces heat in such devices as toasters, electric stoves, and light bulbs because of resistance in the filaments. Chemical energy produces heat through burning.

Heat is transmitted through *conduction*, *convection*, or *radiation*. Conduction most often occurs in solids, though it also occurs in liquids and gases. In conduction, heat moves from warmer areas to cooler areas along the material that transmits the heat, such as a wire or a metal rod. Different metals have different abilities to conduct heat; gold, silver, copper, and aluminum are the best. Materials such as glass and wood do not conduct heat and are termed *insulators*.

Convection occurs in liquids and gases as they circulate due to temperature differences. In convection, heat is transferred through collisions of the molecules. Molecules move faster in the area near the source of heat, and this motion is transferred to neighboring molecules, which transfers the motion to other neighboring molecules, and so on. Convection is used to heat houses. Radiation occurs in gases and empty space such as outer space. In radiation, heat is transmitted in the form of *infrared* radiation. (See p. 420 and Figure 12.6.) Infrared radiation is similar to visible light, except that its wave length is longer than that of red light, and it cannot be seen by the human eye. When infrared radiation strikes a solid object, the molecules of the solid absorb the radiation and begin to vibrate faster, causing heat. This is the principle by which the sun heats the earth. Infrared radiation travels from the sun through space and the earth's atmosphere, ultimately striking the surface of the earth. The earth's surface gets warm as it absorbs the infrared radiation, and the atmosphere warms through convection of heat from the surface. Thus, the earth's atmosphere warms from the bottom upwards. That is why it is cold in the upper levels of the atmosphere, and it is why it is colder at higher elevations than at sea level.

Sound

Sound is caused by vibrating objects: wind chimes being struck, a horn being blown, nails being hammered, crickets rubbing their hind legs together. The instruments of the orchestra show the complete range of ways sound can be produced. Sound can be produced by vibrating columns of air, as in woodwinds, brass instruments, organ pipes, and so on. In reed instruments like clarinets and oboes, players vibrate the column of air by vibrating the reed; in brass instruments like trumpets and trombones, players vibrate their lips; in flutes and piccolos, players blow across the instruments like a soda bottle. Sound can be produced by vibrating solids, such as drums, cymbals, triangles, castanets, xylophones, and so on. Sound can be produced by vibrating strings such as violins, cellos, guitars, banjos, pianos, and so on.

The vibratory nature of sound can be shown by striking a tuning fork and touching the tines gently to the surface of water. The water splashes because of the vibration of the tines.

The more rapid the vibration, the higher the pitch of the sound. When sound is produced by moving columns of air, the shorter the column of air, the higher the pitch. Thus, organ pipes that produce high pitches are short, and those that produce low pitches are very long. The piccolo is short whereas the tuba is made of a tube so long it has to be wrapped around itself in order to be manageable.

The pitches of sounds made with percussion instruments are varied by changing the tension on drum heads, changing the thickness of the material being struck, and changing the size of the material. A bass drum produces a lower sound than a tom-tom. The kettle drums are changed in pitch by changing the tension on the drum heads. Large cymbals produce a lower pitch than small cymbals.

The pitch of stringed instruments depends on the tension, the thickness, and the length of the string. The shorter the string, the higher the pitch. The strings of a violin are shorter than the strings on cello, and produce higher pitches. The guitarist plays different notes by putting his fingers on the strings, changing the length that is allowed to vibrate. The tighter a string is stretched, the higher the pitch. This can be seen in a shoe box guitar where rubber bands are stretched to make the different pitches. The thinner the string, the higher the pitch. In the shoe box guitar, the thicker rubber bands produce lower pitches than the thin rubber bands if they are stretched the same.

Sound travels through solids, liquids, and gases, but sound *must* have a medium to travel through; it cannot travel in a vacuum. To demonstrate that sound travels through solids, tap on a desk with your ear pressed close to the surface of the desk. You can tell that sound travels through liquids when you are swimming under water and someone cracks two stones together under the water.

A vibrating object produces sound by causing a succession of compressions and rarefactions of the surrounding molecules. The compressions and rarefactions are transmitted to the next layer of molecules, which, in turn, transmits them to the next layer, and so on. This produces a wave called a *longitudinal wave*. A longitudinal wave is a series of compressions and rarefactions that travel spherically outward from the source of sound. The distance between compressions or rarefactions is the *wave length* of the wave. Eventually, the compressions and rarefactions reach the ear, and cause the parts of the ear to vibrate the same way the compressions and rarefactions were vibrating, and we hear the sound. Longitudinal waves can be seen by using a slinky. Stretch a slinky in the air and pluck one end. The compressions and rarefactions travel the full length of the slinky.

A vibrating tuning fork generates a series of compressions and rarefactions in the air.

MODEL OF SOUND WAVES

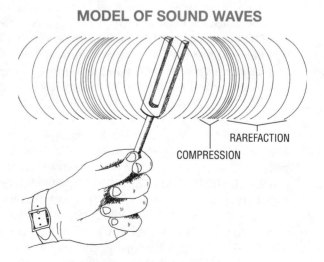

RAREFACTION

COMPRESSION

FIGURE 12.4 A vibrating tuning fork generates a series of compressions and rarefactions in the air

Sound has three basic characteristics: pitch, amplitude, and quality. Pitch is how high or low the sound is, and depends on the rate of vibration; the faster the vibration the higher the pitch. Amplitude is the loudness of the sound, and is caused by the force with which the sound is produced. The greater the force, the louder the sound. Quality refers to the special characteristics of a sound that enable us to tell what its source is. Quality is caused by the presence of overtones which are sounds of different wave lengths mixed together. The presence of these overtones causes differences in sound quality and makes it possible for us to tell what produces a given sound.

The speed of sound depends on how closely packed the molecules are. Sound travels fastest through solids. Sound travels through liquids fairly rapidly, and it travels slowest through gases such as air. The speed of sound in air at 20° Celsius is about 1129 meters per second, or about 505 miles per hour (1088 feet per second). In air, sound travels a mile in five seconds.

The human ear can only hear sounds caused by objects that vibrate between about 20 vibrations per second and 16,000 vibrations per second. Ultrasonic waves are sound waves that vibrate very fast. Their frequencies are too high to be detected by the human ear, though animals such as dogs and bats can hear these high frequencies. Ultrasonic sound waves have greater penetrating power than audible sound waves, and can be used to see *in-utero* fetuses and the functioning of human hearts.

Light

Light travels in straight lines called *rays*. Light travels through anything that is transparent or translucent. In a vacuum it travels at a speed of 186,000 miles per second, or 300,000 kilometers per second. The more dense the medium, the slower the speed of light. Thus, light travels slower in air than in outer space, and it travels slower through water than air, and slower through glass than water.

Light travels in the form of *transverse waves*. Transverse waves resemble the waves produced when you drop a pebble into a pool of still water. Each wave has a series of crests and troughs. The distance between the crests or between the troughs is called the *wave length*. (See Figure 12.5.)

Light is an electromagnetic wave. Electromagnetic waves are created by causing the electrons of the atoms that make up materials to move rapidly and emit energy. This occurs in light bulbs where the electrons of the filament are heated causing the electrons to move fast, giving off light. It also happens in fires, where the heated particles of burning material give off light.

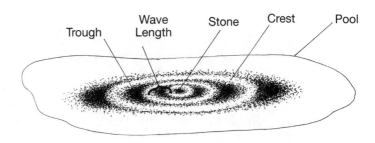

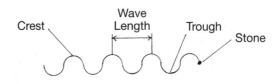

FIGURE 12.5   Transverse waves

Visible light is only one small segment of a very wide range of electro-magnetic radiations which can occur as the result of exciting the electrons of atoms. The electromagnetic spectrum is shown in Figure 12.6, and includes radio waves, microwaves, infrared waves, visible light waves (including the colors red, orange, yellow, green, blue, indigo, and violet), ultraviolet waves, X rays, and gamma rays. The wave length of the radiation decreases from left to right on the electromagnetic spectrum. The shorter the wave length, the higher the frequency of the radiation. Thus, red light has a lower fre-quency and a longer wave length than violet light or ultraviolet radiation or gamma rays. The shorter the wave length, the higher the frequency of the radiation. It takes more energy to produce higher frequencies than lower frequencies. Thus, it takes much more energy to produce gamma rays than it does to produce red light or radio waves.

Reflection of light is caused when light rays bounce off a surface. If the surface is very smooth, such as in a mirror or a very smooth table top, images will be reflected. Mirrors can be plane (flat), concave (curved inward), or convex (curved outward). Concave mirrors, such as those found in make-up mirrors, magnify images; convex mirrors, such as garden reflector balls, produce smaller images. If the surface is not smooth, as in a painted wall, the light will be reflected but images will not.

Refraction refers to the bending of light rays as they pass from a material of one density to a material of a different density. Lenses make use of the principle of refraction. The broken appearance of a pencil in

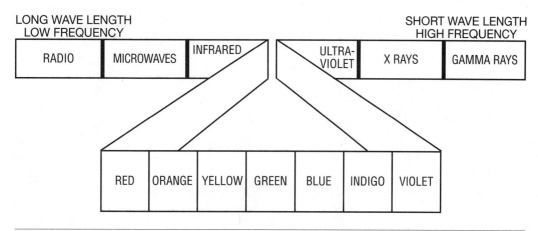

FIGURE 12.6 The electromagnetic spectrum

a glass of water is caused by refraction of the light rays as they move out of the water into the air.

The sun is the major source of light energy for the earth. The sun and stars radiate the full electromagnetic spectrum, from radio waves through gamma rays. Very high frequency radiation such as X rays and gamma rays are stopped by the earth's atmosphere. The shortest ultraviolet radiation is stopped by the ozone layer. Infrared radiation is absorbed by the earth, causing heat. Some of the visible light may be reflected by objects on the earth. However, some may be absorbed causing heat. Dark objects are better absorbers of light than light objects. Thus, dark materials get warmer in sunlight than light colored objects, for the dark objects absorb the light energy and turn it into heat, whereas the light colored objects reflect the light energy.

Electricity and Magnetism

Magnets have two poles termed the north pole and the south pole. Like poles (north-north and south-south) repel when brought near each other, and unlike poles (north-south) attract. All magnets have these two poles, though they are more apparent on bar magnets and horseshoe magnets than on other kinds of magnets. Ring magnets have one pole in the center and the other on the outside edge. Magnetic "refrigerator" strips have a parallel series of many north-south pole lines. (See Figure 12.7.)

Materials that are attracted to magnets are said to be magnetic. Most metals that are magnetic, such as steel, have iron in them. Copper, nickel, aluminum, silver, and gold are **not** magnetic.

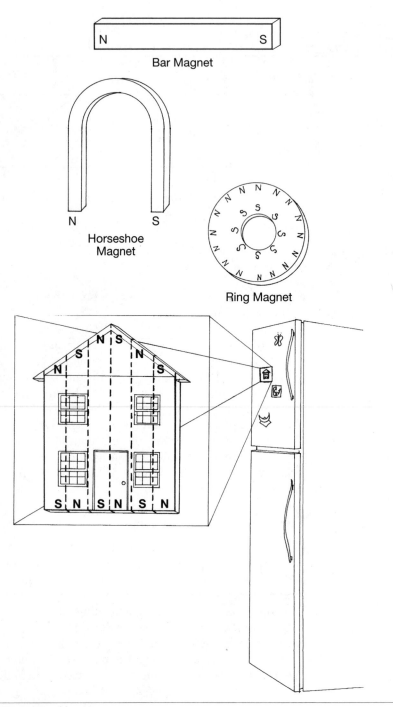

FIGURE 12.7 Magnets

Static electricity is an accumulation of electric charges that does not flow through a circuit. The largest displays of static electricity occur as lightning in thunderstorms and are caused by the discharge of huge accumulations of charged particles on clouds. The discharges can occur by the lightning moving from one cloud to another cloud, from the cloud to the ground, or from the ground to a cloud.

When we rub a hard rubber rod with fur, we produce a static charge called a negative charge on the rod; the fur is left with an equal positive charge. When a glass rod is rubbed with silk we produce a positive charge on the rod, and the silk carries an equal negative charge. (The terms "positive" and "negative" were first used by Benjamin Franklin.) The charges on the rubber rod or the glass rod can be transferred to metal balls suspended with thread by touching the balls with the rods. Crumpled-up balls of aluminum foil, light styrofoam balls, and small pieces of styrofoam such as the styrofoam "popcorn" used for packing also can be used. Balls with the same charges on them (two positively-charged balls or two negatively-charged balls) repel each other. Balls with unlike charges (a positively charged ball and a negatively charged ball) attract each other when they are brought close to each other. Static electricity investigations must be undertaken on dry days; on humid days, the atmosphere contains water molecules which tend to absorb the static electricity, with the result that the rods, the fur, the silk, and the aluminum balls are left with no charges.

Electricity flows through conductors. An electric conductor is a material that will let an electric current flow through it. Most metals are electric conductors. The best electric conductors are copper, aluminum, gold, and silver. Most plastics, rubber, wood, and pure water do not conduct electricity. Materials that do not conduct electricity are called insulators. Water with impurities such as salt or vinegar dissolved in it becomes a good conductor of electricity because the dissolved material *ionizes* (breaks up) in the water and provides a "path" for the electric current. However, water with sugar dissolved in it is not a good conductor because the sugar molecules do not ionize in the water. Pure water does not conduct electricity.

There are two requirements for a complete electric circuit: a source of electrical energy and a conductor. The source of electrical energy typically is a battery, and the conductors typically are wires. The amount of push given to the current is called the voltage. Batteries come in many voltage ratings; the $1^1/_2$-volt batteries are satisfactory for most investigations into electricity, and do not give an electric shock. Note that batteries do not *create* electricity; rather, they push and pull existing electrical charges to and from the terminals. The amount of electricity that flows through a conductor is called the *amperage*. Most circuits have such devices as light bulbs, motors, fans, and so on included in them called *resistances*. The resistance causes the electron flow to do some work such as lighting a bulb or running a motor. The more the resistance in an electric circuit, the lower the amount of electricity (or amperage) that can flow through the circuit.

Circuits with several elements such as two or more light bulbs can be connected in series or in parallel. In series circuits, the resistances are connected next to each other, one following the other. If one is disconnected, the circuit is broken, and the whole circuit is disabled. Old fashioned Christmas tree lights were wired in series; if one went out, they all went out. In parallel circuits, each device is connected to the main circuit with its own sub-circuit. The flow of electricity continues through the rest of the circuit even if one device is disabled.

If an insulated wire is wound around a metal rod and an electric current flows through the wire, the metal rod becomes a magnet. This

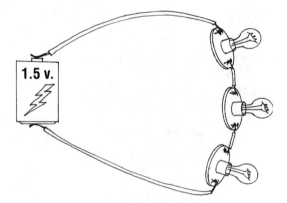

Three bulbs connected in series

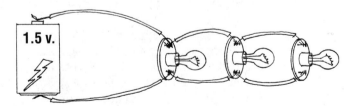

Three bulbs connected in parallel

FIGURE 12.8 Series and parallel circuits

effect is called electromagnetism. The strength of an electromagnet depends on the amount of current flowing through the wire or the number of turns of wire around the metal rod, or both; the higher the current and the more the turns, the stronger the electromagnet. Electromagnetism is the basic principle underlying motors, generators, transformers, and sound systems.

Nuclear Energy

The atom consists of three basic particles: protons, neutrons, and electrons. Protons and neutrons make up the atom's nucleus, and the electrons surround the nucleus in a haze. In radioactive substances, particles in the nucleus change form and release energy. The disintegration of the original nucleus forms the nucleus of a different kind of element; alpha particles (protons), beta particles (electrons) or gamma rays are emitted and shot forth from the nucleus with considerable energy. The half life of a substance is the length of time it takes half of the atoms in a given quantity of that substance to disintegrate.

Radioactivity has many uses. In medical diagnosis, special detectors are used to follow the path radioactive substances take in the body to pinpoint the sources of potential medical problems. Radioactive materials are used to find sources of water and gas leaks. Radioactive materials are used for generating electricity; radioactive uranium is put in nuclear reactors where the radiation it emits is used to heat water which, in turn, is used to power generators.

There are two basic kinds of nuclear reactions: fission and fusion. *Fission* involves breaking down the nuclei of atoms as has been described above. Nuclear reactors and the atomic bomb use fission reactions. *Fusion* involves smashing two or more nuclei together with such force that a they combine to form a different kind of nucleus. Since it takes much less energy to hold the new nucleus together than it took to hold the original nuclei together, the excess energy is released as radioactivity and heat. Fusion is the reaction that occurs on the sun, and is the reaction used in the hydrogen bomb and other contemporary nuclear warheads.

Matter and Chemical Energy

Materials have definite properties such as weight, size, shape, color, texture, and luster. Materials can be elements, compounds, or mixtures. An element is the simplest form of matter, and is made of atoms. In the universe, there are 92 naturally-occurring elements (some of which are unstable and disintegrate radioactively in very short periods of time) plus another 15 that have been made by man on earth (which also are radioactive). All materials in the universe are made of these same elements. Each element has a unique *atomic number* which is the number of protons in its nucleus. The elements are organized in the *Periodic Table of the Elements* in order of atomic number such that elements with similar characteristics occur in the same vertical columns. Elements can be metals such as sodium, potassium, copper, iron, gold, and silver. Elements can be non-metals such as oxygen, nitrogen, sulfur, chlorine, fluorine, and phosphorus. Elements can be metalloids which sometimes behave as metals and sometimes behave as non-metals; examples of metalloids are carbon, silicon, and arsenic. There are six elements that do not react with other elements or compounds under normal circumstances; these are the inert (or noble) gases, and include helium, neon, argon, krypton, xenon, and radon.

Compounds are made of *molecules*, which consist of two or more atoms, usually of different elements, chemically combined. Compounds are often classified as acids, bases, and salts. An *acid* is a compound that turns litmus paper pink, tastes sour, and can react with other materials sometimes violently. A *base* is a compound that turns litmus paper blue, feels slippery, and can react with other materials sometimes violently. Vinegar is an example of an acid, and soap is an example of a base. A *salt* is a compound that does not change the color of litmus paper, and is formed either directly or indirectly from the reaction between an acid and a base. Table salt and copper sulfate are examples of salts.

Elements combine to form compounds through chemical reactions causing rearrangement of atoms to form different substances. Examples of compounds are carbon dioxide, sodium chloride (salt), copper sulfate, and sugar. Inorganic compounds are those that do not have carbon as the basic element; organic compounds are those that have carbon as the basic element. There are many more organic compounds than inorganic compounds.

Chemical reactions occur when electrons of elements change places. There are several distinct kinds of chemical reactions. *Single replacement* reactions occur when an element in one compound or a free element replaces an element in a different compound. An example of a single replacement reaction is the replacement of chlorine in sodium chloride (salt) with fluorine to form sodium fluoride, a material used in the prevention of tooth decay. *Double replacement* reactions occur when the two parts of each of two compounds change places. An example of a double replacement reaction occurs when a solution of sodium chloride (salt) is mixed with a solution of silver nitrate. The sodium and the silver atoms change places, resulting in sodium nitrate and silver chloride. The silver chloride is insoluble in water, and precipitates out as a white substance that turns dark when exposed to light similar to photographic film. *Analysis* reactions occur when compounds break up into component parts. An example of an analysis reaction is breaking water into hydrogen and oxygen by running an electric current through it. *Synthesis* reactions occur when two or more elements or compounds combine to form a third composite compound. An example of a synthesis reaction is the combination of nitrogen and hydrogen to form ammonia.

Mixtures are the result of mixing two or more materials together without chemical reaction. Alloys, solutions, and air are mixtures.

Solutions contain a *solvent* (the material that does the dissolving) and a *solute* (the material that is dissolved). Water is called the "universal solvent" since it dissolves many substances. In general, the warmer the solvent, the more solute can be dissolved. A solution is said to be *saturated* when it contains all the solute dissolved in it that can be dissolved at that temperature. It is *supersaturated* if it contains more than it should, and it is *unsaturated* if it contains less. The presence of water vapor in air forms a solution and is called humidity.

Life Science Principles

Life science is the study of living things and is organized around several basic themes: (1) the nature and diversity of life; (2) the cellular theory of life; (3) the structure and function of plants; (4) the structure and function of animals; (5) reproduction, life cycles, and heredity; (6) genetics and evolution; and (7) ecology.

The Nature and Diversity of Life

There are over 1,800,000 different species of living organisms known to exist on earth, and additional species are being identified and described every year. Living things are classified into five Kingdoms.

1. Kingdom Monera, with over 10,000 species, contains bacteria which are single-celled organisms without nuclei.
2. Kingdom Protista, with up to 200,000 species, contains single-celled organisms with nuclei, and includes algae, slime molds, and protozoans such as amoeba, euglena, and paramecium.
3. Kingdom Fungi, with over 100,000 single-celled and multicellular species, contains organisms that cannot manufacture their own food and live on decomposing matter.
4. Kingdom Plantae with a half million species contains multicellular plants and includes liverworts and mosses, ferns, cone-bearing plants, and flowering plants.
5. Kingdom Animalia with over a million species contains multicellular animals. Kingdom Animalia is divided into ten large phyla. (See Figure 12.9.)

PHYLA OF THE ANIMAL KINGDOM

PHYLUM	REPRESENTATIVE ANIMALS
PORIFERA	Sponges
COELENTERATA	Jellyfish, Coral, Sea Anemones
PLATYHELMINTHES	Flatworms
NEMATODA	Roundworms
BRACHIOPODA	Lampshells
MOLLUSCA	Clams, Snails, Octopi, Squids
ANNELIDA	Segmented Worms
ARTHROPODA	Insects, Spiders, Crustaceans
ECHINODERMATA	Starfish, Sea Urchins
CHORDATA	Fish, Amphibians, Reptiles, Birds, Mammals

FIGURE 12.9

The major subdivisions in naming organisms are as follows:

Kingdom
Phylum
Class
Order
Family
Genus
Species
Subspecies

In the binomial nomenclature system, each organism is identified by the name of its genus and species; the genus is capitalized, and both words are underlined or italicized. Thus, the taxonomic name for the domestic cat is *Felis catus*, and the name for humans is *Homo sapiens*.

Living things exhibit several common characteristics:

1. They are made of **protoplasm** organized into **cells**.
2. They use **energy**.
3. They are capable of **growth**.
4. They have definite **lifespans**.
5. They **reproduce**, giving rise to **similar organisms**.
6. They are **affected by the environment**.
7. They can **adapt to the environment**.
8. They can **respond to the environment**.

Living things are found everywhere on earth, from grasslands to forests, from lakes and rivers to the depths of the sea, from the hottest and driest deserts to the polar caps. To survive in these diverse surroundings, organisms must be able to adapt to their environment; special characteristics enable them to live where they do.

The Cellular Theory of Life

Living things are made of cells. Some organisms such as a bacterium, an amoeba, and *Paramecium* are made of single cells. Organisms such as spirogyra and certain algae occur in colonies of cells that work together for the common good, though each cell independently carries out its own complete life functions. Complex organisms are made of different kinds of cells specialized to carry out specific functions, all working together to accomplish the total needs of life. In the human, for example, there are cells specialized for growing hair, secreting digestive juices, making bones and muscles, and carrying oxygen.

A group of similar cells forms a *tissue*. Examples of human tissues are muscle tissue, blood tissue, and bone tissue. A group of tissues working together forms an *organ*. Examples of human organs are the stomach, the biceps muscle, and the heart. Several organs working together form a *system*. Examples of human systems include the circulatory system, the digestive system, and the muscular system. All the systems make up the *organism*. Organisms can be single celled or multicellular.

The cell is the fundamental unit of life. It is a tiny structure made of protoplasm, enclosed by a plasma membrane, and containing organelles. The *plasma membrane* provides form and structure for the cell, and permits materials the cell needs to pass in and waste products to pass out. The *nucleus* is the control center of the cell, and contains the *chromosomes* which are made of genes, which, in turn, are made of DNA. Most directions for cellular activity are given by the DNA in the nucleus. The *cytoplasm* in the cell includes all material outside the nucleus.

Several specialized structures are found in the cytoplasm. The *endoplasmic reticulum* connects the cell membrane to the nucleus, functioning as a network of canals to transport material to the nucleus through the cytoplasm. *Ribosomes* are tiny structures that manufacture proteins. The *mitochondria* are sausage-shaped structures that release energy to the cell through the chemical reactions that occur in them. The *lysosomes* are tiny spheres containing enzymes that break down molecules for use by the cell. The *Golgi apparatus* packages the proteins made by the ribosomes and transports them throughout the cell. *Vacuoles* are used to store food, water, and minerals. (See Figure 12.10.)

TYPICAL ANIMAL CELL AND TYPICAL PLANT CELL

Typical Animal Cell

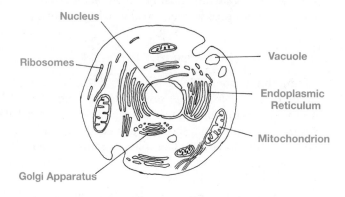

Typical Plant Cell

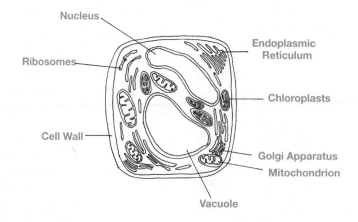

FIGURE 12.10

Plant cells have structures in addition to those described above to help them carry out their special functions. In plant cells, the plasma membrane is surrounded by a cell wall made of cellulose to provide rigidity for the cells since plants do not have a skeletal structure. Plant cells also contain plastids, tiny colored bodies that provide color and are used for storage or as chemical factories. Chloroplasts are plastids that contain chlorophyll which is used in making food. When the green leaves die in the autumn, the chlorophyll fades, and other plastids can be seen, resulting in the brightly colored fall foliage. (See Figure 12.10.)

Cells can be seen under microscopes. Prepared slides are stained to highlight special structures. Living protozoans can be seen by preparing hay infusions. Collect some swamp water (the more dank it is the better), and put it in a jar with leaves and debris. Place the jar in a warm, dark place to let the organisms grow and reproduce, and then use an eyedropper to place one small drop of the liquid on a slide. Many species of protozoa can be seen in a drop of this infusion. Plant cells can be seen by obtaining a sprig or two of a seaweed known as *elodea* (available where fresh water aquariums are sold). Select a light green leaf from the tip of a sprig, and place it on a slide. Children can see the cell wall, chloroplasts, cytoplasm, and nucleus. Staining the cell with a drop of iodine will highlight the structures.

Some materials are transported into or out of cells by diffusion. During diffusion, materials move from areas of higher concentration to areas of lower concentration; in cells, this can occur through the plasma membrane. The plasma membrane is selectively permeable, and permits certain materials to diffuse into the cell if there is a higher concentration of that material in the fluids surrounding the cell than there is inside the cell. The reverse can occur as cells get rid of the products they manufacture or waste materials.

Cells have basic living functions, some of which are: (1) to manufacture proteins and other materials to help build the cell; (2) to manufacture energy; and (3) to reproduce.

Cells manufacture proteins through complex chemical reactions directed by the DNA genetic material in the nucleus. Raw materials in the form of amino acids are transported to the ribosomes where the manufacturing process occurs. Products include proteins for enzymes, cell growth, and reproduction.

In addition to the protein manufacture that occurs in all cells, plants have the unique capability of manufacturing their own food from water and carbon dioxide. Water and minerals are absorbed through the roots and are transmitted through the stems to the leaves. Carbon dioxide is absorbed from the atmosphere through the leaves. The chlorophyll absorbs light energy which enables plants to make glucose using carbon dioxide, water, and minerals as the raw materials. The by-products of the reaction are oxygen which is released through the leaves, water, and other food materials. The glucose may be stored in the leaves or may be transported to the stems or roots for storage as starch. Examples of plants that store food in their leaves are lettuce and spinach; plants that store food in their stems include celery and asparagus; plants that store food in their roots include sweet potatoes, carrots, and beets.

The manufacture of energy starts in the cytoplasm and continues in the mitochondria. Both oxygen and glucose are used in energy production. The products of this reaction are energy, water, and carbon dioxide. The process by which cells obtain oxygen and release carbon dioxide is called gas exchange. With very few exceptions, all cells, including animal and plant cells, use oxygen for manufacturing energy and release carbon dioxide as a waste product. Thus, oxygen is used by both plant and animal cells, and carbon dioxide is given off by both plant and animal cells. As can be seen, plants use and release both oxygen and carbon dioxide, and carbon dioxide is a product of both plant energy manufacture and plant respiration.

When cells reach their optimum size, they reproduce through mitosis to make two cells. Thus, the organism grows.

Structure and Function of Plants

Plants contain organs called roots, stems, leaves, and flowers. The *roots* provide anchorage for the plant and, through tiny root hairs, enable plants to absorb water and nutritional elements from the soil. The *stems* transport the nutrients to the leaves through cells that are specialized for transport. The *leaves* are the food-manufacturing sites of the plants.

Flowers are the sexual reproductive organs of the plants. The petals attract insects and birds to help disperse pollen for cross-fertilization. The male reproductive organ is the *stamen* which manufactures the pollen. The female reproductive organ is the *pistil* which has a sticky top called a *stigma* to capture the pollen, a *style* to transport the pollen nucleus to the ovary, and the *ovary* which manufactures the *ovules*. When the pollen nuclei join the ovule nuclei, fertilized seeds result. There are two kinds of seeds: those that come with two food storage parts, such as beans and peas, and those that come with one food storage part only, such as corn. The two-part seeds have tiny embryos embedded between the two halves. Seeds that come in one part have the embryo embedded within the seed. If a seed is kept wet, the embryo uses the water and the food stored in the seed to germinate and grow.

Ripened ovaries of flowers are called fruits, and include such delectable delights as apples, tomatoes, and watermelons. Vegetables come from the roots, stems, leaves, and flowers which store food.

Plants move in response to gravity, light, and touch. If you allow a seed to germinate, and then turn it upside down so its roots point up, the plant will grow so its roots point down and the stem points up, showing that plants respond to gravity. Plants also tend to grow toward areas with the most light, causing them to bend. Thus, house plants bend toward the light and forest plants grow tall, reaching for the sun. Certain plants, such as the *Mimosa* have leaves that quickly close when touched.

Mung beans are excellent to show characteristics of plant germination, growth, and response. If kept damp, they germinate within a day or two, and the resulting plants, called bean sprouts, grow very rapidly.

Structure and Function of Animals

In order to live and to survive as a species, animals must support the workings of each of their individual cells and also grow, reproduce, and interact with the environment as complete organisms. The basic functions of all animals include the following:

Nutrition
Respiration
Excretion
Circulation
Response
Movement
Regulation
Reproduction

The study of an individual animal involves investigating how that animal is specialized to accomplish these body functions in its environment. The more complex the structure of an animal, the more removed its cells are from the external environment. Consequently, more complex animals have systems to serve the needs of individual cells. The digestive system takes food in, processes it for use by cells, and eliminates undigestible materials. The respiratory system is adapted for extracting the required oxygen either from the air or from water and removing carbon dioxide. Excretion is accomplished through kidneys and other excretory organs that extract liquid waste from body fluids and eliminate it from the organism. A complex circulatory system ensures that nutrients, gases, and regulatory hormones are transported from the specialized systems to each individual cell and that wastes can be removed from each cell and delivered to the excretory and respiratory system organs. Regulatory glands secrete hormones to keep all cells working harmoniously. An intricate network of nerves and often a central brain structure coordinate all systems and permit movement, thought, and interaction with the environment. The muscular system allows the organism to move. A skeletal system provides rigidity in animals that do not otherwise have the required structure. Skeletons may be made of bone, cartilage, or water (such as the hydroskeletons in worms). Some

animals such as crayfish and lobsters have *exoskeletons* (external skeletons) that are made of *chitin*. Reproduction is accomplished either sexually or asexually through specialized organs and specialized systems that
ensure perpetuation of the species.

Reproduction, Life Cycles, and Heredity

The purpose of reproduction is to enable organisms to grow and to per-
petuate species. Reproduction occurs in two ways: asexually and sexually.

In asexual reproduction, the genetic material in a cell first reproduces
itself to form identical pairs of chromosomes. As the cell splits into two
cells, one of each of the identical pairs of chromosomes moves to each of
the new cells where the new nuclei form around the chromosomes; each
nucleus is identical to the original nucleus. This process is called *mitosis*,
and is the process by which cells divide. In lower plants and animals,
specialized organs produce cells by mitosis which are released from the
original organism and grow into new identical organisms. This process of
reproduction where organisms are derived from only one parent is called
asexual reproduction. Asexual reproduction occurs in bacteria, algae, molds,
fungi, many lower plants, protozoans, sponges, and coelenterates as well
as in a few higher order animals.

Sexual reproduction requires the union of a male *gamete* (reproductive cell) and a female gamete. These gametes are formed in specialized
organs through the process of *meiosis*; following meiosis, each gamete
contains one-half of the chromosomes. When the two gametes unite,
each contributes its half of the chromosomes to the new nucleus, restor-
ing the full chromosome count to the fertilized egg.

Chromosomes are made of genes which are composed of strands of
DNA (deoxyribonucleic acid). DNA carries the code of life which is the
code for protein production. Chromosomes come in pairs with a gene for
each trait on each member of the pair; thus each trait is determined by
two genes which may be dominant or recessive. If both of the two genes
for a given trait are dominant genes, the organism exhibits the dominant
trait. If both are recessive, the organism exhibits the recessive trait. If one
is dominant and one is recessive, the organism exhibits the dominant
trait. Dominant traits in humans include unattached earlobes, brown eyes,
curly hair, polydactylism (more than ten fingers or toes), and the ability
to curl one's tongue. Recessive traits include attached earlobes, blue or
hazel eyes, straight hair, the normal number of fingers and toes, and the
inability to curl one's tongue.

Living organisms move through definite life cycles: they come into
being, they grow, they may metamorphose, they mature, they reproduce,
and they die. In lower animals, the fertilized egg cell may develop into
an organism entirely different in appearance from the adult. These juve-

nile stages carry out their life functions while preparing to metamorphose into adults. Life cycles exhibiting larvae or other juvenile stages are seen in frogs, most insects (including butterflies), and many aquatic species including worms, mollusks, and arthropods. The fertilized eggs of frogs develop into tadpoles which develop into frogs. The butterfly's eggs hatch into caterpillars which grow and encase themselves in a *pupa* where they undergo complete metamorphosis into the butterfly. In higher species, the fertilized egg develops directly into the adult shape which then grows, matures, reproduces, and dies.

Genetics and Evolution

Whereas the vast majority of offspring are genetically similar to their parents, abnormalities sometimes occur. When gametes are formed, abnormal (or *mutant*) genes can be formed by erroneous duplication of the DNA, by physical transformation of the positions of molecules making up the DNA strands, or by external causes such as radiation, X rays, or gamma rays. Often the presence of these mutations makes it impossible for the fertilized egg to develop into a living organism. However, occasionally mutations enable offspring to survive better or have a better chance of successful reproduction than offspring without these mutations. If that happens, then eventually all or most of the species will come to possess the mutation. Because the mutation gives the offspring an advantage in adapting to its environment, it has a better chance of survival. For example, animals with white coats are better able to survive in arctic climates than similar animals with dark coats. Camouflaged green insects that feed on leaves have a better chance of survival than they would if they were yellow.

The basic principle of evolution is "survival of the fittest." This means that the individuals best adapted to the environment generally produce the greatest number of offspring. Most organisms produce far more offspring than can possibly survive. On average, those offspring that possess traits that adapt them most favorably to the environment survive and reproduce. Consequently, organisms with favorable adaptations accumulate by natural selection; those with less favorable adaptations eventually die out.

The Theory of Evolution offers an explanation for the immense diversity of life found on earth, namely, that through the process of natural selection, organisms become better adapted to their environments.

Ecology

Ecology is the study of the interactions of organisms with their environment and with each other. The environment in which living organisms exist is called the *biosphere*, and includes land, water, and air.

The basic unit of ecological study is the *ecosystem* which includes a *community* of living organisms and their non-living environment, all of which interact with each other. It is the environment through which energy flows and minerals recycle. Ecosystems can be large, such as deserts, tropical rain forests, and the ocean, and they can be small, such as a backyard, a school playground, or a pond. A balanced ecosystem has three fundamental characteristics: (1) There is a relatively constant source of energy (the sun); (2) The sun's energy is converted to glucose which is needed by the living organisms; (3) Organic matter and nutrients are successfully recycled. The study of ecosystems involves investigating the manner and extent of these factors.

The ultimate source of energy on earth is the sun, and ecosystems vary widely in their ability to utilize solar energy. Solar energy is a primary factor in the formation of hot regions such as deserts, and cold areas such as the polar regions, each of which have their own unique community of living organisms adapted for life in that environment. Solar energy penetrates to limited depths in the seas, resulting in different life forms in shallow areas than in deeper layers. Solar energy drives the water cycle which, in turn, regulates the amount of moisture available to an ecosystem. Organisms that need large amounts of water are found in wet regions; organisms found in deserts are adapted to arid climates. Forests are characterized by a canopy of tall trees which compete for the sun's energy needed to sustain their life, resulting in a shaded floor which sustains organisms that can thrive in the shade.

Energy is transmitted through an ecosystem primarily by means of the food chain. Ultimately, the source of all food in any ecosystem are the plants which manufacture their own food. Some animals eat plants and other animals; some eat only plants; and some eat only animals.

Recycling of organic matter and nutrients within an ecosystem occurs as plants and animals excrete waste materials back into their environment and die, and microorganisms recycle all material in the organisms back to the environment.

If the supply of energy is changed, the food cycle is interrupted, or needed organic matter and nutrients are increased or decreased, the ecosystem loses its balance. It must then adjust to the new conditions, with the result that a different ecosystem may be formed as existing organisms die out or migrate to other ecosystems, and new organisms migrate into the ecosystem.

Changes in ecosystem balance can be caused by a variety of factors. Natural disasters such as floods, earthquakes, and tornadoes may completely destroy an existing ecosystem. Natural disasters in one part of the world may affect ecosystem balance in other parts of the world. For example, when volcanoes erupt, huge amounts of dust and ash are spewed into the atmosphere and circulate around the globe in a band, altering the amount of sunlight available to ecosystems in its path. Natural phenomena such as El-Niño, the large-scale warming of the Pacific Ocean, may cause long-term climatic and temperature changes which result in ecosystem changes.

Humans contribute in significant ways to the upset of the delicate balance in the ecosystems. Air and water pollution introduce new materials to the ecosystem that change the balance of recycling organic materials and nutrients; some of these materials may be poisonous to the organisms, killing them. Increased levels of atmospheric carbon dioxide may cause localized or global warming, upsetting the balance of energy. Increased chlorofluorocarbon levels reduce the thickness of the atmosphere's ozone layer, allowing increased levels of short ultraviolet radiation to enter the atmosphere, causing significant changes in the balance of energy. Improper disposal of solid wastes produces land pollution which, in turn, upsets the balance of materials in the ecosystem in the area. Mining, tree cutting, and other resource-depleting activities, when performed to excess, remove needed materials from an affected ecosystem, often resulting in total destruction of the ecosystem and extinction of species. Much remains to be learned about the effects of civilization on the balance of nature; however, most experts agree that we need to take immediate and drastic action to stop the wanton destruction of ecosystems.

Earth and Space Science Principles

Earth and space sciences involve the studies of the non-living environment including the earth and its place in space. Earth science can be divided into seven broad areas of study: (1) the structure of the earth; (2) plate tectonics; (3) constructive and destructive forces; (4) the rock cycle; (5) weathering and the water cycle; (6) oceanography; and (7) historical geology. Space science includes studies of the solar system, the universe, and space exploration.

Structure of the Earth

The earth is approximately 8000 miles (12,800 km) in diameter at the equator. Due to its rapid rotation on its axis, its diameter at the equator is 26 miles greater than its diameter from north pole to south pole, giving it a slight equatorial bulge. The planet earth consists of four concentric spheres: the *inner core*, the *outer core*, the *mantle*, and the *crust*. The inner core is solid and the outer core is molten; both are rich in iron. The mantle is a solid rocky layer; its deeper regions flow in a plastic manner due to enormous forces of stress. The crust ranges in thickness from 3 miles (5 kilometers) under the oceans to 25 miles (40 kilometers) under the continents. The surface of the earth consists of the lithosphere (solid areas), the hydrosphere (areas of water), and the atmosphere. The continents and oceans lie on plates of the lithosphere.

Plate Tectonics

The *Theory of Plate Tectonics* is a refinement of the older continental drift and sea-floor spreading theories, and came into existence in the mid-1960s as a unifying theory. The explanatory power and the implications of this theory are so widespread that it is considered the basic framework from which most other geologic processes are viewed.

According to the theory of plate tectonics, the earth's crust is divided into about twenty plates of various sizes and thicknesses that continually drift very slowly at rates of two to five centimeters per year. These plates are made of crustal material and the underlying solid and rigid outer portion of the mantle. The plates beneath continents (called continental plates) are thick, ranging from 100 to 400 kilometers in thickness, and the

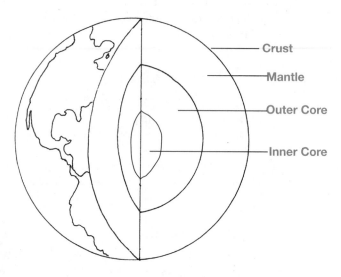

Thickness of crust is exaggerated.

FIGURE 12.11   Cross section of the earth

plates beneath the oceans (called oceanic plates) are thinner, ranging between 80 and 100 kilometers in thickness. As the plates move, some plates are pulled under others, and become re-melted into the material of the mantle. Gaps created by plates moving away from each other are filled with molten rock called magma that originates in the mantle and becomes solidified into new crustal rock. This currently is occurring on the floor of the Atlantic Ocean which is split in the middle as its two halves drift away from each other. The resulting Mid-Atlantic Ridge is the site of continual oozing of magma from the mantle to fill the widening gap. Thus, rock from the mantle is recycled over a period of millions of years as plates drift under each other and melt into the magma and new magma emerges in gaps to form new rock.

When continental plates collide with each other, the result is the formation of mountains. Most recently (about 40 million years ago) this occurred when the north-moving Indian Plate collided with the Eurasian Plate, causing the formation of the Himalayan Mountains. All of North America is on the same continental plate except for western California which rests on the Pacific Plate which is moving northward relative to the North American Plate at a rate of about 2 centimeters per year. The landward boundary between these two plates is marked by the San Andreas fault, and the motion of the Pacific Plate and the North American Plate relative to each other is one reason for the earthquake activity along this fault. Though two centimeters of movement per year may not seem significant, in a span of geologic time, this movement is very significant. In the 2 million years since the beginning of the Ice Age, plates have been displaced some 25 to 50 miles. The current position of continents on the globe is thought to be the result of the break-up and subsequent movement of the plates making up the supercontinent, *Pangea*, about 250 million years ago. Pangea, in turn, is thought to have formed from the collision of continents formed from the original crust of the earth which started moving around $2^{1}/_{2}$ billion years ago.

Constructive and Destructive Forces

The surface of the earth undergoes continuous cycles of building structures and tearing them down. Several forces cause the build-up of earth structures. As we have seen, continental plates colliding with each other cause mountains to form. Volcanic activity causes volcanic cones of several types to form. Sediments settling onto lake beds and ocean floors and subsequently becoming compacted and cemented, form vast sedimentary rock layers. Glaciers pick up materials as they march over land masses, and deposit these materials in the form of mountains, drumlins, and thick deposits.

No sooner are landforms constructed than forces of destruction begin to wear them away. The chief destructive forces are water, gravity,
wind, and vegetation. The term *weathering* refers to the process of wearing structures down, and the term *erosion* refers to moving the weathered
material.

Water is the most powerful of the geologic destructive forces. Running water in the form of rivers exerts tremendous force on the material
it encounters, breaking particles away from riverbeds and ransporting
them downstream where they accumulate as sedimentary deposits. These
deposits can be in the form of river deltas or can end up in lakes or
oceans where they eventually settle on the floors. Water also dissolves
some of the material it encounters. Canyons, gullies, and valleys are the
result of weathering and erosion by rivers and streams. One of the most
famous examples of this phenomenon is the Grand Canyon, which was
formed by the Colorado River cutting its way through rock and forming
a canyon over a mile deep.

Water in the form of ice exerts a tremendous destructive force. When
water freezes, it expands; water trapped in cracks in rocks aidin breaking
the rocks into fragments when it freezes. Glaciers are masses of ice that
can be over 4 kilometers (2.5 miles) thick, flowing slowly downhill in
response to gravity. As they move, they carve out huge chunks of land
which they carry with them and leave behind when they melt. In North
America, the Great Lakes and the Finger Lakes of New York State are
examples of the results of glacial erosion; the fjords in Scandinavia also
are the result of glacial activity. When glaciers flow toward open seas, the
leading edges crack off to form icebergs. Thousands of glaciers exist on
earth today. In the mountainous areas they carve out glacial valleys,
glacial lakes, cirques, and horns. Huge continental glaciers cover most of
the island of Greenland and a large portion of Antarctica; their combined
area represents nearly 10 percent of the earth's land.

Gravity causes loosely consolidated material to move downhill.
Rockslides, mudslides, and landslides are examples of this devastatingly
destructive flow.

Though wind is a very powerful force, its role as a destructive geologic force is minor. Wind erodes by blowing loose particles away. Only
relatively light particles the size of grains of sand or smaller can be
picked up by the wind, and they generally are carried only short distances. However, particles of dust can be carried for miles before they
settle. The primary way wind weathers rocky materials is through natural sandblasting of rocks by the particles carried by the wind. Since wind-
blown particles cannot be carried to heights much over one meter, a
typical formation resulting from wind weathering is the "balancing rock."

Winds over large bodies of water create water waves which weather and erode shorelines.

Vegetation causes surface weathering of rocky formations. Seeds trapped in the crevices and cracks of rocks germinate and, when they grow, tend to exert destructive forces on the rock, breaking it into smaller particles which can be carried away by water, gravity, or wind.

Earthquakes are tremendously destructive forces, both in geologic terms and in terms of human life and property damage. Earthquakes are vibrations of the earth caused by movement of land masses along faults. The vibrations reverberate through neighboring rocks like a bell, causing the land to move and shake. Earthquake severity is measured on the Richter scale; the higher the Richter number, the more severe the earthquake. The Richter scale and its interpretation are shown in Figure 12.12.

The Rock Cycle

All rocks on earth come from the mantle. When the earth first cooled, some 4.6 billion years ago, the molten material of the earth solidified into igneous rocks such as granite and basalt. Igneous rocks are produced today from magma solidifying when it oozes from the earth's mantle or erupts from volcanoes as lava. Common igneous rocks are granite, basalt, obsidian, and pumice. Granite is coarse-grained and is made of the minerals feldspar, quartz, mica, and hornblende. It is the principal rock forming the upper layers of the continents. Basalt is fine-grained and is found in the lower layers of continents and on ocean floors. Obsidian (natural glass) and pumice (frothy natural glass) are products of volcanoes.

As rocks are acted upon by the destructive forces of weathering and erosion, they break into smaller and smaller particles. Eventually these

THE RICHTER EARTHQUAKE SCALE

RICHTER MAGNITUDE	EARTHQUAKE EFFECTS
Less Than 3.5	Barely felt
3.5 – 5.4	Felt; minor damage
5.5 – 6.0	Some damage to structures
6.1 – 6.9	Destructive in populous regions
7.0 – 7.9	Major earthquakes; serious damage
Greater than 8.0	Great earthquakes; can produce total destruction

FIGURE 12.12

particles are transported by water to lakes and oceans where they settle. The sediments become compressed and become cemented with materials formerly dissolved in the water and left behind when the water evaporates, resulting in sedimentary rocks. Examples of sedimentary rocks and their composition are given in Figure 12.13.

Metamorphic rocks are formed from the transformation of igneous, sedimentary, or other metamorphic rocks. When rocks are subjected to intense pressure and high temperatures, they melt, recrystallize, and often rearrange in layers. Metamorphic rocks often are characterized by large and well-defined crystals, broken edges of particles, strong cementation, and layering. Examples of metamorphic rocks and their origin and characteristics are given in Figure 12.14.

SOME SEDIMENTARY ROCKS

SEDIMENTARY ROCK	COMPOSITION
Sandstone	Grains of sand
Limestone	Grains of calcium carbonate (calcite)
Conglomerate	Many kinds and sizes of grains
Shale	Particles of mud
Gypsum	Calcium sulfate
Coal	Partially decomposed plants
Rock Salt	Salt
Coquina	Shells cemented together

FIGURE 12.13

SOME METAMORPHIC ROCKS

METAMORPHIC ROCK	ORIGIN AND CHARACTERISTICS
Slate	From shale; splits into layers
Quartzite	From sandstone; grains well cemented
Marble	From limestone; crystalline in appearance
Schist	Many fine layers; easily split
Gneiss ("nice")	Coarse layers

FIGURE 12.14

Weather and the Water Cycle

The earth's atmosphere extends some 625 miles above the surface of the earth. The atmosphere is composed of 78 percent nitrogen, 21 percent oxygen, 1 percent carbon dioxide, argon, neon, helium and methane, and traces of other gases. Weather occurs in the *troposphere*, the lowest layer of atmosphere, which is 6 to 12 miles thick.

Three basic natural phenomena contribute to weather: (1) solar radiation, (2) earth movements, and (3) the water cycle.

Solar radiation is heat energy transmitted to the earth in the form of infrared radiation which is converted to heat when it strikes the earth's land or water surfaces. (See also p. 421.) The earth revolves about the sun in an elliptical (oval-shaped) orbit once every 365$^1/_4$ days. Furthermore, the earth's axis is tilted to the plane of its revolution at an angle of 23$^1/_2$ degrees, with the earth's axis pointing to the North Star (*Polaris*) in the northern sky at all times. (There is no such convenient marker in the southern sky.) Thus, during the course of one revolution about the sun, the northern and southern hemispheres sometimes are tilted toward the sun and sometimes are tilted away from the sun. Times of maximum tilting toward or away from the sun are called the *solstices*. The summer solstice in the northern hemisphere occurs when the northern hemisphere is at its maximum tilt *toward* the sun; the winter solstice occurs when the northern hemisphere is at its maximum tilt *away* from the sun. The same is true for the southern hemisphere. Twice during one revolution, there is no tilt at all relative to the sun; these times are called *equinoxes*. (See Figure 12.15.)

Seasons are caused by the tilt of the earth on its axis as it revolves about the sun. When a hemisphere is tilted toward the sun, the solar radiation it receives is more direct and thus more intense than when it is tilted away from the sun, and the season is summer. When a hemisphere is tilted away from the sun, the solar radiation it receives is less direct and thus less intense, and the season is winter. (See Figure 12.16.) The seasons between are spring and fall. Atmospheric temperatures are caused by the atmosphere heating through convection from the heated earth. The more the sunlight and the more direct its rays, the warmer the earth gets, and thus the warmer the atmosphere gets.

In addition to its revolution about the sun, the earth also rotates on its axis from east to west at the rate of once every 24 hours. Friction between the atmosphere and the earth causes global winds to blow around the earth in the opposite direction of its rotation—from west to east. If solar radiation everywhere on earth were the same, we would have a single wind blowing constantly from west to east all around the globe.

ORBIT OF THE EARTH AROUND THE SUN

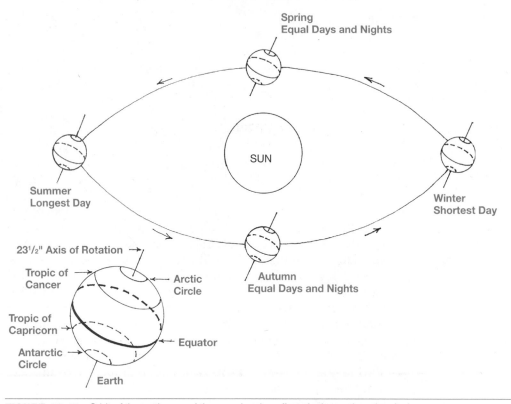

Spring
Equal Days and Nights

SUN

Summer
Longest Day

Winter
Shortest Day

Autumn
Equal Days and Nights

23½" Axis of Rotation →

Tropic of
Cancer

Arctic
Circle

Tropic of
Capricorn →

Antarctic →
Circle

← Equator

Earth

FIGURE 12.15   Orbit of the earth around the sun showing effects in the northern hemisphere

FINDING THE TROPIC OF CANCER

FIGURE 12.16   Children shine a flashlight beam on a tilted balloon representing the earth to find the Tropic of Cancer

But solar radiation varies, with some areas becoming warmer than others. Equatorial regions consistently are warmer; average atmospheric temperature decreases with distance from the equator.

Furthermore, warm air rises, and cool air falls. As the warm equatorial air rises, it cools, spreads out, and then falls. These rising and falling cells of air, coupled with the earth's rotation, cause major bands of winds in each hemisphere: the *Trade Winds* near the equator, the *Westerlies* in the middle latitudes, and the *Easterlies* in the polar regions. (Note that winds are named for the direction *from which* they blow.) Local temperature differences cause localized winds.

The *water cycle* is the natural cycle in which water evaporates, condenses to form clouds, and returns back to earth as precipitation. The temperature of the atmosphere together with the amount of water already present in the atmosphere (*humidity*) determine the rate of evaporation; the hotter and drier the air, the faster the rate of evaporation. As the humid air cools, the water vapor it holds condenses back to water. If this happens near the surface, *dew* is formed. If this happens in the cool higher air, the water condenses on dust particles to form *clouds*. Clouds that become saturated with condensed water droplets drop the water as

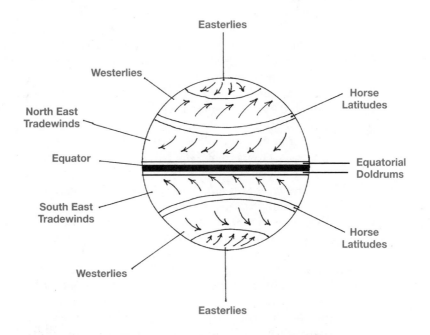

FIGURE 12.17 Global wind patterns

precipitation. The type of precipitation produced depends on the temperature of the atmosphere, and includes rain, sleet, hail, and snow.

The phenomenon called *weather* is caused by the complex interactions of temperature and winds which act to form high and low pressure
systems, and atmospheric water which is the source of precipitation.
Severe storms such as hurricanes and tornadoes are the result of localized wind patterns.

Oceanography

The study of oceanography involves investigating the interrelationships
between aquatic life and the oceanic environment.

Oceans occupy 71 percent of the earth's surface and account for about
97 percent of the earth's water. There are three major units in ocean bot-
toms: the *continental margins*, the *deep-ocean basins*, and the *mid-ocean ridges*.

Continental margins are extensions of the continents bordering oceans,
and slope from the exposed continental land to the deep-ocean basins in
three distinct phases. The *continental shelf* is the portion of the continental
margin that is the immediate extension of the continental land surface
into the ocean, and is shallow and very gently sloping. The continental
shelf is followed by a steep *continental slope*, and then a gently sloping
continental rise that merges with the oceanic crust. The continental margins consist largely of accumulations of sedimentary material often several kilometers thick that work their way seaward from the edges of the
continents and the shallow regions of the continental margins.

The *deep-ocean basins* occupy a submarine area roughly equal to the
land area of the earth. Most of these regions are extraordinarily flat,
though they are sprinkled with underwater volcano peaks that rise hundreds of meters above the ocean floor, and trenches that often exceed 10
kilometers in depth. The Hawaiian Islands were formed by undersea
volcanic activity that resulted in volcanic cones extending above the
surface of the water.

The *mid-ocean ridges* are sites of ocean floor spreading. They divide
oceans into sections, and represent edges of plates that are moving apart.
They are elevated above the surrounding terrain, and form a continuous
submarine mountain range some 40,000 miles long, winding around the
ocean floors of the earth much as the seam of a baseball winds around
the baseball.

The nature of life forms found in the seas depends on the amount of
sunlight that can penetrate and the amount of oxygen available. The
greatest diversity of aquatic life is found in the waters of the continental
shelves. The coral reefs, the most picturesque of the submarine ecosystems, form in warm, shallow waters that have clear exposure to sunlight.

Coral reefs can be very large, forming entire islands like the coral atolls in the South Pacific Ocean.

At middle depths, organisms rely on wave motion to replenish the supply of dissolved oxygen. The depth at which organisms are found varies considerably, and depends on the penetration of the sun and the available oxygen.

At greater depths, living organisms are adapted to living in darkness and existing on small amounts of oxygen. In the deepest parts of the oceans, bacteria and other organisms that do not require oxygen are found near underwater plumes that spew hot sulfur-rich gases which these organisms are adapted to use for cellular functions instead of oxygen.

Historical Geology

The study of historical geology involves investigating how the earth and its life forms have developed over time. Two fundamental principles govern the study of geologic history. (1) The *principle of uniformitarianism* says that the scientific laws that operate today have operated since the beginning of time, and that "the present is the key to the past." (2) The *law of superposition* states that, unless a rock formation has been deformed in some way, the oldest rocks and events are found at the bottom of the formation and the youngest rocks and events are found at the top. Various radioactive dating methods, coupled with these two principles, have enabled geologists to piece together the *Geologic Time Scale*. A generalized Geologic Time Scale is shown in Figure 12.18.

Geologic time is divided into two eons. The *Precambrian* eon is the period of time between the formation of the earth some 4.6 billion years ago and the emergence of life forms similar to present-day life forms. Precambrian time occupies a span of almost 4 billion years. The *Phanerozoic* eon encompasses the rest of the time, and is divided into *Paleozoic* (early life), *Mesozoic* (middle life), and *Cenozoic* (late life) eras. Shell-like organisms lived during the early Paleozoic era, and fish, amphibians, and seed plants rose and thrived during this era. The Mesozoic era, sometimes called the age of dinosaurs, saw dinosaurs rise, thrive, and become extinct. The Cenozoic era is characterized by the presence of primates, flowering plants, and, most recently, humans.

The Solar System

The solar system includes the sun and all bodies that revolve about the sun. There are nine planets: Mercury, Venus, Earth, Mars, Jupiter, Saturn, Uranus, Neptune, and Pluto. All planets revolve about the sun in the same plane called the *ecliptic*. It is as though the sun were a basketball in

GEOLOGIC TIME SCALE

EON	ERA	PERIOD	EPOCH	BEGINNING (Years Ago)	LIFE FORMS	LAND FORMS
P H A N E R O Z O I C	C E N O Z O I C	QUATERNARY	Recent (Holocene)	10,000	Modern Man	
			Pleistocene (Ice Age)	2 Million	Rise of Australopithecus	
		TERTIARY	Pliocene	5 Million	Rise of Hominids	
			Miocene	24 Million		Himalaya Mtns.
			Oligocene	37 Million		India and Asia
			Eocene	58 Million	Rise of Horses	
			Paleocene	66 Million	Rise of Primates	
	M E S O Z O I C	Cretaceous		144 Million	Extinction of Dinosaurs Rise of Flowering Plants	Alps and Rockies
		Jurassic		208 Million	Rise of Birds	Pangea Fragments Start to Drift
		Triassic		245 Million	Rise of Mammals Rise of Dinosaurs	Pangea Breakup; Atlantic Ocean
	P A L E O Z O I C	Permian		286 Million	Rise of Reptiles	Pangea Together; Appalachian Mtns.
		Carboniferous	Pennsylvanian	320 Million		
			Mississippian	360 Million		
		Devonian		408 Million	Rise of Amphibians, Insects, Seed Plants, Trees	
		Silurian		438 Million	Rise of Land Plants	
		Ordovician		505 Million	Rise of Fish and Vertebrates	
		Cambrian		570 Million	Trilobites Shells Mollusks Brachiopods Echinoderms	
P R E C A M B R I A N		Proterozoic		2.5 Billion	Multicellular Soft-body Organisms Algae "Jellyfish" "Worm Tubes"	Latest Start of Plate Movement
		Achean		3.8 Billion	Bacteria Cells without Nuclei	Crust Development
		Origin of Earth		4.6 Billion		

FIGURE 12.18

the middle of a huge pizza, and all the planets moved around the basketball on the surface of the pizza. For this reason, when looking at the night sky, all the planets are seen on the same arc in the sky which can be identified easily as the arc connecting the sun and the moon. The planets move in *elliptical* orbits, which means their paths around the sun are oval-shaped. Pluto's orbit is the narrowest ellipse, causing it to be positioned at times closer to the sun than Neptune. This, together with its small size, has led astronomers to hypothesize that Pluto once was a moon of Neptune and that it escaped Neptune's gravitational field to orbit the sun as a planet.

The *asteroids* occupy a band between Mars and Jupiter. These are large chunks of planetary matter, irregular in shape, that are thought to have resulted from some catastrophic disintegration of a planet that originally occupied the same orbit. Their orbits are irregular, with several coming closer to the earth than Mars.

Meteoroids are stony or metallic particles that revolve about the sun. They are thought to be the remains of comet nuclei that have disintegrated. Most are very small, about the size of a grain of sand, and are visible only when they enter the earth's atmosphere and burn, resulting in the bright streak of light we see. When meteoroids are burning through the atmosphere, they are called *meteors*. Occasionally meteors are very large, and fall to the ground as *meteorites*. Astronomers believe these objects are debris in the solar system; their exact source is unknown.

Comets revolve about the sun in sharply elongated elliptical orbits that are widely inclined to the plane of the ecliptic. A comet possesses a tail and a nucleus. As it revolves about the sun, the tail points away from the sun because of *solar wind*. Often the gravitational field of the sun or planets it passes during its orbit cause the breakup of a comet's nucleus. When this happens, debris is left behind. When the earth passes through a zone of this debris in its path around the sun, we experience meteor showers. Such is the case each August 12th when we experience the Perseid Meteor Shower.

The earth has one moon, 2160 miles in diameter, which revolves about the earth at a distance of about 250,000 miles. The moon takes one lunar month of about 28 days to make one complete revolution about the earth. The moon also rotates on its axis; the period of rotation is exactly the same as its period of revolution, causing us to see the same side of the moon at all times. The moon does not emit its own light; instead, it reflects light from the sun. Phases of the moon are caused by the position of the moon relative to the position of the sun. If the sun is behind or nearly behind the moon, it is the back face of the moon that is illuminated by the sun, and we do not see the illuminated surface. This is the *new moon*. If the sun is on the opposite side of the earth from the moon, the entire surface of the moon we can see is illuminated; this phase is the *full moon*. As the moon revolves around the earth, it changes position relative to the sun, and we see phases that go from new moon to crescent, quarter, gibbous, and then full. This is repeated in reverse order as the moon continues its path around the earth. (See Figure 12.19.)

The surface of the moon is peppered with craters thought to have occurred as the result of impact of meteors and other interplanetary debris. It has no atmosphere, and its pull of gravity is approximately 1/6 that of earth.

Eclipses of the moon (lunar eclipses) occur when the moon passes through the earth's shadow; these eclipses occur during the full moon. Eclipses of the sun (solar eclipses) occur when the moon passes between the sun and the earth causing its shadow to fall on the earth. Since the moon appears to be exactly the same size as the sun when viewed from earth, during a solar eclipse, the moon can completely block off the light of the sun.

The Universe

The Universe is thought to have originated some 20 billion years ago from a huge amount of densely compacted matter that underwent a

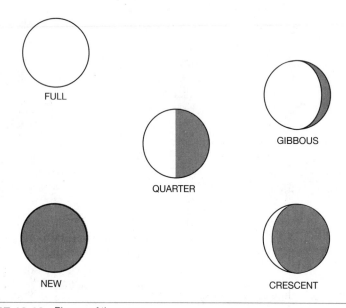

FIGURE 12.19 Phases of the moon

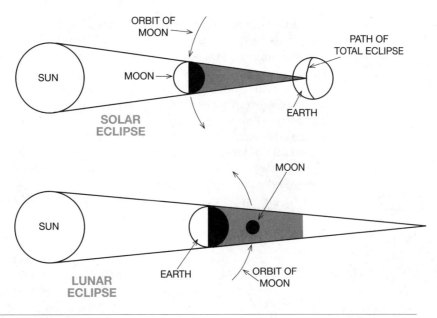

FIGURE 12.20   Lunar and solar eclipses

catastrophic explosion sending primal material out in all directions from this central region. Much of the material coalesced to form stars in huge regions which we know as galaxies. The galaxies, in turn, tended to hold together in galactic clusters. The Milky Way Galaxy is the galaxy in which our sun and our solar system is located. Our galaxy is spiral in shape and spins like a pinwheel, with the sun near one of the trailing edges. The galaxy rotates (and the sun and earth rotate with it) at a speed of 482,000 miles per hour. When we look at the night sky, everything we can see with the naked eye is located in our own Milky Way Galaxy. There is one exception—a faint galaxy that can barely be seen with the naked eye. This is the great Galaxy of Andromeda in the constellation, Andromeda, the closest galaxy to the Milky Way, approximately 2.2 million light years away. The closest star to our sun is Alpha Centauri which is 4.3 light years distant. It is thought that there are planetary systems on other suns; the closest such planetary system is associated with the star Alpha Centauri. Astronomers believe they may have discovered a Jupiter-sized planet orbiting a star some 235 trillion miles from earth in the constellation Pegasus (Begley, 1995, p. 86).

A *light year* is the distance light travels in one year; it can be calculated by multiplying the speed of light (186,000 miles per second or 300,000 kilometers per second) by 60 seconds in a minute, and then by

60 minutes in an hour, times 24 hours in a day, times 365$\frac{1}{4}$ days in a year. This turns out to be nearly 6 million million miles.

Astronomers have divided the night sky into regions called *constellations*. A constellation is to the night sky what a state is to a country: it is simply an artificial boundary. Somewhere within each constellation is a familiar grouping of stars after whose common name the constellation region is named.

In addition to stars and galaxies, space contains *nebulae*, some of which are clouds of gas coming together under gravitational force to form new stars. Other nebulae are the remains of stars that have completed their life cycles and have exploded because of mechanisms associated with the end of their life cycles, such as weakening gravitational forces.

Space Exploration

With the advent of the rocket, space travel became a matter of engineering and technology. Rockets are governed by Newton's Third Law of Motion which states that for every force there is an equal and opposite force. (See p. 408.) The huge rockets that launch space ships develop enough force to propel them into orbit. Artificial satellites remain in orbit because the force of their momentum equals the force of earth's gravity. Space vehicles effectively overcome the force of gravity, and, once in space, minor amounts of jet force can propel them great distances and can correct their paths. Space ships and artificial satellites that are in orbit around the earth remain in orbit because of the earth's gravitational pull; in this respect, they behave much like the moon or the planets as they revolve about the sun.

The space program is very expensive, and a continuing debate rages as to the advantages and disadvantages of expending huge sums of money on the program. Certainly communications technology is aided by artificial satellites placed in orbit around the earth. Weather forecasting is far more accurate with the weather satellites than it was before the space program. The Hubble Telescope has provided vast amounts of information about the nature of the Universe from its vantage point above the interference of the earth's atmosphere. However, space travel is time consuming; it takes a space vehicle nearly a year to reach Mars, our closest planetary neighbor. Should the space program be continued? This is a question individuals must answer for themselves.

References

Begley, S. (1995). Now there are 10. *Newsweek,* October 30, 1995.

Poincaré, H. (1902). *La Science et l'hypothèse.* Paris: E. Flammarion.

CHAPTER 13

The Elementary Science Education Professional

And gladly wolde he lerne, and gladly teche.

Geoffrey Chaucer,
The Canterbury Tales
(c. 1387), 1. 308

To teach is to learn twice over.

Joseph Joubert: *Pensées*
(1842)

As a teaching professional, you have tremendous opportunities to share successes, to contribute to discussions on open issues with other professionals, and to exert your professional influence on the direction education takes. You also have the responsibility for providing the best possible education for each individual child, for meeting the educational needs of the school, the community it serves, and the nation, and for keeping up with new curricular materials, new ideas about pedagogy, and current developments in the profession.

This chapter offers suggestions on how you can take advantage of the opportunity to influence education through making and justifying curriculum and methodology decisions, keeping up with new developments, and contributing to your personal professional growth and the growth of science education.

Decisions About Methodology

One of the most significant contributions you can make to your profession lies in the decisions you make about methodology and the manner in which you justify these decisions. In this text, many issues have been raised about elementary science teaching methodology, such as the following:

- Doing science *vs.* learning about science
- Deciding on goals of elementary science education
- Instructing from a constructivist perspective *vs.* imparting knowledge
- Teaching in an inquiry *vs.* an expository mode
- Identifying and accommodating individual learner differences
- Assessing children's accomplishments authentically
- Developing interdisciplinary studies *vs.* using a discipline-centered approach
- Including reading and writing in science
- Considering the influence of state and federal goals and state and district mandates
- Considering the role of standardized tests
- Keeping classroom order

We have urged you to weigh all sides of each issue with an open mind, and to formulate your own ideas concerning each issue.

CONSTRUCTING YOUR IDEAS 13.1
Explaining Your Science Program

Divide the members of your class into groups: pairs, small groups, or halves. One group takes the role of the new teacher in a school who has decided to implement a science teaching methodology developed as a result of this course. The other group takes the role of an administrator. The opening question of the administrator is, "Tell me what you plan to do with your science program, and why." Role play this for a while, and then reverse roles. Critique the discussions.

Did the teacher have a sound methodology in place? Was she able to justify it? Did she cite experts in the field? Professional societies? Research? Was she cognizant of opposing views? Was she sensitive to the needs of the local school and community? Had she considered all aspects, both pro and con? Was she thoroughly prepared? Was she able to provide satisfactory answers to the "administrator's" questions?

This exercise enables you to refine the philosophy of science education you have been developing, and state it in operational as well as theoretical terms, giving you a committed and firm foundation for the successful implementation of your elementary science program.

You now (or shortly will) have the opportunity to explain your methodological approach to colleagues, parents, administrators, concerned citizens, and other professionals. It is hoped that every teacher will be able to explain and defend his or her methodological decisions based on personal constructions of the research and the various positions, arguments, and situations.

Let us return to the concept of the metaphor. In Chapter One you were asked to select a metaphor for your role as an elementary science teacher. Look at it. Is it still valid? Or do you want to change it? Re-think this metaphor now, and decide on what it is to be. Remember that metaphors have been shown to be strong internal referents for teacher behavior, and that the metaphor chosen subtly but powerfully drives teachers' professional actions and decisions. Talk about the metaphor you now choose, trying to isolate all its implications. Then make your final decision.

Decisions About Curriculum

As has been suggested previously, there are three sides to the education triangle: what to teach, how to teach, and how to assess. This text is concerned primarily with how to teach and how to assess. However, there must be congruence between methodology and curriculum; thus attention also has been given to what to teach.

We have suggested it is better to teach the processes than the products of science. We have suggested that the products in the form of facts, concepts, generalizations, theories, and laws can be used as vehicles for process mastery—vehicles through which children learn to *do* science. We have suggested that integrated interdisciplinary approaches are more representative of real-world situations than the compartmentalized approach where science is taught separately and the three main branches of science are taught in isolation from each other.

Volumes have been written about the reform of science education; much of this material is concerned with the reform of science curriculum. The nation's leading science educators urge abandoning product-oriented science programs in favor of process-oriented inquiry constructivist approaches that teach children how to do science, and interdisciplinary approaches that are closely aligned with the way scientists do science, that capture children's interest, and that are meaningful to children.

However, in spite of decades of persuasive argument and overwhelming agreement on the part of educators, many science programs remain content-oriented. This is caused, in part, by the role standardized achievement tests have in driving the curriculum. It also is the result of public reaction to reports of declining achievement test scores, and the basic reluctance of policy makers and legislators to take the leap of faith to something new.

Today's elementary science teachers are faced with a curriculum dilemma characterized by forces of constraint and dedication to teaching science products on the one hand, and the relentless forces of science reform on the other.

Contemporary science education seeks to achieve three overarching goals:

1. Science as a process of inquiry and problem-solving
2. Sufficient working knowledge of science to deal effectively with societal and technical issues
3. Preparation of the next generation of scientists

To accomplish these goals, contemporary science curriculum development is guided by several broad considerations:

1. Process is more important than content.
2. Discipline boundaries among the sciences are softened.
3. Science is integrated with the rest of the curriculum.
4. Science is attached meaningfully to life.
5. Science content is based on fundamental scientific principles and concepts.

As a professional educator, you have the opportunity to participate in this continuing professional dialog about elementary science curriculum and to make informed decisions about what to teach in your elementary science program.

As William Glasser said, "We should never forget that people, not curriculum, are the desired outcomes of schooling. What we want to develop are students who have the skills to become active contributors to society, who are enthusiastic about what they have learned, and who are aware of how learning can be of use to them in the future" (1992, p. 694).

The Elementary Science Teacher as Researcher

Every teacher is a researcher. At a minimum, teachers reflect on lessons, assess the good points and the areas that were weak, and make changes to strengthen them. They revise the instruction to accommodate the changing needs of children. They reconstruct lessons to ensure that every child is successful. They develop assessment techniques that are authentic. They share successful teaching strategies with colleagues.

The time may come when teachers want to try out a whole new system, such as a different methodology or a different approach to curriculum. They often do this informally, comparing the results of two classes, or this year's class with last year's class. If the results seem to be better, the new system may be adopted.

Often, however, the research done by teachers never leaves the classroom or the school. It is considered experience, not research. Yet it is these very ideas that have been tried and proven in individual teachers' classrooms that can comprise a large portion of the research base. The ultimate goal of all effective research in science education is improving classroom practice. How do children best learn science? What works? What doesn't work? How effective are various teaching techniques and new and innovative teaching strategies? Teachers can and should play a significant role in that research.

Much research is conceived, planned, controlled, executed, and analyzed by college- and university-based researchers. They use children in teachers' classrooms for their subjects, imposing experimental conditions and controls to ensure validity. They select the questions to be investigated, design the experimental method, and formulate conclusions from the application of statistical procedures to show the significance (or lack of significance) of outcomes on the research hypothesis. The studies are published in journals teachers probably do not read, using language and statistical manipulations unfamiliar to teachers, about problems teachers probably are not faced with in the first place, suggesting solutions teachers probably would not find useful to implement.

Research tends to be a "one-way process that is done to teachers; their personal knowledge is discredited, and the researcher assumes an expert role as one who produces knowledge. As a result, the teacher's understanding of the classroom is unchanged and the researcher is not able to benefit from the teacher's personal knowledge and insights" (Gitlin, 1990, p. 445).

Many investigations are perceived by teachers as not relevant, and much of the research fails to help science teachers improve their science teaching.

> There is little reason to do research in science education unless there is a pay-off in the classroom. But this rarely happens. Teachers view most research findings as impractical, difficult to interpret, and rarely possible to implement (Hurd, 1986).

One solution to the dilemma about irrelevant and meaningless science education research is for teachers to become involved in research.

There are many ways teachers can get involved in research. One way is for them to collaborate with university researchers, providing their views and input.

Another, more powerful, way is for teachers to do it themselves. The National Association for Research in Science Teaching has coined the phrase, "Every Teacher a Researcher" (ETR) to demonstrate commitment to the notion that a large amount of meaningful, relevant, and valid research can be done by teachers in their own classrooms.

The research done by teachers researching their own classrooms is called *action research* or *applied research*. This type of research seeks to determine effectiveness of classroom practice. The term "action" comes from the idea that the teacher is a participator in the development of new knowledge. The study occurs while the teacher is teaching, and the teacher is part of the group under study. Action research is essential if changes to teaching practices are to occur, for it is action research that determines the ultimate effectiveness of any proposed change in classroom practice.

In action research, you systematically inquire into practice in your classroom and document the results following the paradigm of scientific inquiry. However, common sense investigation is not enough; to qualify as research, investigations must possess validity, and this occurs through systematic inquiry, documentation, and analysis of data. The steps are as follows:[1]

1. **State the problem or hypothesis.** The hypothesis may be a simple statement of what you think will happen as a result of doing what you plan to do, such as, "If I implement a hands-on approach, children should become more interested in science." Or it may be a statement of a problem such as, "I wonder what would happen if I took children outdoors every day to observe their natural surroundings?" In action research, the hypothesis or problem frequently emerges when a teacher notices a reaction to something being done

in the classroom, such as "I notice that when I provide simple hands-on activities, children get very involved in their own inquiries."

2. **Read the current literature** available on the subject to see what others have found out and how they proceeded.

3. **Identify the information needed to solve the problem.** This may include changes in student achievement, attitude, and interest, or changes in teacher attitude and interest, or, frequently, both.

4. **Select or develop instruments to gather the needed information.** It is important to identify the kinds of information available to you that will help you answer your question. Many objective tests are available to help the researcher gather quantitative data. Or you may wish to design your own. Attitude and interest surveys can be used. Videotaping, student journals, open-ended interviews, teachers' journals, observations, children's work samples, written records of formal discussions, numbers of times children go to the science center on their own, numbers of trips taken with parents to local museums, and so on, are all valid kinds of information that can be collected.

5. **Select the sample or group.** In action research, the group most often used is your class. Much has been written about the questionable validity of researchers using pre-selected samples of children such as the researcher's own class. There normally is nothing that can be done about this situation, and the consensus within the educational research community is that the disadvantages of a pre-selected sample are outweighed by the insights gained from action research. Since you are using your own class, you must be careful to be as objective as possible; be sure your own feelings do not color the data or conclusions. You also must be careful not to generalize the results of your work to all children. What worked in your class may and may not work in someone else's class. However, your research makes a significant contribution to the literature, and when many action researchers have studied the same type of problem, generalizations can be made; these generalizations often are more valid than those made from carefully selected random sampling of subjects in one location.

6. **Design the procedure for collecting the data.** In action research you do not need to utilize complicated statistical techniques; instead, you can utilize a qualitative approach which involves systematic and thorough descriptions of what you did and what the responses were. Keep notes, student portfolios, grades, records, student work, opinion polls, attitudinal assessments, and so on. Most action researchers keep daily journals in which they record their daily procedure and reflective interpretations. Videotapes of lessons can be analyzed

objectively when it comes time to analyze the data. It is well to collaborate with another teacher when doing action research, for your colleague often will be able to lend an objective eye to your data; this practice offers a reliability check referred to as *triangulation*. Your colleague can also run the camcorder for you, focusing on scenes that are germane to what you are seeking to learn, freeing you to concentrate on the teaching. You will have to spend time designing your investigation; your review of the literature may give you ideas. You will need to consider many factors such as when to implement the new system, what time of day to collect information, whether you need help (camcorder operator, objective observer, etc.), the format for the data (journal formats, test formats, questionnaire formats), and so on. The key to this step is to have an advance plan for how you will analyze the information. Then, you can work backward to be sure you get the right kind of data to enable you to do the analysis. However, in qualitative action research, the design of the study may emerge during its implementation. As you proceed, if what you are doing does not seem to be answering your question, you can revise the procedure.

7. **Collect the data.** This is the implementation phase. You might want to get used to the idea that Murphy's Law will be in full force during this stage: "If anything *can* go wrong, it *will*." Many action researchers do a short version of the project called a *pilot study* before they do the full-fledged implementation, to work out the snags. However, you must be certain that whatever you do as a pilot program does not provide either the children or you with preconceived notions that could contaminate the data once you start the real procedure.

8. **Analyze the data.** This involves pouring over all the information you obtained to see what makes sense. You have already planned how you are going to analyze the information, so now you do it. However, much new data that you never considered previously will present itself. Thus, it is entirely possible that you may find unexpected results. Sometimes these results are valid and become part of the analysis; sometimes they suggest additional avenues of new research or ways of continuing the original research. Enlisting the assistance of a colleague to examine the data independently helps ensure valid interpretations.

9. **Prepare the report.** Whatever research you do, it is imperative that you get the results out to others. This could mean sharing your work with focus groups at your school. It could mean publishing the work in professional journals or presenting it at professional conferences (or both). The typical research report contains the following elements:

■ Statement of problem or hypothesis
■ Survey of relevant literature
■ Detailed description of procedure, with instruments identified, the kinds of data they collect, and an indication of the reliability and validity of each
■ Your analysis of the data
■ Implications for the classroom teacher

In evaluating quality of research, the researcher looks at the following:[2]

1. The match between the research questions and the method employed
2. The match between the research questions and type of data collected and the analysis of the data
3. Successful and appropriate application of data collection and analysis techniques
4. Value—can the research be usefully applied
5. Ability to withstand critical analysis (Conclusions have to be warranted from the data presented; are there additional or different conclusions or explanations?)[3]

Student teaching is a good time to work on an action research project. Select a mentor from your college, and ask your cooperating teacher for permission and assistance.

A word of caution is in order. Research is different from trying out new ideas or new activities which fall under the category of novel ideas, and that are implemented primarily to lend spice and uniqueness to your class. New ideas, hints to the teacher, and the like describe better, new, or unique ways of doing something already known to have an effect. For example, one might try out a new way of teaching the types of clouds, and find it "works" better than other ways. This would be an improvement on teaching clouds, and should be published. In research, the goal is to try to establish some degree of cause and effect or to provide explanations for why something may have occurred: the understandings and insights that emerge from field work and subsequent analysis. For example, a research project might be undertaken to see if a more hands-on approach to science would result in improved student attitudes toward learning science. Or a research project might seek to describe the attitudes of children engaged in an active recycling project.

Professional Organizations

Teachers of elementary grades are given an impossible task. They are expected to know about all subjects and to teach all things well. No one can possibly keep up with everything! So, in this age of specialization, it is suggested you single out one area that has become of particular interest to you on which to focus your continued professional development. Become an expert in that area; others will look to you for expertise in your area, and you will find yourself assuming a leadership role in that field.

The area may be subject-specific, such as mathematics, language arts, reading, music, science, physical education, social studies, and so on. Or it may focus more on specific methodologies, such as teaching learning-disabled or gifted children, preschool children, or children with special needs. You have the opportunity to assume an active role in the field where your interest lies. You can join the professional societies, subscribe to their publications, submit manuscripts for publication, and attend their national, state, and regional meetings as participant and as presenter of the results of your work.

This section describes the professional organizations which elementary teachers interested in science might wish to consider.

The National Science Teachers Association (NSTA) is the largest science teacher's organization in the nation. Its purpose is to stimulate, improve, and coordinate science teaching and learning.

NSTA publishes four journals, all of which welcome teachers' classroom ideas and reports of teachers' action research. *Science and Children* is devoted to science teaching in preschool through middle school. Articles include descriptions of innovative projects and programs, descriptions of hands-on activities, reports of research in science education, informational pieces, and helpful hints.

Science Scope focuses on the unique needs and characteristics of children of middle and junior high school age. Articles include ideas for laboratory activities and demonstrations, and discussions of issues important to teachers of middle level science.

The Science Teacher focuses on high school science, and the *Journal of College Science Teaching* focuses on the teaching and learning of science in college.

In addition, NSTA publishes a bi-monthly newsletter, *NSTA Reports!* which contains articles of current interest and importance to all science educators.

NSTA holds an annual conference attended by thousands of teachers from all grade levels, at which thousands of presentations are made, many by classroom teachers presenting new and innovative classroom teaching ideas and the results of individual research projects. NSTA also holds several regional conferences each year. Each state has its own state science association concerned with helping classroom teachers at all levels improve their teaching of science and children's learning of science. Most states have annual association meetings at which classroom ideas, papers on current paradigms, and issues in science education, classroom ideas, and results of action research projects are presented.

The National Association for Research in Science Teaching (NARST) promotes scholarly research and discussion of issues in the field of science education. The association publishes a monthly journal, the *Journal of Research in Science Teaching*, containing manuscripts of research on science teaching. The articles are thoroughly researched and thoroughly reviewed, and seek to impact science teaching practice. NARST hosts an annual conference where panel discussions, position papers, and research papers dealing with science education are presented.

The Association for the Education of Teachers in Science focuses on research in science education teaching and learning and the application of research in the classroom. AETS publishes two journals. *Science Education* contains descriptive articles and research reports dealing with curriculum, instruction, assessment, science teacher education, learning, current issues and trends, and international science education. The *Journal of Science Teacher Education* contains articles on methodology, instructional design, current science education issues, position statements, new ideas, and consolidated research findings and critical reviews of literature pertaining to professional development in science teaching. Both journals publish results of action research.

AETS holds an annual meeting at which papers about new developments in science education are presented. There are several regional associations affiliated with AETS, and each of those holds its own annual conference; these conferences provide excellent forums for classroom teachers to present the results of their action research. Certain of the regional associations publish their own journals; for example, the *Journal of Elementary Science Education* is published by the Southeastern Association for the Education of Teachers in Science (SAETS).

Each state has an Academy of Science which provides a forum for interaction among professors, students, and teachers on a variety of scientific topics; many have sections devoted to science education. Each state also has a Junior Academy of Science which promotes science among elementary, middle grade and secondary students.

There are literally dozens of additional science-oriented organizations, some with specialized focus such as the Sierra Club and the Audubon Society. The elementary science teacher desiring to get involved with science will not have a difficult time finding the organization the best suits her needs and interests.

Excellence in Science Teaching

What constitutes excellence in elementary science teaching? Penick and Yager (1993) found several common characteristics:

1. Excellent science teachers give up on textbook-oriented science and develop their own programs that are relevant and responsive to the needs of children and the community. Programs are discovery in orientation and hands-on in nature.
2. Excellent elementary science programs focus more on process than on content. The teachers develop materials and kits and package them for easy distribution to all teachers.
3. Excellent elementary science programs provide much inservice training, and have strong central and building administration support.
4. Excellent elementary science programs are considered to be in a continuous state of evolution.

Yager (1988) formed additional generalizations:

1. Effective teachers tend to reach out and to seek new ideas.
2. Increased preparation in science content is not a significant factor in differentiating between the most and the least effective science teachers.
3. Effective teachers elect to participate in several professional growth experiences per year, such as in-service programs and conferences.

Teaching science in the elementary grades is not difficult. Children love science, and successful teachers encourage them to wonder, to explore, and to construct their own meanings. Excellent elementary science teachers stimulate children to ask their own questions about phenomena that are meaningful and interesting to them, to develop their own methods of investigating these questions using the scientific processes, and to validate their conclusions through connections with their prior knowledge and through the presence of both explanatory and predictive power. Excellent elementary science teachers challenge children to do science the way scientists do science, using the world and all fields of knowledge as the arena for the development of scientific literacy. Excellent elementary science teachers involve *all* children in scientific inquiry, regardless of gender, ethnicity, academic ability, or any other factor.

By using the constructivist approach suggested in this book, you can develop an elementary science program that meets the needs of all children, provides the foundation for the academic challenges that lie ahead, and prepares them for a lifetime of successful learning.

Conclusion

The professional educator makes decisions about curriculum and methodology based on sound pedagogical theory, research, and the standards of the professional societies, and is responsible for keeping up with new curricular materials, new ideas about pedagogy, and current developments in the profession. Many opportunities are provided by national, state, regional, and local science teachers associations for elementary science teachers to attend conferences where they can share their experiences and expertise with each other. Research in science education is vital to establishing best ways of teaching science and most appropriate curriculum. The professional educator is in a unique position to undertake action research projects and share the results of this research with the professional community through conference papers and publications. Through such activities, the professional elementary science teacher engages in lifelong learning.

CHAPTER 13   Additional Questions for Discussion

1. Cite the current professional literature that supports the system of elementary science education you have constructed, and describe the nature of each.
2. Prepare a statement of philosophy that will guide you in teaching elementary science. (See Constructing Your Ideas 2.11, p. 53, for guidance.)
3. Discuss the desirability of preservice teachers becoming involved in action research during their field experiences. Discuss the extent to which teachers can get involved in action research during their first one or two years of service.

Notes

1. Adapted from Ary, D., Jacobs, L. C., & Razavieh, A. (1990, p. 381).

2. From a seminar on Contemporary Research Paradigms held at the annual meeting of the National Association for Research in Science Teaching, Boston, MA, March 12, 1992.

3. The National Science Teachers Association has adapted a position statement urging that research in science education be relevant, meaningful, rigorous, and readily accessible to teachers," (National Science Teachers Association, 1992).

References

Ary, D., Jacobs, L. C. & Razavieh, A. (1990). *Introduction to research in education,* Fourth edition. Forth Worth, TX: Holt, Rinehart and Winston, Inc.

Chaucer, G. (1995). *The Canterbury Tales.* San Marino, CA.: Huntington Library Press.

Gitlin, A. D. (1990). Educative research, voice, and school change. *Harvard Educational Review,* 60(4), 443–466.

Glasser, W. (1992). The quality school curriculum. *Phi Delta Kappan,* May, 1992, 690–694.

Hurd, P. D. (1986). Issues linking research to science teaching. ERIC Information Bulletin No. 1. ERIC Document No. ED 271 293.

Joubert, J. (1966). *Pensees.* Paris: Union General D'Editions.

Penick, J. E. and Yager, R. E. (1993). Learning from excellence: Some elementary exemplars. *Journal of Elementary Science Education* 5(1), 1–9.

Research in science education. (1992). *NSTA Reports!.* National Science Teachers Association, 1742 Connecticut Avenue, N.W., Washington, D.C. 10009.)

Yager, R. E. (1988). Differences between most and least effective science teachers. *School Science and Mathematics,* 88(4), 301–307.

PART III

Back to the Future

CHAPTER 14

A Model of Teaching
By Listening

In this text, you have constructed your own meaningful and valid conceptualizations of the elementary science program. You have taken innumerable factors into account in coming to these constructions, such as the process-oriented inquiry methodology, the amount and kind of science content used to teach the processes, methods of assessment, and the enormously wide and varied differences among children in the classroom. It has been proposed that children learn best that which is meaningful to them; yet not all children consider the same topic meaningful at the same time. It has been suggested that children begin their understanding of science with preconceived notions, and that they construct and reconstruct these ideas in increasingly sophisticated forms as they experience new phenomena; yet each child comes to the class with a different set of preconceived notions and prior experiences. It will occur to the perceptive student that the ultimate in science education would be for each child potentially to be studying something different at the same time.

This chapter offers a model of teaching science so that it is maximally meaningful to all children: *a model of teaching by listening*.

A CONSTRUCTIVIST EXPLORATION OF MOTORS

I once had a group of four eighth grade boys in junior high school science who, for seven years, had been learning that they weren't very smart, that they couldn't succeed because they couldn't (or wouldn't) read, and that they needed constant watching because if they were left alone, even for a moment, they would cause trouble.

You can imagine that these boys really felt great about themselves. But, in fact, they did! They were the most popular boys in school because of the things they did and got away with. They were highly creative. With the kinds of restrictions placed on them by family and school, it took a great deal of creative planning for them successfully to pull off some of the things they got by with.

But academically, they were a most unhappy lot.

One day, early in the class, I talked with them, trying to find out what would motivate these boys in science. I reasoned they were not learning any science out of the textbooks, anyway, so, if we could find something they were interested in, they just *might* learn something.

They responded that they wanted to study motors. Not out of books, but out of motors.

They outlined their goals—what they wanted to learn. Their goals were fuzzy, but basically they wanted to find out how each part of the motor worked. Not only the pistons, but *all* the parts.

So we requisitioned an abandoned V-8 engine and secured it in the back of the science classroom. The boys brought in tools from home, and they started taking the thing apart. As each part came off, they examined it and tried to figure out how *that* part fit in with the whole engine, understanding that without each part, the engine would not work. They were successful for some time, but eventually the day came when they could not figure out what a certain part was for. I knew next to nothing about automotive mechanics, and was unable to help. So they had to find out in a different way. They looked in the textbooks, but none had information about motors. So they borrowed automotive repair manuals to read about how the component works and how it relates to the rest of the motor. Reading??? For those boys???

They delighted in explaining the motor to onlookers, verbalizing what they had learned and teaching the onlookers something they might not otherwise have learned. They decided to write descriptions of how the parts operated; the descriptions were not lengthy, but they were accurate and concise.

There were no discipline problems—lots of noise, but no behavior problems. The boys were far too busy investigating the motor to be bothered with trying to get attention or create difficult situations for the teacher.

They pursued this project for some three months, and when it was over, at their request, an automotive mechanic quizzed them on their understanding of how motors work. They passed with flying colors (Martin, 1975).

The Need for a Different Model

Consider this scenario. It is early in the spring, and the pollen in the air is profuse. Children are asking questions about what pollen is, what it looks like, and why it causes allergies to act up. So you decide to capitalize on the children's demonstrated interest and provide a lesson on pollen. You collect pollen from several different kinds of plants—pine trees, hardwood trees, flowering plants, and grass—and you set up a microscope so the children can examine the pollen. The idea is for children to observe what pollen looks like and to observe and describe the subtle but definite differences among the various kinds of pollen. You also plan to extend this concept to air pollution in general; for the next lesson, you will have children paint a thin layer of clear petroleum jelly on one-foot-square pieces of black paper which they will suspend outdoors in various locations. They will count the number of grains that stick to the paper after, say, one full day, and use the data to formulate hypotheses about the relationship between location and concentration of impurities in the air.

During the pollen lesson, a child unexpectedly begins asking questions about frogs. It seems he has discovered that a pond near his house is home to many frogs, and he wonders how they got there, what they eat, how they reproduce, and so on.

CONSTRUCTING YOUR IDEAS 14.1
How Can Teachers Accommodate the Interests of All Children?

What can you do about this situation? Before you go any further, discuss this as a class.

There are several ways you can handle this situation. (1) You can tell the child to wait until the topic of frogs comes up. (2) You can tell the child that you will be happy to begin a study of frogs after the study of air pollution is complete. (3) You can suggest that child spend his free time pursuing references on frogs. (4) You can try to integrate the subject of frogs with the current lesson. None of these options encourages the child to pursue his own interest. Your responses seek to preserve the integrity of the lesson you have planned. They send the message that the lesson you have planned is more important than some quixotic interest the child happens to have at the moment. Your hope is that the child will pursue the investigations of pollen and air pollution you have planned, even though he seems to be more interested in frogs.

There is another solution. You could encourage the child to begin an independent study of frogs instead of continuing with the lesson you had planned. This, of course, means that you will have two lessons going on at the same time: one on pollen and air pollution for most of the children in the class, and one on frogs for one child.

CONSTRUCTING YOUR IDEAS 14.2
Reaction to Multiple Simultaneous Inquiries

What is your reaction to the solution presented above? Discuss this as a class.

All teachers are faced with these situations; most try to resolve the issue by developing the most interesting lessons they can to capture the full attention of the children. However, the question remains in the back of the teacher's mind: would children do better in science if they were studying what *really* interests them?

A Model of Teaching By Listening

The model of teaching by listening addresses this very issue.[1]

The science education research agenda has focused, for many years, on how to provide *meaning* to science education. A significant indicator of meaning is *interest*. This is not new. Ausubel said that the most important factor influencing what a child learns is what he already knows (Ausubel, Novak & Hanesian, 1978). Marlene Scardamalia said, at a Holmes Group seminar in 1988, "The way you start is by asking students what they want to know" (1988). Jack Easley proposed that teachers *listen* rather than *talk* to students (1990). He called this concept "Teaching by Listening," and it is this term that provides the title for the model.

The Model of Science Teaching by Listening is predicated on the idea that topics which are of interest to the children carry inherent meaning, and that only the children themselves know what is interesting to them. Teachers must *listen* to children to find out what is meaningful. Novak (1992) defined meaningful learning as the constructive integration of thinking, feeling, and acting leading to human empowerment. *Meaningfulness* of science thus becomes child-centered and child-generated. It becomes relevant and non-imposed. Teachers listen not only to children's interests, but also to what they are thinking, how they are constructing information, and how they are validating the conceptualizations they construct. Children talk first, and teachers facilitate as necessary.

The model is cyclical and involves four phases: (1) topic selection, (2) plan of action, (3) activities, and (4) evaluation.

The model involves close and continuous interaction between groups of children investigating the same topic and their teacher. Initially a team is formed of the teacher and several children with similar interests. In the

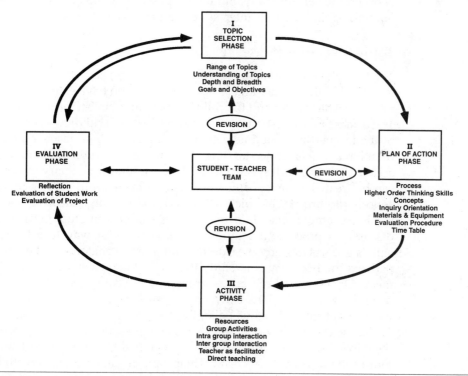

FIGURE 14.1 A model of teaching by listening

topic selection phase, this team establishes the specific topic to be studied based largely upon interest expressed by the children.

Next, a *plan of action* is developed by the team and details the specific activities to be pursued. Children's abilities, learning style preferences, the availability of materials, resources, and facilities, and the teacher's prior knowledge of the children and academic goals for the class influence the choice of activities. A time table and methods of reporting progress and achievement are established during this phase.

During the *activities* phase, the teacher acts as facilitator of the children's learning. The children work in groups while the teacher observes and listens, offering helpful guidance and clarification as required. During this phase, much valuable information about process skill mastery, content acquisition, personal learning style, and other factors is obtained by both children and teacher to help guide the direction of current and future studies.

The *evaluation* phase completes the cycle, and serves as the transition between the current study and the proposed new topic. New groups are formed, again based on interest, and a new cycle begins.

Topic Selection Phase

The first phase is the topic selection phase. To get started, an *ad hoc* team is formed of the teacher and several children who have expressed similar interests. The teacher and the children meet to establish the specific topic. The teacher asks questions of the children, and the children ask questions of the teacher in a safe interactive dynamic until both teacher and children have a clear understanding of what is to be studied. Topics can be selected from the full spectrum of science or interdisciplinary topics, and can be treated in many different ways, from in-depth studies of single concepts to broad, "big picture" overviews of a large area.

For example, one child may express interest in studying frogs. As discussions proceed, it may emerge that the best way to achieve the child's goals is to study the external and internal anatomy of the frog. Or, perhaps the best way is to study the frog's interaction with its environment. Or, perhaps both are warranted. In addition, as other children overhear the discussions between the teacher and the child, they may want to get involved, thus enlarging the group.

In the case of the boys who studied engines, the topic of engines was the only interest they had. All four of them had the same interest, and all four of them worked as a team. Their topic began as a detailed study of a very large area of inquiry: the way engines work.

The teacher with a new class possesses limited information about the children. However, as the children work, both child and teacher gain more and more insight into the educative process for that child. The teacher plays a critical role in helping children organize inquiry skills, process skills, higher order thinking, and so on, into their proposed studies.

Concurrent with topic selection is determining one or more goals or objectives to be accomplished as a result of having studied the proposed topic. Indeed, when a group of children works on the same topic, the objectives often differ for each child in the group. Studies may be qualitative or quantitative in nature. They are always investigative and always inquiry-oriented. Membership of the group may change during this initial phase as the congruency between their interests and the emerging topic of study is seen.

Factors influencing selection of the topic to be studied include at least the following:

Child-Oriented Considerations
- Interest
- Meaningfulness of topic
- Abilities
- Developmental needs
- Social interaction needs
- Experience with group work
- Reading ability
- Personal factors: gender, age, intelligence, socioeconomic status, culture
- Home factors
- Attitudes

Academic Considerations
- Prior science experiences
- Prior science achievement
- Academic needs and goals: process skills and content
- Problem solving needs
- Level of understanding
- Higher-Order thinking skills
- Understanding of scientific values
- Academic outcomes: Program goals, scientific and technological literacy

---

Plan Of Action Phase

The next phase of the model is the Plan of Action phase. Having established the topic to be studied and the goals or objectives of the study, the team formulates a plan of action. This plan details the specific activities to be pursued. Children have their own ideas of what to do, and the teacher has her own idea of what the children ought to do in the way of developing process skills, higher order thinking, conceptual understandings, and so on. The activities might include reading, performing lab activities, doing computer work, viewing videos, working with interactive computer and videodisc set-ups, and a whole host of other learning experiences.

The specific activities are listed, together with the resources to be utilized for each activity. The specific activities planned depend to a large extent on what material is available. A check-list of resources to be considered includes at least the following:

- Books
- Audio-Visual Materials (charts, maps, drawings, models, videos, films, filmstrips, etc)
- Computers
- Computer-Assisted Instruction programs
- Home computers with modems
- Interactive videodiscs
- Library materials
- Concept maps
- Laboratory materials and equipment
- Lectures and demonstrations on videotape and audiotape.
- People

Various learning strategies are considered, such as the following:

- Independent study
- Group work
- Grouping by interest
- Cooperative learning
- Question and answer and discussion sessions in groups or with the teacher
- Teacher demonstrations
- Inquiry and guided discovery activities
- Whole-class activities

During this phase, the team decides how to evaluate the work and how the children will report progress to the teacher. Reporting options available include at least the following:

- Written and verbal reports
- Demonstrations
- Tapes
- Video productions
- Drawings
- Model construction
- Concept map development
- Poster presentations
- Class presentations
- Panel discussions

A time line for activities and completion is also established. It is important to note here that this plan of action is not set in cement—it is the team's best approximation at the time. Revision is crucial to the success of the program.

Activity Phase

Children now start their investigations. In a well laid-out classroom, children know where the resources are, and they assemble what they need: table space, materials, things they bring in from home, reference books, visuals, models, videos, computer programs, CD-Roms, videodiscs, and so on.

The classroom is busy. One group is dissecting a frog, using models, lab manuals, and drawings to guide their work. Once they perfect the technique, they plan to do demonstration dissections for children in the lower grades. Another group of children is watching a video (with earphones) or a filmstrip on the human circulatory system, relating what they see and hear to what they read in texts in their efforts to develop understanding of how the human body functions. Still another group is drawing charts of observations of the night sky they made over the past two or three nights, checking their charts against the references. There is a group dissecting a worm; it is their first dissection, so from time to time, they seek guidance from the group dissecting the frog. Another group is investigating friction using inclined boards with various surfaces. Some children are taking notes. Some are writing in their journals. Some are drawing. Some have left the room to utilize other resources. Locations may include the classroom, study carrels, the hallway, resource rooms, playground, school grounds, home, and computer modem connections between home and school or on-line resources

The teacher is very busy, moving from group to group, listening to the children, asking questions, probing for understandings, and challenging new understandings. The room is noisy, but everyone soon gets used to the din as they focus on their own activities. Children are busy figuring out things for themselves.

Groups visit other groups and individual children get ideas about what they want to do and what they do not want to do. Groups welcome these visits, for it gives them an opportunity to explain what they are doing and studying.

Revision is the key to this phase. The teacher understands the children better, and the children increase their awareness of themselves, each other, and the topics under study. As a result, the plan, the objectives, or even the topic itself may be revised to reflect this new and increased understanding.

For example, a group of children deciding to study the human circulatory system may find the topic is too specific, and revise their topic to include the interaction of the circulatory system with other systems of the body. A group working on friction may find they do not understand how to isolate the variables in complex systems, so decide to focus on a simpler inquiry such as the relationship between degree of incline of a board and the time it takes a cart to roll down the board. Once they gain familiarity with isolating variables, they will return to the friction investigations.

From time to time, a team forms a huddle, and they rethink a topic, or they hold an evaluation session. Or, a newly-formed group may need to begin their topic selection and plan of action phases. Sometimes the teacher pulls the whole class together for an item of interest to all—a demonstration, a guest speaker, a contemporary event. Now and then, the teacher provides direct instruction for a group.

Evaluation Phase

The final phase in this cyclical model is the evaluation phase. When the investigation or project is complete, the children submit the agreed-upon evaluation, and the team spends a few minutes reflecting on the just-completed topics: understandings, thinking, processes, concepts, strengths, areas for improvement, work habits, acceptance of responsibility, most effective activities, least effective activities, and so on.

The evaluation is a continuous process. Under teacher encouragement, the children are constantly evaluating themselves with respect to academic goals, inquiry skills, processes, thinking, learning styles, and so on.

At the conclusion of the project and its evaluation, the teacher prepares a formal assessment which documents (1) the child's performance relative to self (Were the objectives met? Were the developmental goals met? Were the time goals met?) and (2) performance relative to norms based on standardized test results, criterion-referenced test results, and national norms (science content, processes, concepts, understandings, and thinking and reasoning skills attained). In the post-project conference, children and the teacher discuss the children's overall performance, focusing primarily on mutually increased understanding of each child's academic needs, developmental needs, interests, abilities, and attitudes. A progress report is sent to parents (Figure 14.2), and the information is recorded in a permanent file (Figure 14.3) which forms a record of the child's progress and is forwarded to the science teacher in the next grade.

The Next Cycle

Many academic and developmental factors emerge as a result of a study, and these factors are taken into account when the next topic is planned. When the boys who investigated the workings of the V-8 engine had passed their "final exam," it was time for them to select the next topic. You will recall that, though they never had read for information in the past, they found it necessary to read to obtain enough information to answer their questions about the workings of the engine. This project helped those boys to accomplish a heretofore impossible goal: to want to read for information. This desire to read for information became apparent as they selected their next topics. All four boys chose topics which required substantial reading such as archaeology and astronomy. In my planning conferences with them, I explained that the topics they had selected would require a lot of reading. That was fine with them. They had always wanted to learn about these things.

Management

As this system progresses, the teacher builds a repertoire of projects undertaken by prior groups in the form of outlines that list activities done previously and materials available for the study. These are used to form the basis of similar studies for other groups interested in the same topic so the teacher does not have to start from scratch each time. It also may be possible to enlist the help of other teachers (especially if you are in a team-teaching situation), parents, and older children.

It is well to start on this type of science program very slowly. You might want to limit the diversity of projects in your classroom to accommodate only those who are having difficulty with the material you are presenting. To scrap the class-oriented approach and move to this model in one fell-swoop is folly. It takes time to prepare; it takes time for children to assume their responsibility; and it takes time for children to become adjusted to this way of doing business. Children need much

TEACHING BY LISTENING PROGRESS REPORT

Pupil _____ Date _____

Unit Studied _____ Time Period _____

PART I—COMPETITION WITH SELF

This part shows how well your child has been working and learning compared with ability as shown on standardized test results and classroom performance.

During this time period, your child's success in fulfilling potential is rated as follows:

_____   Your child is performing within ability range.
_____   Your child's performance has been exceptionally good.
_____   Your child is performing below ability range.

PART II—RELATIVE PERFORMANCE

This part reflects your child's achievement level in learning experiences compared with the achievement levels for the class as a whole.

At this date, your child's relative achievement is rated as follows:

_____   Above average
_____   Average
_____   Needs improvement

CONFERENCE NOTES

_____   I feel that a conference with you would be helpful. Parents are invited to initiate conferences at any time and may do so by calling the school office.

COMMENTS:

_____

_____

_____

_____   _____
Teacher Signature   Date

FIGURE 14.2

TEACHING BY LISTENING CUMULATIVE RECORD

CUMULATIVE RECORD OF PROGRESS IN SCIENCE

Name _____ Year _____ Grade _____

Inferred Academic Ability _____ based on _____

Demonstrated Interest in Science _____

Standardized Test Results

Test							
National Score							

Time Period	Unit	Progress In Regard to Self [1]			Progress In Regard to Norm [2]			Comments And Conference Notes
		S	EX	BR	AB	AV	NI	

(1) S: Satisfactory progress
     EX: Exceptional progress
     BR: Below ability range

(2) AB: Above average
     AV: Average
     NI: Needs Improvement

FIGURE 14.3

modeling at first to show them how to make decisions and perform investigations with minimal teacher help, especially if they have grown accustomed to learning about science and doing science activities by the numbers.

I found that daily journal entries helped keep children focused on their project, and helped remind them each day where they left off the day before so they did not have to ask the teacher every time. However, children need help at first in making journal entries. I also found that providing storage space for each child helped them keep track of their materials; when the time for science is over, children merely slide their things into the designated area, knowing it will be there the next time they have science.

Behavior management ceases to be a problem, for all children are interested in what they are doing, and they pursue their studies with a vigor and intensity seldom seen in traditional settings. However, it is impossible to insist on silence. The room is noisy, but creatively noisy.

Concluding Remarks

Children can only learn what is meaningful to them. In science, there are so many topics to choose from that every child can find topics that are meaningful. Yet, science educators persist in covering certain prescribed content out of fear that, if children are not exposed to every science topic in a systematic manner, their science education will be lacking, the United States will continue to plummet on the international science report card, and we will continue to register declines in world "scienceship."

Leaders in education and business for many years have urged defocusing from content-oriented science programs and, instead, working toward a science education that teaches "less so it can be taught better" (American Association for the Advancement of Science, 1989); that teaches science not as a body of knowledge, but as a way of thinking (Sagan, 1989); that focuses on children rather than teachers (Glasser, 1990). Outcomes of science education are described today in terms of the "what," and "how" and "why" of scientific investigation rather than the accumulation of facts (Aldridge, 1989), and in terms of scientific literacy (Hurd, 1986). Ingenious instructional techniques designed to engage children more actively in the learning process are being advanced. Teachers are urged to take hard looks at the nature of learners and to use their findings to devise appropriate teaching strategies that teach all children how to do science, and encourage all children to make choices about scientific values. Integration of science with other subject matter, innovative instructional practices, and the unification of topics in science, technology, and society are among the contemporary goals for quality science education.

The literature abounds with descriptions of individual differences among learners: learning style, cognitive style, learning modality, intelligence, creativity, reasoning ability, special physical and cognitive needs, and on and on and on. No teacher can possibly know each and every individual difference which characterizes each and every individual child. Teachers, however, are urged to teach such that each individual child can learn maximally, given the child's unique learning style. Expository teaching methodologies, of necessity, are directed at the non-existent middle-of-the-road child. Free discovery teaching may leave children so much in charge of their own learning process that they may fail to advance to full potential or to meet specific objectives.

The Model of Teaching by Listening is a child-focused science teaching strategy which takes into account scientific processes, scientific content, the myriad of individual differences among children, and learning by doing. The basic assumption of the model is that if children are studying something that interests them, they are more likely to learn than if they are required to study something solely because the teacher said so. The certainty of each child learning *something* is preferable to the possibility of children *not* learning.

There are concerns with this model. The most frequently addressed deal with children's freedom and the lack of methodical coverage of content. These concerns are more a matter of perception than reality. Children are not treated permissively. They have the freedom to choose, but they also have responsibility and accountability for their studies. Concerning content coverage, it has been my experience that children do, in fact, study the traditional amount of content. They may cover it in different ways, and it may take longer, but they do cover it.

Teaching in this manner is difficult. But, as Glasser says, "Being an effective teacher may be the most difficult of all common jobs in our society" (1990).

> *The true scientist never loses the faculty of amazement. It is the essence of his being.*
>
> Hans Selye, *Newsweek*, March 31, 1958

Note

1. I am indebted to Dr. Edward C. Lucy, Professor of Science Education, Georgia State University, for guidance in preparing this chapter.

References

Aldridge, B. G. (1989). *Essential changes in secondary school science: scope, sequence, and coordination.* Washington, DC: National Science Teachers Association.

American Association for the Advancement of Science. (1989). *Project 2061: Science for all Americans.* Washington, DC: American Association for the Advancement of Science.

Ausubel, D. P., Novak, J. D., and Hanesian, H. (1978). *Educational psychology: A cognitive view,* Second Education. New York, NY: Holt, Rinehart and Winston, p. iv.

Easley, J. (1990). Guest Editorial: Could we make a breakthrough for an at-risk nation? *Journal of Research in Science Teaching, 27*(7), 623–624.

Glasser, W. (1990). The quality school. *Phi Delta Kappan,* February, 1990, 52–62.

Hurd, P. D. (1986). Perspectives for the reform of science education. *Phi Delta Kappan,* January, 1986.

Martin, D. J. (1975). Individualizing junior high science. *The Science Teacher, 42*(3).

Novak, J. D. (1992). The current status of Ausubel's assimilation theory of learning. Paper presented at the 65th annual meeting of the National Association for Research in Science Teaching, Boston, MA, March 23, 1992; personal communication same date.

Sagan, C. (1989). Why we need to understand science. *Parade Magazine.* September 10, 1989.

Scardamalia, M. (1988). From *Tomorrow's Schools, Seminar One: Models of Learning, A Summary.* The Holmes Group, 501 Erickson Hall, East Lansing, MI 48824-1034.

Selected Sources of Free and Inexpensive Materials

American Association for the Advancement of Science
1333 H Street, NW
Washington, DC 20005

> The AAAS sponsors a number of educational programs and also maintains networks of scientists who visit elementary school classrooms. Write for information.

American Chemical Society
Education Division
1155 16th Street, NW
Washington, DC 20036

> Free materials on teaching chemistry are available.

American Gas Association
Public Relations
1515 Wilson Boulevard
Arlington, VA 22209

> Free educational materials are available on energy and the gas industry.

American Nuclear Society
555 North Kensington Avenue
LaGrange Park, IL 60525

> Ask for teaching materials; specify general age range. Also request to be placed on the mailing list for *re-Actions*, a newsletter on atomic energy published five times a year.

American Textile Manufacturers Institute
1801 K Street, NW
Washington, DC 20006
> Free and inexpensive teaching materials are available on manufactured dry goods.

Biological Sciences Curriculum Study
830 North Tejon Street, Suite 405
Colorado Springs, CO 80903-4720

> Ask to be placed on mailing list for BSCS Newsletter, *BSCS—The Natural Selection*. Contains recent information on life sciences and inquiry science teaching.

Friends Of the Earth
530 7th Street, SE
Washington, DC 20003

> Materials concerning the preservation of the rainforests of the world are available.

The Garden Club of America
598 Madison Avenue
New York, NY 10022

> Write for free information on water conservation.

Invent America
U. S. Patent Model Foundation
1331 Pennsylvania Ave., NW
Washington, DC 20004

> This organization sponsors an annual invention contest for elementary schools and provides materials for classroom programs.

Marine Debris Information Center
1725 De Sales St., NW
Washington, DC 20036

> This group offers free educational materials concerning preservation of our waterways.

National Aeronautics and Space Administration

> NASA operates Teacher Resource Centers throughout the country to provide educators with NASA-related materials for use in the classroom. Materials include classroom activities, lesson plans, teacher guides, slides, audio tapes, and video tapes. Contact the NASA center that serves your state, or
>> George C. Marshall Space Flight Center
>> One Tranquility Drive
>> Huntsville, AL 35807

National Oceanic and Atmospheric Administration
Department of Commerce/NOAA
Education Program Branch
11400 Rockville Pike
Rockville, MD 20852

> Maps, posters, charts, and pamphlets about the oceans and weather are available.

National Science Foundation
1800 G Street, NW
Suite 527
Washington, DC 20550

> Ask to be placed on mailing list to receive information about science events pertinent to your grade level.

National Science Teachers Association
1840 Wilson Boulevard
Arlington, VA 22201-3000

> *NSTA Science Education Suppliers* is an annual catalog of educational services, computer software, media materials, and print materials endorsed by the NSTA.

> NSTA also publishes *NSTA REPORTS!* Each issue contains several pages of sources of free and inexpensive materials.

Natural Resources Conservation Program
(Formerly The Soil Conservation Service
of the USDA)

Check the federal government pages of your telephone directory for local listings.

Materials are available on the uses and conservation of water.

Northern Textile Association
230 Congress Street
Boston, MA 02110

Free and inexpensive teaching materials are available about manufactured dry goods.

Polystyrene Packaging Council
1275 K Street, NW, Suite 400
Washington, DC 20005

Free classroom materials about plastics and the environment are available.

Rainforest Action Network
466 Green Street, Suite 300
San Francisco, CA 94133

Materials concerning preservation of the rainforests of the world are available.

Scientific American Frontiers
Connecticut Public Television
P. O. Box 260240
Hartford, CT 06126-0240

Ask to be placed on mailing list to receive announcements and teacher materials for the PBS telecasts *Scientific American Frontiers*.

Sierraecology
Sierra Club Public Affairs
730 Polk Street
San Francisco, CA 94109

Free environmental education materials for teachers. Materials also are available that describe successful environmental programs in the United States.

The Smithsonian Institution
National Science Resources Center
Arts & Industries Building, Room 1201, MRC 403
Washington, DC 20560

> Ask to be put on mailing list for *NSRC Newsletter*. The NSRC collects and disseminates information about exemplary teaching resources, develops curriculum materials, and sponsors activities to help schools develop hands-on science programs.

Office of Elementary and Secondary Education
Smithsonian Institution
Arts and Industries Building
Room 1163, MRC 402
Washington, DC 20560

> Write for free Resource Guide for Teachers that offers a listing of media available for the classroom for language arts, visual and performing arts, science, and social studies.

> Also ask for free quarterly publication, *ART to ZOO*. Each issue covers one topic and includes general background information, lesson plans, classroom activities, and resources for teachers. An English/Spanish page is included.

State Departments of Natural Resources often have excellent collections of free or inexpensive materials about state natural resources and state parks. Ask for information.

The Ohio State University
ERIC/CSMEE
1929 Kenny Road
Columbus, OH 43210-1080

> CSMEE stands for ERIC Clearinghouse for Science, Mathematics, and Environmental Education. Ask to be placed on mailing list for *The CSMEE Horizon*, a newsletter that describes new publications on science and mathematics education available through ERIC.

The Weather Channel
2600 Cumberland Parkway
Atlanta, GA 30339

> Free materials are available on weather and teaching weather. Many documentary videos are available for dubbing; write for information.

United States Department of Commerce
National Oceanographic and Atmospheric Administration
Office of Ocean and Coastal Resource Management
Looe Key National Marine Sanctuary
Rt. 1, Box 782
Big Pine Key, FL 33043

> Information about coral reefs and teaching about marine ecology is available.

U. S. Environmental Protection Agency
401 M Street, SW
Washington, DC 20460

> Write for a list of educational materials. A wide variety of available information about the environment is free or very inexpensive.

U. S. Fish and Wildlife Service

> This is a branch of the U. S. Department of Interior. Check the federal government pages of your telephone directory for local listings.

> Free information about U.S. wild life is available. This organization also produces beautiful posters.

U. S. Geologic Survey
582 National Center
Reston, VA 22092

> Some free materials. Ask for address and telephone number of your local office of the USGS. Many materials are available to help children pursue earth science topics.

Wool Education Center
200 Clayton Street
Denver, CO 80206

> Free and inexpensive materials are available about wool processing.

Activities Cross-Referenced to Basic Scientific Concepts and Principles

HEAT ENERGY AND STATES OF MATTER

SOUND ENERGY

LIGHT

ELECTRICITY AND MAGNETISM

NUCLEAR ENERGY

MATTER AND CHEMICAL ENERGY

LIFE SCIENCE CONCEPTS AND PRINCIPLES

EARTH AND SPACE SCIENCE
CONCEPTS AND PRINCIPLES

CONSTRUCTIVE AND DESTRUCTIVE FORCES

THE ROCK CYCLE

WEATHER AND THE WATER CYCLE

OCEANOGRAPHY

HISTORICAL GEOLOGY

GENERAL PRINCIPLES AND CONCEPTS

APPENDIX C

Listing of Children's Literature

Author Index

Subject Index

References to activities are *italicized*.
References to figures are shown in **bold face**.